# Julius Caesar
## Man, Soldier, and Tyrant

# JULIUS CAESAR

## MAN, SOLDIER, AND TYRANT

❖

## Major-General J.F.C.Fuller

WORDSWORTH EDITIONS

First published in 1965 by
Eyre & Spottiswoode (Publishers) Ltd
22 Henrietta Street, London WC2

Copyright © 1965 J.F.C.Fuller

This edition published 1998
by Wordsworth Editions Limited
Cumberland House, Crib Street, Ware,
Hertfordshire SG12 9ET

ISBN 1 85326 692 2

© Wordsworth Editions Limited 1998

Wordsworth® is a registered trade mark of
Wordsworth Editions Limited

Printed and bound in Great Britain
by Mackays of Chatham plc, Chatham, Kent.

# CONTENTS

# GAUL
## GALLIC TOWNS AND FRENCH EQUIVALENTS

| | |
|---|---|
| *Agedincum* | Sens |
| *Alesia* | Alise–Sainte–Reìne |
| *Aquae Sextiae* | Aix-en-Provence |
| *Avaricum* | Bourges |
| *Bibracte* | Mont Beuvray |
| *Bibrax* | ? Vieux-Laon |
| *Bratuspantium* | ? Breteuil |
| *Cabillonum* | Chalon-sur-Saône |
| *Cenabum* | Orléans |
| *Decetia* | Décize |
| *Durocortorum* | Rheims |
| *Gergovia* | Gergovie |
| *Gorgobina* | Unidentified |
| *Lemonum* | Poitiers |
| *Lutetia* | Paris |
| *Massilia* | Marseilles |
| *Matisco* | Mâcon |
| *Narbo* | Narbonne |
| *Nemetocenna* | Arras |
| *Noviodunum of the Aedui* | Nevers |
| *Noviodunum of the Suessiones* | Pommiers |
| *Portus Itius* | ? Boulogne or Wissant |
| *Samarobriva* | Amiens |
| *Tolosa* | Toulouse |
| *Uxellodunum* | Puy d'Issolu |
| *Vellaunodunum* | ? Montargis |
| *Vesontio* | Becançon |
| *Vienna* | Vienne |

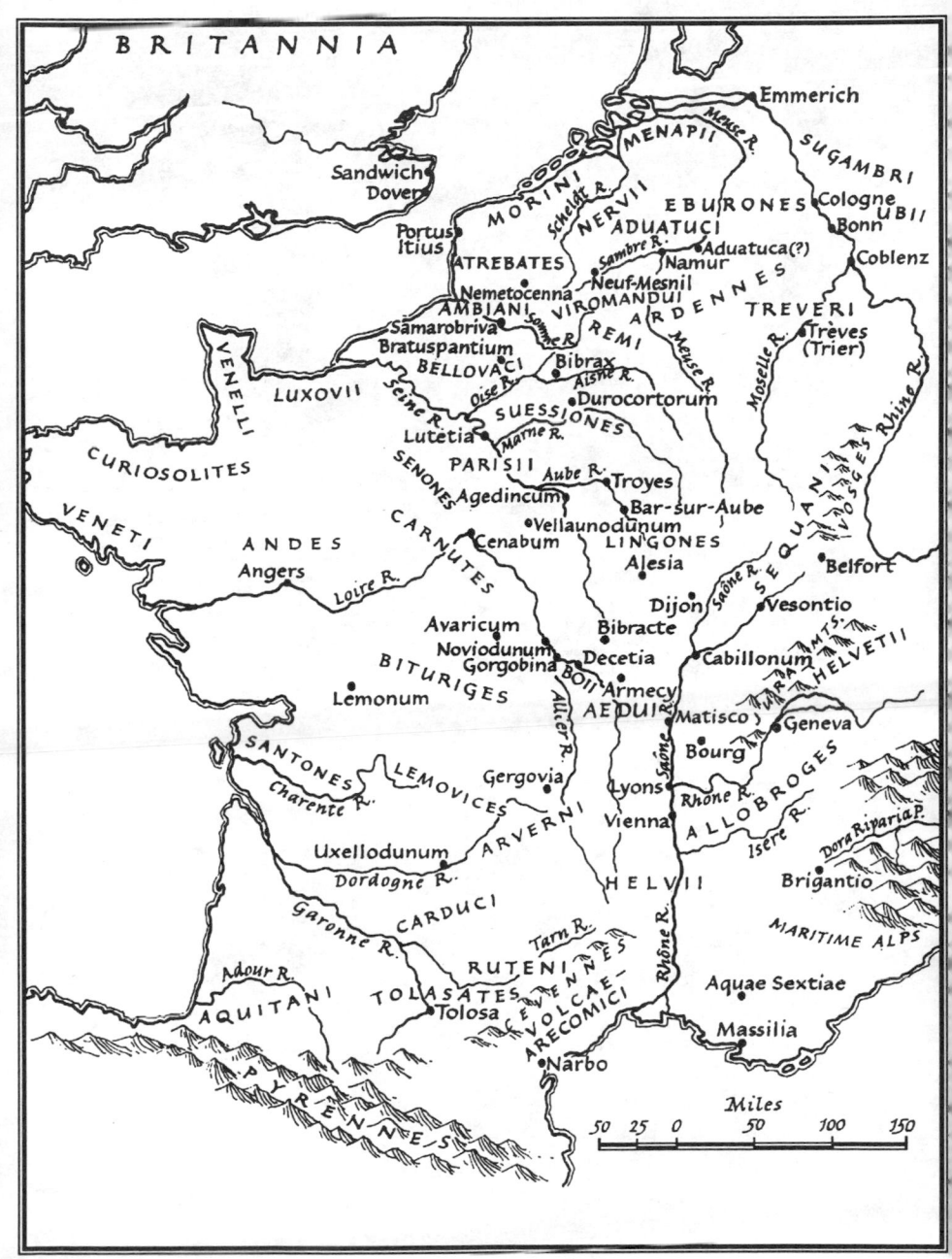

Map of Gaul

# Preface

'So very difficult a matter is it to trace and find out the truth
of anything by history, when, on the one hand, those who
afterwards write it find long periods of time intercepting their
view, and, on the other hand, the contemporary records of
any actions and lives, partly through envy and illwill, partly
through favour and flattery, pervert and distort truth.'

PLUTARCH

As Plutarch points out, one of the great difficulties in history is
to disentangle the true characters and activities of outstanding
personalities from the distortions of their legends. Through
repetition these legends become *idées fixes*, not only in the popular mind
but frequently also in the minds of the most conscientious of historians.
This is especially noticeable in such emotional crises as revolutions and
civil wars, in which the virtues, vices, and deeds of their leading partici-
pants are so magnified or belittled that from human beings they are
transformed into mythical creatures – travesties of their actual selves.

In our own history we have Oliver Cromwell; anathematized until
the nineteenth century, then acclaimed the greatest of our parliament-
arians, and today honoured by a statue outside Westminster Hall, the
doors of which he bolted and locked!

More cogent – from the point of view of this book – is the American
Civil War general Robert E. Lee, concerning whom, and most appropriately on the day I sat down to write this preface, I received a letter
from an American correspondent in which he informed me that he was
'midway through the second reading' of my *Generalship of Ulysses S.
Grant*. Then he went on to write:

'Born and raised south of the Mason–Dixon Line, and nurtured on
the twin-truisms that the earth is round and General R. E. Lee was (and
still is) the greatest ever, it required some time for even the sheer weight
of inexorable fact and cold logic to convince this person that maybe,
just maybe, "he wasn't". If you have ever travelled the area – especially
south of the Potomac River – you will understand that it is neither

polite nor safe to express such heretical views there, regardless of the company.'

The thought that I should discover a comparable example of myth-making when I set out to write this book was far from my mind. Not until I had marshalled my notes into some order did it become apparent to me that the Caesar as depicted by many scholars and modern historians was in several important respects very different from the self-revealed Caesar of the *Commentaries* and the Caesar of the classical historians. Whereas Lee's exaggerated fame was war-born and grew rapidly after the Civil War, it would appear that Caesar's apotheosis as a superman did not begin to take form until the Renaissance, and, then, soon became an *idée fixe* – an historical obsession. When Shake-speare wrote his *Julius Caesar*, he made Cassius say:

> Why man he doth bestride the narrow world
> Like a Colossus, and we petty men
> Walk under his huge legs and peep about
> To find ourselves dishonourable graves.

Related to this superhuman vision are the apparitions conjured forth by some of the historians consulted or referred to in this book, and no doubt a search through the works of others would reveal similar historical sorceries.

Theodor Mommsen's opinion is, that 'Caesar was the entire and per-fect man'; and 'Perhaps there never was an army which was more per-fectly what an army ought to be' than his.[1] James Anthony Froude affirms that 'perhaps no commander who ever lived showed greater military genius.'[2] Dr T. Rice Holmes considers him 'the greatest man of the world', and 'the greatest man of action who has ever lived'.[3] Colonel Theodore A. Dodge holds him to be 'the greatest man in antiquity' and that 'We are gauging the work of perhaps the greatest man the world has ever seen.'[4] Prof. E. L. White asserts that he was 'the greatest man the earth has ever produced.'[5] Prof. Hugh Last, with more sobriety, declares that 'His triumphs were so much the product of his personality that he left behind him no single advance in the art of war. He bequeathed to the generals who followed him no receipt

[1] *The History of Rome* (Everyman's edit.), vol. IV, pp. 430 & 343.
[2] *Caesar a Sketch* (1896 edit.), p. 550.
[3] *Caesar's Conquest of Gaul* (1911), pp. xii & 42.
[4] *Caesar*, vol. II, pp. 767 & 691.
[5] *Why Rome Fell* (1927), p. 136.

for victory except one beyond their reach – to be Caesar . . . he made no single innovation in the technique of Roman soldiering.'[1] And Sir Frank Adcock states that why he did not do so 'was because he did not need to',[2] which implies that Caesar's army could fulfil all tactical requirements demanded of it.

Classical sources present a far less exalted being: an unscrupulous demagogue whose one aim was power, and a general who could not only win brilliant victories but also commit dismal blunders, so costly to himself that – in spite of his encomium – Dodge correctly remarks: 'If the months be counted, it will be seen that more than half of Caesar's campaigns were consumed in extricating himself from the results of his own mistakes.'[3]

To have to spend over half a long war in extricating oneself from difficulties created by the enemy may or may not be good generalship; but to have to do so because they are due to one's own mistakes is incontestably bad generalship, even when the extrications are brilliant. Therefore, although I have read a considerable number of modern histories on both the Roman Republic and Caesar, my views on him as man and soldier are based solely on classical sources; and, so far as I am aware, I have in no way twisted them to reinforce some theory of my own. When, in 1958, I began to collect notes for this book, I certainly held no theory. Now that I have written it, the theory, if it can be called that, is: It is reasonable to suspect that, at times, Caesar was not responsible for his actions, and toward the end of his life not altogether sane.

For the political background of Caesar's rise to power I have relied on Dr T. Rice Holmes more than on any other modern historian, not only because of his eminence as a classical scholar, but also because of the elaborate notes appended to his history of the Roman Republic, in which the opinions of no less than 277 modern commentators are discussed. His volumes are encyclopaedic, and have saved me much time in consulting the works of many other modern authorities.

Nevertheless, I have been informed that, since Dr Holmes's works were published, some of his views have been challenged. I venture to suspect, not because the sources of classical history are so vast that new knowledge is constantly being mined, but because they are frequently so fragmentary that almost unlimited scope is given to scholastic

---

[1] *The Cambridge Ancient History*, vol. IX, p. 705.
[2] *The Roman Art of War Under the Republic* (1940), p. 123.
[3] *Op. cit.*, vol. II, p. 692.

speculation and argument. Fortunately, however, Caesar's activities as a soldier have been so well documented by himself, by some of his subordinates and at times by Cicero, that further evidence on his generalship is unlikely to be forthcoming, and so far as I am aware no recent reassessment of it has been made. Therefore I have not attempted to keep pace with the unending speculations, conjectures and arguments of the scholars, nor am I capable of adjudicating between them. And it was for that very reason I selected Dr Holmes as my guide.

In brief, this book is a study of the power politics of an extraordinary man, who first as a demagogue of reckless ambition won over the rabble of Rome, and then as a soldier, who looked upon war as a political instrument, with matchless boldness made himself *tyrant* of the Roman world. A word which in classical times denoted the irregular way in which political power was gained – whether by fraud or force – rather than the way in which it was exercised. Today it is called 'Caesarism', and once again it is troubling the world. That, I hope, gives additional interest to this book, which is likely to be my last one.

J. F. C. FULLER

*January 1964*

# I

# The Background

## I. THE EARLY CONSTITUTION OF THE REPUBLIC

ACCORDING to tradition, Rome was founded in 753 B.C. as a city state. Its king was chief priest, chief judge, and supreme war lord, and was advised by a council of heads of leading families – the Senate.[1] The people (*populus*), which included the less privileged classes (plebeians and clients), were divided into *curiae* – probably kinships[2] – and, when assembled as an army, into *centuriae* (nominal hundreds) The grouping by centuries was based on property qualifications; the richer citizens, those who owned a horse, known as *equites* (knights), were allotted to the cavalry, and the poorer divided into five classes of which the first three were infantry of the line and the last two light armed troops; those without property were not privileged to bear arms. Assemblies of the people were known as *comitia*, and voting was not by individuals but by groups: the majority in each *curia* or *centuria* decided how it was to vote, and the majority of groups decided the issue.[3]

When toward the end of the sixth century B.C. the patricians expelled Tarquinius Superbus, the last of the kings, and transformed the monarchy into a republic, a problem was born which was to vex the Romans until the days of Augustus. It was how to organize and control the armed forces so that, while the Republic would be safeguarded against foreign aggression, the liberties of its citizens would not be infringed, as apparently they had been under the monarchy. But the solution sought by the patricians was not directed toward that end,

[1] According to Livy (I, 8) Romulus created 100 senators called 'fathers', and their descendants were called 'patricians'. Under the Republic they were increased to 300, and remained so until the days of Sulla.

[2] A *curia* was one of the ten parts into which Romulus is reputed to have divided each of the three traditional Roman tribes.

[3] In republican times the *curia* was largely replaced by the *tribus* (tribe), a division founded on a territorial basis.

instead they monopolized the kingly power – his *imperium* – and vested it in two of their fellows, first known as praetors (leaders) and later as consuls, who were elected yearly by the Assembly of the People. Like the kings, they were endowed with the power of selecting new members of the Senate, and of summoning the Assembly at which their successors were elected.[1] Their powers were limited by the brevity of their term of office and the veto they exercised on each other's proposals.

The power of the Senate was grounded in its permanence (senatorship was for life) and since the consuls were exclusively chosen from among the senatorial families, the position of the Senate was strongly entrenched, and particularly so in wartime, when so many of the citizens were enrolled under the consuls. Its weakness lay in that, while in all probability the king's personal body-guard kept order within the city, in the Republic no steps were taken to maintain a police force, possibly due to fear that it might establish a tyranny. Eventually this became one of the causes which ruined the Republic, and after its establishment the lack of such a force must have greatly assisted the plebeians[2] in their struggle with the patricians, which began in 494 and lasted until 287 B.C.

Their revolt was directed against senatorial monopoly of government, as well as to gain social and economic justice. Although they constituted the bulk of the people, who in theory were the source of all authority, they were deprived of political power; they neither participated in the *imperium* of the magistracy, nor could they protect themselves against its abuses. The procedure they adopted to secure reform was secession; they organized themselves into a separate corporation, which held its own assemblies (*concilia plebis*), appointed its own officers, the tribunes (*tribuni plebis*),[3] and secured their inviolability by a collective undertaking to protect them. At times of abnormal stress they withdrew *en masse* from Rome; between 494 and 287 B.C. five such secessions are recorded, and there may have been others.

During the 200 years of the struggle, the *concilium plebis* and the tribunes – patricians were excluded from both – were incorporated in

---

[1] The consulate not only conferred dignity on its holders for life, but it ennobled their families for ever.

[2] *Plebs* was the name given to the general body of Roman citizens as distinct from the privileged *patricii*.

[3] In 459 B.C. two, soon after increased to ten. Not to be confused with the *tribuni militum*, officers of the army.

the State, and although the *concilium* did not include the whole of the people, and therefore could not legally pass laws, its resolutions (*plebiscita*) were eventually given the force of law. Thus, by 287 B.C., when the last secession took place, the plebeians won right of admission to all offices, and hence to the Senate. Like the consuls, the persons of the tribunes were sacrosanct during their yearly term of office, and like them each tribune had power to initiate laws and to veto not only consular proposals but also those of his colleagues. In brief, two sets of rulers were established to carry out simultaneously the duties of government, but not as a democracy, which under this dual system was impossible.

Two further innovations of importance must be mentioned. The first was that, in 366 B.C., a praetor was elected to supervise the administration of justice in Rome; later the number of praetors was increased in order to provide governors for oversea provinces, when to all intents and purposes they were endowed with full consular powers. The second was that in 327–326 B.C., because the siege of the Greek city of Neapolis (Naples) lasted for more than one year, in order to retain the consul commanding the besieging army in office, he was appointed by the Assembly to act as proconsul – that is, to carry on the siege as though he were still a consul. This device of increasing the number of officers with *imperium*, without altering the number of consuls and their annual term of office, came increasingly into use, and eventually became a leading factor in the civil wars which wrecked the Republic.

## 2. INFLUENCES OF OVERSEAS EXPANSION

During the 226 years which separate the victory of the Romans over the Latin cities at Lake Regillus in 498 B.C., and the submission to them of the Greek cities of Tarentum (Taranto) and Regium (Reggio) in 272 B.C., Rome gradually extended her rule over the whole of Italy south of the Apennines. The many wars waged between these dates were fought to establish her security within Italy; but once Regium was occupied, her problem became how to secure Italy from without, and as no more than three and a half miles of water separated the Romans from the Carthaginians in Sicily, the impulse of security led to the First and Second Punic Wars.

In the first, fought between 264 and 241 B.C., Rome acquired Sicily, the first of her provinces, and in 238 B.C., with doubtful faith, she deprived Carthage of Sardinia, which together with Corsica became her second province. Next, in 218 B.C., came the Second Punic War, which in 202 B.C. was ended by the defeat of Hannibal at the hands of Scipio Africanus at Zama. In accordance with the terms of peace, the whole of Spain was annexed to Rome and organized into two provinces. Thus Rome became mistress of the Western Mediterranean.

During the Second Punic War Philip V of Macedon entered into treaty with Hannibal and took up arms against Rome. This led to the First Macedonian War (214–205 B.C.), a conflict of small account. But immediately after the Roman–Carthaginian peace Philip's aggressive policy precipitated the Second Macedonian War (200–194 B.C.) and, in 197 B.C., led to his defeat at Cynoscephalae. Out of that conflict emerged a series of wars, which occupied the next half-century. First, a war with Antiochus III of Syria (192–190 B.C.) and his defeat at Magnesia. Next, the Third Macedonian War (171–168 B.C.) with Perseus, son and successor of Philip V, who was defeated at Pydna and whose kingdom became a Roman province. Then came the Third Punic War (149–146 B.C.), which led to the destruction of Carthage and to Africa being added to the provinces; and lastly to a war with the Achaean League in 148 B.C., which two years later resulted in the destruction of Corinth, Thebes, and Chalcis. Thus, fifty-six years after Zama, Rome became mistress of the Eastern Mediterranean.

The impact of these wars on the Republic was profound. Because the popular assemblies were incapable of arriving at quick decisions, and because the people were ill-informed and scattered, the conduct of war automatically passed into the hands of the Senate, which from an advisory body developed into a supreme war council. The sovereignty of the people was so completely subordinated to its will that the Assemblies were no longer even asked to agree with its decisions. Further, the successful outcome of the wars added enormously to the prestige of the Senate.

Simultaneously other changes supervened, which ultimately undermined the authority of the Senate and corrupted the Republic. The most important was the emergence of a capitalist class, and with it the growth of a money economy.

Wars of the ancient world differed from those of today in that frequently they were highly profitable. After coinage became a medium of exchange, the need for bullion grew more and more pressing, and as the mining of the precious metals was rudimentary, and because the Romans never took to industry, war was the main means of obtaining them. Further, shortage of money led to high rates of interest, to un-redeemable debts and agitation for their remission; and when the demand for money outstripped its supply, as Mommsen says, war became 'a traffic of plunder'.

Tenny Frank has computed that between 200 and 167 B.C., the Roman generals brought back in booty 31,000 lb. of gold and 669,000 lb. of silver, besides which the Roman treasury received in indemnities something like £5,000,000.[1] In addition to this, the generals and their armies, as well as the tax-gatherers, appropriated in perquisites vast sums of money. So considerable were the profits accruing from the wars in the East that, in 167 B.C., all direct taxes in Italy were discontinued, and henceforth the expenses of the State were met by the tribute of the provinces.

As corrupting as the influx of precious metals was the enormous extension of slavery which, because slave power was the classical equivalent of modern steam power, led to economic and social changes as profound as those which emerged out of the Industrial Revolution in the nineteenth century.

Although, since times immemorial, slavery had existed among the Romans, it was only after the Second Punic War that it took a steep upward course. Unlike in modern wars, prisoners were not looked upon as an encumbrance, but as an indemnity toward meeting the cost of a campaign, and frequently their capture was more profitable than the loot acquired. It is, therefore, no surprise to learn that armies were followed by bands of speculators in the slave trade who made vast fortunes out of the prisoners auctioned. On occasions the number made available is staggering: after the battle of Pydna, Aemilius Paullus sold into slavery 150,000 of the free inhabitants of Epirus; after the battles of Aquae Sextiae and Vercellae 60,000 Cimbri and 90,000 Teutoni respectively were sold by Marius; and on one occasion during his Gallic War Caesar sold 53,000. The trade in human flesh became so profitable that slave breeding grew into a lucrative business.

In the early days of the Republic a nobleman was contented with one man servant and a maid; but, in the epoch under review, the Roman slave market became so glutted and the price of a slave fell so low that even comparatively poor men could afford to buy at least 10 and the wealthy 200 or more. Unlike those captured in the West, who

---

[1] 'The Public Finances of Rome, 200–167 B.C.', *American Journal of Philology*, vol. LIII, 1932, pp. 3–4. Throughout, all money values, when converted into pounds sterling, are based on 1913 value.

for the most part were rude barbarians, many from the East were cultured men and skilled craftsmen: rhetoricians, grammarians, architects, artists, engineers, physicians, goldsmiths, weavers, metal workers, singers, dancers, actors – men and women of every conceivable occupation.

The influx of these enslaved men and women had two great social effects: on the one hand it progressively hellenized Roman culture; on the other the Latin stock was increasingly mongrelized as Greeks, Asiatics, Spaniards, Gauls, and others were absorbed through manumission and became citizens.

The long war with Hannibal created within Italy an economic vacuum into which the outpourings of wealth from the East were sucked. Agriculture had been disrupted and in the south destroyed; many landowners had fallen in battle, and many more had had to serve so long in the army that they had mortgaged and lost their farms. In addition, cheap corn from Sicily, Sardinia, and Africa rendered home-grown wheat in the vicinity of the coastal areas unremunerative, and on the more productive lands it was superseded by the olive and the vine, the cultivation of which demanded capital, the one thing the small farmer so seldom had. The result was that there was much land on the market, and as slaves were abundant, all that was needed to turn it to profit was credit wherewith to purchase them.

Because immediately before the outbreak of the Second Punic War senators had been forbidden by law to engage in commerce and business, during the war army contractors – who had to be wealthy men – were recruited from the knights. These men made vast fortunes, and in the wars which followed they established themselves so firmly as money-lenders and bankers that usury became the scourge of Italy and the provinces. In Italy and Sicily they rented huge tracts of public land, and added to them the small farms of their poor neighbours, either by purchase or force, and because slaves were cheaper than free men, the latter were ousted; besides slaves were exempt from military service. These large estates were known as *latifundia*.[1]

Because the Republic had no machinery with which to collect the provincial revenues, the farming of them was sold by auction almost exclusively to the knights, and as few single persons were wealthy enough to advance sufficient security, syndicates of financiers were formed to carry out the collection. Notwithstanding that no magistrate or provincial governor was allowed to take shares in a syndicate, many

[1] According to Pliny (*Nat. Hist.*, XVIII, 35) they were 'the ruin of Italy'.

frequently did so, with the result that the provinces were as often as not ruinously exploited, and should a governor on completion of his term of office be prosecuted for extortion, bribery of the jurors generally led to his acquittal.

Many senators, *sub rosa*, became their partners, and 'The financiers,' writes Sir Ronald Syme, 'were strong enough to ruin any politician or general who sought to secure fair treatment for provincials or reform the Roman State through the re-establishment of the peasant farmer.'[1] Thus it came about that the capitalists pervaded all aspects of public life; in the opinion of the elder Cato there was no great difference between a money-lender and a murderer, and in Mommsen's opinion 'the Roman capitalists beyond doubt contributed quite as much as Hamilcar and Hannibal to the decline in vigour and numbers of the Italian people.'[2]

Those who had lost their farms, or who had been ousted from them, flocked to Rome and other cities to form a turbulent proletariat which soon discovered that a source of profitable gain was to sell their votes in the magisterial elections, and, to win the support of the voters, candidates for the consulships vied with each other in the magnificence of the games and gladiatorial contests they gave at elections; in proportion to the splendour of which their fitness was commonly measured by the populace. As the cost of these displays and the vote-buying was prodigious, normally they had to be paid for with money borrowed from the bankers, who by their loans established a lien on the consuls elected. By corrupting senators, magistrates, generals, soldiers and the proletariat, money became the dominant power in the State. Thus Sallust writes:

'As soon as riches came to be held in honour, when glory, dominion, and power followed in their train, virtue began to lose its lustre, poverty to be considered a disgrace, blamelessness to be termed malevolence. Therefore as a result of riches, luxury, and greed, united with insolence, took possession of our young manhood. They pillaged, squandered; set little value on their own, coveted the goods of others; they disregarded modesty, chastity, everything human and divine; in short, they were utterly thoughtless and reckless.'[3]

[1] *The Roman Revolution* (1956), p. 14.
[2] *The History of Rome* (Everyman edit.), vol. II, p. 370.
[3] *The War with Catiline*, XII, 2-3.

## 3. INAUGURATION OF THE CENTURY OF REVOLUTION

Of the many changes provoked by expansion, the most serious was the steady decline of the farming population in Italy. Since the landless city rabble and the slaves were not conscripted, it was the sole source of recruitment, and unless the number of the legions could keep pace with the demands of expansion, and their wastage be made good, the whole structure of the Republic was in peril of collapse.

The solution of this problem was sought by Tiberius Sempronius Gracchus, a nephew of Scipio Africanus. In 134 B.C., he stood for the tribunate, and when elected brought before the Assembly an agrarian bill in which he proposed that the public lands should be parcelled into farms for the landless. It led to violent opposition, because most of these lands were either rented by or had been appropriated by the rich, and when the bill came to the vote its opponents induced Marcus Octavius, one of the other tribunes, to veto it. In retaliation Tiberius made use of his tribunician power, he suspended all administrative business, and unconstitutionally carried a motion which deprived Octavius of his office. That done, the bill was passed by the Assembly and commissioners were appointed to reallot the land.

Aware that his adversaries could do nothing until he laid down his office, Tiberius decided to seek re-election, which was either illegal or contrary to custom, and as he feared defeat, on the day of the elections he was prepared to overcome opposition by force. A riot ensued, in which he and some 300 of his followers were killed. Of it Appian writes: 'This shocking affair, the first that was perpetrated in the public assembly, was seldom without parallels thereafter from time to time.'[1] Thus the century of revolution was born.

The second phase in the struggle was opened by Tiberius' younger brother, Gaius, when tribune in 123 and 122 B.C. He restored to his brother's agrarian commission the judicial power it had meanwhile been deprived of and enacted a series of popular measures, including the sale of cheap corn and the establishment of colonies in Italy. To win the support of the knights he excluded senators from service as knights, and gave definite political functions to the class from which the knights were drawn, and thereby created a rival body to the Senate. He enacted a law by which the jurors of the jury courts, hitherto exclusively composed of senators, were henceforth to be selected from the knights, a measure which opened to them a field for unlimited extortion.

[1] *The Civil Wars*, I, 17.

Another of his proposals was to admit Italians to the Roman franchise, and as it was repugnant to the aristocracy it brought the struggle between him and the Senate to a head. In 122 B.C., the bill was violently opposed by the consul Gaius Fannius, who asserted that, were citizenship conferred upon the Latins, there would be no room for anyone else at the public meetings, nor at the games and festivals. As these specious forebodings appealed to the people, the Senate persuaded one of the tribunes to veto the bill. In December, 122 B.C., Gaius again stood for the tribunate, was defeated, and reverted to private citizenship.

The details of what followed are obscure, but it would appear that, although the Senate had triumphed, it recognized that its victory was likely to prove ephemeral unless, like his brother, Gaius was eliminated for good and all. The step taken to effect this was to recommend that the law by which he had established a colony at Carthage, a project he had set his heart on, should be repealed. Determined to oppose this, Gaius came to the Assembly with a band of armed followers, and appeared so threatening that the consul, Lucius Opimius, one of his most bitter enemies, called upon the Senate to defend the constitution. It was an unprecedented act, which later became known as the *Senatus Consultum Ultimum* ('Ultimate Decree') – virtually a declaration of martial law. Opimius was instructed to defend the commonwealth, and when Gaius rejected his summons to appear before the Senate, the position he had taken up on the Aventine was stormed, and he and his followers slaughtered.

When calm had been restored, 'the Senate ordered the building of a temple to Concord in the forum.'[1] It was the monument to a hollow victory, not only because the problem of the Gracchi remained unsolved, but because protean-like it had changed its form. From a question of land for the landless it had developed into a struggle for power between the Senate and the knights. Henceforth, they were always rivals and often enemies, because a money economy was replacing the old agricultural economy, and it was through bribery more than through the reallotment of land that the votes of the proletariat could be captured. It enabled the knights to hold the balance of power; yet it was as impossible for them to establish a purely plutocratic government as it was for the Senate to maintain a senatorial government unless either could depend on the loyalty of the army – the basis of political power.

Under the old agricultural economy the Senate was supreme,

1 Appian, *The Civil Wars*, I, 26.

because the soldiers were recruited from the small farmers, who were an integral part of the economy. But when this source of military power began to dry up, recruiting was increasingly shifted on to a monetary footing, not by augmenting the soldier's pay, but by offering him the prospect of plunder, and unless plunder could permanently be assured, and through it the good will of the legions retained, any form of government would be nothing other than an incipient anarchy. Because anarchy is the one condition a people will not tolerate for long, it is the forcing-ground of civil wars, in which whoever gains military supremacy becomes master of the state. Sallust is just off the right track when he writes: 'To restore power to the plebs [the proletariat] was to prepare the way for monarchy.'[1] But it was not restored, nor could it be, because in all ages the rabble is no more than the tool of power. Instead the anarchy, which the proletariat and the knights helped to create, coupled with the loss of senatorial prestige, led directly to the establishment of a stratocracy – that is, government *by* military power in contrast with government *based on* military power. In other words, the foundations became the superstructure. It is this revolutionary change that marks the next period.

## 4. RISE OF MARIUS AND HIS ARMY REFORMS

After the death of Gaius Gracchus, with the acquiescence of the knights the Senate regained power; but, soon after, a break between the two orders was precipitated by a dynastic dispute in Numidia, which Sallust described as 'the beginning of a struggle which threw everything, human and divine, into confusion, and rose to such a pitch of frenzy that civil disorder ended in war and the devastation of Italy.'[2] During it, Jugurtha, grandson of Masinissa – the ally of Scipio Africanus at Zama – gained the upper hand; but unfortunately for him, when in 112 B.C. he sacked the city of Cirta (Constantine), many Italian traders were massacred.

This caused an explosion in Rome, and the knights, who were furious at the fate of the traders, compelled the unwilling Senate to send the consul L. Calpurnius Bestia with an army to Africa. Bribed by Jugurtha – who was convinced 'that at Rome anything could be bought'[3] – Bestia patched up a peace with him and returned to Rome. Because at the time hordes of Cimbri and Teutoni, who had defeated two consular armies, were moving from Illyricum westward toward Gaul, the

---

[1] *The Jugurthine War*, XXXI, 8.
[2] *Ibid.*, V, 2-3.      [3] *Ibid.*, XX, 1.

Senate accepted the peace rather than press the war. This infuriated the knights who, supported by the clamour of the people, forced the hands of the Senate, and, in 110 B.C., the consul Spurius Postumius Albinus was sent out to take command of Bestia's army. He found it in a state verging on mutiny, handed it over to his brother Aulus, and returned to Rome to preside at the consular elections.

If Sallust is to be believed, the state of the army was appalling. He tells us that Jugurtha set about to bribe certain of its centurions and cavalry leaders to desert. 'One cohort of Ligurians and two squadrons of Thracians,' he writes, 'went over to the king, while the chief centurion of the Third legion gave the enemy an opportunity of entering the part of the fortifications [of the camp] he had been appointed to guard.'[1] To save the army, Aulus agreed that it should pass under the yoke and quit Numidia within ten days. This was an indignity no true Roman could stomach.

The war was now resumed in earnest under the consul Q. Caecilius Metellus, an able aristocrat. He took with him on his staff Gaius Marius, an experienced soldier, who had worked his way up to the propraetorship in Spain, and had married Julia, aunt of Julius Caesar. Disgusted with the length of the war, the knights and the tribunes backed Marius in the consular elections of 107 B.C. He was triumphantly returned, and although the Senate had prolonged Metellus' command, on a motion of a tribune the Assembly voted that Marius should supersede him. At once Marius set about to recruit his army.

Sallust tells us that 'He . . . enrolled soldiers, not according to the classes . . . but allowing anyone to volunteer, for the most part the proletariat,'[2] an innovation which, as Professor Hugh Last writes, 'did more than any other single factor to make possible that series of civil wars which only ended in the establishment of the Principate'.[3] A brief comparison between the old and the new systems of recruitment will make this clear.

The old militia was designed for economy and short service. Its recruits were sufficiently wealthy to provide their own arms and equipment, and their service in the ranks was sufficiently short that, during their absence, their farms could be maintained by their families. This was undercut when wars became of long duration, and the longer they grew the greater was the deterioration of the soldier's property likely to be; therefore the one thing the legionary looked for was his

---

[1] Ibid., XXXVIII, 6.    [2] Ibid., LXXXVI, 2.
[3] The Cambridge Ancient History, vol. IX, p. 133.

discharge, and the more it was delayed the more unpopular the conscription became.

Marius was well aware that a sufficiency of recruits was not forthcoming from the classes, and that should he fail to raise an army powerful enough to end the Numidian war rapidly, his popularity with the people would decline. His innovation was by no means novel, because the property qualifications had by now been so reduced that it had become customary to recruit the legions in part from the proletariat. Further, long before his day, extra-Italian subjects, such as Thracian and African cavalry, Ligurian light infantry, and Balearic slingers, had been recruited in ever-increasing numbers. What was novel was that the conscription of the classes was suspended, and that the volunteers, instead of looking upon service as a tiresome interruption of their normal lives, regarded it as a profitable profession. In the old system, demobilization at the earliest opportunity was what the soldier yearned for; in the new – it was the one thing he wished to avoid. Therefore, what normally happened was, when at the close of a campaign an army was disbanded, the majority of its men at once re-enlisted. To all intents and purposes it then became a standing army on a peace-footing, which, in the event of war, was brought on to a war-footing or reinforced by newly raised legions.

Another innovation was that, while in the days of the militia the men were drafted to fight under a leader appointed by the State, these newly raised legions were enlisted to serve a particular general, more often than not a popular favourite.[1] Therefore their fortunes were intimately linked with his own, and when a campaign ended they looked to him either to find a pretext to start another war, and so keep them employed in gathering fresh spoil, or, as no system of pensions was introduced, to provide them with land to settle on when their campaigning days were over. Whether a war was, or was not, for the benefit of the State did not concern them, their loyalty was to their general and not to the State – they were mercenaries. Therefore, as Sir Ronald Syme states: 'The general had to be a politician, for his legionaries were a host of clients. . . . But not veterans only were attached to his cause –

---

[1] Because the soldiers served mainly for plunder, naturally they preferred to enlist under a general of acknowledged ability. Therefore, when the government was in need of an army, such a man was chosen to command it, because his reputation stimulated recruiting. In the days of the militia, a general (consul) was elected, not for his military abilities, but because he represented a political faction: hence the numerous defeats the legions sustained.

from his provincial commands the dynast won to his allegiance and personal following (*clientela*) towns and whole regions, provinces and nations, kings and tetrarchs.'[1] As in the Persian satrapies, the commands of the generals became states within the State.

Thus, out of Marius' elementary and necessary change in recruitment, and other innovations, the basis of political power passed from the government to the generals, and when two or more were simultaneously in the field civil war became endemic. Marius was, as Last says, 'the first Roman who made military prowess a claim to direct the civil government and the earliest precursor of the soldier-emperors of the third century A.D.'[2]

When Marius arrived in Africa he pressed on with the war, but with no greater success than had Metellus.[3] At length, after a defeat in 105 B.C., Jugurtha sought refuge with his brother-in-law Bocchus, King of Mauretania. It was then that Marius' quaestor, L. Cornelius Sulla, a young officer of outstanding ability, suggested to him that the speediest way to end the war was to bribe Bocchus to betray Jugurtha. At the risk of his life Sulla went secretly to Bocchus and promised him Western Numidia in exchange for the Numidian king. The offer was accepted and the war brought to an end.

Marius was again elected consul for 104 B.C., an office he successively held in 103, 102 and 101 B.C., and on his return to Rome he was called upon to face a more formidable foe than the elusive Numidians. The Cimbri and Teutoni, who by now had crossed the Rhine into Gaul and had defeated three consular armies, decided between themselves that while the Teutoni moved through Transalpine Gaul (the Province) and crossed the Maritime Alps, the Cimbri would move eastward, and by way of the Brenner Pass descend into Transpadane Gaul. In 102 B.C. Marius annihilated the former at Aquae Sextiae (Aix-en-Provence), and in the year following he and his colleague, Q. Lutatius Catulus, routed the latter at Vercellae (Vercelli). These two victories made Marius the idol of the people.

Intoxicated by his successes, he looked forward to equal triumphs in the Forum. So long as he retained his army his chances were bright, but foolishly he disbanded it, and when he found himself unable to honour the promises he had made to his veterans, he set out to woo the

---

[1] *The Roman Revolution* (1956), p. 15.

[2] *The Cambridge Ancient History*, vol. IX, p. 158.

[3] See Sallust's *The Jugurthine War*, L, LI, for a description of how Marius was nonplussed by the tactics of the Numidians.

*populares*,[1] and entered into a compact with their leaders, Appuleius Saturninus and Servilius Glaucia.

In 101 B.C., he stood as a candidate for his sixth consulship, and with the aid of Saturninus and Glaucia, by dint of bribery, riot, and murder, was elected. Between them they revived the colonial projects of Gaius Gracchus, and introduced an agrarian bill to provide land for Marius' disbanded veterans. Besides colonies in Sicily and Macedonia, the lands of the Celtic tribes in Transpadane Gaul were claimed, and because the new occupants were to include Italians as well as Romans, the former were placed on a footing of equality with the latter. This antagonized the Senate and the people.

The knights, who so far had supported the *populares*, also took fright and abandoned them, and Saturninus and Glaucia, when they found that Marius was an inept politician, threw him over, decided on a *coup d'état*, and in the consular elections of 99 B.C., murdered the senatorial candidate. The Senate once again resorted to the ultimate decree, and Marius, disgusted with the general disorder, put himself at the head of the senators and knights and quelled the revolt, during which Saturninus and Glaucia were murdered. Now that he had alienated all parties, Marius sensed that the Senate and the knights would abandon him, so he discreetly took a prolonged trip to Asia.

## 5. THE FIRST CIVIL WAR

With the departure of Marius, the tide flowed in favour of the Senate; but a few years later the abuses of the knights, who now had complete control of the courts, led to a fresh upheaval. In 91 B.C., M. Livius Drusus,[2] an aristocrat of immense wealth, who had bribed his way to tribunician office,[3] proposed to return the jury-courts to the Senate, double the Senate by the inclusion of 300 knights, and enfranchise the Italians. He carried this legislation *en bloc*, and as it was contrary to law to pass more than one measure at a time, the Senate declared it invalid, and Drusus was assassinated.

When the Italians learnt of his murder, 'they decided to revolt from the Romans altogether, and to make war against them with all their

---

[1] The *populares* were those who sought the support of the proletariat. Their opponents, who were called *optimates*, were an ultra conservative and wealthy caucus which had great influence in the Senate.

[2] Son of Livius Drusus, who wrecked Gaius Gracchus' colonial project.

[3] This was effected by being adopted by a plebeian, see *infra*, Chapter III, pp. 71–72.

might.'[1] Their revolt, known as the Social War[2] (91–88 B.C.) – virtually a civil war – started in Picenum and quickly spread throughout central Italy, Samnium, and Campania. To direct their operations the rebels established their headquarters at Corfinium (Pentima), which significantly they renamed Italia.

In the spring of 90 B.C., one of the consuls took the field in the north with Marius, who had returned from the East, as one of his legates, while the other consul, among whose legates was Sulla, advanced against the Samnites in the south. Next, Etruria and Umbria joined the rebels, and the Roman situation grew so precarious that full citizenship was granted to those allied communities who had not revolted, as well as to all who forthwith laid down their arms. This brought Etruria and Umbria to heel, but in other parts the rebellion continued, and a further concession, which provided that all Italians who returned to their allegiance within sixty days should receive citizenship, reduced the rebellion to the Samnites, who continued the struggle to the bitter end.

While the rebellion was in progress, Mithridates VI,[3] king of Pontus, seized the opportunity to overrun the Roman possessions in the East, a task rendered easy and rapid, because he was welcomed by the people as their deliverer from the exactions of the Roman tax-farmers and money-lenders, of whom thousands were slaughtered.

To meet this new emergency, the Senate entrusted Sulla, consul in 88 B.C., with the direction of the war against Mithridates. But Marius, eager to regain his old popularity and harvest the fabled treasures of Pontus, backed by many of the knights, determined to oust Sulla and replace him. To effect this, he and his backers found a ready tool in the tribune P. Sulpicius Rufus, a bankrupt aristocrat whom they bribed, and when Sulla left Rome to rejoin his army, which at the time was besieging Nola in Campania, Sulpicius passed several laws, one of which conferred the Eastern Command on Marius; orders were then sent to Sulla to surrender his troops. Unfortunately for Marius, the change he had made in recruitment now recoiled on him; for Sulla had no intention of complying with this law. The loyalty of the soldiers he had recruited was assured, it was to him and not to the State; besides

---

1 Appian, *The Civil Wars*, I, 38.

2 The war was so named because it was between the Romans and their allies (*socii*).

3 Mithridates VI (the Great) was one of the most remarkable characters of antiquity, around whom an extensive mythology was created.

they were as eager as he himself was to plunder the East, so at the head of his army he marched on Rome.

As the mob in Rome was powerless to back up Marius, Sulla occupied the city without a fight. Once in control, the Sulpician laws were annulled, and Marius and Sulpicius were proclaimed public enemies; the former escaped, and the latter was killed. Next, Sulla strengthened the Senate by a law which provided that no bill could be brought before the Assembly without the approval of the Senate. Then he held the consular elections, in which L. Cornelius Cinna and Gnaeus Octavius were elected for 87 B.C., and although he suspected Cinna to be untrustworthy, so eager was he to set out against Mithridates that he sailed with his army for Greece.

Sulla was not mistaken in his suspicions of Cinna, for no sooner had he left Italy than a quarrel arose between Cinna and Octavius over the enfranchisement of the Italians; wild rioting followed, and Cinna was deposed by the Senate from his consulship and driven out of Rome. In retaliation, he appealed to the Italians, whose cause he had championed, and the troops in Campania went over to him. Meanwhile Marius, who had come out of hiding, raised an army of slaves in Etruria, and proposed to Cinna that together they should pinch out Rome by a combined attack simultaneously delivered from the north and the south. This was agreed; Ostia, the port of Rome, was captured, and as its loss deprived the city of its food supply, the bulk of Octavius' soldiers deserted to Marius and Cinna. Rome was then occupied for the second time.

Cinna's first act was to rescind the decree outlawing Marius, and Marius, lusting for vengeance, let loose his armed slaves in the city. Octavius was butchered, and for five days and nights Rome was subjected to a reign of terror in which all enemies, real or imaginary, were ruthlessly slaughtered. The heads of the murdered senators were displayed from the *rostra*, and their bodies left unburied to be devoured by dogs.

When the terror subsided, Cinna and Marius declared themselves elected consuls for 86 B.C. They forthwith outlawed Sulla, repealed his legislation, confiscated his property, and forced his family to seek safety in Greece. This was the last act of Marius, for a few days after he had assumed his seventh consulship he was found dead in his bed; and his army of bandits soon followed him. Their orgies of murder had revolted Quintus Sertorius, a leading Marian, and under the pretext of paying them he surrounded them with his Celtic troops and slaughtered them *en masse*: at least 4,000 are said to have perished. For the next three years peace was restored in Italy under the successive consulships of Cinna.

Meanwhile Sulla refused to be distracted by events in Rome; from Epirus he advanced into Boeotia and defeated Mithridates' generals Ariston and Archelaus. Next, he invaded Attica, laid siege to Athens, cut it off from the Piraeus and took it. While thus engaged, another Pontic army invaded Boeotia, and after a sharp tussle was defeated at Chaeronea. In the spring of 85 B.C., Mithridates hurled yet another army into Greece; Sulla came up with it at Orchomenus, and in a desperate battle routed it. He then crossed into Asia in pursuit of an army under L. Valerius Flaccus which, in 86 B.C., had been sent out by Cinna by way of Greece. In Asia Flaccus was murdered by his legate, C. Flavius Fimbria, and when Sulla caught up with the latter, Fimbria's men deserted to him and Fimbria committed suicide. With Greece lost and Asia in turmoil, Mithridates opened peace negotiations with Sulla, who himself was eager to end the war. Peace was concluded in 85 B.C.

Sulla then set to work to restore order in Asia. He imposed an indemnity of 20,000 talents[1] on the province, and as this sum was beyond the resources of the inhabitants, recourse had to be made to the money-lenders, who again brought the province to despair. Once order had been restored, Sulla addressed a letter to the Senate, in which he informed the conscript fathers that he was about to return to Italy to punish those guilty of crimes against him, but that the innocent had no reason to fear.

This announcement caused consternation in Rome. The Senate attempted to negotiate with Sulla; nevertheless Cinna and his colleague, C. Papirius Carbo, prepared for war. Rather than await him in Italy, they decided to send an army to Greece, and in the spring of 84 B.C., when Cinna attempted to force the unwilling soldiers to embark, he perished in a mutiny. Carbo then abandoned the enterprise, and took command of Cisalpine Gaul. Resistance in the south was left to the consuls L. Scipio Asiaticus and Gaius Norbanus, both of the Marian party, and so incapable that, when in the spring of 83 B.C., Sulla landed his army at Brundisium (Brindisi), he was unopposed.

---

[1] An Attic talent of silver was worth £243-15-0. Besides selling a vast number of Asiatics into slavery, and appropriating an enormous amount of loot for himself and his soldiers, Sulla paid into the Roman treasury 15,000 lb. of gold and 115,000 lb. of silver.

At once Calabria and Apulia declared for him, and from all quarters scattered remnants of the *optimates* flocked to his camp. Among them were Q. Caecilius Metellus Pius and M. Licinius Crassus, and in Picenum the youthful Gnaeus Pompeius – better known as Pompey – raised a considerable force in his support.

Soon after he had landed, Sulla set out along the Via Appia to meet the two consuls, who were then hastening toward him; but instead of uniting their forces they moved separately, which enabled Sulla to tackle them in turn. In Campania he defeated Norbanus near Capua, after which he advanced up the Via Latina and met Scipio at Teanum; but Scipio's army was so badly shaken by Norbanus' defeat that, after an abortive armistice, which would appear to have added to its demoralization, it went over to Sulla. Next, instead of marching on Rome, Sulla spent the remainder of 83 B.C. in consolidating his position. He sent agents to all parts of Italy to raise troops, and to conciliate the Italians and win them to his cause.[1]

The consuls for 82 B.C. were Carbo and Marius the Younger, who successfully recruited large forces in Cisalpine Gaul, Etruria, and Samnium: Carbo took command in the north, while Marius was responsible for Rome and the south. When fighting was resumed, Sulla sent Metellus and Pompey north to hold back the former, while he himself marched against the latter. He routed Marius in the battle of Sacriportus – between Signia (Segni) and Praeneste (Palestrina) – and drove him and his shattered remnants into Praeneste, where Quintus Ofella was left to invest him. Next, Sulla occupied Rome, but immediately after pressed on north and met Carbo near Clusium (Chiusi), where an indecisive battle was fought. In the meantime Metellus invaded Cisalpine Gaul, and Pompey and Crassus defeated the Marians in Umbria. Carbo's men now became so demoralized that Carbo lost heart, abandoned his army and sought refuge in Sicily.

While still in the field, Carbo had made attempt after attempt to raise the siege of Praeneste, and now that he had fled, help in earnest came from southern Italy; an immense army of Samnites and Lucanians, under Pontius of Telesia and Marcus Lamponius, set out to reinforce the Marians who were attempting to raise the siege. When Sulla learnt of this, he hastened to Ofella's support, and on his arrival, Pontius and his colleagues decided to abandon the enterprise and instead

---

[1] 'Sulla made a league with the states of Italy, lest he should be suspected of intending to deprive them of their constitution and the right of suffrage, which had been lately conceded to them' (Livy, *Epit.*, LXXXVI).

march on Rome. Early on November 1, 82 B.C., they set out for the capital.

Directly this unexpected move became known to Sulla, he ordered his cavalry with all speed to head off Pontius; next, he hastened forward his legions, and at about noon came up with his enemy outside the Colline Gate, at the extreme north of the city. Not pausing to rest his weary men – they had marched over 20 miles – he drew up his line of battle and attacked. The battle was stubbornly contested and lasted into the night. Sulla's left wing, under his personal command, was driven back in disorder against the city wall, and so critical was his situation that he believed the battle lost; but his right wing, under Marcus Licinius Crassus, broke through its opponents. Little quarter was given, and the next day, 4,000 Samnites, who had been made prisoners, including Pontius and two other generals, were herded together near the temple of Bellona, where the Senate was in session, and butchered.

Praeneste forthwith surrendered, was given up to pillage, and Marius committed suicide. Pompey was then ordered to subdue the Marians in Sicily and Africa, and soon after, except for Spain, to where Sertorius had, in 83 B.C., been sent by the Marians as praetor, Sulla's authority was supreme over almost all the Roman world.

The proscription which followed the occupation of Rome put into the shade the slaughterings of Marius, not that it was more brutal, but more systematic and widely spread: all who at any time had opposed Sulla, or had aided the Marians, were either outlawed or butchered on the spot. It would appear that either 4,700 or 6,000 names of victims were published in the official lists; and, according to Appian, they included those of 90 senators, 15 consulars and 2,600 knights;[1] probably many more were done away with privately. Their property, to the value of 350 million sesterces (£3,500,000), was confiscated to provide allotments for 120,000 discharged soldiers, and whole communities were punished: Etruria was disfranchised and reduced to the status of a colony, and throughout its length and breadth Samnium was ruthlessly devastated. To control the turbulent rabble in Rome and to have a body-guard ready at hand for an emergency, Sulla manumitted and enfranchised 10,000 young and vigorous slaves of the proscribed, known as Cornelii,[2] and armed and quartered them in the city.

As the two consulships were now vacant – Carbo had since perished in Sicily – to give a legal complexion to his authority, Sulla instructed

---

[1] *The Civil Wars*, I, 103.    [2] *Ibid.*, I, 100 and 104.

the Senate to appoint an *interrex*,[1] who, at his instigation, carried a law in the Assembly – an unprecedented act – by which Sulla was elected dictator for life, and all his acts were ratified in advance. 'It was,' writes Mr A. W. Gomme, 'the first example of a law for the delegation of the imperium to one man for an unlimited period, the basis therefore of the later principate.'[2] Thus Sulla, all but in name, restored the monarchy, and his problem was – how should he make use of his regal power?

Two pressing problems had emerged from out of the Social and Civil Wars, and although the discord which had distracted the Republic since the days of the Gracchi might be temporarily suppressed by force, neither problem could be solved as long as its causes remained vital. The one was, how to create a government which would do justice to all classes; and the other, how to prevent the army becoming the tool of rival generals.

The enfranchisement of the Italians had added vastly to the electorate; nevertheless, as long as the elections continued to be held at Rome, it was meaningless, because the distances to be travelled by the new electors prohibited the bulk of them from casting their votes in the capital. Therefore, unless voting was decentralized and polling carried out in towns and groups of villages, however extensive the electorate might become, the elections would normally continue to be decided by the rabble in Rome, or rather by the party which bought its votes.

Sulla made no attempt to solve this problem; his policy was purely reactionary. It was to restore to the Senate its old authority, which meant that its predominance over the magistrates and the people must be assured. His means of accomplishing this was to suppress all possible opposition to the Senate, and not to redress the evils which had led to the Social and Civil Wars.

He deprived the knights of their privilege of jurors, who henceforth were to be selected from the Senate alone, and as the Senate had been depleted by wars and proscriptions, and even at its old strength of 300 could not supply the requisite number of juror, sas previously proposed by Drusus, he added to it 300 new members, mostly knights. Further,

---

[1] Originally the *interrex* was a magistrate appointed by the senators on the death of a king to exercise provisional authority. Under the Republic, on the death or incapacity of both consuls, he was appointed until new consuls were elected. He exercised full consular powers.

[2] 'The Roman Republic', *European Civilization, its Origin and Development* (1935), vol. II, p. 140.

he enacted that the members of the enlarged Senate were to be maintained without the sanction of the censors.[1]

He revived his earlier law which forbade the submission of any bill to the Assembly until it had received senatorial sanction, and enacted that no tribune should be eligible for any other office. Further, the tribunes were forbidden to convene meetings of the people, and although their right of veto was not abolished, presumably because the Senate might find it convenient in order to check an obstructive consul, it was restricted.

He enacted that no man might be elected praetor unless he had served as quaestor, and as consul unless he had served as praetor, with an interval of two years between promotions; and that no man might be re-elected consul, praetor, or tribune, until after an interval of ten years.

These changes were little more than administrative trimmings; in no way did they solve the first of the above two problems.

As regards the army, Sulla left things much as they were. By now it had become customary to appoint pro-magistrates instead of magistrates as governors of the provinces. He standardized this, ruled that consuls and praetors should remain in Italy during their year of office, and that in the following year they should be sent as proconsuls and propraetors to govern the provinces. As there were now ten provinces in all,[2] he increased the number of praetors from six to eight, so that with the two consuls there would be sufficient pro-magistrates. As hitherto, the command of the army was to be entrusted to the provincial governors, who were forbidden to leave their provinces or engage in war without the authority of the Senate. He made no attempt to modify the system of recruitment, to provide pensions or erect barracks, and although in normal times the armies of the provincial governors were too small for them to cause serious trouble, the danger remained that in a war of magnitude there was nothing to prevent an ambitious governor from emulating the part Sulla had himself played in the Civil War. 'Once and for all he had showed,' writes Professor Last, 'that an elaborate programme of legislation, of the sort which the

---

[1] The censors (there were always two) were magistrates responsible for the census of those liable for cavalry service. They possessed the right of striking off the names of those who no longer merited the privilege of fighting as knights, including senators.

[2] Sicily, Sardinia and Corsica, the two Spains, the two Gauls, Africa, Macedonia, Asia, and Cilicia.

Gracchi had lamentably failed to carry through with the support of the Concilium Plebis, could be enacted in all its parts by one who relied upon the army.'[1] This, and not his enactments, was the legacy he bequeathed to the Republic.

In 80 B.C., to his dictatorship he added the consulship, and took as his colleague Metellus Pius. A year later he declined re-election as incompatible with his own ordinances, and at the opening of that year resigned his dictatorship, confident of the loyalty of his supporters, veterans, and *Cornelii.* In 78 B.C., in his sixtieth year, and while writing his memoirs, he suddenly collapsed and died. On his tomb in the Campus Martius was engraved the epitaph he had himself composed: 'No friend has ever served me, no enemy has ever wronged me whom I have not repaid in full.'[2]

[1] *The Cambridge Ancient History*, vol. IX, p. 312.
[2] Plutarch, *Sulla*, XXXVIII.

# II

# *The Rise of Pompey*

## I. HIS PERSONALITY AND CHARACTER

BARELY was Sulla dead than the Senate found itself faced with yet another crisis. The consuls for 78 B.C. were Q. Lutatius Catulus and M. Aemilius Lepidus. The latter had been elected in spite of the warnings of Sulla, and no sooner was he in office than he set about to win the leadership of the counter-revolutionary forces, whose aim was the annulment of the Sullan constitution. Encouraged by his election, the Italians in northern Etruria revolted and evicted Sulla's veterans from their settlements at Faesulae. In reply, the Senate instructed Lepidus to raise an army and suppress the insurrection; but no sooner had he recruited it than he went over to the insurgents and marched on Rome to demand a second consulship and the full restoration of the tribunate. This threw the Senate into consternation, and as Catulus was no soldier, he was instructed to hold Rome, and Pompey was called from retirement to raise an army and march against Lepidus.

Pompey, who from now on will figure largely in this book, was born on September 29, 106 B.C., and, as we have seen, was one of the first to join Sulla when he landed at Brundisium in 83 B.C. He served him so ably that Sulla saluted him *Imperator*, and in the following year, as already mentioned, he entrusted him with the task of destroying the remnants of the Marians in Sicily and Africa. This he did so speedily that he was carried away by his success, and, although no more than twenty-four years of age, he demanded the honour of a triumph and the right to use the title of *Magnus* ('The Great') as a surname. When Sulla reminded him that his request for a triumph was unprecedented, because it was only given to dictators, consuls, and praetors who had defeated a foreign enemy, Pompey retorted, unabashed: 'More men worship the rising than the setting sun.' As Sulla did not catch what he said, a bystander repeated Pompey's words, whereupon Sulla replied: 'Let him triumph,'[1] and forthwith retired him from public life.

In this episode is to be found the key to Pompey's ultimate failure. Though a soldier of marked ability, he was lacking in political sense.[2] On this occasion, he failed to realize that dictators do not welcome possible competitors; that ambition in their subordinates is not what they look for; and that when serving such men, modesty rather than arrogance pays best. As the story is unfolded, we shall see that, while Pompey, the soldier, could, like a second Sisyphus, push his military rocks to the top of the hill, Pompey, the politician, kicked them down again. But for his lack of political acumen, there might never have been a Julius Caesar as he is known to history.

It is difficult to assess Pompey's worth as a general, because the records of his campaigns are so lacking in detail. Frequently called a lucky general, he was less so than Caesar, and, in spite of good luck, his achievements are sufficiently remarkable to warrant the verdict that, until he met Caesar, he was the outstanding general of his day. Mommsen's estimate of him is that, although he was 'An intelligent, brave and experienced, thoroughly excellent soldier, he was still, even in his military capacity, without trace of any higher gifts. It was characteristic of him as a general, as well as in other respects, to proceed with caution bordering on timidity, and, if possible, to give the decisive blow only when he had established an immense superiority over his opponent.'[3] This, as later will become apparent, is a fairly just estimate of his generalship; to it, may be added that his successes, like strong wine, went to his head.

Although an able administrator, as a statesman he was an unqualified failure, 'constantly tormented', as Mommsen says, 'by an ambition which was frightened of its own aims.'[4] In great matters he was shortsighted, and although his politics were Sullan, he was little at home in the optimate party. His flatterers, so Plutarch tells us, likened him to Alexander the Great, and whether because of this or not, the great Macedonian would appear to have been constantly in his mind. His

---

[1] Plutarch, *Pompey*, XIV, 3.

[2] Sir Tenny Frank (*Roman Imperialism* (1914), p. 318) remarks: 'He never had a political policy of his own; in fact, he never in the least understood the art of politics.'

[3] *Op. cit.*, vol. IV, p. 10. In this respect his generalship may be compared with that of Ulysses S. Grant and Viscount Montgomery.

[4] *Ibid.*, vol. IV, p. 12.

respect for womanhood is comparable with Alexander's, and Plutarch mentions that, when the concubines of Mithridates were brought to him, 'he used not one, but restored them to their parents and kindred.'[1] Another similarity was, he treated the corpse of Mithridates in a kingly way, as Alexander treated the corpse of Darius, 'provided for the expenses of the funeral and directed that the remains should receive royal interment.'[2] Also, like Alexander, he founded many cities and repaired many damaged towns;[3] searched for the ocean, which was thought to surround the world,[4] and rewarded his soldiers munificently.[5] To these likenesses Mommsen adds, that he was 'the first to depart from the barbarous custom of putting to death the captive kings and generals of the enemy after they had been exhibited in triumph'[6] – a deed which would have been abhorrent to Alexander. And Appian mentions that in his triumph he is said to have worn 'a cloak of Alexander the Great;'[7] though certainly a figment should the actual cloak be meant, it fittingly clinches the comparison.

Such was the man whom the Senate called upon to crush Lepidus, and from then on the sun of Pompey was to blaze in the political heavens until it set at Pharsalus.

## 2. HIS CAMPAIGN AGAINST SERTORIUS

While Catulus held Rome, Pompey advanced north and defeated Lepidus' subordinate, M. Junius Brutus – father of the tyrannicide – in Cisalpine Gaul. Next, he moved south, came up with Lepidus at the port of Cosa in Etruria and defeated him; but because he failed to pursue him, Lepidus with 20,000 infantry and 1,500 cavalry escaped to Sardinia. Soon after, Lepidus died, and his army, under Vento Perpenna, sailed to Spain to join Sertorius.

When, in 83 B.C., Sertorius arrived in Spain,[8] he set about to recruit an army of Celtiberians and resident Romans, to win and hold that country for the Marians. In the following year he was compelled to seek refuge in Mauretania (Morocco); but in 80 B.C. he returned to head a revolt in Lusitania (Southern Portugal). Alarmed by this insurrection, in 79 B.C., Sulla appointed Metellus Pius governor of Further Spain; but he was no match for Sertorius, a commander of

---

1 *Pompey*, XXXVI, 2.  
3 *Ibid.*, 115.  
5 *Mithridatic Wars*, 116.  
7 *Mithridatic Wars*, 117.  

2 Appian, *Mithridatic Wars*, 113.  
4 Plutarch, *Pompey*, XXXVIII, 2.  
6 *Op. cit.*, vol. IV, p. 10.  
8 *Supra*, Chapter I, p. 33.

genius, and by the end of 77 B.C., Sertorius was master of Spain from the Sierra Morena to the Pyrenees, with influence extending into Aquitania and Transalpine Gaul. About this time he was reinforced by Perpenna, and the Senate, fearful lest, like a second Hannibal, he might attempt to invade Italy, both to reinforce Metellus and to be rid of Pompey, who after the departure of Lepidus had refused to disband his army, at Pompey's request appointed him proconsul of Nearer Spain to co-operate with Metellus.

Pompey set out in the autumn of 77 B.C., wintered north of the Pyrenees, and early in 76 B.C., opened his campaign, but was out-generalled by Sertorius who was an adept in guerrilla warfare. Nevertheless, in the following year, through force of numbers the tide began to turn against Sertorius. Still worse for him, as his prestige declined, dissensions broke out among his followers, which culminated in a plot contrived by Perpenna, and in 72 B.C., he was assassinated. 'So ended,' writes Mommsen, 'one of the greatest men, if not the very greatest man, that Rome had hitherto produced – a man who under more fortunate circumstances would perhaps have become the regenerator of his country.'[1]

## 3. OUTBREAK OF THE THIRD MITHRIDATIC WAR

While Pompey was in Spain, Nicomedes IV of Bithynia died, and, according to the Romans, he bequeathed his kingdom to them. This was unacceptable to Mithridates VI of Pontus, and as he was aware that the Romans had their hands full with Sertorius in Spain, and that the inhabitants of Bithynia, rendered frantic by the Roman tax-collectors, were ready to welcome him,[2] in 74 B.C. he invaded Bithynia, and started the Third Mithridatic War.

To meet this emergency, the Senate sent out the consuls M. Aurelius Cotta and L. Licinius Lucullus, the former with a fleet and army to occupy Bithynia, while the latter was assigned Cilicia and Asia. A series of campaigns followed, and in 71 B.C. Mithridates was so badly defeated by Lucullus at Cabeira (Niksar) that he fled to Armenia to seek the assistance of King Tigranes. Lucullus demanded his surrender, and when it was refused he invaded Armenia. In 69 B.C., he laid siege

---

[1] *Op. cit.*, vol. IV, p. 33.

[2] Plutarch in his life of Lucullus (IV, 1, and XX, 4–5) writes, that by now the fine of 20,000 talents imposed by Sulla on the province of Asia had by usury been advanced to 120,000 talents, and to meet their taxes the people were compelled to sell their sons and daughters.

to Tigranocerta;[1] defeated Tigranes when he attempted to relieve it; then stormed the city, and some time later advanced on Artaxata (Adresh), capital of Armenia. But the hardships of the campaign were so great that his men refused to follow him, and Lucullus withdrew to Nisibis (Nisibin). Tigranes then recovered most of his kingdom, and in the spring, or early summer, of 67 B.C., at Mount Scotius, a few miles north of Zela (Zilleh), Mithridates surrounded Lucullus' lieutenant, L. Valerius Triarius, routed his insubordinate army, regained most of Pontus, and withdrew to the fortress of Talaura (site unidentified). At the time, Lucullus was on his way from Nisibis to join Triarius, but instead of investing Mithridates at Talaura, he decided to complete the subjection of Tigranes. But when his troops learnt that Acilius Glabrio (consul 67 B.C.)[2] had been appointed to supersede Lucullus in Bithynia and Pontus, at the instigation of Publius Clodius – Lucullus' brother-in-law – his troops mutinied,[3] and Tigranes plundered Cappadocia. Thus ended the first phase of the Third Mithridatic War.

## 4. REVOLT OF SPARTACUS

Barely had Lucullus left for the East than the most devastating of all her slave wars broke out in Italy. Spartacus, a Thracian gladiator in the gladiatorial training school at Capua, with seventy of his comrades determined to make a bid for freedom. They overcame their guard, armed themselves with daggers and clubs, and took refuge in the crater of Mount Vesuvius, where they were joined by many fugitive slaves. The troops – 'forces picked up in haste and at random'[4] – sent against them, under one of the praetors, were ignominiously routed; a victory which encouraged so many malcontents to flock to Spartacus that, according to Appian, his army soon numbered 70,000 men.

In 72 B.C., both consuls took the field against him and were defeated, after which the rebels ranged unchecked over Italy, and in panic the Senate ordered M. Licinius Crassus, one of the praetors for 72 B.C., to raise six new legions and suppress the insurrection. Crassus succeeded

---

[1] The site of Tigranocerta is disputed. Dr Holmes (*The Roman Republic*, vol. I, p. 425) considers that it may have stood upon the site of Tel Ermen, some 30 miles west of Nisibis.

[2] Already in 68 B.C., the consul Q. Marcius Rex had superseded Lucullus in Cilicia.

[3] Dio Cassius, XXXVI, 14-15.

[4] Appian, *The Civil Wars*, I, 116.

in driving Spartacus into Bruttium, and, when he attempted to escape to Sicily, he blockaded him in the toe of Italy by means of an immense earthwork which stretched from shore to shore. In spite of this prodigious work, Spartacus broke out, and the Senate, more terrified than ever, called upon Pompey, who with his army had just returned from Spain, to assist Crassus in quelling the rebellion.

When Spartacus learnt of this, he set out for Brundisium in order to escape by sea to Epirus, but when he discovered that the port was garrisoned, he abandoned the attempt, and soon after was brought to battle in Lucania by Crassus, was defeated and slain. Five thousand of his followers, as they were attempting escape, fell in with Pompey, who exterminated them, and 6,000 captured by Crassus were crucified along the Appian Way between Capua and Rome.

When the insurrection ended, two unemployed armies were left in Italy, and although the mutual dislikes of their leaders – Crassus and Pompey – were pronounced, neither wanted to start a civil war by fighting the other. Instead, both looked for a consulship in 70 B.C., and to gain it each needed the support of the other. Crassus' assets were that he was fabulously rich,[1] and half the Senate was indebted to him; Pompey's, that he was the idol of the people. Therefore, were they to support each other's candidature, they had little to fear from either the people or the Senate.

So they set their differences aside, provisionally linked arms, and to make certain of the voters they promised the people to restore to the tribunes their former powers, and won the support of the knights by offering to hand the jury-courts back to them. As long as they did not disband their armies the Senate was paralysed; therefore, on the pretext of awaiting their triumphs, they maintained them, and camped them outside Rome. Thus, once again, the devotion of the legions to their leaders became the key of office.

They were duly elected, and on January 2, 70 B.C., the day after they assumed their consulships, by what process is unknown, they disbanded their armies without trouble. Then they repealed the legislation of Sulla, and the old regime was restored. At the close of their consulships they retired into private life; Crassus to his money-making, and Pompey, who could expect nothing from the Senate, to contemplate how best he could return to public affairs.

[1] Crassus' wealth was derived from Sulla's proscriptions, money-lending and speculations in real estate, etc.

## 5. HIS CAMPAIGN AGAINST THE PIRATES

Until recent times piracy has flourished in the Mediterranean, but at no time more so than during the revolutionary period of the Roman Republic, when from mere freebooters the pirates organized themselves into a piratical state with headquarters in Cilicia and Crete. This was due partly to the turmoil of the times, which hindered policing the seas, and partly also to the influence of the Roman slave dealers and tax-gatherers who tolerated the pirates as wholesale purveyors of slaves. According to Plutarch, at the time of the Third Mithridatic War the pirate fleets numbered 1,000 ships, and Appian writes that they operated 'in squadrons under pirate chiefs, who were like generals of an army'.[1] They raided coastal roads, laid seige to coastal towns, had recently vanquished two Roman praetors in naval engagements off Sicily, and had 'assailed the coasts of Italy around Brundisium and Etruria, and seized and carried off some women of noble families . . . and also two praetors with their very insignia of office.'[2] But most damaging of all, they intercepted the Roman corn fleets plying between Sicily, Sardinia, and Africa and the ports of Italy. As this raised the price of grain and led to famine and rioting in Rome, it became a political question.

Pompey was astute enough to realize that, were he to exploit the situation, and gain the support of the people, more particularly the rabble in Rome, who were the chief sufferers, he would be in a position to override senatorial opposition to his return to office. Therefore, in January, 67 B.C., he put up one of his supporters, the tribune Aulus Gabinius, to propose a bill in the Assembly which empowered the people to select among the senators of consular rank a dictator of the seas to suppress piracy. He was to be appointed, not for the customary six months, but for three years; be given a fleet of 200 sail; authorized to raise as large an army as he thought fit; be supplied with 6,000 talents in coin; be allowed fifteen legates, with power of *imperium*, and be allotted as his area of operations the whole Mediterranean and its coasts up to 50 miles inland. No so all-embracing a command had ever before been allotted to a Roman general.

The people were overjoyed with these proposals, but since it was obvious that the man of consular rank could be no other than Pompey, the Senate vigorously opposed the bill. The people then stormed the

[1] *Mithridatic Wars,* 92.
[2] *Ibid.,* 92–93.

senate house, and the bill was carried in the Assembly in spite of senatorial opposition. Pompey was elected, and the first thing he did was to persuade the Assembly to grant him power to increase his forces to 500 ships, 120,000 legionaries, 5,000 cavalry, and 24 senators who had been generals of armies and two quaestors.[1] The immediate result was a fall in the price of grain, and the most significant that, as Professor F. B. Marsh writes: 'From the day the bill was passed in 67 B.C., till Pompey disbanded his army in 61 B.C., he was the Emperor of Rome all but in name.'[2] Or, as Plutarch puts it: 'not an admiral, but a monarch.'[3]

Pompey's plan was an able one: it was first to close the strait of Gibraltar, the Dardanelles and the Bosporus; next to divide the Mediterranean into areas of operations – Plutarch mentions thirteen and Appian nine – to each of which was assigned a squadron under an admiral. All areas were to be swept simultaneously, in order to prevent the pirates from concentrating, and the impetus was to be from west to east, so that they would progressively be driven from area to area eastward, until they could finally be rounded up in the north-east corner of the Mediterranean.

The campaign opened early in 67 B.C., and as Pompey was anxious to end it as rapidly as possible – other ideas were brewing in his head – to strike terror into the pirates he first dealt with all prisoners ruthlessly, and then, once he had thoroughly terrified them, when he had driven those who had escaped his net to their lairs in Cilicia, he offered a free pardon to all who voluntarily submitted, which they did in droves. He then distributed them in various parts of Asia Minor, in Achaia and elsewhere, and allotted to them deserted cities and land in the hope that they would take to a settled life. From start to finish this remarkable campaign took three months, and rightly it added enormously to Pompey's prestige.

The speed with which Pompey reduced the pirates was largely due to his desire to add at as early a date as possible Lucullus' command to his own. Therefore, once his campaign was at an end, instead of returning to Italy, he remained in Asia, while his agents in Rome secured the appointment for him. There could be little doubt that they would succeed, because Marcius Rex and Acilius Glabrio had proved themselves to be worthless soldiers, and there was no other Roman who approached Pompey in fame.

[1] *Pompey*, XXVI, 2.
[2] *The Founding of the Roman Empire* (1927), p. 68.
[3] *Pompey*, XXV, 2.

## 6. HIS CAMPAIGN AGAINST MITHRIDATES

At the beginning of 66 B.C., with the whole-hearted support of the *populares*, the tribune Gaius Manilius proposed a bill by which Pompey was to be entrusted, in addition to the powers he had already received, with the government of Asia, Bithynia, and Cilicia, and the chief command against Mithridates and Tigranes. Pompey's prestige won the day; the bill was passed with little opposition.

When, in 66 B.C., Pompey opened his first campaign, Mithridates was probably in the vicinity of Cabira, and as he was not strong enough to meet Pompey in the field, he fell back, devastated the country as he withdrew, and at length occupied a formidable hill position, probably near the future Nicopolis. Because Pompey became aware that Mithridates was determined not to come out of his entrenchments, he carried out a remarkable night assault and routed him. Mithridates, however, succeeded in effecting his escape, and when Tigranes refused him refuge, he withdrew to Colchis on the north-eastern corner of the Black Sea. After his victory Pompey pushed on to Artaxata, where Tigranes surrendered to him, and, on payment of 6,000 talents, was reinstated by Pompey as an ally of Rome to hold Armenia as a buffer state.

Next, Pompey crossed the Araxes (Aras) river and wintered in the valley of the Cyrus (Kur). His intention was, before following up Mithridates, to secure his rear by first subduing the Albanian and Iberian tribesmen of the Caucasus. He did so, and then set out westward for the Crimea, where Mithridates had retired; but when he found the road to be impracticable he returned to Pontus. At the fortress of Talaura he spent thirty days in making out an inventory of the treasures stored there; founded Nicopolis (near Purkh) in commemoration of his victory over Mithridates; restored many towns; settled his time-expired soldiers in colonies, and organized Pontus as a Roman province.

In the spring of 64 B.C., he set out for Syria, proclaimed it a Roman province, and, early in the following year, quitted Antioch to invade Palestine. There he laid siege to Jerusalem, and after three months took it by storm.

Some time before the siege opened, and when on the march toward Petra – south of the Dead Sea and near modern Elji – Pompey learnt that Mithridates' son, Pharnaces, had rebelled against his father, and that Mithridates, after failure to commit suicide by taking poison, had ordered one of his Galatian officers to kill him, which he did. 'So died Mithridates,' writes Appian, '. . . the sixteenth in descent from Darius, the son of Hystaspes, king of the Persians.'[1] He had warred against Rome for twenty-four years.

The Third Mithridatic War was at an end, the conquest of the East was finished, and Pompey, after he had settled affairs in Syria, returned to Pontus to instate Pharnaces king of Bosporus (the land adjoining the strait of Kerch) as a reward for having brought to his death the most formidable opponent Rome had faced since the days of Hannibal.

## 7. HE DISBANDS HIS ARMY

The war made Pompey the uncrowned emperor of the East, and it endowed him with power and authority possessed by no Roman before his day. Although, like every Roman conqueror, he exploited the lands he conquered, nevertheless he gave their peoples peace such as they had not enjoyed since the fall of the Persian empire; and to the ancient world the consequences of his conquests were as great as those of Caesar's Gallic Wars.

His homeward journey was the progress of an absolute king. On his way, Plutarch writes, he treated all cities he passed through with a royal munificence, so that he might 'set foot in Italy with a reputation more brilliant than that of any other man.'[2] At Ephesus, before his soldiers embarked, he distributed to them in prize-money 384 million sesterces (£3,840,000), and still had 480 million (£4,800,000) left to pay into the treasury.[3]

In December, 62 B.C., he disembarked his army at Brundisium, and, except for a small personal escort, he forthwith disbanded it; whereupon the cloud of fear which had hung so heavily over Rome dispersed.

Why did he take this fatal step? Fatal, not because he deprived himself of power to establish a tyranny; but fatal because, without an army to back him, he could not compel the Senate and the people, should they refuse to do so, to ratify his *acta* – the treaties he had made with the Oriental princes – and provide the land he had promised his discharged soldiers.[4] Possibly, such a contingency never troubled his mind; possibly, he relied on his men flocking back to him should he need them. But what would seem more probable is what Mommsen

[1] *Mithridatic Wars*, 112.
[2] *Pompey*, XLII, 6.
[3] Besides this he augmented the annual tributary revenue of Rome from 200 million to 340 million sesterces, and vastly enriched himself.
[4] Dio (XXXVII, 20) overlooks this in his praise of him for disbanding his army 'on his own initiative'.

suggests. 'He was one of those men who are capable it may be of a crime, but not of insubordination; in a good as in a bad sense, he was thoroughly a soldier.'[1] The bad sense was, that he was oblivious of the political implications of his act, which it is unlikely he would have been had there existed at the time a rival general to awaken them. His unique position would appear to have been his stumbling-block, he could not see beyond himself and was blinded by his own glory.

In September, 61 B.C., he held his triumph. In it inscriptions in advance of the procession were carried, which informed the spectators that he had triumphed over Pontus, Armenia, Cappadocia, Paphlagonia, Media, Colchis, Iberia, Albania, Syria, Cilicia, Mesopotamia, Phoenicia, Palestine, Judaea, and Arabia; had destroyed 1,000 pirate strongholds; had founded 39 cities, and had placed 20,000 talents of coined money in the treasury.[2] Three hundred and twenty-four captives, royal princes, princesses, satraps, generals, pirate chieftains and others, followed behind their conqueror. And what redounds to Pompey's credit is his disregard of precedent; he did not allow his captives to be led to execution. All, except the royal personages, who were interned, were sent back to their homes at the public expense. Also it redounds to his intelligence that, except for the privilege of wearing the laurel wreath and general's cloak at the public games, he refused all other honours, because they 'were liable to bring him merely envy and hatred, even from the very givers, without enabling him to benefit anyone or to be benefited.'[3]

The wise course for the Senate to take was to win Pompey's friendship, if only to have him at call should his services be needed in the future. The price was a moderate one, it was the ratification of his acta, and the granting of land to his discharged soldiers, for the purchase of which there was now ample money in the treasury. Instead, the Senate set out to humiliate him; it haggled over his acta one by one, and quibbled over the cost of land for his men.[4]

Thwarted by the Senate, Pompey turned to the Assembly, and in January, 60 B.C., the tribune L. Flavius introduced on his behalf a land purchasing bill. But the urban voters were not interested in it, and, as in the days of the Gracchi and Marius, their enthusiasm for their former idol had volatilized. Therefore, six months later, Pompey allowed Flavius to drop the bill. 'Thus he learned that he did not possess any

[1] *Op. cit.*, vol. IV, p. 182.    [2] Plutarch, *Pompey*, XLV, 3.
[3] Dio, XXXVII, 21, 3–4, and 23, 4.
[4] Dio, XXXVII, 49, 1–2.

real power . . . and he repented of having let his legions go so soon and of having put himself in the power of his enemies.'[1]

Throughout, Pompey displayed a lack of political acumen which is difficult to understand in so great a soldier and administrator, for were his soldiers not provided for, their loyalty to him would be lost. He had relied upon his prestige, and had overlooked that, unless prestige is backed by force, it is no more than tinsel. Once he had, like Samson, lost his locks, he was at the mercy of the Senate and the people. To refuse to ratify his *acta* and provide land for his soldiers was a purblind thing to do. The oligarchs had learnt nothing from the revolutionary period, and had forgotten nothing of their heydays which had preceded it. They could not see that their humiliation of Pompey was unlikely to be overlooked by the next great general. And were he not to overlook it, and were he faced with a rival, as Marius had been with Sulla, then another civil war was inevitable. They had not long to wait for this man, he was already in Rome, and his name was Gaius Julius Caesar.

[1] Dio, XXXVII, 50, 5-6.

# III

# *The Rise of Julius Caesar*

## I. HIS PERSONALITY AND CHARACTER

CAESAR was the product of what may be called the Roman Renaissance which, since the days of the Scipios, had influenced Roman society as profoundly as the Medieval Renaissance was to influence Italian society; both were rooted in the learning and culture of classical Greece.

He would have admired the Italian despots, and have approved of what Machiavelli meant by *virtù* – not goodness, but vigour, ability, and above all success. Like the Medici, he was an artist of power, indifferent to moral distinctions, and, in consequence, he was possessed of an extraordinary versatility of mind. Like them, he was a generous and intelligent patron of learning and the arts, with a taste for the magnificent. As ruthless and unscrupulous as they were in gaining power, like many of them he could be just and considerate once power had been gained. When supreme power was his, he exercised it with an unexpected degree of moderation, and Suetonius tells us: 'The resentment he entertained against any one was never so implacable that he did not very willingly renounce it when opportunity offered.'[1]

A realist to his fingertips, he was not led astray by ideals and ideologies. Astute, rather than imaginative, he dissected things into their constituent parts; was clear-sighted rather than long-sighted; saw the immediate problem; set out to solve it, and never discarded a possible advantage for a problematically more attractive aim, thereby risking making the best the enemy of the good. Dio Cassius' opinion of him is illuminating:

'For he did not act in such a way [he writes] as to seem to be defending himself against anybody, but so as to arrange everything to his own

[1] Suetonius, *Div. Iul.*, LXXIII.

advantage while arousing the least hatred. Therefore he visited his retribution secretly and in places where one would least have expected it, both for the sake of his reputation, in order to avoid seeming to be of a wrathful disposition, and also to the end that no one should learn of it beforehand and so be on his guard, or try to inflict some serious injury upon him before being injured. For he was not so much concerned about what had already occurred as he was to prevent future attacks. As a result he would pardon many of those, even, who had vexed him greatly, or pursue them only to a limited extent, because he believed they would do no further injury. . . .'[1]

And further:

'. . . he showed himself perfectly ready to serve and flatter everybody, even ordinary persons, and shrank from no speech or action in order to get possession of the objects for which he strove. He did not mind temporary grovelling when weighed against subsequent power, and he cringed as before superiors to the very men whom he was endeavouring to dominate.'[2] Also he was aware 'that the multitude often purposely [cast] many idle [slurs] upon their superiors, in the effort to draw them into strife, so that they might seem to be their equals and of like importance with them . . . and he did not see fit to make anybody his rival in this manner.'[3]

His clear-sightedness, which amounted to intuition, was largely due to his mind being undisturbed either by recollections or by expectations, and to the fact that he was seldom led away by illusions concerning the abilities of men or the appearance of events. He was a supreme opportunist, whose self-confidence, combined with his faith in his fortune, his audacity and his subtlety, enabled him to take chances unimagined by others. Possessed of a magnetic personality and boundless egotism he lacked both fear and scruple; a man whose end governed his means, and a man who would allow nothing to stand in his way.

As a patrician and an aristocrat, his *dignitas* (honour) demanded that it was his duty to reward and protect his friends and clients. When, toward the end of his life, he was censured, because he promoted some of his faithful adherents of low origin to the Senate, he replied: 'Had I been assisted by robbers and cut-throats in the defence of my honour,

---

[1] Dio, XXXVIII, 11, 4–6 (see also XLIII, 12, 3, and 13, 1–2).
[2] *Ibid.*, XXXVII, 37, 2–3. Appian (*Civil Wars*, II, 10) calls him 'a master of dissimulation'.
[3] Dio, XXXVIII, 11, 1–2.

I should have made them the same recompense.'[1] – 'He was Caesar and he would keep faith.'[2]

From his youth he avoided quarrels, not only because they aggravated present troubles, but because they compromised the future; and when worsted his malice was disguised. Instead of showing resentment, he chaffed the pirates who captured him, and thereby lulled them into a false sense of security.[3] Although, as Suetonius implies, he was sensitive to slander, 'When C. Calvus, after publishing some scandalous epigrams upon him, endeavoured to effect a reconciliation by the intercession of friends, he wrote to him, of his own accord, the first letter. And when Valerius Catullus, who had, as he himself observed, fixed such a stain upon his character in his verses upon Mamurra[4] as never could be obliterated, he . . . invited him to supper the same day. . . .'[5] Metaphorically, instead of hitting him on the jaw, he patted him on his stomach – surely a more effective way of putting a stop to his scurrilous lampoons.

Cicero's frequent opposition he tolerated with equanimity, not only because of his genuine admiration for him, but because he was the greatest orator of his age, and therefore a dangerous opponent to quarrel with. It was always Caesar's end in view which governed his behaviour; with him first things came first – why ruffle a potential enemy with invective or sarcasm, when a honeyed word would tranquillize him? This was something Cicero never learnt, and in the end it was responsible for his death. In addition to these reasons, he attached great importance to winning Cicero over to his cause, in order to give it a semblance of legality and respectability. Early in the Civil War he even went so far as to meet Cicero, and tell him that his decision not to join his government 'was a slur on him, and that others would be less likely to come, if he did not come.'[6]

---

[1] *Div. Iul.*, LXXII.    [2] *The Spanish War*, 19.    [3] See *infra*, p. 57.

[4] Catullus, XXIX and LVII: Mamurra of Formiae was a Roman knight, and Caesar's chief of engineers in Gaul. He made a vast fortune out of the war, and, according to Catullus, was an abnormally repellent homosexual.

[5] *Div. Iul.*, LXXIII. It should be remembered that in Roman times there was no law of libel; therefore, the 'smearing' of political opponents was a daily practice. When Cicero was about to conduct his canvass for the consulship, his brother Quintus advised him to 'contrive, if possible, to get some new scandal started against your rivals for crime or immorality or corruption, according to their characters' (cited by Rice Holmes in his *The Roman Republic*, vol. I, p. 239). Cicero's orations are probably replete with libels and gross exaggerations.

[6] *Letters to Atticus*, IX, xviii (March 29, 49 B.C.).

Caesar's two great political weapons were money and oratory. The first was an essential in an age when bribery and lavish expenditure on public games and gladiatorial contests were the common means of winning the votes of the rabble. He bribed his way to the position of *Pontifex Maximus*; purchased the support of G. Scribonius Curio at a cost little short of half a million sterling; and the splendour of his entertainments was of a kind never before witnessed in Rome. Plutarch says: 'He was so profuse in his expenses that, before he had any public employment, he was in debt thirteen hundred talents, and many thought by incurring such expense to be popular he changed a solid good for what would prove but a short and uncertain return; but in truth he was purchasing what was of the greatest value at an inconsiderable rate'[1] – namely, political power which, when backed by an army, made him the wealthiest man in the Republic, and eventually its dictator.

His debts, which at times were enormous – in 62 B.C., they amounted to 25 million sesterces ($£250,000$)[2] – were paid out of the spoils of his provinces.

'For the discharge of his debts [writes Suetonius], at the point of the sword he plundered some towns of the Lusitanians. . . . In Gaul he rifled the chapels and temples of the gods. . . . In his first consulship he purloined from the Capitol three thousand pounds weight of gold. . . . He bartered likewise to foreign nations and princes, for gold, the titles of allies and kings. . . . He afterwards supported the expense of the civil wars, and of his triumphs and public spectacles, by the most flagrant rapine and sacrilege.'[3]

Dio says much the same: in 47 B.C., before leaving Asia for Rome, he collected along his way great sums of money from everybody, 'and upon every pretext. . . . In short, he showed himself a money-getter, declaring that there were two things which created, protected and increased sovereignties – soldiers and money – and that these two were dependent upon each other.' When he arrived in Italy 'he collected large amounts, partly in the shape of crowns and statues . . . and partly by "borrowing".' A term he applied to levies of money, which he

---

[1] *Caesar*, V, 3–4.

[2] This was not exceptional. According to Mommsen (vol. IV, p. 486), Mark Antony, at the age of twenty-four, owed 6 million sesterces, and fourteen years later 40 million; Curio owed 60 million sesterces, and Milo 70 million.

[3] *Div. Iul.*, LIV.

exacted in a high handed way, 'and it was his intention never to repay them.'[1]

Tacitus points out that the art of oratory 'flourishes to the most advantage in turbulent times', and that the orator 'delights in clamour and tumult',[2] because they enable him to display his fine feathers in the Forum and win the applause of the rabble. For this Caesar was superlatively well endowed, as Cicero – no mean judge – affirms. 'He is a master of an eloquence,' he writes, 'which is brilliant and without suggestion of routine, and which in respect to voice, gesture, and the speaker's whole physique, possesses a certain noble and high-bred quality.'[3] And in a letter to Cornelius Nepos he wrote of Caesar in the following terms: 'What! of all orators, who, during the whole course of their lives, have done nothing else, which can you prefer to him? Which of them is more pointed or terse in his periods, or employs more polished and elegant language?'[4]

Caesar's oration at the funeral of his aunt Julia (widow of Marius) was largely a piece of political propaganda, directed toward his own aggrandizement by winning the support of the plebs. Not only did he have an effigy of Marius carried in the procession, but, according to Suetonius, in his oration he outlined to his listeners the pedigree of the Julian family, and in conclusion proclaimed: 'We therefore unite in our descent the sacred majesty of kings, the chiefest among men, and the divine majesty of gods, to whom kings themselves are subject.'[5] What more could the people demand than to be befriended by such a man?

On the evidence of Suetonius, Caesar is described to have been in stature tall – that is for a Roman – his complexion fair, and his eyes

---

[1] Dio, XLII, 49, and 50, 2–3. According to Cicero (De Officiis, I, 25) Crassus remarked: 'No man with political ambitions is now sufficiently wealthy unless he can support an army on his own income.'

[2] A Dialogue Concerning Oratory or the Causes of Corrupt Eloquence, 37 and 39. He also writes: 'If there was a government in the world free from commotions and disturbances, the profession of oratory would be as useless as that of medicine to the sound.' And: 'What is the expediency of haranguing the populace, where public affairs are not determined by the voice of an ignorant and giddy multitude, but by the steady wisdom of a single person?' (41). Cicero corroborates this. In a letter to Papirius Paetus, dated July 23, 46 B.C., he wrote: 'now that the law-courts have been abolished . . . I am no longer King of the Forum' (Ad. Fam., IX, xviii, 1).

[3] Brutus, LXXV, 261.          [4] Div. Iul., LV.

[5] Ibid., VI. Nevertheless, according to Suetonius (LIX), 'No regard for religion ever turned him from any undertaking.'

black and piercing. Although Plutarch mentions that he was subject to epilepsy,[1] he is said to have enjoyed excellent health; throughout his life his physical endurance was phenomenal. We are told that he was particular of his personal appearance and dress, was clean shaven, kept his hair short, and to disguise his premature baldness, of which he was sensitive, he combed it forward and frequently wore a chaplet of laurels. His contemporaries agree that he ate and drank with moderation, that his manner was always courteous, and his conversation both easy and pleasing. Throughout his life his gallantries were notorious, though probably exaggerated by his political opponents.

Among his mistresses, Suetonius mentions the wives of Servius Sulpicius, Aulus Gabinius, Marcus Crassus, Pompey, and of Bogud, king of Mauretania. Servilia, a woman of ready wit, half-sister of Cato and mother of Marcus Brutus, the tyrannicide, would appear to have been a special favourite; he bought for her a pearl for which, according to Suetonius, he paid the colossal sum of 6 million sesterces (£60,000).[2] Of all his mistresses, the most famous was Cleopatra, who would appear to have completely enthralled him. He had a statue of her placed next to that of the goddess in the temple of Venus Genetrix, which he built in commemoration of his victory over Pompey at Pharsalus. Both Plutarch and Suetonius affirm that he had by her a son whom she named Caesarion, and although the evidence for this has been questioned, Augustus had no doubts; he spared Cleopatra's children by Antony, but Caesarion he put to death.[3]

Few great men can have been more versatile and many-sided than Caesar. Not only was he an outstanding general, and a soldier who in horsemanship and skill at arms could compete with the best of his men, but he was also a remarkable orator, an astute politician, a demagogue of genius, a writer, a patron of the arts, and a man interested in astronomy.

Of his writings, his *Commentaries* on the Gallic and Civil Wars up to the Alexandrian War have survived. Their clear and direct narrative reveals an unemotional and objective writer whose aim was to produce

[1] *Caesar*, XVII, 2. See also Appian, *Civil Wars*, II, 110, and Suetonius, *Div. Iul.*, XLV.

[2] *Div. Iul.*, L. Though a high figure, it is not exceptional. Suetonius states that Caesar bought gems, statues, and other works of art 'at any cost'. On one occasion he bought two pictures costing 80 talents (£19,200), and on another commissioned Cicero to purchase for him land in Rome valued at 60 million sesterces (£600,000).

[3] Suetonius, *Div. Aug.*, XVII. Holmes (*The Roman Republic*, vol. III, pp. 503–6) considers that the evidence 'is irrefragable'.

a summary rather than a history of those wars. As literature, they have been acclaimed models of their kind, and Cicero compared them with '. . . nude figures, straight and beautiful; stripped of all ornament of style as if they had laid aside a garment'.[1] But as history, more particularly for the student of war, because of the paucity of detail, tactical and topographical, frequently they are not easy to follow. Some quite minor incidents are elaborated at length, while others and more important ones are given short shrift. They were probably, as Aulus Hirtius, who it is thought may have written the final book of *The Gallic War*, states, hastily compiled from despatches,[2] and a contemporary criticism of them is illuminating. It is supplied by Suetonius:

'Asinius Pollio[3] thinks,' he writes, 'that they were not drawn up with much care, or with a regard to truth; for he insinuates that Caesar was too hasty of belief in regard to what was performed by others under his orders; and that he has not given a very faithful account of his own acts, either by design, or through defect of memory; expressing at the same time an opinion that Caesar intended a new and more correct edition.'[4]

This would appear to be a just criticism, except that Caesar is unlikely to have wilfully falsified the more important events, if only because there were too many living witnesses of them. What is more probable is, that he soft-pedalled his failures, exaggerated the numbers of his enemies, and omitted incidents which might have reflected adversely on himself. Yet, on the whole, he is amazingly frank; and in one respect his frankness reveals the essential difference between his generalship in the Gallic War and in the Civil War. In the one, the atrocities he perpetrated on the unfortunate Gauls have seldom been exceeded by a civilized soldier; in the other, his leniency toward his enemies has seldom been equalled even in more recent civil wars. This again reveals his amorality. He was a man totally governed by his end, and whether the means he employed to gain it were good or evil meant exactly nothing to him, as long as he considered they would lead to

---

[1] *Brutus*, LXXV, 262.   [2] *Div. Iul.*, LVI.

[3] C. Asinius Pollio (consul 40 B.C.), a soldier of note, fought on Caesar's side in the Civil War, and wrote an account of that war which was used by Plutarch and Appian.

[4] *Ibid.* Mr H. J. Edwards, the translator of the Loeb edition of *The Gallic War*, is of opinion that this work is a popular edition 'of the despatches (*epistulae*) sent by Caesar to the Senate at the end of each year of operations', in which probably were incorporated despatches received by him from his generals and staff officers. Today this would be the normal procedure.

success. His end justified his means – he was the supreme Machiavellian of his age.

## 2. HIS YOUTH AND EARLY MANHOOD

In spite of the implicit statements of Plutarch, Suetonius, and Appian that Caesar was fifty-six years old when he died, and therefore was born in 100 B.C., Mommsen has proved to his own satisfaction that he must have been born two years earlier, and the scholars have been in argument ever since.[1]

His family was of patrician rank, which traced its legendary descent from Iulus, the founder of Alba Longa, son of Aeneas and grandson of Venus and Anchises. Most of its members belonged to the *optimates*, but from early life Caesar himself was a *popularis*; the determining factor undoubtedly was that Marius married his aunt Julia. When a boy he was placed under the tutorship of M. Antonius Gnipho, a free-born native of Gaul, whom Suetonius describes as a man of considerable learning, well read in Greek and Latin and of an obliging and agreeable temper.[2] In 84 B.C., Marius and Cinna appointed young Caesar priest of Jupiter (*flamen dialis*), an office of considerable dignity and subject to many restrictions, and two years later, when eighteen years of age, he definitely identified himself with the *populares* by marrying Cinna's daughter Cornelia. In spite of the political implications of the union, it would appear to have been a genuine love match.

Soon after his return from the East, Sulla ordered both Pompey and Caesar to divorce their wives; Pompey complied, but Caesar refused to do so. This so angered Sulla that he seized Caesar's property as well as his wife's dowry, and deprived him of his priesthood. Aware that his life was in danger, Caesar sought refuge in Samnium, but was tracked down by a party in search of Marian refugees and captured; he saved his life by bribing its commander. Through the intercession of the Vestal Virgins and his relatives, Sulla yielded to their appeals to spare him. He said to them: 'Your suit is granted, and you may take him among you; you know,' he added, 'that this man, for whose safety you are so extremely anxious, will, some day or other, be the ruin of the party of the nobles, in defence of which you are leagued with me; for in this one Caesar, you will find many a Marius.'[3] Should the story be true, then Sulla must have been a remarkably good judge of character.

[1] See Mommsen, *op. cit.*, vol. IV, pp. 14–16, and Holmes, *The Roman Republic*, vol. I, pp. 436–42.

[2] *Lives of Eminent Grammarians*, VII.          [3] *Div. Iul.*, I.

Apparently, in spite of his reprieve, Caesar still felt unsafe, because in 81 B.C. we find him in the province of Asia on the staff of the praetor Minucius Thermus. By him he was entrusted with a mission to the king of Bithynia, and at the storming of Mitylene was awarded the much-prized decoration of a civic crown for saving the life of a soldier. Some time after he served for a month or two under the proconsul Servilius Isauricus in Cilicia, and when, in 78 B.C., he learnt of Sulla's death, he returned to Italy. First he considered whether or not to join Lepidus, then in rebellion, but although he received a tempting offer from him, he distrusted his leadership and refused it.

Like so many highly educated Romans, he next set out to gain notoriety as a jurist, and selected as his victim C. Cornelius Dolabella, who had been consul in 81 B.C., and in 82 B.C., proconsul of Macedonia, and arranged for a charge of extortion to be preferred against him. Although Dolabella was acquitted, Caesar's eloquence won him many admirers, and he became so well known in the fashionable world that, to perfect his oratory, in 75 B.C., he left Italy again, this time to study rhetoric at Rhodes under Apollonius Molon, a celebrated master, who also taught Cicero. What immediately followed is related by Plutarch.[1]

On his way out he was captured by pirates off the island of Pharmacussa (Fermaco) near Miletus, who demanded of him twenty talents in ransom. Caesar laughed at this, and to impress them with his importance, suggested that fifty talents would be a more appropriate sum. It must have won their respect, for we are told that when he had a mind to sleep he sent orders to them to keep quiet, and for the best part of six weeks he joined in their games, practised his rhetoric on them, called them illiterate barbarians, and in raillery promised to have them crucified – the normal punishment meted out to pirates. As soon as his ransom arrived from Miletus, they kept their word and released him. He also kept his; at Miletus he hired and manned several galleys; surprised the pirates in their lair; took most of them prisoners, recovered the ransom money, and fulfilled his promise by crucifying the lot. Suetonius adds, that before he did so, to spare them the torture of a lingering death, he first had their throats cut,[2] which is an example of his lack of vindictiveness once he had gained his end.

On the outbreak of the Third Mithridatic War he crossed from Rhodes to Caria, recruited a force of volunteers and chased the king's governor out of that province, after which he set out on his return to Rome, and was elected a military tribune, 'the first honour he received

---

[1] *Caesar*, II and III.   [2] *Div. Iul.*, LXXIV.

from the suffrages of the people'.[1] Of what he did in that capacity we are not told, but we are informed that he assisted those who were agitating for the restoration of the tribunician authority, and took part in obtaining the recall of his wife's brother, Lucius Cinna, who had allied himself with Lepidus, and after his death had sought refuge with Sertorius in Spain.

From 73 B.C., practically nothing is known of his life until 69 B.C., when he was elected quaestor, and in the following year served as such on the staff of C. Antistius Vetus, praetor of Further Spain. Shortly before he set out to take up the appointment he lost both his aunt and his wife.

His quaestorship would appear to have been uneventful. The only item of interest recorded is that, when at Gades (Cadiz), he saw a statue of Alexander the Great in the temple of Hercules, and when he contemplated it 'he sighed deeply, as if weary of his sluggish life, for having performed no memorable actions at an age at which Alexander had already conquered the world. He, therefore, immediately sued for his discharge, with the view of embracing the first opportunity which might present itself in the city of entering upon a more exalted career.'[2]

On his way home he passed through Cisalpine Gaul, which had been proclaimed a province, probably by Sulla, and whose people south of the river Po had been granted Roman citizenship; but those who lived north of it, the Transpadanes, had only Latin rights, and at the time they were agitating for full citizenship. Caesar, who whenever a chance occurred to champion a popular cause, seized it, travelled from town to town and exhorted the people to fight for their rights. The commotion he stirred up must have been considerable, because, according to Suetonius, the consuls delayed the departure of the legions which had been raised in Cisalpine Gaul for service in Cilicia.

It was probably immediately after his arrival in Rome that he took as his second wife the wealthy Pompeia, daughter of Quintus Pompeius Rufus, an aristocrat, killed by Marius in 88 B.C., and a grand-daughter of Sulla. It was certainly a strange marriage for the nephew of Marius

---

[1] *Div. Iul.*, V.

[2] *Ibid.*, VII. Plutarch (*Caesar*, XI, 3) and Dio, XXXVII, 52, 2, refer this incident to the year 61 B.C., when Caesar was propraetor in Spain. Suetonius' date is to be preferred, because, as he held that Caesar was born in 100 B.C., in 68 B.C. he would be approximately the same age as Alexander when he died; whereas in 61 B.C. he would be seven years older.

and the son-in-law of Cinna to make, and Ferrero is of opinion that Caesar contracted it because he was anxious to ally himself with the conservative nobility. 'His marriage,' he writes, 'shows that Caesar was at this moment in no way preoccupied by the fresh outbreak of hostilities between the Conservatives and the popular party, and did not regard it as sufficiently important to impede the gradual process of conciliation between all classes and parties which had been going on since the death of Sulla.'[1] What would seem more probable is that at the time political conditions did not favour the popular cause, and therefore, like Lenin in after years, he decided to take one step back to gain two steps forward at the appropriate moment; in other words, his second marriage was politically a tactical move in order to gain an eventual strategic advantage. Whatever may have passed through his mind, at the opening of 67 B.C., he stepped on to the threshold of his political career.

### 3. HIS RISE TO POLITICAL POWER

Since the spring of 83 B.C., when Sulla returned from the East, Crassus and Pompey had been rivals; both were competent soldiers who had served Sulla with ability, and Crassus was bitterly envious of Pompey's spectacular rise to power. When, in 66 B.C., the Manilian law gave Pompey supreme command in the East, to envy was added fear, for should Pompey on his return follow in the footsteps of Sulla, Crassus can have had no illusions who would head his proscription list. How could he overcome that danger? His money would help, but in itself it was insufficient unless backed by an army powerful enough to command his rival's respect. In spite of the numerous senators indebted to him, he could not expect to secure an army as long as Pompey retained the good will of the people; therefore Crassus set out to woo the popular cause, and as he lacked the qualities of a demagogue, he decided to purchase for hard cash an alliance with Caesar, and employ him as his political agent. With his assistance, control of the popular party might be secured and through it an army. In spite of the vagueness of our authorities, such would appear to have been Crassus' aim at the time.

Although, on his return from Spain, Caesar had been the sole member of the Senate to vote for the Gabinian law,[2] and later had voted

---

[1] *The Greatness and Decline of Rome* (1909), vol. I, p. 219.
[2] Plutarch, *Pompey*, XXV, 4.

for the Manilian,[1] Crassus must have been aware that his reason for doing so was not love of Pompey but in order to ingratiate himself with the people and win their votes in his forthcoming election for an aedileship – the first rung on the political ladder. It required not only oratory, which Caesar possessed, but also money, which Crassus could amply provide; hence the alliance between them was a *mariage de convenance*.

In 66 B.C., Crassus stood for one of the two censorships for 65 B.C., and was elected with Q. Lutatius Catulus as his colleague. Caesar was also elected as one of the *curule aediles*, and because, when the time came to present themselves for a praetorship, one of their duties was to super-intend the public games, to secure the good will of the people Caesar set about to outdo all his predecessors in the splendour of his contests and displays. Among other things, he redecorated the Forum, hired 320 gladiators, and armed criminals to fight wild beasts in the arena: 'he gained,' writes Plutarch, 'so much upon the people, that everyone was eager to find out new offices and new honours for him in return for his munificence.'[2]

In 66 B.C., there occurred the first Catilinarian conspiracy,[3] which Crassus persuaded the Senate to hush up, probably because he hoped to make use of the conspirators at a later date. And in 65 B.C., as censor, he brought forward two measures designed toward achieving his aim.

The first was to grant the Transpadanes full Roman citizenship, which, as we have seen, Caesar was already interested in. Its probable hidden purpose was to secure popularity in an area in which army recruits could readily be raised. Although the measure was blocked by Catulus, it at least made clear to the Transpadanes who were their friends.

The second measure was based on a pretext to raise an army, and

[1] Dio, XXXVI, 43, 2. Caesar not only supported the Manilian Law to favour Pompey; but because, according to Dio, it 'paved the way to a similar vote to be passed some day in his own interest'.

[2] *Caesar*, V, 5.

[3] In 66 B.C., P. Cornelius Sulla, a nephew of the dictator, and P. Autronius Paetus were elected consuls, and on conviction of bribery they forfeited their offices. Not disposed to submit, with L. Sergius Catiline, who had not been allowed to put forward his name as a candidate, it is alleged that they concerted to murder the new consuls when they took office on January 1, 65 B.C. The plot was exposed, and through Crassus' persuasion the senatorial enquiry was abandoned.

this Crassus found in the will of Ptolemy Alexander II of Egypt[1] who, on his death in 81 B.C., had, so it was alleged, bequeathed Egypt to the Roman people. Because Egypt possessed a superabundance of grain, and as recently there had been a severe food shortage in Rome, Crassus expected that the annexation of Egypt would be popular, and if so he was prepared to follow it up with the proposal that Caesar should be made governor of Egypt, which meant that he would require an army to secure it. The design was an astute one, because it would place an army on Pompey's flank. But, like the first, it was opposed by Catulus, and on a stalemate arising between him and Crassus, as Plutarch informs us, 'they laid down their offices by consent'.[2] This somewhat spiritless shelving of the measure may have been due to the discovery that the people were uninterested in the annexation; they were now, thanks to Pompey, well supplied with corn, and as always took no heed of the morrow. Also, the knights were apathetic, because Pompey's conquests in the East would provide them for the time being with ample opportunities to plunder without adding Egypt to their hunting-grounds.

In spite of this, Crassus and Caesar did not abandon their efforts, and in preparation to relaunch their scheme, they set about to secure for two of their partisans, Catiline and C. Antonius, the consulships of 63 B.C. This brought on them a violent attack from Cicero, who insinuated that both Crassus and Caesar had been involved in the first Catilinarian conspiracy, and the result was that out of the five competitors for the consulship – one of whom was Cicero – Catiline was among the defeated, and Antonius and Cicero successful. Cicero then won over Antonius by bartering his future province of Macedonia for Cilicia, which by lot had fallen to Antonius.

To mitigate this rebuff, and also, it may be suspected, to square his account with Catulus, toward the end of 64 B.C., on the death of Metellus Pius, the Chief Pontiff (*Pontifex Maximus*), Caesar came forward as a rival candidate of Catulus for the vacancy. The office was a life appointment, and carried with it considerable political as well as religious power. To whittle down Catulus' chances of election, Caesar persuaded Titus Labienus, at the time a Pompeian tribune – later to become his own second-in-command in Gaul – to sponsor a bill by which the appointment, which belonged to the college of pontiffs, should be restored to the people, who had been deprived of it by

[1] See *A History of Egypt under the Ptolemaic Dynasty*, J. P. Mahaffy (1899), p. 224.          [2] *Crassus*, XIII, 1.

Sulla. The bill was passed, and on March 15, 63 B.C., when the elections were held, Caesar was so overwhelmed with the debts he had incurred in bribing the electors, that when his mother, Aurelia, kissed him as he went to the Assembly, he said to her: 'Today, mother, you will see your son either Chief Pontiff or an exile.'[1] He was returned with a bumper majority.

At about the time when Labienus introduced his bill, Crassus and Caesar decided on yet another line of approach. They bribed a tribune, Publius Servilius Rullus, to propose a bill which was designed to procure for them a position somewhat similar to Pompey's under the Gabinian and Manilian laws. It was an agrarian measure of vast proportions, and as its nominal aim was to purchase land in Italy on which to settle the indigent poor and discharged soldiers, it had the appearance of being a popular measure. According to the bill, the purchase money was to be raised by selling vast tracts of land and real estate in nine of the provinces,[2] and to administer the law ten commissioners, each with special *imperium*, were to be appointed with the right to raise an army to enforce their decisions. With the obvious intention of excluding Pompey, a provision of the bill required that candidates for the commission had to give in their names in person. Because both Crassus and Caesar were certain to be elected commissioners, once the bill became law there was nothing to prevent them from reviving their claim on Egypt and raising an army to annex it. Further, as the commissioners would have at their disposal extensive tracts of land in Italy, on Pompey's return they would be in a position to bargain with him over the settlement of his disbanded soldiers.

On January 1, 63 B.C., the first day of his consulship, Cicero, who guessed that Rullus was a cat's-paw and acted in the interest of Crassus and Caesar, violently attacked the bill. He pointed out that it was a cunning device to create ten kings to dispose of the empire; that the proposal to settle old soldiers on the land was aimed at filling Italy with garrisons; and he concluded with the warning that the real object of the bill was to raise an army against Pompey.[3] When a tribune announced that he would veto the bill, it was dropped by the Assembly.

Soon after this, Catiline decided to stand as a candidate in the next consular elections. As he was overwhelmed with debt, his only chance of restoring his fortunes was to procure a province to plunder, and

[1] *Div. Iul.*, XIII.
[2] Sicily, Spain, Africa, Cyrene, Achaia, Macedonia, Asia, Bithynia, and Cilicia.
[3] Cicero's *De lege agraria*, No. 1, V–VI, and No. 2, IX–X.

should he fail to be elected he determined to resort to violence. He knew that there were many like him, including impoverished senators and knights, and that they would be ready to support him. Also he knew that there were many of Sulla's old soldiers who were now destitute; they had either squandered their property or had been deprived of it by the usurers.[1] They were, writes Plutarch, scattered among the cities of Etruria, and 'entertained themselves with dreams of new plunder and rapine amongst the hoarded riches of Italy'.[2]

In 63 B.C., the consular elections were held in early October instead of in June, and because Catiline again failed to be elected, he forthwith decided to strike. His plan was that, while Gaius Manlius raised a revolt in Etruria, P. Cornelius Lentulus, then praetor for the second time, was to carry out a *coup d'état* in Rome. He was to fire certain quarters of the city, massacre a number of prominent citizens, including Cicero, and create a pandemonium under the cover of which Manlius would march on Rome and, presumably, Catiline would set up a dictatorship.

Shortly before the elections Cicero got wind of what was brewing from the mistress of one of the conspirators, and immediately after the elections, apparently to clear themselves from suspicion of complicity with Catiline, Crassus and Caesar provided Cicero with fuller information; the former visited him secretly by night and gave him letters which compromised the conspirators.[3]

On the following morning Cicero convened the Senate, and on the next day the ultimate decree was passed, and Cicero was authorized to raise an army to suppress the projected revolt. A few days later Manlius took the field, and simultaneously the slaves revolted in Capua and Apulia. When the news of this reached Rome, Catiline fled to Etruria, was outlawed, and after a considerable delay, caused by collecting evidence against them, Lentulus and his four chief accomplices were arrested.

The question then arose – what should be done with them? And in the senatorial debate, Caesar, after he had pointed out that were the conspirators to be executed without fair trial a dangerous precedent would be created, advised that their lives should be spared, that they

[1] Gaius Manlius, a poverty-stricken Sullan centurion and chief subordinate of Catiline in Etruria, said: 'We are wretched and destitute, many of us have been driven from our country by the violence and cruelty of the money-lenders.' (Sallust, *The War with Catiline*, XXXIII, 1.)

[2] *Cicero*, XIV, 1.

[3] Plutarch, *Crassus*, XIII, 3. See also Suetonius, *Div. Iul.*, XVII, and Dio, XXXVII, 31, 1.

be imprisoned for life and their property confiscated.[1] Cato then rose, praised Cicero, hinted that Caesar was involved in the conspiracy, and that leniency would embolden the rebels while severity would dishearten them; lastly he demanded sentence of death and was wildly applauded.[2] His motion was put to the vote and carried by a large majority. Cicero then had Lentulus and his companions led to the Tullianum and strangled.

Cato's surmise proved to be correct, for when the news reached Catiline's army that Lentulus and his companions had been executed, desertions reduced it from 12,000 to 3,000 men. Nevertheless, Catiline put up a desperate resistance, and when ultimately he was cornered, he and his 3,000 desperadoes sold their lives to a man.[3] His head was cut off and sent to Rome, and Cicero was acclaimed 'the father of his country'.

Since 65 B.C., when Caesar went into partnership with Crassus, it would appear that he looked upon his partner's scheme to oust Pompey as no more than a gamble, and that his co-operation with him centred in his own self-interest more than in Crassus' aim. Ever since he had supported the Gabinian and Manilian laws he had had a second string to his bow, and directly it became apparent to him, as Dr Holmes affirms, that Catiline, 'whom he had planned to mould in the event of his becoming consul . . . was doomed',[4] he decided to twang it. Pompey was about to return, and as with Caesar first things came first, he abandoned his policy of attempting to counter-balance Pompey's authority and substituted for it the winning of his good will.

An opportunity toward setting this policy in motion arose soon after the Catilinarian revolt broke out. When Pompey learnt of the outbreak, he sent Metellus Nepos as his agent to Rome to stand for the tribuneship, and as soon as Metellus was elected in December he demanded the recall of Pompey to suppress Catiline. When his demand was rejected by the Senate, Metellus brought it before the Assembly, and Caesar who, on January 1, 62 B.C., had become urban praetor, at once supported him; not that he favoured the bill, as it would give Pompey supreme power in Italy – the last thing he can have desired – but because he was certain that it would be rejected, as it was by the veto of Cato, then a colleague of Metellus in the tribunate. He foresaw that the rejection of the bill would widen the breach between Pompey

[1] Plutarch, *Cicero*, XXI, 1; Sallust, LI, 1–7; and Dio, XXXVII, 36, 1.
[2] Sallust, LII, 36, and LIII, 1; Plutarch, *Cicero*, XXIII, 2.
[3] Dio, XXXVII, 40, 1.                    [4] *The Roman Republic*, vol. I, p. 284.

and the Senate, and thereby open the road for an alliance between Pompey and himself. This was not to abandon Crassus, but to achieve their common end through friendship instead of hostility.

Meanwhile an incident occurred which was to have wide repercussions. Yearly, in the first week of December a religious ceremony, known as *Bona Dea* ('Good Goddess'), was held in the house of the chief magistrate in Rome, under the leadership of his wife assisted by the Vestals; from it men were strictly excluded. In 62 B.C., just before Pompey landed his army at Brundisium, because Caesar was city praetor, it was held in his house, and during it Publius Clodius – alleged to be the lover of Caesar's wife – dressed in woman's clothing, was discovered among the celebrants. The scandal this aroused led to the appointment of a commission to try Clodius for sacrilege, and Caesar immediately divorced Pompeia. When the trial took place, Clodius' defence was that at the time he was some 90 miles from Rome, which was at once disposed of by Cicero, one of the witnesses, who in his evidence stated that three hours before the ceremony was held Clodius had paid him a visit. Caesar, called as a witness, said that he knew nothing about the affair, and when asked by the prosecutor, 'Why then did you divorce your wife?' he replied: 'Because my wife must be above suspicion.'[1] The evidence against Clodius was so overwhelming that his conviction appeared certain. Though *de jure* this was so, *de facto* it was not, because both Crassus and Caesar resolved to save him in the now normal Roman way. Crassus bought out a majority of the jurors and Clodius was acquitted; but he never forgave Cicero.

The repercussions of this trial will appear later; but here it is of interest to consider Caesar's conduct at it, because it reveals so clearly his amorality.

When the scandal was first made public, Caesar must have been intensely annoyed; but after he had divorced his wife, whether she were guilty or not, because she became a thing of the past, to wreak vengeance on Clodius was to think and act in terms of the past. Better to look to the future and profit by the incident. If Clodius were bold enough to commit sacrilege, which he certainly had done, and probably had seduced, or attempted to seduce, the wife of the Chief Pontiff, he must be a man of astonishing audacity, and as such men are not to be picked up at every street corner, would not it be more profitable to befriend him, as the gold of Crassus had enabled Caesar to do, than to

[1] Plutarch, *Caesar*, X, 6. It should be remembered that Caesar was Chief Pontiff.

make him a deadly enemy? Might not so bold a scoundrel prove a useful instrument in the future? From a purely self-interested point of view the answers are uncontradictably in the affirmative.

On the expiration of his praetorship Caesar was allotted the pro-praetorship of Further Spain; but his departure was delayed both by the trial of Clodius and his own debts; for when he was about to set out his creditors seized his carriages and refused to let him go until he had paid them.[1] This is scarcely to be wondered at, as he is reported to have said that he was in need of 25 million sesterces (£250,000) 'to be worth exactly nothing at all'.[2] Fortunately for him Crassus again came to his relief and placed at his disposal 830 talents (£200,000), sufficient to satisfy his most pressing creditors, and some time before midsummer 61 B.C., he left Rome for his province.

On his arrival in Spain 'he took money from the proconsul, who was his predecessor ... and from the Roman allies ... for the discharge of his debts',[3] presumably for part or all that remained unpaid. Then he set out on a campaign against the Lusitanians and Callaeci, who inhabited the region between the Tagus and the Douro; at the same time he sent a naval expedition from Gades (Cadiz) to Brigantium (Coruña), and in these operations he subjected the tribes along the Atlantic coast.

Dio is the sole classical historian who has attempted to describe this campaign, but unfortunately his account is unintelligible. Among other things he says that, as Caesar 'was eager for glory', in order to be chosen consul he purposely provoked war by demanding of the people things he knew that they would refuse to do.[4] Appian says, that he 'sent much money to the public treasury at Rome', and that 'for these reasons the Senate awarded him a triumph'.[5] Ferrero holds that he 'devoted him-self systematically to the amassing of money',[6] and Holmes doubts whether there was booty in Lusitania 'worth the trouble of removal'.[7]

After his campaign, Caesar returned to Gades, and as his province was overburdened with the debts contracted during the Sestorian War, he arranged that creditors should receive no more than two-thirds of their debtors' yearly incomes, and that the latter should not be deprived of the remaining third as long as the debts remained unpaid.[8] In this he was assisted by the local knowledge of Cornelius Balbus, a Gadi-

---

[1] Plutarch, *Crassus*, VII, 6; and Suetonius, *Div. Iul.*, XVIII.
[2] Appian, *Civil Wars*, II, 8.    [3] *Div. Iul.*, LIV.
[4] Dio, XXXVII, 52, 3.    [5] *Civil Wars*, II, 8.
[6] *The Greatness and Decline of Rome*, vol. I, p. 308.
[7] *The Roman Republic*, vol. I, p. 302.    [8] Plutarch, *Caesar*, XII, 2.

tanian upon whom Pompey had conferred Roman citizenship; as he was an exceptionally able man, Caesar made him his staff officer.[1]

When this had been done, and 'without waiting for the arrival of his successor',[2] he hastened back to Rome to hold his triumph and present himself for the consulship.

## 4. HIS FIRST CONSULSHIP

Because a victorious general had to remain outside Rome until granted permission to retain his *imperium* within the city on the day of his triumph, and because a candidate for the consulship had to enter the city to register his name, in order not to forfeit his triumph, Caesar asked leave to do so by proxy. As he was a popular favourite who was bound to be elected, here was a heaven-sent opportunity to win him over as a counterpoise to Pompey; but instead of granting his request, the Senate allowed Cato to talk the motion out.[3] Caesar then forwent his triumph and appeared in person at the hustings.

This foolishness was followed by another which, although understandable, was still more annoying for Caesar. To act as a brake on him, should he be elected, the Senate resorted to bribery, which Cato – the incorruptible – acclaimed 'was for the public good',[4] and saddled him with M. Calpurnius Bibulus, a man bitterly opposed to him, as his colleague. Were this not sufficient, on the eve of the elections, when the provinces were selected for the prospective consuls, the Senate converted the 'Civil Department of Forests and Cattle-Drifts' into a province to be administered by the two successful candidates jointly.[5] To deprive Caesar of a normal province, and thereby of the sole means of meeting his debts, was to ruin him both financially and politically.

Caesar's riposte, which might well have been foreseen, was to enter into secret negotiations with Pompey, still smarting from his senatorial rebuffs, and for his support Caesar promised to obtain land for his discharged soldiers and ratify his *acta*. Pompey agreed, and immediately after Caesar and Bibulus had been elected, Caesar set out to rope in Crassus, whose financial support was not lightly to be abandoned. He

[1] In 40 B.C., he became Rome's first foreign-born consul.

[2] *Div. Iul.*, XVIII.

[3] Plutarch (*Cato the Younger*, V, 2) writes: 'he often would speak a whole day and never stop.'

[4] *Div. Iul.*, XIX.

[5] From early times the Senate retained the right 'to declare any department of public business outside of Rome, a province for any year' (*A History of the Roman World, 146–30 B.C.*, F. B. Marsh (edit. 1957), p. 178).

was astute enough to realize that, in spite of Pompey being Crassus' bugbear, rather than be left single-handed to face so powerful a combination as he himself and Pompey, Crassus would be prepared to set aside his quarrel with Pompey and join the alliance. To effect it, Caesar promised to obtain for Crassus a rebate on the Asian tax contracts in which he was interested, and which the Senate had refused to sanction; besides, this would greatly enhance Caesar in the eyes of the knights. Crassus agreed, possibly, as Dio writes, because he thought 'that Caesar was going to rise to great heights', and that he desired to set him and Pompey in opposition to each other, 'in order that neither of them would get the upper hand'.[1] Thus, unsuspected by the Senate, the all powerful but fragile First Triumvirate came into being. It was in fact a state within a state: Pompey had the veterans, Crassus the money, and Caesar the idolatry of the people. So long as the three co-operated, it was irresistible.

When, on January 1, 59 B.C., Caesar entered upon his consulship, he brought forward an agrarian bill to provide land for Pompey's soldiers and to relieve the congested population of Rome. As he did not want to frighten the Senate, it was purposely a modest and a reasonable measure, and he proposed that the land required should be purchased out of existing taxes and the revenue Pompey had enriched the State with. He took the precaution first to read it to the Senate; he knew that they would loathe it, therefore he argued in such a way that, were they openly to object to it, the rabble of Rome would decide in their stead. He asked each senator to raise any objection to it, but none did. Nevertheless, the Senate was lukewarm, did nothing, and 'fruitless delays and postponements kept arising'. Then Cato, who on principle 'disapproved of any innovation', rose, relied on his usual tactics, and began to talk the measure out. Caesar had him seized and dragged out of the house; but when others began to follow Cato, he released him, adjourned the Senate and said: 'I have made you judges and masters of this law, so that if anything did not suit you, it should not be brought before the people; but since you are not willing to pass a preliminary decree, they shall decide for themselves.'[2]

Soon after, Caesar brought his bill before the Assembly, and to give it teeth he added to it a clause which, should the bill become law, required all senators to swear non-resistance to it on pain of exile. At the time there were a considerable number of Pompey's old soldiers in Rome, and Caesar had obtained Pompey's consent to have a party

[1] Dio, XXXVII, 56, 4.     [2] *Ibid.*, XXXVIII, 3, 3.

of them at hand should he need a few rioters. He called upon Crassus
and Pompey to speak; they did so in favour of the bill, and Pompey
concluded his speech by saying: 'If any one dares to raise a sword, I
also will snatch up my shield.'[1] When the bill was put to the vote,
three tribunes vetoed it, and Bibulus announced that he would 'watch
the skies' for the remaining days of the year, which meant that the
people could not legally meet in their Assembly until the heavenly
omens were declared to be propitious. Caesar paid no attention to this
piece of archaic humbug, instead he unmasked his batteries: he called
in his soldiers; they swept his opponents out of the Forum, and in the
tumult a basket of dung was emptied over the head of Bibulus. So well
had the secret of the coalition been kept that, when this incident revealed
it, the Senate was completely nonplussed; it dared not pass the ultimate
decree and order Bibulus to restore order, because he had no troops
at his disposal. Caesar had, and therefore was master of the field. The
bill became law.

A few weeks later Caesar brought forward a supplementary agrarian
bill. The need for it may have been due to a miscalculation in the first
one; but it would seem more in consonance with Caesar's character
that the land demanded in it had on purpose not been referred to in the
first, so as not to frighten the Senate. Should this be so, then it would
appear that the first was no more than a preliminary canter to stretch
the legs of the second – the *Campanian Law*. Its aim was to acquire the
leases of the public lands in northern and central Campania, which
included Capua, and to assign them to Pompey's soldiers and destitute
fathers with families of three or more children. Of the latter Appian
says that 'twenty thousand . . . came forward at once',[2] and Dio adds:
'For this reason Capua was then for the first time considered a Roman
colony.'[3] We are not told what happened to the thousands of tenant
farmers who were evicted, some of whose forbears had been lease-
holders since the Second Punic War. Of these evictions George Long
writes: 'This monstrous, this abominable crime was committed to
serve a party purpose; and the criminal was a Roman consul . . . too
intelligent not to know what he was doing, and unscrupulous enough
to do anything that might serve his own ends.'[4]

That is sound comment, and is sufficient to explain why the Campania was omitted from the first bill. Notwithstanding, in an age of
violent power politics, to condemn Caesar as a criminal is no insult. He

---

[1] *Ibid.*, XXXVIII, 5, 5.     [2] *Civil Wars*, II, 10.     [3] Dio, XXXVIII, 7, 3.
[4] *Decline of the Roman Republic* (1864), vol. III, p. 424.

was playing for higher stakes than the judgement of the settled Victorian era would seem to have been aware. To achieve his end – the acquisition of power – it was imperative for him to fulfil his promise to Pompey; therefore he acted as a general so often does when faced with a critical situation: as long as he can win he does not haver over the costs.

The bill was passed with little opposition, and the entire Senate, with the exception of one of its members who went into exile, took the oath to observe the law.

Next, Pompey's *acta* were ratified *en bloc* 'with no opposition',[1] and the promise to Crassus was honoured in a bill which released the Asian tax farmers from the third part of their contracts. 'For this unexpected favour,' Appian writes, '. . . the knights extolled Caesar to the skies. Thus a more powerful body of defenders than that of the plebeians was added to Caesar's support through one political act.'[2]

As Caesar had now fulfilled his obligations toward his two colleagues, he set about to consolidate his position and prepare for his proconsulship. To please the people, he borrowed money on an extensive scale and entertained them lavishly. To bind Pompey as firmly as he could to him, probably in May, he gave his daughter Julia to him in marriage, and although it was a purely political union, it turned out to be a very happy one. Also, about this time, he and Pompey decided on the consulships for 58 B.C.; they selected two of their supporters, L. Calpurnius Piso and Aulus Gabinius – the proposer of the Gabinian law – and to strengthen Piso's fealty Caesar married his daughter Calpurnia; whereupon Cato 'cried out that the government was debauched by marriages'.[3]

The two agrarian bills had been introduced by Caesar himself, and those which concerned Pompey's *acta* and Crassus' tax contracts by his right-hand man, the tribune Publius Vatinius. The remainder of Vatinius' legislation is of no great importance, except for his bill, known as the *Lex Vatinia de Caesaris Provincia*, upon which depended the future of Caesar's career. It is generally believed to have come before the Assembly in either May or June. By it the Senate's selection of consular provinces for 58 B.C. was set aside, and Caesar was allotted the governorship of Cisalpine Gaul and Illyricum.[4] By the terms of the bill Caesar's

---

[1] Dio, XXXVIII, 7, 5.     [2] *Civil Wars*, II, 13.     [3] *Ibid.*, II, 14.

[4] Because no troops were allowed to be stationed in Italy proper, whoever commanded the legions in Cisalpine Gaul dominated both Italy and Rome. And because Illyricum was as yet only partly conquered, it offered Caesar the immediate prospect of a war in which his reputation might be enhanced, his legions salted and booty gained.

proconsulship was conferred upon him for five years instead of the normal two; he was authorized to nominate his own staff and to found colonies at his discretion. Soon after it was passed occurred one of those strokes of good fortune which so frequently favoured Caesar: Metellus Celer, when on his way to take over the governorship of Transalpine Gaul, suddenly died, and under pressure of the Assembly the province was allotted to Caesar – presumably on a five years' basis – in addition to Cisalpine Gaul and Illyricum. Without it, it would not have been possible for him to have conquered Gaul; but its conquest was as yet unthought of.

Because the Vatinian law empowered Caesar to recruit an army, opposition to him became too dangerous to be contemplated; it was replaced by bitter resentment toward him on the part of the senatorial party. In July Cicero wrote to Atticus that although everyone was complaining no one dared to suggest a remedy, 'for we do not think resistance possible without a general slaughter, nor see what the end of concession is to be except ruin'.[1] As the sun of Caesar rose in the ascendant, the shadow of a Sullan proscription grew darker and darker; yet, like an eclipse, might not it pass away once Caesar had left Rome?

Caesar was well aware of what was in the minds of his opponents, and, to frustrate opposition after his departure, he determined to open an inner front against the Senate. To do so he needed a man as audacious and unscrupulous as himself, who would not only support him, but would cause so much trouble in Rome that the Senate would be too fully occupied to intrigue against him during his absence. Such a man was to be found in Publius Clodius: that he was alleged to have attempted to debauch the wife of the Chief Pontiff was no impediment, it was his strongest recommendation. A man who could do such a thing was capable of anything, and as Vatinius' tribuneship would expire in December, Caesar decided to secure Clodius as his successor, and by means of him muzzle Cicero and in all probability Cato as well. Already in 'a very gentlemanly manner', so writes Cicero to Atticus, Caesar had invited him 'to act as a *legatus* to himself' in Gaul, and he adds: 'I don't like running away; I am itching to fight.'[2] In the end he refused, and from persuasion Caesar resorted to craft. Only one thing stood in the way of Clodius' tribuneship; it was that by birth he was patrician, and because of it he could not stand for that office unless he was adopted by a plebeian and his adoption confirmed by the *Comitia*

[1] *Letters to Atticus*, II, 20.  [2] *Ibid.*, II, 18; and II, 19.

*Curiata* under the Chief Pontiff.[1] This Caesar arranged with the assistance of Pompey who, as an augur, officiated at the ceremony, and shortly before Caesar's consulship expired Clodius was elected a tribune for 58 B.C.

In 59 B.C., the triumvirs had by law and on payment of 6,000 talents (£1,440,000) recognized Ptolemy Auletes as the rightful king of Egypt,[2] but they had left in suspense the kingship of Cyprus, which was held by Auletes' brother. According to Plutarch, no sooner had Clodius assumed office than, in preparation for an attack on Cicero, he determined first to rid himself of Cato. As he could find no pretext to prosecute him, he decided to have him sent on a foreign mission, and he offered him the governorship of Cyprus. When Cato hesitated to accept it, Clodius threatened to bring a decree before the Assembly and enforce acceptance. This resulted in Cato agreeing to go, and he did not return until the end of 56 B.C.

While Cato was being got rid of, Clodius brought forward a number of new laws; their object was to win the support of the urban proletariat. Then, probably in February or March, he tabled a bill by which anyone who had put to death a Roman citizen without trial should be 'interdicted from fire and water' – that is, outlawed. Although the bill was couched in general terms, no one could fail to see that it was directed against Cicero, and that it referred to the death sentences he had passed on Lentulus and his co-conspirators without trial, a deed which Cicero had never ceased to boast about. Cicero, who had so violently attacked Clodius at his trial, forthwith collapsed; he sent entreaties to Caesar, cast himself at the feet of Pompey, and appealed to the consuls Gabinius and Piso, but in vain. On about March 20, the eve of the day upon which the vote was to be taken, he so completely lost his nerve that he hurriedly left Rome.[3] The law took effect, he was banished and for-

---

[1] In republican times the *Comitia Curiata* was only held to confer *imperium* on consuls and praetors, and carry out certain other formalities including adoption.

[2] A few months later, exasperated by the taxes imposed in order to pay the debt, his subjects expelled him, and his daughter, Berenice, usurped the throne. In 55 B.C., on his promise to pay an additional 10,000 talents (£2,400,000) Aulus Gabinius, proconsul of Syria, defeated Berenice's army, restored him, and left him a body of Gallic and German troops to wring from his subjects the price of his restoration. By his will he bequeathed his kingdom to the elder of his two daughters (Cleopatra) and the elder of his two sons (Ptolemy XIII) and 'adjured the Roman people in the name of all the gods and the treaties which he had made at Rome to carry out these provisions' (Caesar, *The Civil War*, III, 108).

[3] He did not return until the late summer of 57 B.C.

hidden to reside within 500 miles of Rome, his property was confiscated and his house was razed to the ground.

Simultaneously, Caesar received the startling news that the Helvetii intended to migrate into south-western Gaul by way of the Province, and that they had fixed upon March 28 as the day upon which their forces were to muster opposite Geneva, the first town of the Allobroges across the Helvetian border. Without a moment's delay he and Labienus set out from Rome, and 'by as rapid stages as possible arrived at Geneva'.[1]

[1] *The Gallic War*, I, 7. Ordinary travellers averaged about 50 miles a day by *reda* (a light four-wheeled vehicle) and official couriers could in cases of urgency cover 160 miles in 24 hours. Suetonius (*Div. Iul.*, LVII) records that, on occasion, Caesar travelled 100 miles a day by *reda*.

# IV

## The Roman Army

### I. ITS CHARACTER

THE grandeur and extent of the Roman Empire have led many to assume that, as an instrument of conquest, the Roman army was superior to any which preceded it. This is not so, because in composition and tactical arrangement it cannot compare with the scientifically organized army of Philip of Macedon and of his son Alexander, or with those of Alexander's immediate successors. *Pace* Livy (IX, 19), any one of those armies would have annihilated a numerically equal force of Romans in a brief morning's engagement.

What were its deficiencies? The outstanding one was that it was basically an infantry army, and throughout Roman history the astonishing thing is that, although the Romans were fond of horses and horse racing, they never attempted to develop an efficient cavalry arm as the complement of their infantry. It was a one-armed army, which again and again was defeated because of its lack of efficient cavalry, and ultimately at Adrianople, in A.D. 378, was erased from the pages of history by barbaric Gothic horsemen.

Out of this crucial limitation arose its second major deficiency – lack of generalship. An infantry army, particularly in an age in which battles were hand-to-hand contests, was a simple force to command. So much depended upon drill, upon the maintenance of an unbroken front and ability to replace quickly and without confusion an exhausted front rank by a fresh rear rank, that any good drill-master was a good general. But tactical ability demands more than drill-mastership, and in set battles – major engagements fought in a terrain which permits of the deployment of large forces of infantry and cavalry – it can only be developed when their respective powers are combined: of infantry which can resist with cavalry which can press – that is, of both a stable and a mobile element, the combination of which is the tactical base of true generalship.

Because an all but purely infantry army is simple to command, in the earlier days of the Republic generalship was little more than sergeant-majorship; therefore consuls and praetors, as long as they knew their drill, could without any great risk be selected by lot. Although, today, this may seem fantastic, and would have seemed equally so to Philip and Alexander, or to Antigonus and Eumenes, it appeared reasonable to the Senate and Roman people, because they completely lacked the cavalry idea. What is even more extraordinary is that, when in the late Republic the *condottiere* type of generals emerged, men like Marius, Sulla, Lucullus, Pompey and Caesar, who were far in advance of drill-masters, not one of them had any conception of the supreme value of highly trained cavalry.

The reader may well ask: Granted that the Roman army was so defective in tactical organization and command, how came it that it was the instrument which established one of the greatest and most permanent of empires?

The most important military reason was that, although the Senate was consistently averse to wars of expansion, paradox though it may seem, instead of warfare being restricted, it became devastating. Mommsen, after an outline of the Third Mithridatic War, pertinently remarks:

'That distrust of her own readiness to fight and preparation for fighting, which had for long governed the policy of Rome – a distrust which the want of standing armies and the far from exemplary character of the collegiate rule render sufficiently intelligible – made it, as it were, an axiom of her policy to pursue every war not merely to the vanquishing, but to the annihilation of her opponents. . . .'[1]

Although it would have been comprehensible to Alexander, to the Romans the remark Montesquieu once made, 'that nations ought to do each other the most good during peacetime and the least harm during wartime without harming their true interests',[2] would have had no meaning, because when they went to war their aim was to wage war to end war – that is, to annihilate the possibility of its recurrence in the theatre in which it was fought. All said and done, a nation whose army is destroyed, and whose ability to recover is sterilized by extortionate taxation, is likely to be permanently incapacitated. Therefore, it should not be overlooked that empires can be built by wars of annihilation, which beat enemy after enemy into a set mould, as well as by wars with

1 *Op. cit.*, vol. IV, p. 47.
2 Polybius (xviii, 3) says much the same thing.

more positive aims; those which, if they are to be remunerative, require in varying degrees the co-operation and good will of the subjected peoples. Nevertheless, both types demand a long period of gestation in which to attain their aims, and in the history of Rome, the period extended from the Punic Wars to well into the days of the Principate. During it the empire was not merely won, but nation after nation was compressed into the Roman mould. Eventually, through lack of opposition, the masses became soulless and they and the mould crumbled into dust.

A collateral factor which favoured the expansion of the empire was that, except in Parthia and to a lesser extent in Numidia, the legionaries were never, until toward the end of Rome's supremacy, called upon to face efficient cavalry. In the first of these countries, the 53 B.C. campaign of Crassus ended in utter disaster;[1] that of Antony, seventeen years later, in a severe defeat; and after it, Augustus, rather than risk further calamities, wisely reached a *modus vivendi* with his mounted enemy. In the second, it is doubtful whether the Romans would have succeeded in subduing the Numidians had they not recruited larges forces of African horsemen.

There were, of course, other assets and defects, but the above should be sufficient to illustrate the character of the Roman army.

## 2. ITS DEVELOPMENT

Caesar does not tell us in his *Commentaries* how his army was organized, trained, and supplied, other than by requisitioning, presumably because he considered these things too commonplace to mention, and, as is frequent in military history, historians pay but a passing attention to them. Nevertheless, we can assume that, as the Romans were a conservatively-minded people, and because military development before the introduction of firearms was exceedingly slow, Caesar's army was not very different from that of Marius, and as the latter's was based on the military organization described by Polybius (*c.* 203?–120 B.C.), to begin with it is as well briefly to summarize what he has to say about it.[2]

He begins by stating that all Roman citizens rated at above 4,000 *asses* (about £1–6–8) had to serve for ten years in the cavalry and

---

[1] As an example of how history repeats itself, because so seldom its lessons are taken to heart, in A.D. 297, close by Carrhae, where Crassus met his doom, the army of the emperor Galerius was destroyed in an identical way.

[2] VI, 19–42.

twenty in the infantry up to the age of forty-six. Though he does not mention it, service in the Republican Army was not continuous, because the legions were raised and disbanded yearly. Therefore, it would be more correct to say that a cavalryman was liable to serve for ten yearly periods, and an infantryman for twenty.

A typical example of a legionary's service is given by Livy. He cites the case of a soldier, by name Spurius Ligustinus, who had a family of six sons and two daughters, and whose father had left him one acre of land and a small cottage.

'I became a soldier [says Ligustinus] in the consulate of Publius Sulpicius and Caius Aurelius (204 B.C.). In the army which was sent over into Macedon I served as a common soldier, against Philip, for two years; and in the third year, Titus Quintius Flamininus, in reward of my good conduct, gave me the command of the tenth company of spearmen. When Philip and the Macedonians were subdued, and we were brought back to Italy and discharged, I immediately went as a volunteer, with the consul Marcus Porcius (195 B.C.) into Spain. . . . This commander judged me deserving of being set at the head of the first company of spearmen. A third time I entered as a volunteer in the army which was sent against the Aetolians and King Antiochus; and Manius Acilius (191 B.C.) gave me the command of the first company of first-rank men. After Antiochus was driven out of the country, and the Aetolians were reduced, we were brought home to Italy, where I served the two succeeding years in legions that were raised annually. I afterwards made two campaigns in Spain; one under Quintus Fulvius Flaccus, the other under Tiberius Sempronius Gracchus (180 B.C.) praetors. I was brought by Flaccus among others whom he brought home from the province to attend his triumph, out of regard to their good services. At the request of Tiberius Gracchus, I went with him to his province. Four times within a few years was I first centurion of my Corps; thirty-four times I was honoured by my commanders with presents for bravery. I have received six civic crowns, I have fulfilled twenty-two years of service in the army, and am upwards of forty years of age.'[1]

Polybius restricts his observations to the four consular legions – two for each consul – which, whether there was a war or not, were raised yearly; each comprised 4,200 infantry and 300 cavalry. At the time of their recruitment, the consuls instructed the magistrates of the allied

---

[1] Livy, XLII, 34.

cities in Italy (*socii et Latini*) to raise an equivalent number of allied infantry and twice the number of allied cavalry. Therefore the troops raised each year numbered in all 33,600 infantry and 3,600 cavalry: these figures are formal.

Besides these troops, and increasingly so during the last two centuries of the Republic, mainly to make good deficiencies in cavalry and light-armed troops, contingents, known as *auxilia*, were recruited from provincials who had not received the franchise and from independent allies. They already had begun to appear in the First Punic War; in the Second, Numidian cavalry turned the scales at Zama, and during the civil wars the *auxilia* increased rapidly until entire legions, such as Caesar's *Alaudae* ('the Larks'), raised in Transalpine Gaul, came into being. Later, under Augustus, the strength of the *auxilia* rose to some 130,000 men.[1]

A legion was organized in three lines of infantry one behind the other, the *hastati*, *principes*, and *triarii*. The men were selected according to age; in the *hastati* were the youngest and in the *triarii* the oldest. There were 1,200 men in each of the first two lines and 600 in the third. Besides these men, 1,200 of the poorest citizens, known as *velites*, were indifferent light infantry, normally split up among the maniples.

The legion was divided into thirty maniples, ten to each line; each consisted of two centuries under two centurions; the senior commanded the maniple, which was the tactical unit. Each maniple was provided with a standard (*signum*), a pole crowned with a twist of hay would appear to have been the earliest type; it was used by the maniple commander to transmit orders by signal and to rally his men. Besides the centurions, a legion had six military tribunes, employed on administrative duties and less so in tactical command.

According to Polybius, the *hastati* were equipped with the full panoply. Their shields were of a rectangular semi-cylindrical shape, two and a half feet broad and four feet in length; they were made of two layers of wood glued together and covered with canvas and leather; their upper and lower edges were rimmed with iron to resist a sword stroke, and in their centre was a metal boss. They wore a brass helmet and a breast-piece, or coat of mail, and their weapons were a sharp pointed two-edged Spanish sword two feet in length, slung on the right side, and two javelins; they also carried a dagger. The *principes* and the *triarii* were similarly equipped and armed, except that, instead of the javelins the *triarii* carried long spears. The *velites* were armed with

[1] See *The Auxilia of the Imperial Roman Army*, G. L. Cheesman (1914).

a sword, two javelins and a round shield of three feet diameter; their head-dress was of wolf's skin.

The 300 legionary cavalry were divided into ten squadrons, each commanded by a *decurio*; the troopers were equipped in Greek fashion, wore armour and helmet, and carried shield, spear, and sword; they preferred to fight on foot. In order of battle their place was on the flanks of the infantry.

While the battle order of the phalanx was in a single line, that of the legion was in three lines, one in rear of the other, and each of moderate depth. Mommsen suggests, 'in ordinary cases of only four files',[1] and with intervals between the maniples, the whole being drawn up in chequer, or chess-board, fashion – that is, the second-line maniples covered the intervals in the first line, and the third line those in the second. It has frequently been held that the intervals were adopted to enable the front-line maniples, when exhausted, to withdraw through the intervals in the second line without disordering it. But whether this was so has been questioned, and it is highly unlikely that the first line had intervals, because, and particularly so in hand-to-hand fighting, it is essential to maintain an unbroken front. Were a line of maniples with intervals between them to attack or be attacked, its front would be penetrated at the first shock. It is only necessary to picture a legion with a morcelated front met by an onrushing horde of Gallic warriors to realize what would happen; it would be like water pouring through a colander.

Like the Spanish short sword and cavalry armament, the javelin (*pilum*) was a foreign importation. It was probably copied from the Gallic javelin, and as it was *par excellence* the missile weapon of the legion, it is as well to give a brief description of it. Polybius mentions two types, a 'thick' and a 'thin', but with the exception of a hand-grip on the former they would appear to have been identical. From actual specimens recovered from Alesia and elsewhere, the haft was four feet six inches in length, and the skewer-shaped iron head three feet; but as half of it was sunk into the haft, the total length of the javelin was six feet, the same as the short pig-sticking spear. Its head was barbed, like that of an arrow, so that on impact with a shield it was difficult to remove, and should several catch fast they weighed the shield down. Further, the skewer-like shank of the head bent on impact, and this prevented the javelin being used by the enemy until the shank had been straightened.

[1] *Op. cit.*, vol. I, p. 434.

The javelin could be hurled with or without a throwing thong (*amentum*), a leather loop bound to the shaft behind its centre of gravity, through which the first and second fingers were inserted. 'As the javelin leaves the hand the pull on the amentum gives the javelin a half turn, and like the rifling of the gun imparts to it a rotatory motion which not only helps it to maintain its direction, but increases its carry and penetrating power.'[1] In experiments carried out by Napoleon III, it was found that an unpractised thrower could cast a javelin 25 metres, and could increase his throw to 65 metres by using the *amentum*. According to Gardiner, the *amentum* does not appear to have been used in the Roman army after the Punic Wars. If so, the reason probably was that, as obviously it was to the advantage of the legionaries to follow up their javelin attack as quickly as possible with a sword assault, a short throw suited that best. Couissin's comments are of interest. He points out that, although it is generally agreed that Marius replaced the spear (*hasta*) by the *pilum*, and that Caesar frequently mentions the *pilum*, but never once the *hasta*, the *hasta* is constantly shown on the monuments and the *pilum* seldom. In all the discoveries of Roman weapons at Alesia, Osuna, Saalburg, and elsewhere, 'the *pila* are much less numerous than the heads of spears and ordinary javelins. Certainly, many of the javelins may have belonged to the barbarians, others to the auxiliaries, cavalry or infantry. Nevertheless the number is relatively so high, not only on the battlefields, but in all places at which the legions were stationed, that it appears impossible not to assign them to the legionaries.' Couissin therefore concludes that probably the legions remained partly armed with the *hasta*, and that they were carried in the baggage column for use when required.[2]

Besides abolishing recruitment by classes, Marius recast the organization of the legion. While he maintained the centuries and the maniples for administrative purposes, he increased the legionary infantry from 4,200 to 6,000 and divided the legion into ten cohorts, each of which consisted of three maniples. It was not an entirely novel innovation, because three-maniple cohorts had first been formed by Publius Scipio

[1] *Athletics of the Ancient World*, E. Norman Gardiner (1930), p. 173.

[2] *Les Armes Romaines* (1926), pp. 278–9. Tacitus (*The Annals*, XII, 35) mentions that while the Roman heavy-armed (i.e. legionaries) fought with short swords and *pila*, the auxiliaries fought with long swords and spears. Therefore many of the spearheads unearthed may be those of auxiliaries, and as Caesar's Gallic horsemen were armed with javelins, some of the javelin heads may have belonged to them.

in the Second Punic War; and it would appear that from now on the cohort, nominally of 600 men, became the tactical unit of the legion.

Each cohort retained the six centurions of its three maniples, they were the *pilus prior, pilus posterior, princeps prior, princeps posterior, hastus prior*, and *hastus posterior*; and probably the cohort was commanded by the first of the six. Further, the standard of the first maniple of each cohort became the standard of the cohort, and to encourage morale Marius gave each legion an eagle of silver as the legionary standard; it was carried by the *aquilifer*. It symbolized the majesty of the legion, and its loss in battle sometimes entailed the legion's disbandment.

Strange to say, Marius took no steps to raise cavalry and light troops from Roman citizens, and from his day on contingents of men from the *auxilia*, client states, and at times recruited from enemy peoples during a campaign, supplied these deficiencies. The cavalry were organized in wings (*alae*), each from 500 to 1,000 strong, and the light troops in cohorts.

Henceforth the order of battle of the legion became either two lines of five cohorts each (*duplex acies*) – virtually a return to the phalangial order – or more frequently three lines, of four cohorts in the first, and three in the second and the third (*triplex acies*). It is unlikely that there were any intervals between cohorts, and the number of files in a cohort may have been six, but this has not been recorded.

## 3. CAESAR'S ARMY

Although some historians have gone to considerable pains to reconstruct the organization of Caesar's army, and to describe its drill and battle movements in detail, their labours are speculative. All we know is, that his legions were organized in cohorts, that as in the days of Marius the cohort was the tactical unit, and we may assume that drill must have been what drill always has been, a series of time-saving and orderly movements of lines into columns, of columns into lines, of echelons and squares, and in battle of the replacement of exhausted units and men by fresh ones.

So far as is known, other than the tightening up of discipline, and instilling morale and *esprit de corps*, Caesar accepted the Roman military organization as he found it, and saw so little need to change it that he made no attempt to provide his legions with efficient cavalry and light-armed troops. For the first, he relied on contingents of foreign horsemen, who served for booty and normally were led by their tribal chieftains – mere cossacks – and for the second, on archers, slingers, and javelin-men recruited from various parts of the empire. For the most part these men were undisciplined, frequently ill-armed, and more often than not they must have spoken languages unintelligible to the legionaries: brave, probably; unreliable, inevitably; and brutal, certainly. In spite of all his high qualities as a soldier, Caesar was no military organizer, and in that respect cannot compare with his uncle Marius.

As *imperator*,[1] Caesar had under him, besides his *quaestor*, who combined the duties of quartermaster-general and chief of staff, a number of legates, men usually of senatorial rank and nominated by him. During wartime they acted either as his General Staff, or were entrusted with important subordinate commands. In the Gallic War the most prominent was Titus Labienus, Caesar's second-in-command, who at times was employed as an independent army commander, and who commanded the entire army in Caesar's absence. As in the days of Marius, each legion had six military tribunes, who occasionally were given command of a group of cohorts; also thirty centurions, of whom those of the first cohort were regularly summoned to councils of war. Like every *imperator*, Caesar had a body-guard (*cohors praetoria*), which was extra-legionary.

In the early Roman army there were two separately organized centuries of *fabri*, smiths and artificers, who repaired arms, and armour; but long before Caesar's day they had been absorbed into the ranks, and when not engaged on their technical tasks, they fought as ordinary legionaries; a wasteful employment of skilled craftsmen, which Caesar made no attempt to remedy. Evidence for this is that, when on landing in Britain forty of his ships were damaged in a storm, to repair them he 'picked out artificers from the legions, and ordered others to be fetched from the Continent'.[2] Besides repairing arms and armour, the *fabri* superintended the construction of camps, fortifications, and siege works; supervised the building of hutments and bridges, and probably worked the military hurling engines – catapults and *ballistae*.

As is not unusual in military history, there is but the meagrest information on Caesar's service of transport and supply. Holmes notes that nowhere in his *Commentaries* does Caesar mention that he used wagons or carts, and that it has been estimated that each legion required

[1] A generic title for a victorious Roman general. Caesar first used it permanently, and 'From him this title has come down to all subsequent emperors, as one peculiar to their office, just like the title "Caesar".' (Dio, XLIII, 44, 4.)

[2] *The Gallic War*, V, 11.

at least 300 or 600 mules to carry its baggage.[1] This is not an excessive number, even should it be restricted to first-line transport;[2] but quite inadequate should second-line transport be included. Should it be a fact that the legions were unprovided with the latter, and that requisitioning of corn, etc., was done by carts hired or impressed in the districts traversed, it would be difficult to imagine a more inefficient and precarious system. Yet, from the *Commentaries*, this would appear to have been so, because we learn that on one occasion during the African War, when Caesar left his army's baggage – presumably his pack-train – at Ruspina, and set out with a force in light order to forage in the surrounding country, he instructed the townsfolk 'that all their carts and draught animals must go with him'.[3] Pompey, we know, made use of wagons, because Plutarch records that he 'supplied himself with provisions and beasts of burden and wagons and everything else that an army requires';[4] and we are told also that Antony in his Parthian campaign of 36 B.C. had with him 300 wagons to carry his siege engines.[5] Also, the author of Caesar's African War mentions that, on one occasion, Labienus – then opposed to Caesar – 'ordered his wounded to be carried in carts'.[6] When it is borne in mind that, like most Roman colonial campaigns, those of Caesar in Gaul were largely looting expeditions, and that loot has to be carried; that a vast number of spades, picks, axes, saws, and other tools were required by the legionaries to dig their frequent entrenched camps, construct siege works, bridge rivers and make roads, even when the carriage of their rations and tents is omitted, it is hard to believe that Caesar could have waged his wars as successfully as he did without a wagon train.

Of the medical services nothing is known other than that, in the days of Augustus, superior officers were at times attended by private surgeons,[7] and – somewhat dubiously – Holmes adds that 'medical aid

1 *The Roman Republic*, vol. I, p. 120. This is not strictly correct, because Caesar mentioned the use of wagons in his *The Civil War*, I, 51 and 54, but they may have been local ones.

2 The loads carried by 600 pack animals represent about 20 lb. per man in the legion.

3 *The African War*, 9.

4 *Pompey*, VI, 4. Also the author of *The Spanish War*, 6, states that Gnaeus (Pompey the Younger) 'retired to Corduba with a numerous train of carts and laden mules'.

5 Plutarch, *Antony*, XXXVIII, 2.          6 *The African War*, 21.

7 Suetonius, *Div. Aug.*, XI.

of some sort was provided for the rank and file'.[1] If so, then it was probably found from among the host of camp followers, sutlers, and slaves who followed the army.

On the monuments the legionaries are depicted at their best; therefore we should beware of assuming that Caesar's soldiers resembled them in detail. Not only were many of his legions hastily raised, but in the chaos of the Civil War it must have been well-nigh impossible for his men, who had to provide their own arms and equipment, to do so with strict uniformity. Like most things concerning Caesar's army, little is recorded on its men's equipment.

It is generally held that his soldiers were close cropped and clean shaven; that they wore long, sleeveless woollen shirts, and in cold weather woollen drawers, puttees, and a blanket-like cloak, which was fastened together on their right shoulder. Except for metal helmet, large rectangular shield, and possibly a greave on the right leg, which was unprotected by the shield, nothing further is definitely known of their defensive weapons. Caesar nowhere mentions the *lorica*, or metal cuirass; therefore it is assumed that in its place the legionary wore a stout leather jerkin across the breast and back of which iron bands were fastened. But even this is in doubt, because during the siege of Dyrrachium Caesar mentions that, in order to protect themselves against arrows, 'all the soldiers had made themselves jerkins or other protections out of felt, quilt, or hide',[2] which suggests that previously they were not worn. Their offensive weapons were a Spanish sword, a dagger, and a *pilum*.[3]

This armament represented only part of the load carried by the soldier on the line of march. 'Over his left shoulder,' Holmes writes, 'he bore a pole to which were fastened in a bundle his ration of grain, his cooking vessel, cup, saw, basket, hatchet, sickle, pick, and spade. For it was necessary that he should be woodman and navvy as well as a soldier.'[4] Granted that these articles were necessary, the legionary,

---

[1] *The Roman Republic*, vol. I, p. 121. When Quintus Cicero was in Gaul in 54 B.C., Dio (XL, 8, 1) mentions: 'They were unable to care for their wounded through lack of the necessary appliances.'     [2] *The Civil Wars*, III, 44.

[3] On the surviving monuments one *pilum* is shown, but two may still have been carried.

[4] *The Roman Republic*, vol. I, p. 119. This apparently is based on Josephus (*The Wars of the Jews*, III, v, 5), who writes of the legionary of A.D. 69: 'The foot soldiers have a spear, and a long buckler, besides a saw and a basket, a pick axe and an axe, a thong of leather, and a hook, with provisions for three days: so that a footman hath no great need of a mule to carry his burthens.'

like all infantry before his day and since, was grossly overloaded. Cicero says he carried 60 lb. Even a Goliath could not have marched any appreciable distance with such a load carried in so cumbersome a way. Therefore it would appear more probable that, as H. J. Edwards writes, the soldier 'carried his kit (*sarcinae*) and food in a bundle, on a crutch strapped to his shoulders – called after its inventor *mulus Marianus*',[1] and that the woodman-cum-navvy's Christmas tree outfit, mentioned by Holmes, was relegated to the pack animals.

The soldier's staple food was wheat, issued in the grain, ground by him in a portable hand mill – another gadget he had to carry – and made into a rough kind of bread, probably resembling a chupatty baked on hot stones or embers. He seldom ate meat, was allowed no wine, and drank vinegar when obtainable. His corn ration and clothing were charged against his pay, which Caesar increased from 120 *denarii* (about £4-15-0) a year to 225 (about £9-0-0); he also allowed his men 'corn, when it was in plenty, without any restrictions'.[2] That the Roman soldier could march and fight as he did on so meagre a ration certainly redounds to his astonishing physical endurance.

## 4. ITS TACTICAL ORGANIZATION

The three essential elements in tactics are: to guard (defensive), to hit (offensive), and to move (mobility), and the simplest tactical organization is the phalanx of spearmen. When two such bodies met, the tactical aim was also of the simplest; it was to push each other over with their spears – a tug of war in reverse. The defensive consisted in maintaining an unbroken front, and the offensive in breaking through the opposing front.

When Philip II of Macedon (359–336 B.C.) reorganized the Macedonian army, because the low mobility of the phalanx and its need to fight on level ground rendered it an insufficient instrument of conquest as opposed to inter-city brawls, his tactical idea was to base his reorganization on mobility. He, therefore, separated his small force of cavalry, which hitherto had protected the flanks of the phalanx, from the phalanx, increased its strength and converted it into his offensive striking force. Simultaneously he limited the phalanx to a defensive role. From an offensive force it became a defensive one: to hold the enemy's phalanx by clinch, or threat of clinch, while the cavalry manœuvred for the decisive blow; thus the phalanx became the tactical

[1] Appendix A, p. 604 of his translation of *The Gallic War*.
[2] Suetonius, *Div. Iul.*, XXVI.

base of cavalry action. Besides this, he made the phalanx more flexible by dividing it into battalions, and because an army of conquest would have to fight over every sort of ground and against an irregular as well as a regular enemy, he added to his phalanx and cavalry bodies of trained light horse and light infantry. These were his essential changes, and all were aimed at increasing mobility. His tactics may be summed up in Napoleon's dictum: 'The whole art of war consists in a well-reasoned and extremely circumspect defensive, followed by rapid and audacious attack.'

The Romans, when they changed over from phalanx to legion, continued to rely on their infantry as their offensive arm; they made no changes in the tasks of their small cavalry force, which as previously were to guard the flanks of the legion, to reconnoitre, to forage and to pursue. To render the legion more flexible than the phalanx, and also to economize the endurance of its men in battle, they divided it into three bodies – a fighting line, a support line, and a reserve line.

In hand-to-hand fighting physical endurance is all-important. In the phalanx all its men were in the fighting line, and although of its eight to sixteen ranks only the leading four or five in the Macedonian phalanx were engaged, those in rear of them – like all soldiers in close contact with danger – became emotionally if not physically exhausted as the battle proceeded. Compared with this, the legion, organized as it was in three separated lines, was able to hold two-thirds of its men outside the danger zone – the zone of demoralization – in which the remaining third was engaged. Therefore, until required to replace or reinforce the front line, the legion had both physically and morally fresh troops at its disposal.

Nevertheless, when compared with Philip's system, the legionary system had certain serious defects. While Philip's mobility was incomparably higher, and because of his efficient light troops, horse and foot, the security of his army could at all times be guaranteed, in the legionary system this was far from being so, because its light troops were seldom efficient or reliable. Unlike Philip's army, a legionary army, opposed to a bold enemy, risked being surprised, both at rest and on the line of march. To guard against the first risk, the Romans resorted to entrenchments as their main means of protection, and their legions became the greatest entrenching army in history. On campaign, not only did every legion construct an entrenched camp[1] at the end of each

1 Normally the camp was built to accommodate two legions, with cavalry and auxiliaries. When the ground permitted, it was square in shape; each of its sides

day's march, a task which, although it afforded ample security, reduced mobility by three to four marching hours a day, but at times trenches were dug on the battlefields themselves in order to protect the flanks of the infantry against cavalry attack.[1] So completely did the spade dominate tactics, that the legions seldom accepted battle unless there was an entrenched camp close at hand, and not a few Roman campaigns may be described as mobile trench warfare. Further, lack of mobility, due to lack of efficient light cavalry and light infantry, rendered the legionary system unsuited against guerrillas.[2]

While the horse dominated Philip's organization, the spade dominated the legionary organization. In the one the aim of battle was the decisive cavalry assault followed by a pursuit à outrance; in the other the aim was methodical attrition followed by a general massacre, or enslavement.

That no Roman army developed the mobility of the Macedonians under Alexander the Great is understandable. Besides lack of cavalry and entrenching, it was also due to dependence on requisitioning – that is, living off the enemy country as it advanced. Though, as will become apparent, Caesar fully appreciated the value of speed, because of his primitive method of supply, not one of his campaigns, nor even that of any other Roman general, can compare with Antigonus' in 319 B.C., against Alcetas. Notwithstanding that the latter with some 20,000 men lay encamped 287 miles away, Antigonus moved his whole army, horse, foot, and elephants, about 50,000 men in all, at an average speed of 41 miles a day for seven days on end, surprised his unsuspecting victim and routed his army.[3] 'Such a feat,' writes Sir Frank Adcock, 'would seem incredible were it not that in this period an accurate record was kept of each day's march by officers appointed for the purpose.'[4]

---

was about 2,000 feet in length, and consisted of a 12-foot rampart crowned with a palisade, and protected by a ditch 8 feet deep and 15 feet wide. In the centre of each side was a wide gateway with material at hand to block it.

[1] At the battle of Orchomenus, in 85 B.C., because the Romans were in terror of the enemy's cavalry, Sulla entrenched the flanks of his army with ditches 10 feet wide (Appian, *The Mithridatic War*, 49).

[2] For example: In 146–140 B.C., Viriathus, a guerrilla leader in Spain, on one occasion with 1,000 horsemen held an entire Roman army at bay for two whole days because it lacked light cavalry. For his exploits, see Appian, *The Wars in Spain*, 60–75. And Plutarch (*Sertorius*, XII) describes how in the Sertorian War Metellus' army was incapable of operating against guerrillas.

[3] Diodorus, XVIII, 44–45.

[4] *The Greek and Macedonian Art of War* (1957), p. 78.

That this march was possible can only be explained on administrative grounds. There cannot have been any time for requisitioning, and because Antigonus had to march light, his army must have had a most efficient supply train, probably accompanied by spare draught animals to replace those which became exhausted. Had Antigonus been compelled to secure his army each night in an entrenched camp, and had his men been loaded up with spades, picks, axes, etc., lashed to a pole, it is highly improbable that it could have covered a third of the distance it actually did. The secret of his success was that he relied on mobility, not only to surprise his enemy, but to prevent his enemy from surprising him; for, as Diodorus writes: 'He escaped the notice of his enemy because of the rapidity of his march.'[1]

From this it must not be inferred that the Roman legionaries were poor marchers; in all probability they were every bit as good as, if not better than, Antigonus' Greeks and Asiatics. The reason must be sought in the Roman system of warfare. In accordance with it, it took Caesar eight years to subdue Gaul, in extent but a fraction of the Persian empire, which under the Macedonian system was subdued by Alexander in nine. Although the conditions in which these two great conquests were made differed widely, the question remains, could Caesar, or any other general who adhered to the Roman system, have emulated Alexander? The spade will answer this: a soldier cannot simultaneously dig and march, and should he spend between three and four hours out of every twenty-four in digging, to an enemy who understands the tactical value of time he will make a gratuitous gift of one day out of every seven.

It was fortunate for Rome that she never had to match her generals against Alexander or his immediate successors; also it was fortunate that when her legions first appeared in the East, they were faced with a degenerate phalanx which had reverted to its pre-Philipian offensive role, and had become more tied than ever before to level ground, because the 14-foot *sarissa* (pike) with which Philip armed his phalangites had been lengthened to 21 and even to 24 feet, and was so heavy and cumbersome that it could only be wielded with difficulty, even on level ground, by men in armour.

The two Roman battles which most clearly reveal the inferiority and superiority of the legion engaged with the phalanx of late Hellenistic times are Magnesia and Pydna. The first was fought at the close of 190 B.C., between the Romans under L. Cornelius Scipio and Gnaeus

[1] XVIII, 44, 2.

Domitius Ahenobarbus and the Syrian army of Antiochus the Great. The second was fought on June 22, 168 B.C., between the Romans, commanded by L. Aemilius Paullus, and the Macedonian army of Perseus, king of Macedon. In the one cavalry and infantry were engaged on both sides, in the other infantry only.

At Magnesia, fortunately for the Romans, they were supported on the right of their line by 2,800 excellent cavalry commanded by Eumenes II of Pergamum. The battle was opened by Antiochus, who at the head of his cavalry charged the Roman left wing and routed it. Next, Eumenes, after his light troops had driven the Syrian chariots back on to the troops in rear of them, under cover of the confusion charged and broke through the Syrian left wing. He then wheeled his horsemen to the left, charged Antiochus' massive phalanx in flank, while Domitius Ahenobarbus advanced his legions and plied its front with *pila*. The credit for this victory must go to Eumenes.

It was the first great battle of the Romans in the East, and also the last won by the tactics of Alexander. Once again boldly handled cavalry had shown themselves to be the arm of decision. Nevertheless, the Romans learnt nothing from this battle.

At Pydna, after an initial skirmish, the Macedonian phalanx slowly advanced toward the Roman camp entrenched on a low hill, and at the sight of 'the bristling rampart of outstretched pikes', Aemilius 'was stricken at once with astonishment and terror'; never before had he seen so fearful a spectacle.[1] As long as the ground was level the phalanx drove all before it; but when it became broken its front began to bend and gaps opened in it. Aemilius took advantage of this; he split up his cohorts into groups, and 'ordered them to plunge quickly into the interstices and empty spaces in the enemy's line and thus come to close quarters, not fighting a single battle against them all, but many separate and successive battles.'[2] This they did, and the phalanx rapidly dissolved.

In his analysis Polybius writes: '. . . the Macedonian phalanx is difficult, and sometimes impossible to handle, because the men cannot act in squads or separately. The Roman order on the other hand is flexible: for every Roman, once armed and on the field, is equally well equipped for every place, time, or appearance of the enemy.'[3] This is true, as long as the enemy happens to be infantry; but it is certainly not true should he be cavalry. The front of a well-dressed phalanx was

[1] Plutarch, *Aemilius*, XIX, 1, and Polybius, XXIX, 17.
[2] Plutarch, *Aemilius*, XX, 4.
[3] Polybius, XVIII, 32.

invulnerable to a charge of heavy cavalry; but the front of a legionary army, either in line or in columns, was not, and particularly so after the legions had dispensed with that most effective anti-cavalry weapon, the spear, and replaced it by the *pilum* which, because of its fragile construction and inferior length, was an indifferent substitute when used as a spear.

Fortunately for the Romans, in the West they were never called upon to face efficient cavalry; their problem was to overcome hordes of Iberians, Gauls, and Germans, whose infantry was undisciplined, and whose horsemen were little other than mounted brigands. Nevertheless, until the Romans had developed their tactical drill, they proved to be formidable antagonists.

In the early battles between Romans and Gauls, the latter, armed with the long cutting-sword – an excellent weapon in the initial assault, but an indifferent one in the hand-to-hand mêlée – rushed with terrifying yells upon the manipular columns and beat down the shields of their leading divisions so rapidly that time was insufficient for the ranks in rear to replace those in front. The result was that frequently the columns became completely demoralized, and to avoid being cut down where they stood, their men took to their heels and massacre followed.

We know that to overcome this the Romans bound the upper and lower rims of their shields with metal; but in itself this was not sufficient, for though it enabled the legionary to protect himself more effectively, it did not add to his endurance – to his staying-power in battle.

It should not be overlooked that classical infantry battles consisted of a series of close order individual duels, in which only the men of the leading rank, or ranks, were engaged. The belief that the power of a mass of men resides in its depth is erroneous, not only because the ranks, or masses, in the immediate rear of the actual fighters instinctively recoil from danger, but because were they to push forward, the inevitable result would be that the leading rank would be thrown into confusion. The true purpose of mass-depth is to maintain the fighting front at maximum strength; therefore to fill vacancies in it as its men are killed or wounded, and to relieve those who become exhausted. Also it must not be overlooked that in hand-to-hand fighting the physical endurance of the fighters is brief, and that, therefore, irrespective of casualties, the need for a steady replacement of the men in the front rank by those of the ranks in rear is imperative. For instance, should a body of men be ranged in six ranks, and should the fighting endurance of the front rank men be fifteen minutes, then, omitting casualties, its collective endurance will be an hour and a half, by when the exhausted men will be rested. Ardant du Picq puts this succinctly:

'The Romans,' he writes, 'believed in the power of the mass, but from the moral point of view. They did not multiply their ranks to add to the mass, but to endow the combatants with confidence in being supported and relieved; and the number of ranks was calculated according to the duration of the moral pressure the latter could sustain.'[1] He should have added – and physical also.

Although no details of the Roman battle drill of Caesar's days have survived, it stands to reason that it must have included these relay movements, which endowed the legionaries with an overwhelming tactical superiority over the Gauls and other barbarians, who believed that fighting power increased in proportion to the size of the mass. Therefore they threw all their warriors into the initial assault, and had no organized reserves in hand to replace them when their endurance was exhausted.[2]

In brief, against their like, as well as against barbaric warriors, the techniques of the legionary battles may be summarized as follows:

(1) To engage the minimum number of combatants necessary to wage the initial fight.

(2) To support the fighting front with reliefs and replacements stationed immediately in rear of it.

(3) To hold a reserve well outside the zone of demoralization, in order to feed the supports when required, or to clinch victory by a final assault with fresh troops.

As far as purely infantry fighting is in question, this was an advance on anything that had preceded it, and in modified form it is still adhered to in the present age. The legion was a tactical organization of genius; nevertheless limited in tactical effect, because of the lack of an efficient cavalry arm.

---

[1] *Études sur le combat* (7th edit., 1914), p. 20.

[2] At the battle of Vesontio, in 58 B.C., Appian (*The Gallic History*, 3) writes of the Germans: 'It seems that they were without patient endurance in their battles, and did not fight in a scientific way or in any regular order, but with a sort of high spirit simply made an onset like wild beasts, for which reason they were overcome by Roman science and endurance.' (See also Polybius, II, 29, 30 and 33, for Gallic tactics.)

## 5. ITS SIEGECRAFT

Throughout history there have been three ways of taking a walled city or fortress: by starving it into surrender; by fomenting treachery within its walls; and by batter and storm. The third constitutes siegecraft proper, and all the Romans knew of it was borrowed from the Greeks, who borrowed from the Carthaginians, whose masters were the Assyrians and Babylonians.

In the classical age, there were three ways of overcoming a defended wall. It could be breached by battering-rams; its foundations could be undermined by tunnelling; and command of its summit could be gained by means of scaling-ladders, mounds of earth, and movable towers.

Because all these tasks entailed close contact with the wall, the initial problem was how to approach it under protective cover; and, once it was neared, how to protect the besiegers from the missiles of the besieged. This was solved by the use of mantlets and penthouses.[1]

The mantlet (*pluteus*) was a large shield constructed of hurdlework or planks, and sometimes of cable mats, or mattresses, suspended on a frame. It resembled a huge snowplough mounted on wheels, and was pushed forward by men in rear of it.

The penthouse (*vinea*) was a shed, or hut, with open ends. Normally its two sides were of hurdlework and its roof of timber, both protected against fire by a covering of raw hides. It was moved forward on rollers by the men inside it, and was either used singly or in chains – that is, end to end – so as to form a continuous covered way. When so used, they were the equivalent of modern siege saps.

The movable tower was generally built of scaffolding and hurdlework; it was divided into storeys, and protected against fire by raw hides, sometimes by plates of metal. Vitruvius mentions that the smallest were 60 cubits[2] in height and 17 cubits in width at the base, and the largest 120 cubits and $23\frac{1}{2}$ respectively; both contracted at their tops by one-fifth of the width of their bases.[3] Actually, there can have

[1] Vitruvius, in Book X, Chapters X–XVI, of his *Treatise on Architecture*, supplies much detail on siege apparatus, mainly of a technical and historical nature. He would appear to have served under Julius Caesar in his African War. His treatise was written in the reign of Augustus.

[2] According to Sir William Tarn, the Greek cubit was $18\frac{1}{4}$ inches and the Macedonian from 13 to 14 inches (*Alexander the Great* (1948), vol. II, pp. 169–71).

[3] *Vitruvius on Architecture* (Loeb edit., 1934), X, xiii, 4–5. 120 cubits appears an exaggeration.

been no fixed size, because each tower must have been built with reference to the height of the wall it was required to command, and to its distance from it, which, should the wall rise from a mound surrounded by a moat, must at times have been considerable. The tower was provided with wheels, and was hauled forward by means of cables, pulleys, and capstans along a prepared causeway by hundreds of men, and sometimes it would appear by thousands. When in position, from its upper storeys and summit archers and catapults fired on the defenders of the wall, while on its ground floor a battering-ram pounded the lower part of the wall. When a tower could be brought close up to the wall, under cover of its archers and catapults, a boarding-bridge was let down from it on to the top of the wall to enable a storming party to gain a footing on its battlements.

Another means of gaining command of a wall was to raise against it a mound of earth (*agger*) – more correctly a ramp – which sloped toward the summit of the wall. The men engaged on it approached it under cover of one or more chains of penthouses, and when at work were protected by mantlets. It was an extremely laborious operation, and frequently thousands of tons of earth had to be carried forward in baskets. When completed, one or more movable towers were at times hauled up the mound so that increased command might be gained.

The ram (*aries*), *par excellence* the 'siege gun' of antiquity, was a beam which resembled a ship's mast crowned with an iron head or beak; it was worked either from within a large penthouse, or, as already described, from the ground floor of a movable tower. It was swung from chains suspended from the roof of its shelter, and when required to span an intervening ditch or moat, was sometimes over 100 feet in length. Appian records that, in 149 B.C., the Romans used a ram against Carthage which required 6,000 men to bring it into action.[1]

Before the introduction of gunpowder, tunnelling and mining of a wall, or tower, was carried out as follows: Under cover of mantlets a gallery was driven under its foundations, and a chamber excavated, the roof of which was shored up with pit props. The chamber was then filled with combustibles which, on being ignited, consumed the props; the roof then caved in and the structure above it collapsed. To frustrate this, the defenders resorted to countermining. According to Appian, when, in 72 B.C., Lucullus laid siege to Themiscyra, its inhabitants cut openings from above into the tunnels, 'and thrust bears and other wild animals and swarms of bees into them against his workers'.[2] This may

[1] *The Punic Wars*, VIII, 98.      [2] *The Mithridatic War*, XII, 78.

be one of the many Mithridatic myths; nevertheless, as late as the First World War, in East Africa an attacking force stumbled upon a bee-farm, and was routed by its inhabitants.

The catapult was developed from the bow, but it had far greater force, range, and accuracy. It would appear to have been invented by the Phoenicians. It resembled the medieval crossbow, and like it the

1. Catapult

bow-string was drawn back by a windlass; unlike it, its power was derived, not from the tension of a bow but from the torsion of two vertically twisted skeins of sinews, or hair, into which bow arms were inserted (see Diagram 1).

There were two types, which varied mainly in size, the light and the heavy; the former, the *catapulta* (Greek *katapeltes*) – a machine that could pierce a shield (*pelta*) – threw feathered javelins, pebbles and small leaden shot; the latter, the *ballista*, which the Greeks called *petrobolos* (stone-thrower), threw stones up to 50 or 60 lb. in weight. The first was very accurate – much more so than the flintlock musket – it could kill a single man at 100 yards, hit a small group of men at 200 yards, and its maximum range was from 450 to 500 yards. The second was less accurate, and although its projectiles could demolish mantlets, penthouses, and movable towers, they had little effect on walls.

Besides these two pieces of artillery, a third, known as the 'wild ass'

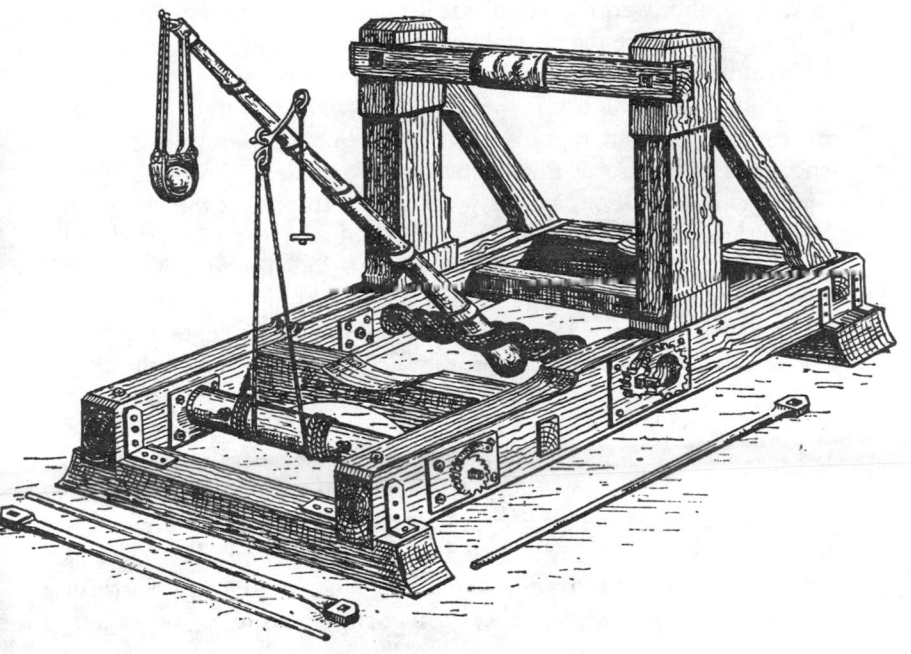

2. Onager

or *onager*, was introduced during Hellenistic times (see Diagram 2). Ammianus Marcellinus describes it as follows:

'In the middle of the ropes [twisted skein] rises a wooden arm like a chariot pole . . . on the top hangs a sling . . . four soldiers on each side of the engine wind the arm down till it is almost level with the ground . . . when the arm is set free it springs up and hurls forth from its sling the stone, which is certain to crush whatever it strikes. The engine was formerly called the 'scorpion', because it has its sting erect, but later ages have given it the name of Onager, or wild ass, for when wild asses are chased they kick the stones behind them.'[1]

It was far less accurate than the catapult, and when compared with it may be classed as a howitzer, which could lob rocks, fire-pots, and other projectiles, over the wall of a city and demolish its houses. We, therefore, find that the main types of land artillery now in use were, in classical times, represented by the ram as siege gun, the catapult as field gun, and the *onager* as howitzer. With the medieval trebuchet – a super-howitzer – they were the world's artillery before the age of gunpowder.

In a classical siege the normal procedure was as follows: First, a line of investment, or of contravallation, was drawn round a city in order to cut its garrison off from relief and supply. Next, were it likely that the enemy would attempt to relieve it, the line of contravallation was encompassed by a second line which faced outwards; it was called the line of circumvallation, and its purpose was to protect the besiegers. When these lines had been dug, the points of assault were selected and the method of attack agreed. Should it be to tunnel or breach, lines of mantlets were pushed forward, under cover of which archers were assembled to fire at the defenders on the walls. Next, under their covering fire, chains of penthouses were advanced in order to establish secure forward communications; simultaneously movable towers and a mound were built, and lastly the battering-rams were emplaced. These various tasks entailed the employment of vast numbers of men, and normally the inhabitants of the entire district in which the city was located were impressed to assist the soldiery. When Sulla invested the Piraeus in 87 B.C., Plutarch informs us that his siege engines called for a daily employment of '10,000 yoke of mules';[2] and in Antony's Parthian campaign of 36 B.C., he states that his siege engines required 300 wagons to transport them.[3]

---

[1] *Roman History*, XXIII, iv, 5–6. Josephus records that at the siege of Jerusalem in A.D. 70, stones weighing a talent (about 60 lb.) were thrown by the Roman catapults (? *onagri*) a distance of two or more stades, 400 to 450 yards (*Wars of the Jews*, V, vi, 3).

[2] *Sulla*, XII, 2.           [3] *Antony*, XXXVIII, 2.

# V

# *The Pacification of Gaul*

## I. GAUL AND ITS INHABITANTS

IN Caesar's day Gaul included the whole of modern France and Belgium, parts of Holland and Switzerland, and all of Germany west of the Rhine. Camille Jullian believes that its population was only a little less than in the days of Louis XIV – that is, between 20 and 30 millions[1] – and Jérôme Carcopino suggests at least 12 millions.[2] Because these are conjectural figures, all that can be said is that, in the first century B.C., Gaul would appear to have been a well-populated country, a proof of its prosperity and wealth.

Its inhabitants were of mixed origin, but throughout the greater part of the country the Celts were the dominant race. Probably they entered Gaul in the seventh century B.C., but by the first century language differences caused Caesar to divide them into three main groups, the *Celtae* or *Galli*, the *Aquitani*, and the *Belgae*. The first were located between the Garonne and Seine, the second in modern Gascony, and the third north of the Seine and Marne. Of the three, Caesar held that the Belgae were the most courageous, because they were the furthest removed from the civilization of the Province,[3] and were mixed with barbaric Germans from east of the Rhine. The entire population was divided into 200 to 300 tribes, a few large and many small, and of the latter many were clients of the former. For the most part they lived in villages scattered round a central refuge or town (*oppidum*) normally situated on a hill-top and sometimes fortified. All were semi-civilized, practised agriculture and cattle-breeding, carried on a considerable

---

[1] *Histoire de la Gaule* (1908), vol. II, p. 8.

[2] *Histoire Général* (1936), edit. Gustave Glotz, section Histoire Ancienne, Part III, vol. II, p. 707.

[3] Also called Transalpine Gaul and Gallia Narbonensis, the belt of country between the Cévennes and Maritime Alps, annexed in 120 B.C. It included much of Languedoc and Provence.

commerce either by road, or river, or sea, and were acquainted with money and the Greek alphabet.

The tribes were governed either by kings, or oligarchies of nobles, or elected magistrates; but in Caesar's day monarchies had mostly disappeared. Among the Aedui, who occupied the greater part of modern Burgundy, the chiefs of villages composed a Senate which yearly elected a magistrate, a kind of dictator, known as the Vergobret; but his powers were largely nominal because the people were wont to intervene in everything. Another complication was that, although the Senate elected the civil head of the tribe, the people as a whole elected the war chief. The whole system lacked discipline, so clearly recognized by Caesar. 'In Gaul,' he wrote, 'not only in every state and every canton and district, but almost in each several household, there are parties' under elected leaders, and 'each . . . refuses to allow his own folk to be oppressed and defrauded, since otherwise he has no authority among them. The same principle holds in regard to Gaul as a whole . . . for the whole body of states is divided into two parties.'[1] It was this lack of inter-tribal co-ordination and internal concord which were the main factors that aided Caesar in his subjection of Gaul. Further, he writes: 'Throughout Gaul there are two classes of persons of definite account and dignity,' the nobles, whom he calls 'knights', and the Druids; 'as for the common folk, they are treated almost as slaves.'[2]

Of the Druids he has much to say: they were the ministers of the gods, who differed little from the Greek and Roman; they interpreted the rituals, instructed the young men, and acted as judges and arbiters. One of them was elected Chief Druid for life, and yearly presided over a general assembly of his subordinates at a central point in Gaul, where disputes between the tribes were ventilated and judgements delivered. This priesthood constituted the sole element of unity between the tribes.

Conversely, the knights, or nobles, were the main element of discord. 'Well-nigh every year,' writes Caesar, 'they would either be making wanton attacks themselves or repelling such', because dissensions and rivalries between the tribes were never-ending.[3]

The Germans, writes Caesar, differed much in their way of living. Their whole life was spent on hunting and warlike pursuits. For agriculture they had no liking; no man was permitted to own land; each year the chiefs assigned to the tribes and clans as much land as they

---

[1] *The Gallic War*, trans. H. J. Edwards (Loeb edit., 1952), VI, 11. Referred to as 'B.G.'.    [2] *B.G.*, VI, 13.    [3] *Ibid.*, VI, 15.

deemed necessary, and after a year's tenancy it had to be surrendered. The reason was that, were possession permanent, it was feared that agriculture would be substituted for warlike zeal, and passion for money would arise 'to be parent of parties and of quarrels'. 'It is their aim', Caesar says, 'to keep common people in contentment, when each man sees that his own wealth is equal to that of the most powerful',[1] which would have rejoiced the heart of Marx.

They devastated the land which surrounded their territories, in order to remove 'all fear of a sudden inroad', and looked upon brigandage as a means to diminish sloth. As warriors they were superior to the Gauls, who had become corrupted by contact with civilization. So much so, according to Caesar, that they had grown accustomed to defeat 'and after being conquered in many battles they do not even compare themselves in point of valour with the Germans'.[2]

Of all arms the Germans preferred cavalry, which normally was well-mounted, and occasionally it comprised a number of professional, salaried horsemen. But it would seem that frequently they operated as mounted infantry, because Caesar tells us that 'In cavalry combats they often leap from their horses and fight on foot, having trained their horses to remain in the same spot, and retiring rapidly upon them at need.'[3]

Except for the Nervii of the Sambre, against whom Caesar's most bloody battles were fought, the Gallic infantry was untrained and frequently little more than an armed rabble. The long cutting sword was their chief weapon, little use was made of spearmen and archers, but javelins of various kinds and slings were used. They carried wooden, or wattle, shields, and the true warrior despised armour and fought stripped. The chiefs, however, wore bronze cuirasses, or coats of mail, and highly decorated helmets.

There was no tactical organization other than the tribal group, and few preparations were made for a campaign. There was a total lack of planning; battles were headlong assaults in a rough phalangial order in which the warriors rapidly exhausted themselves and became disorganized; courage shattered itself on the rocks of discipline. No proper commissariat existed, hosts of women and children followed the army with household wagons, and when their contents were exhausted a campaign petered out. When halted, instead of an entrenched camp, the Gallic horde sought security within a wagon laager. Fortified towns were surrounded with a rampart of stones and huge logs which was

[1] *Ibid.*, VI, 22.　　　[2] *Ibid.*, VI, 24.　　　[3] *Ibid.*, IV, 2.

difficult to ram down; they were seldom moated, and when carried by storm the result was more disastrous than the loss of a battle.

## 2. CAMPAIGN AGAINST THE HELVETII, 58 B.C.

The crisis which brought Caesar hot-footed to Geneva arose out of the long-standing rivalry between the Aedui and Arverni for the hegemony of central Gaul. The former who, in 123 B.C., had by treaty been recognized as the friends and allies of the Roman people, dwelt in the Nivernais and western Burgundy, and the latter in Auvergne. In 71 B.C., the Aedui were in the ascendant, and to undermine their power, the Arverni, in conjunction with the Sequani, who inhabited the country between the river Saône and the Jura mountains and the Rhine, sought aid of Ariovistus, a Germanic chieftain east of the Rhine. He responded to their call, defeated the Aedui, and, enchanted with the country, he compelled the Sequani to cede to him the fertile plains of Alsace as the first step toward founding a German kingdom in Gaul. This led to the Aedui and Sequani composing their differences, and with their allies they formed a coalition against Ariovistus who, in 60 B.C., decisively defeated it at Magetobriga (? Moigte de Broie). The Aedui appealed to Rome, but without effect, because at the time the Senate was occupied in suppressing a revolt of the Allobroges, whose territories lay between the Lake of Geneva and the middle Rhône, and bordered on the Province. Next, a faction of the Aedui set out to gain the assistance of the Helvetii, and when this became known in Rome, not wishing to add Ariovistus to their enemies, in 59 B.C., with Caesar's concurrence, the Senate conferred on him the title of 'king and friend of the Roman people'.[1]

The Helvetii were a Celtic people akin to the Gauls; they inhabited western Switzerland, and because they were hard pressed by Germanic tribes on their northern border, and were alarmed that Ariovistus might close in on their western flank, they decided to migrate *en masse* and occupy the fertile region of the Santones (Saintonge) in western Gaul. One of two routes could be followed, a narrow and difficult one between the Jura and the Rhône through the territory of the

---

[1] Concerning this, Tenny Frank (*Roman Imperialism*, p. 335) remarks: 'It is a significant fact that during Caesar's consulship Rome formally recognized Ariovistus as a "friend". That Rome should have recognized as a friend the prince who was oppressing the other "friends", the Aedui, would seem to indicate that Caesar was promoting complications in Gaul in order to pave the way for Roman intervention at the appropriate moment.'

Sequani, and a less difficult one from Geneva by way of the Allobroges and the Roman Province. They decided to take the latter, and were accompanied by a number of allied tribes.

According to Caesar, they and their allies numbered 368,000 people, of whom 92,000 were warriors.[1] Two years were allotted for preparations, during which corn was sown, carts, draught and slaughter cattle collected, and each man was instructed to provide himself with three months' provisions for the journey.[2]

When Caesar arrived at Geneva, as there was but one legion in the Province, he ordered the largest number of auxiliary troops to be raised, broke the bridge the Helvetii had thrown over the Rhône, and was met by an Helvetian embassy, who begged his permission to march by way of the Province. Because he had so few troops at call, in order to gain time he prevaricated and bade the embassy return on April 13, when he would inform them of his decision. Next, he blocked the Rhône valley with a 19-mile-long[3] chain of fortifications, and when the embassy returned he refused to grant them passage.

After several abortive attempts to break through, the Helvetii, through the intercession of their friend Dumnorix, a brother of the Aeduan chief druid Diviciacus, succeeded in obtaining the permission of the Sequani to march through their territory by way of the alternative narrow road.

When Caesar learnt that their destination was Saintonge, which, according to him, 'was not far removed from the borders of the Tolasates', who inhabited the region about Toulouse, 'he perceived that the event would bring great danger upon the Province'.[4] To prevent it he left Labienus in command of the Rhône fortifications and hastened back to Cisalpine Gaul to enrol two new legions and bring

[1] *B.G.*, I, 29. Orosius (vi, 7, 5) says 157,000.

[2] From a logistical point of view, Caesar's figures, although accepted by a number of modern historians, are extravagant. Because little forage could be obtained *en route*, at the lowest subsistence level each group of ten people sharing, let us suppose, one two-ton wagon drawn by two oxen (more probably four) would require 3,600 lb. of rations and forage for a journey of 90 days. This would leave over 880 lb. for household belongings, tools, seed corn, tentage, etc. Therefore, on this low basis, 368,000 people would require 36,800 wagons. The difficulties in marshalling and moving such a number, either in one column or several, along the primitive cart tracks of Gaul would prove almost insuperable to the most efficient present-day commissariat.

[3] All miles cited are Roman, about 1,665 yards.

[4] *Ibid.*, I, 10. By the narrow road the migration was no concern of Caesar's, because the Helvetii would traverse free tribal country distant from the Province.

the three he already had at Aquileia out of winter quarters. With these five legions he set out by forced marches on his return.

Before we scrutinize Caesar's first campaign, which proved to be the initial step in his conquest of Gaul, we must observe that any idea that he contemplated it as such is improbable.[1] But what is not so is, that his plea – were the Helvetii to occupy the lands of the Santones the Province would be menaced – was a fictitious one, because those lands were nowhere near the Tolosates. Actually, in Saintonge, the Helvetii would be less of a menace to the Province than had they remained in Switzerland. What, then, was his aim when he decided on war against them? The answer is to be sought in his previous intrigues with Crassus to gain the government of a province and with it the command of an army. Now that he had an army, we hazard to suggest that his aim was his own personal aggrandizement, for although he does not hint at it, his previous activities do.

To gain dominion over the Roman world, he had first to win the means wherewith to master, not Gaul, or any other country, but Crassus and Pompey. To dominate the one he needed great wealth, and to dominate the other, great renown and a powerful army. These his three provinces should be able to provide him with during his five years proconsulship were he fortunate and skilful enough to turn events to his advantage. To imagine that, in 58 B.C., he dreamt of merely adding another province to the empire is chimerical; equally so is it to suppose that he could attain supreme power without ridding himself of his two partners. Unwittingly the Helvetii opened the door to the attainment of his ambition, and Caesar, seizing Fortune by the forelock, stepped through it.

With his five legions he took the road leading along the valley of the Dora Riparia, crossed the Isère, was rejoined by Labienus and his legion, and on the Rhône, probably at Lyons, was met by deputies from the Aedui and Allobroges who sought his aid against the Helvetii, who had ravaged their lands, and at the moment were crossing the Saône by a bridge of boats. When this was reported to him, he at once broke camp, pressed on with three legions, and when he caught up with the enemy

[1] Tenny Frank does not concur. He writes: 'Taken all in all, the commentaries seem to reveal a plan of campaign, even though the author does not deign to mention it. This plan was apparently formed early in the first year's work, if not – as is more likely – even before Caesar approached Gaul. In the main it contemplated a rapid conquest of the whole of Gaul up to the Rhine' (*op. cit.*, p. 339). If so, why at the start did not Caesar take all his legions with him?

he found that three-quarters of them had already crossed; so he fell upon the quarter that had not and annihilated it. Next, he bridged the river, and set out in pursuit of the main body.

To reach a practical road to the valley of the Charente in the land of the Santones, the Helvetii had turned northward toward Bibracte (near Autun on Mount Beuvray), the principal town of the Aedui, and to keep touch with them Caesar sent forward the whole of his cavalry, 4,000 in all, raised in the Province from the Aedui and their allies, of which the Aeduan contingent was commanded by Dumnorix. In a skirmish it took panic and was repulsed by 500 Helvetian horsemen, after which the pursuit continued for about a fortnight.

During it Caesar learnt from Liscus, the Aeduan Vergobret, that Dumnorix was an ambitious traitor 'of paramount influence with the common folk'; that not only had he caused the panic, but also was preventing corn from being supplied to Caesar's army. Because its supply was essential, Caesar decided to overlook Dumnorix's defection when his brother Diviciacus pleaded for his life, rather than antagonize Diviciacus who, as Chief Druid, had great influence with the Aedui; but he took the precaution to have Dumnorix closely watched.

On the same day, when Caesar learnt from his scouts that the Helvetii had halted close under a height eight miles from the Roman camp, he decided to surprise them. He instructed Labienus with two veteran legions, under cover of night, to occupy a hill overlooking one flank of their encampment, when with the remaining two he would man-œuvre against the other flank. Labienus carried out his task; but due to a blunder on the part of a subordinate, who mistook his forces for those of the enemy, and reported to Caesar that the hill was occupied by the latter, the operation had to be abandoned. The legions then moved on to encamp three miles in rear of the Helvetii near Toulon-sur-Arroux.[1]

This mishap was unfortunate, because the army had no more than two days' supply of corn left, and as its replenishment was imperative, Caesar decided to march away from the Helvetii and make for Bibracte, some 18 miles to the north, which was the largest and best provided of the Aeduan towns. This change of direction was reported by deserters from Caesar's Gallic horse to the Helvetii, who jumped to the con-clusion that the Romans were afraid to face them, and, in order to prevent them from reaching Bibracte, they also changed the direction of their march and attacked the Roman rear guard, according to Stoffel,

[1] Identified by Colonel Stoffel, see his *Histoire de Jules César – Guerre Civile* (1887), vol. II, pp. 439–52.

near the hill of Armecy, which lies about three English miles north-west of Toulon. To check them, Caesar sent out his cavalry, and under their cover he deployed his four veteran legions in triple line on the western slope of the Armecy ridge, with the two newly raised legions and the auxiliary troops in rear of them on the summit, so as to increase the appearance of his strength. In the meantime the Helvetii parked their wagons, and, when they had driven back the Roman horse, they advanced 'in a densely-crowded line' against their enemy.

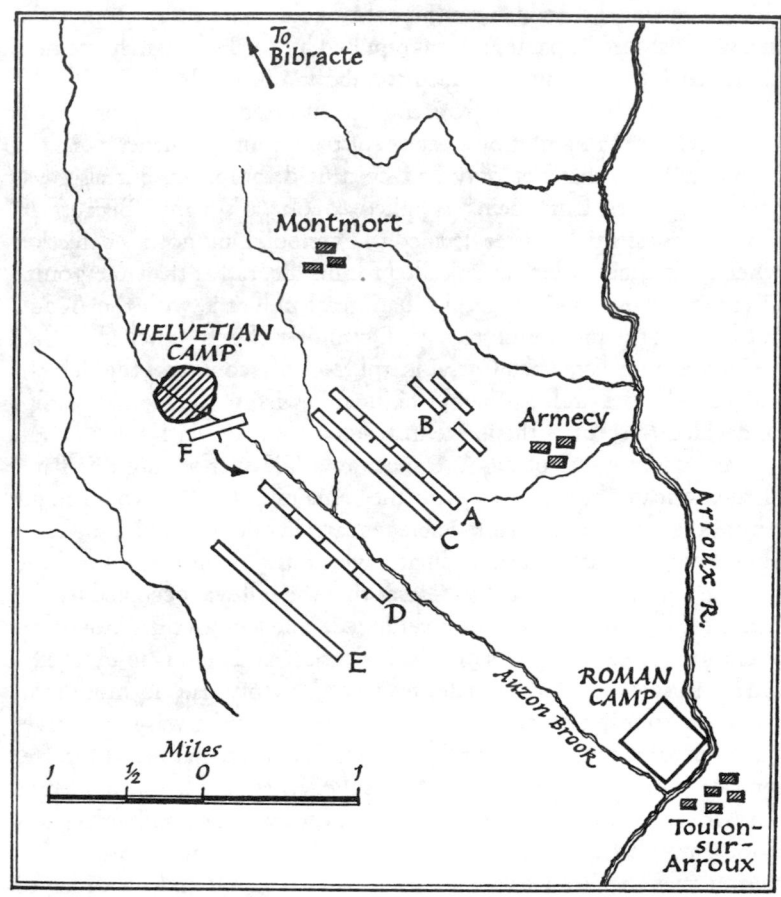

3. The Battle of Armecy

A, 1st position of four veteran legions. B, two recruit legions and auxiliaries. C, 1st position of Helvetians. D, 2nd position of four veteran legions. E, 2nd position of Helvetians. F, flank attack by Boii and Tulingi.

This was to be Caesar's first battle, and his whole future depended, not on winning it but on not losing it. So far, he had had little experience of war; his reputation was still to be made; he was new to his men; his cavalry were untrustworthy, and his four veteran legions, some 20,000 men in all, were faced with an enemy numerically vastly superior to them. But one thing stood in his favour; accompanied as the Helvetian warriors were by vast numbers of women, children, cattle, and wagons, their mobility was severely restricted. Were he to do no more than repulse them, they could not escape him; sooner or later their supplies would fail them, and then they would be at his mercy. Wisely, therefore, his tactics were tempered with caution.

First, Caesar sent his own horse and those of his subordinates to the rear, in order to prevent any sudden flight on their part. Next, he harangued his troops to encourage them,[1] and immediately after the battle opened.

The onrush of the Helvetii was met by a shower of *pila*, many of which stuck in their shields and so weighed them down that they were cast aside. At length worn and wounded they fell back and withdrew to a height about a mile distant,[2] and were followed by the Romans who, as they advanced, were suddenly attacked on their exposed (right) flank by some 15,000 Boii and Tulingi.[3] This brought the Romans to a halt; whereupon the Helvetii descended from the high ground and again assaulted the Roman front, but were repulsed. They then retired on their wagon laager. 'There was no rout,' writes Caesar, 'for throughout the action, though it lasted from the seventh hour to eventide, no one could have seen the back of the enemy.'[4]

The Romans next advanced on the laager, where fighting continued far into the night. Eventually it was stormed and captured, and the surviving Helvetii, 130,000 in all,[5] withdrew, and after three days reached the borders of the Lingones, a tribe which inhabited the country

[1] Classical historians are very fond of introducing pre-battle speeches. At the best, they could only be made to a small group of officers, as it would be impossible audibly to address a single legion, let alone several.

[2] It would appear that this height lay either north or south of the Auxon brook. Although Stoffel accepts the former, other historians accept the latter, as shown on Map 3 (see Holmes, *Caesar's Conquest of Gaul*, p. 627).

[3] As allies, the Boii and Tulingi had joined the migration from its start.

[4] *B.G.*, I, 26.

[5] This means that in the rear guard action on the Saône and in this battle 238,000 Helvetians and their allies, mostly women and children, were slaughtered – an incredible number.

round Tonnerre and Bar-sur-Aube, as well as the plateau of Langres and the neighbourhood of Dijon. There was no pursuit, and after he had rested his men for three days, Caesar resumed his advance.

The inevitable then happened, as Caesar must have foreseen directly the laager was his. The loss of their wagons, or the greater part of them, meant starvation for the Helvetii, who were compelled through lack of provisions to treat of surrender. The main terms decided by Caesar were that the Helvetii were to return to their homeland,[1] and that the Allobroges were ordered to supply them with corn during their journey and while they were rebuilding their villages. His reason for doing so was 'that he did not wish the district which the Helvetii had left to be unoccupied, lest the excellence of their farmlands might tempt the Germans who dwell across the Rhine to cross from their own into the Helvetian borders, and so become neighbours to the Province of Gaul and to the Allobroges.'[2] Further, he was petitioned by the Aedui that the Boii, a tribe of remarkable courage, might be established within their own borders. This he granted, and they were given farmlands on the upper Loire.

### 3. CAMPAIGN AGAINST ARIOVISTUS, 58 B.C.

The results of his first campaign must have surpassed Caesar's wildest expectations. That – according to his own estimate – he had in two engagements destroyed nearly a quarter of a million of his enemy, a figure which probably he widely publicized, must have fired the imagination of the Gallic tribes, in whose eyes he now appeared to be the saviour and not the conqueror of Gaul; this must have added enormously to his prestige. So impressed were they by his victory that deputies from 'well-nigh the whole of Gaul' assembled at his camp to congratulate him. It led to a convention of the tribal chieftains, at which they appointed Diviciacus their spokesman.

He appealed to Caesar to complete his task, and remove the danger of a Germanic invasion under Ariovistus. Recently he had been joined by 24,000 Harudes, and unless Caesar destroyed him, as he had the Helvetii, no option would be left to the Gauls but to emulate them, and seek a new home in some other land. He urged Caesar to defend the whole of Gaul from the outrages of the Germans.

Caesar assured the chieftains that they might rely on him, and he

[1] Caesar (B.G., I, 29) states that a census was taken, and their 'number was found to be 110,000'.

[2] Ibid., I, 28.

promised them that he would concern himself with their request; besides to humble Ariovistus would make him the champion and arbiter of Gaul. Further, he was aware that the Germans were constantly crossing the Rhine, and were they not checked, one day 'a great host of them', like the Cimbri and Teutoni in the days of his uncle Marius, might invade Gaul, and 'break forth into the Province, and push on thence into Italy. . . . All this, he felt, must be faced without a moment's delay.'[1]

To engage in a war with Ariovistus, on whom, with Caesar's concurrence, had been conferred the title of 'king and friend of the Roman people', he had to act diplomatically and justify it in the eyes of his countrymen. So he sent a deputation to Ariovistus and requested a parley. In reply he was told to mind his own business, and should he wish to meet Ariovistus he could come in person to his camp. This impudent invitation was at once rejected, and Caesar assumed a more peremptory tone. He sent back an ultimatum: No German was henceforth to cross the Rhine; the hostages taken from the Aedui were to be returned to them; and as the Roman Senate 'had decided that the governor of the Province of Gaul should protect . . . the Aedui and the other friends of the Roman people, Caesar would not disregard the outrages suffered by the Aedui.' To these terms Ariovistus replied that 'It was the right of war that conquerors dictated as they pleased to the conquered,' and as the Romans were accustomed to do so, so would he.[2] But he warned him that 'no one had fought with Ariovistus save to his own destruction'.

With this message came the news that 'one hundred cantons of Suebi' had assembled on the Rhine and were attempting to cross it. Greatly perturbed by this, because he feared that they might reinforce Ariovistus, Caesar, as soon as he had secured his corn-supply, set out by forced marches to humble the arrogant German.

After an advance of three days, he learnt that Ariovistus intended to seize Vesontio (Besançon), the largest town of the Sequani, which was fortified and provided with abundant munitions of war; so Caesar pressed on by day and night to occupy it before him. When he reached it, he halted for a few days to assure himself of his corn-supply, during which an unexpected event happened. Sensational stories of the incredible valour, ferocity, and skill at arms of the Germans were circulated by the traders and local inhabitants, which so terrified the legionaries that a panic resulted. It started with the tribunes, many of whom had

[1] *Ibid.*, I, 33.  [2] *Ibid.*, I, 36.

had no war experience, and had been appointed for political reasons; from them it rapidly swept through the ranks. Caesar, when he became aware of it, at once assembled his centurions and, like Alexander at Opis, he indignantly reprimanded them; he pointed out how Marius had defeated the Cimbri and Teutoni, and that they themselves had annihilated the Helvetii, who had frequently subdued the Germans. He ended by saying that he intended at once to break camp, and even should no one else follow him, he would march with the 10th Legion alone, as he had complete confidence in its allegiance. Forthwith the men of the 10th Legion responded to his call, and they thanked him for his trust in them. Then the other legions followed suit; they fell into column of route, and after seven days Caesar learnt from his scouts that Ariovistus was within 24 miles of him.

When he was informed of Caesar's approach, Ariovistus sent messengers to him to say that he was now willing to meet him; but as he was aware of the indifference of the Roman cavalry, he stipulated that each side should bring only a mounted escort. Because Caesar could not trust his Gallic horsemen, he mounted the 10th Legion on their horses, and proceeded to the meeting place, a knoll in an extensive plain. There the escorts halted 200 paces from the knoll, and the opposing leaders rode on to it, both accompanied by ten horsemen. A lengthy palaver followed, in which Caesar again set forth his terms, and Ariovistus warned Caesar that, unless he departed, he would consider him his enemy, and should he slay him, pointedly he said '. . . he would gratify many nobles and leaders of the Roman people: this he knew for certain from themselves, by messengers sent on behalf of all whose favour and friendship he could purchase by Caesar's death.'[1]

While they were still speaking, a soldier rode up to Caesar and warned him that a number of German horsemen were edging toward the knoll and some were hurling stones and darts in defiance. Caesar then broke off the parley, rode back to his escort and ordered it not to reply to the enemy's insults, as he did not want to be accused of breaking his word.

Two days later Ariovistus advanced and encamped under a hill six miles from Caesar's camp, and on the next day he led his forces past it and formed a camp two miles from his, so that he might be better placed to cut the road along which the Romans received their corn and supplies from the Sequani and Aedui.

For five days Caesar drew out his legions and offered Ariovistus battle; but, except for some cavalry skirmishes, he refused to engage,

1 Caesar (*B.G.*, I, 44).

and as Caesar could not persuade him to fight, in order to secure his communications he built a second and smaller camp 600 paces distant from his enemy's. 'The first and second line he ordered to keep under arms, the third to entrench the camp', which when built he garrisoned with two legions and part of his auxiliaries. The next day he moved out of both camps, and again challenged Ariovistus, who moved part of his forces out and attacked the lesser camp, but was repulsed. From prisoners captured, the Romans discovered that the reason why so far Ariovistus had refused battle was that the German soothsayers had predicted that the heavens were unpropitious until the new moon (September 20 of the Julian calendar).

On the morning following, after he had detailed sufficient men to hold the two camps, as a show of force, Caesar posted all the allied troops in front of the lesser camp, and then advanced with his six legions in triple line up to his enemy's camp. Then, at last, 'compelled by necessity', which probably means that the Germans were running short of supplies, Ariovistus drew his army up in seven tribal formations, in rear of which he lined up his wagons, so that from them the wives and children of his warriors could urge them to victory.

When Caesar noticed that the enemy's left wing appeared less steady than his centre and right, he took command of his own right wing, and the battle opened by both sides simultaneously charging each other so rapidly and violently that the legionaries dropped their *pila* and closed with their swords. Some leapt on the German shield-wall, tore the shields aside, and soon in complete confusion the left wing dissolved in rout. Meanwhile, through force of numbers, the Roman left wing had been pressed back, and when young Publius Crassus,[1] who commanded the cavalry in rear, noticed it, he galloped forward and on his own initiative brought up the third line to reinforce the struggling troops. This decisive act restored the situation, and soon after the whole of Ariovistus' army took to its heels, and did not stay its flight until the Rhine was reached. Some succeeded in swimming it, others were drowned, and Ariovistus was fortunate enough to find a boat in which he escaped. The rest were caught on the western bank by the cavalry and slaughtered.

The victory was decisive, and when the news of it was carried over the Rhine, the Suebi, who had assembled on its banks, abandoned their projected invasion and turned homeward. With understandable pride Caesar writes: 'Two campaigns were thus finished in a single summer.' He withdrew his legions into winter quarters among the Sequani –

[1] The younger son of the triumvir.

109

probably at Vesontio – placed Labienus in command of them, and set out for Cisalpine Gaul to discharge the civil duties of his province and gain contact with Italy.

## 4. CAMPAIGN AGAINST THE BELGAE, 57 B.C.

It would seem probable that, because of the fickleness of the Gauls and their unceasing inter-tribal quarrels, Caesar had become aware that pacification could only be achieved through conquest. If so, then it must have occurred to him that before he could safely move into the interior, it was incumbent first to secure his rear against Germanic invasions from east of the Rhine. And, because the dense forests of the Vosges restricted large incursions from the middle Rhine, security first demanded the subjection of the Belgic tribes between the Moselle and the North Sea, many of whom ethnically were German.

Although he may not have appreciated this when he left Vesontio for Cisalpine Gaul, soon after circumstances compelled him to. While wintering there he received despatches from Labienus which informed him that the Belgae, fearful that, should all Celtic Gaul be pacified, they themselves would next be subdued, were making ready for war, and that their tribes were exchanging hostages. When he learnt this, he forthwith raised two new legions, the 13th and 14th, and as soon as the grass began to grow he returned to Vesontio, from where he sent out spies who confirmed the reports. Directly he had secured his corn-supply he struck camp, and in about a fortnight reached the borders of the Belgae on the Marne.

His arrival was so unexpected that the Remi, a Belgic tribe who occupied the region around Rheims, Laon, and Châlons, and at the time were subject to a neighbouring tribe, the Suessiones, were surprised and sought his protection; this he immediately granted. They informed him that all the other Belgic tribes were under arms, and had been joined by German contingents from east of the Rhine; that Galba, king of the Suessiones, whose chief town was Soissons, by general consent had been given supreme command over fifteen tribes, who could put into the field some 300,000 warriors; of them the Bellovaci were to provide 60,000, and the Suessiones and Nervii each 50,000.

Whatever the actual numbers may have been, they must vastly have outnumbered Caesar's 40,000 legionaries, and, in order to impede the main contingents from coalescing, he appealed to Diviciacus to lead his tribal levies into the lands of the Bellovaci and ravage them. Next, when he learnt that the main body of the Belgae was advancing against him, he crossed the Aisne by a bridge, probably at Berry-au-Bac,[1] and built a strongly fortified camp on its northern side, with its southern face close to the river, so that it might be better protected. Also, so as to secure his supply route, he fortified and garrisoned the bridge.

During their advance, the Belgae learnt of the defection of the Remi, and to punish them they diverged from their line of march and attacked their chief town, Bibrax (? Vieux-Laon), which lay eight miles from Caesar's camp. Thereupon the Remi appealed to Caesar, and 'in the middle of the night' he sent a force of Numidian light troops, Cretan archers, and Balearic slingers to their assistance.[2] Frustrated by them, the Belgae abandoned their attack, wasted the lands of the Remi, and then moved on to pitch their camp two miles north of Caesar's, from which their watch-fires could be seen 'extended for more than eight miles in breadth'.

At first, 'because of the vast numbers of the enemy and their excellent reputation for valour', Caesar decided to avoid an engagement; but when in the cavalry skirmishes he perceived that his men were in no way inferior to his enemy's, he drew his army out of camp into line of battle. The Belgae did likewise, but as neither side would cross the swampy ground between them – probably the Miette brook, a small affluent of the Aisne – no battle resulted.

Not to be balked, a Belgic force, presumably under cover of night, crossed the Aisne by fords unknown to Caesar, and advanced on the bridge. When this was reported to Caesar, he led out all his cavalry, Numidians, archers, and slingers, and a fierce engagement followed. Frustrated in their attempt to seize the bridge, and because their food supplies were beginning to fail, the Belgae decided to withdraw to their homelands, replenish their stocks, and then reassemble from all quarters to the defence of whichever tribe might be attacked. But this plan was not adhered to, because the Bellovaci had by now learnt of the approach of Diviciacus, and to protect their lands they abandoned the campaign.

At first Caesar believed that the withdrawal was a ruse, but when he discovered its reason he sent forward his cavalry to harass the Belgic rear guard, and next day pressed on by forced marches to Noviodunum (Pommiers) in the territory of the Suessiones, which surrendered to him. Next, he advanced into the lands of the Bellovaci, occupied

[1] See *Caesar's Conquest of Gaul*, T. Rice Holmes (2nd edit., 1911), pp. 659-68.
[2] When he acquired these troops is not stated.

their chief town Bratuspantium (? Breteuil) and demanded 600 hostages. Then he marched into the lands of the Ambiani on the Somme, whose chief town was Samarobriva (Amiens), and after three days reached a point 10 miles from the Sambre, where he encamped. There he learnt that on its far side the Nervii, fiercest of the Belgic tribes, along with the Atrebates and the Viromandui were awaiting his coming, and expected to be joined by the Aduatuci, descendants of the Cimbri and Teutoni who had invaded Gaul in about 110 B.C.

By now Caesar had with him a considerable number of surrendered Belgae – hostages and prisoners – and some of them escaped by night and informed the Nervii of the Roman order of march, which, when distant from an enemy, was that each legion was followed by its own baggage train. They suggested that, when the leading legion reached its new camping ground, those in rear 'in heavy marching order' could easily be ambushed, because their line of march would lead through thickly wooded and hedged country. This plan the Nervii decided to adopt.

As was normal, Caesar sent forward his cavalry to select the next camping ground, which was on a hill, probably close by Neuf-Mesnil, and overlooked Haurmont on the Sambre.[1] But as he was now approaching his enemy he changed his order of march. Instead of each legion being followed by its baggage, he advanced with his six veteran legions 'in light field order', followed by the baggage of the whole army with the 13th and 14th Legions as baggage-guard.

When the leading six legions reached the camping ground, they set about to entrench it and cut timber. Normally this work was done under the protection of a covering force, or of a force kept under arms, as in the Ariovistus campaign; but on this occasion Caesar omitted to do so, probably because he considered the cavalry screen sufficient. It was to prove an error of judgement which nearly led to as great a catastrophe as Varus was to suffer in the Teutoburger Wald in A.D. 9. For, when the legionaries were at work, directly the head of the baggage train appeared over the rise, the Nervii dashed out of the woods, swept the terrified Roman cavalry back over the Sambre,[2]

[1] See *Caesar's Conquest of Gaul*, pp. 671-7.
[2] Because the Nervian camp was at no great distance from the right bank of the Sambre and must have been of considerable size, and because there must have been thousands of the enemy lurking in the woods, it does not speak well of the Roman cavalry that they failed to discover them.

and raced up the slope of the hill on which the legionaries were at work.

Caesar says that he 'had everything to do at one moment': raise the red battle-ensign; sound the alarm; bring in the men who were felling timber, and so on. Two things, however, saved the situation: fortunately the generals had been forbidden to leave their legions until the

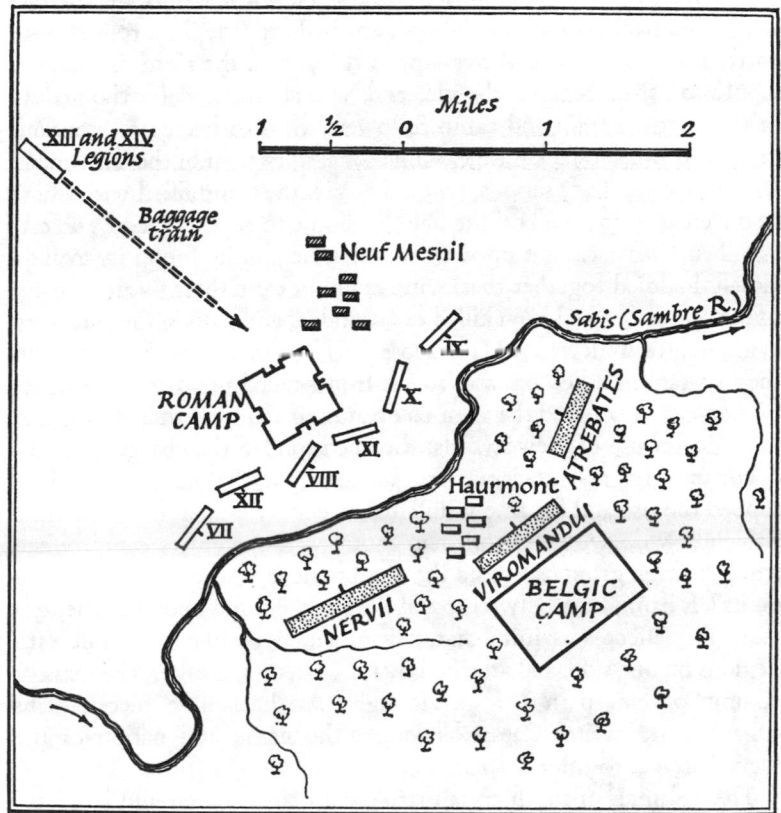

4 The Battle of the Sambre

camp was built; and because the men were highly disciplined, they at once grasped the situation, and, instead of seeking their cohorts, they fell in around the nearest standard and formed a ragged improvised line. As Caesar hurried along it, toward its left he came up with the 10th Legion, and, as the enemy were approaching missile range, he gave the signal to engage. Then he hastened toward the right.

Hurling their *pila*, the 10th, with the 9th on its left, charged the Atrebates who were facing them, drove them pell-mell down the slope and over the Sambre, and then chased them up the rising ground on its far side. At about the same time the 11th and 8th Legions in the centre broke through the Viromandui and drove them back to the river. These movements isolated the 12th and 7th Legions on the right, which were faced by a compact body of Nervii under Boduognatus, their commander-in-chief. They swarmed up the hill toward the partly finished camp, and overlapped the 7th on the right of the line. Confusion then became chaotic, and was augmented by the arrival of the baggage train and camp followers, who rushed terror-stricken in all directions to seek escape, while some horsemen of the Treveri, in the Roman auxiliary service, when they saw the camp filled with a host of the enemy, galloped off the field for home to report Caesar's defeat.

When Caesar caught up with the 12th Legion he found its men so closely huddled together that many could not use their swords; many of the centurions had been killed or wounded, and men in the rear were beginning to slink away. He seized a shield from one of the soldiers in the rear rank, pushed his way to the front, called upon the centurions by name, and ordered the men to open their ranks so that they could make better use of their swords; then he sounded the charge.

Fortunately, at this critical moment, the 13th and 14th Legions topped the rise and became visible to the enemy, and at the same time Labienus, who with the 10th had captured the enemy's camp, when from the high ground beyond the Sambre he saw what was happening on its left bank, hurriedly recrossed the river and fell upon the enemy's rear. The effect was immediate; hemmed in by the 13th and 14th Legions on one side, and attacked by the 10th on the other, the massive column of Nervii in a desperate fight was hacked to pieces. 'This engagement,' writes Caesar, 'brought the name and nation of the Nervii almost to utter destruction.'[1]

The old men of the Nervian tribe, with the women and children, who before the battle had sought security in the estuary of the Scheldt, sent a deputation to Caesar, and as he wished to establish a reputation for clemency, he permitted the survivors to retain their lands, and commanded their neighbours not to molest them. Then he marched eastward against the Aduatuci who, when they learnt of the defeat of the Nervii, had set out for home, and had concentrated in one of their fortified towns, in which they were besieged and surrendered on terms

[1] *B.G.*, II, 28.

similar to those imposed on the Nervii. On the following night a number of them, who had concealed their arms, attempted to escape from the town, but after a fierce struggle they were flung back into it, and in punishment Caesar sold 'three-and-fifty thousand persons' into slavery.

During the same season, Publius Crassus, who had been sent with the 7th Legion against the Veneti and other tribes which bordered upon the Ocean (Atlantic), reported that all those states had been brought into subjection.

'These achievements,' writes Caesar, 'brought peace throughout Gaul, and so mighty a report of this campaign was carried to the natives that deputies were sent to Caesar from the tribes dwelling across the Rhine to promise that they would give hostages and do his commands.'[1]

As Caesar was anxious to proceed to Italy as soon as possible, he bade the deputations return to him early in the following summer, and when the legions had taken up their winter quarters on the middle Loire and lower Seine, he set out for Illyricum, and in Italy a fifteen days' thanksgiving was decreed him, 'an honour that had previously fallen to no man.'

## 5. CAMPAIGN AGAINST THE MARITIME TRIBES, 56 B.C.

When the maritime tribes had surrendered their hostages to Publius Crassus, the 7th Legion went into winter quarters in the country of the Andes (northern Anjou) and of the neighbouring tribes the most considerable was the Veneti in western Brittany. They were skilful seamen, had a powerful ocean-going fleet, and held the monopoly of the carrying trade with Britain.[2] A rumour had reached them that Caesar contemplated an invasion of that island, and fearful that they might lose their livelihood, with seven other maritime tribes between the Loire and the Rhine they formed a coalition to prevent it.

Meanwhile Crassus, when he found that the Andes could not supply him with sufficient corn, sent out officers to requisition more from neighbouring tribes; and the Veneti, who were desirous to recover their hostages before taking up arms, impounded the two sent to them. Two other tribes did the same, and a joint deputation was sent to Crassus 'bidding him restore their hostages if he would receive back his own officers'. Crassus forthwith reported it to Caesar.

The rumour that Caesar intended to invade Britain was true, and the impending revolt played into his hands, because, as Holmes points out,

---

[1] *Ibid.*, II, 35.    [2] Strabo, IV, iv, 1.

'The subjection of the Veneti was a necessary prelude to the invasion of Britain; for Caesar could not safely embark his army unless he had command of the Channel.'[1] Therefore, when he received the report, he at once ordered warships to be built on the Loire and seamen drafted from the Province; then he set out from Illyricum and rejoined the army.

When the Veneti and their allies – supported by a body of auxiliaries from Britain – learnt of Caesar's coming, they prepared for war. 'They trusted that the Roman armies would be unable to remain long in their neighbourhood by reason of the lack of corn',[2] and relied on their fleet to prevent its supply by sea. They decided, therefore, on a war of economic attrition, and to prepare for it 'they fortified their towns, gathered corn thither from the fields, and assembled as many ships as possible in Venetia.'[3]

Although, when he left for Illyricum, Caesar believed 'that all Gaul was at peace again', he was now aware 'that almost all the Gauls were bent on revolution, and could be recklessly and rapidly aroused to war.'[4] No doubt, this was another reason why it was imperative for him to punish the Veneti, since other tribes might emulate them. To meet the situation, he decided on an unusual plan of campaign; instead of concentrating against the Veneti, he split his forces into five detachments: Labienus with a body of cavalry was to proceed to the territory of the Treveri, about Trèves, hold back the Germans and keep the Belgae loyal; Crassus with twelve cohorts and a force of cavalry was to operate in Aquitania and prevent its tribes from co-operating with those of Celtic Gaul; Quintus Titurius Sabinus with three legions was to enter the territories of the Curiosolites, Venelli, and Luxovii, in northern Brittany and Normandy, and impede them from coalescing with the Veneti; Decimus Brutus – the future tyrannicide – was given command of the fleet, which was to assemble in the roadsteads between the Garonne and Loire, and thence set out for Venetia, to which country Caesar himself would proceed with the remainder of the land forces.

The problem of the campaign centred in the defeat of the Venetian fleet, either in a naval action, or by cutting it off from its land bases. The latter course was most difficult, because the bases were strongholds

---

[1] *The Roman Republic*, vol. II, p. 51.

[2] *B.G.*, III, 9. Due either to the coastal districts being more sparsely inhabited, or, possibly, because the people's chief diet was fish.

[3] *Ibid.*, III, 9.                    [4] *Ibid.*, III, 10.

built on tongues of land jutting into the sea, which could not be attacked by land when the tide was in, unless massive moles were built, nor by ships when the tide was out, because of the shoals. Further, should a stronghold be in danger of capture, all the Veneti need do was to remove its garrison at high tide and convey it to some other place.

To defeat the enemy at sea at first appeared to be equally difficult, because of the superiority of the Gallic ships over the Roman. They were stoutly built of oak, which could withstand much buffeting; their keels were flatter than those of the Roman galleys, and could weather shoals at ebb-tide; their prows and sterns were lofty and well-suited for sailing in rough seas; and they depended entirely on sails made of leather, the better to withstand high winds. The only superiority the oar-propelled Roman galleys possessed over them was speed and oar-manship, and their disadvantages are summed up by Caesar as follows:

'Our ships could not damage them with the ram (they were so stoutly built), nor, by reason of their height, was it easy to hurl a pike, and for the same reason they were less readily gripped by grapnels. Moreover, when the wind began to rage and they ran before it, they endured the storm more easily, and rested on shoals more safely, with no fear of rocks or crags if left by the tide; whereas our own vessels could not but dread the possibility of all these chances.'[1]

After Caesar had laboriously taken several strongholds by assault, he decided to await the arrival of the fleet. When it came up, the enemy put to sea in about 220 of their ships and took station opposite to it. At first, because of the disadvantages enumerated by Caesar, Brutus was nonplussed; but as the Veneti were unprovided with archers,[2] his swifter galleys could row alongside their ships with impunity, and the Roman engineers turned this to his advantage by means of a cunning device. They made large numbers of hooks fastened to long poles, and equipped with these the galleys lay alongside the Venetian ships and caught hold of the halyards which fastened the yards to the masts; next the rowers plied their oars until the strain snapped the cordage, when down came the yards and sails.[3] Then, as Caesar says, the conflict became 'a question of courage', and the ships were grappled and boarded.

After several had suffered this fate, the Veneti put out to sea to seek safety in flight, 'when suddenly a calm so complete and absolute came

[1] *Ibid.*, III, 13.    [2] Dio, XXXIX, 43, 1.
[3] According to Strabo (IV, iv, 1): '. . . the Romans rent the sails by means of scythes fixed on long handles.'

on that they could not stir from the spot', and one by one their ships fell prey to the Roman galleys. The battle, which had lasted from about the fourth hour to sunset, 'finished the campaign against the Veneti and the whole sea-coast.' It was decisive, because not only did it win the command of the Channel for Caesar, but the loss of all their ships with their crews deprived the Veneti of the means of defending their towns, and thereby forced their surrender. To make his victory doubly sure, on the pretext that his requisition officers were ambassadors and that their arrest was a violation of international law, he put the whole of the Venetian Senate to the sword, and the rest of the population he sold into slavery.

In spite of this overwhelming victory, and the successful campaigns of Sabinus in the Cotentin and of Crassus in Aquitania, two of the maritime tribes, the Morini and the Menapii, refused to submit. Their territories extended from the river Canche to about Emmerich on the Rhine, and although the summer was almost spent, Caesar, nevertheless, set out on a 400-mile march to subdue the former, who controlled the harbours nearest to Britain. But, instead of meeting him in battle, they scattered in the forests, and on one occasion surprised his troops when they were entrenching their camp, much as the Nervii had done on the Sambre. As the winter set in, the heavy rains made further operations impossible, so Caesar, after he had wasted the land and burnt a number of villages, abandoned the campaign, placed his legions in winter quarters between the lower Seine and the Loire, and once again set out for Cisalpine Gaul.

## 6. CAMPAIGN ON THE RHINE, 55 B.C.

When Caesar was wintering in Italy, two German tribes, the Usipetes and Tencteri, who some years before had been deprived of their homelands by the Suebi, and since had sought some region to settle in, crossed the Rhine near Emmerich and occupied land belonging to the Menapii. Alarmed by the news, and aware that among the Belgae there were many who would welcome the invaders, Caesar 'set out for the army earlier than was his wont.' According to him, the two tribes numbered no less than 430,000 people, a figure which exceeded the Helvetian invasion of 58 B.C. At his headquarters he learnt that his suspicions were not misplaced; that 'deputations [from the Belgae] had been sent . . . to the Germans, inviting them to leave the Rhine, and promising to furnish all things demanded of them.'[1] As this pointed to

[1] B.G., IV, 6.

a coalition more formidable than any so far met, speedy action was imperative. But as his cavalry had been disbanded, he could do nothing until he had replaced them, so he summoned a meeting of Gallic chieftains. At it he concealed his information concerning their doubtful loyalty, 'comforted and encouraged them', and requisitioned 5,000 horsemen.[1]

As soon as he had secured his corn-supply, he set out, and on his way was met by envoys from the two tribes. They informed him that their peoples had crossed the Rhine against their will, and should he grant them land to settle on they would be the friends of the Romans. His reply was that, as long as they remained on Gallic soil, friendship was out of the question; but as he was aware of their plight, they had his permission to settle in the territory of the Ubii – between Coblenz and Bonn – the sole German tribe that so far had submitted to him, and 'he would give orders to the Ubii to this effect.'[2] The envoys replied that they would refer his proposal to their chiefs, and come back with their answer in three days' time; further, they requested Caesar not to advance meanwhile. This he refused to consider, because he suspected that the delay they sought was a pretext to gain time for the return of the bulk of their cavalry, then out foraging. So instead of halting he marched on.

When he was 12 miles from the German camp, the deputies returned, and again besought him not to advance further; also to warn his cavalry not to provoke an engagement, and to allow their leaders time wherein to send envoys to the Ubii to ascertain whether they 'would accept the terms which Caesar offered'.

Still suspicious of their intentions, Caesar promised not to advance beyond a river four miles ahead, where he would await their return on the following morning, and he told them to bring with them as many of their leaders as possible, 'in order that he might take cognizance of their demands'. At the same time he instructed his cavalry commanders 'not to provoke the enemy to an engagement', because secretly he intended to win his campaign by a bloodless ruse. His idea was to go one better than Tissaphernes had after his victory over Cyrus the Younger at Cunaxa, in 401 B.C.;[3] he had separated the generals from the defeated

---

[1] To be compelled to requisition his cavalry from potential enemies conspiring against him, shows in what an impasse Caesar was placed through his lack of Roman recruited cavalry.

[2] *Ibid.*, IV, 8. This seems a poor reward for their submission, and unlikely to encourage other tribes to emulate them.      [3] Xenophon, *Anabasis*, II, 5, 31.

army, massacred them and left their men leaderless. Caesar improved on this piece of treachery: his intention was to corral the generals before a battle was fought. This was low cunning bordering on genius.

The armies were now so close together that hostilities were almost unavoidable, and as Caesar's 5,000 Gallic horsemen – he says 'all the cavalry' were sent ahead – meandered along unsuspecting any danger, because a twenty-four hours' truce had been agreed,[1] suddenly 800 German cavalry fell upon them and scattered them in rout. For Caesar, this was a gift from the gods. He pronounced the attack to be a declaration of war; nevertheless, he told his generals that his purpose was 'not to lose a day in giving battle'. He judged rightly, for on the following morning 'a large company of Germans, which included all the principal and senior men, came to his quarters' to excuse themselves of the mishap 'and get what they could in respect of the truce.' Then we read: 'Caesar rejoiced that they were delivered into his hand, and ordered them to be detained; then in person he led all his troops out of camp.'[2]

The eight miles, which now separated the Germans from him, were so speedily covered that the legions 'reached the enemy's camp before the Germans could have any inkling of what was toward. They were struck with sudden panic by everything – by the rapidity of our approach, the absence of their own chiefs . . .' and no time was given them to take up arms. The legionaries burst into the camp, slew all found there, and 'the remainder, a crowd of women and children . . . began to flee in all directions, and Caesar despatched the cavalry in pursuit. . . . When they reached the junction of the Meuse and Rhine,[3] they gave up all hope of escaping further; a large number were already slain, and the rest hurled themselves into the river, there to perish, overcome by terror, by exhaustion, by the force of the stream.' Thus the Romans, 'with not a man lost and but few wounded', were 'freed from the fear of a stupendous war.' It was one of the most complete victories in history and one of the most inglorious.[4]

---

[1] Truce, or no truce, no cavalry worthy the name would approach an undefeated enemy without taking defensive precautions.      [2] *B.G.*, IV, 13.

[3] Some think that Caesar's '*Mosae et Rheni*' (*B.G.*, IV, 15) should read '*Mosellae et Rheni*' (see *C.A.H.*, vol. IX, p. 558).

[4] *B.G.*, IV, 14–15. The massacre shocked even the Romans, who gloried in bloodshed. According to Plutarch (*Caesar*, XXII, 3) Cato declared that the honour of the Republic should be cleaned by Caesar's surrender to the Germans. And Suetonius (*Div. Iul.*, XXIV) records that 'the Senate passed a decree for sending commissioners to examine into the condition of Gaul.' But the rabble, upon whom Caesar depended for his popularity, undoubtedly were thrilled by the slaughter.

No sooner was the campaign at an end than Caesar decided to cross the Rhine. His reasons were: (1) to show the barbarians that, though an obstacle to them, it was none to a Roman army; and (2) to follow up the cavalry of the Usipetes and Tencteri who, because of their foraging, had escaped the massacre and had retired into the country of the Sugambri, north of Cologne. When the Sugambri refused, or were unable, to surrender them, the Ubii, south of Cologne, offered him a large number of boats to transport his army over the Rhine. But he rejected the offer, as he wished to impress on the barbarians that he did not need boats to do so, and in the vicinity of Coblenz he built a trestle-bridge which, from his detailed description of it, was very similar to modern bridges of that construction. It took ten days to erect, and when the Suebi discovered that it was being built, they ordered all the inhabitants of the towns to seek refuge in the forests, and assemble their warriors at a central point in Suebian territory in order to offer the Romans battle. But judiciously Caesar, whose army was not suited for forest warfare, did not venture to follow them, and after he had ravaged the lands of the Sugambri, and spent eighteen days beyond the Rhine, he withdrew his army, dismantled the bridge, and returned to Gaul.

## 7. THE TWO EXPEDITIONS TO BRITAIN, 55–54 B.C.

Although 'only a small part of the summer was left . . . Caesar was intent upon starting for Britain.'[1] His reason was that in almost all the Gallic campaigns the Britons had furnished support to the Gauls. It is not a very convincing one, since his command of the Channel had made serious support improbable. More cogent ones are: the irresistible attraction of a virtually unknown country, and the fame its submission would win him; also, perhaps, the allurement of loot.[2]

Because the season was advanced, the expedition was no more than a reconnaissance in force, so hastily equipped that supplies of food were not taken. It consisted of the 7th and 10th Legions and their cavalry, carried in eighty infantry and eighteen horse transports, probably assembled at Boulogne and Ambleteuse. It stood out to sea at midnight

---

[1] B.G., IV, 20.

[2] This, in part at least, is substantiated by Cicero in a letter to his friend Trebatius Testa, dated shortly before Caesar's second expedition: 'In Britain I am told there is no gold and silver. If that turns out to be the case, I advise you to capture a war-chariot and hasten back to us at the earliest opportunity' (*Letters to his Friends*, VII, 7).

August 25, and at 9 a.m. the following day the infantry transports cast anchor off Dover,[1] but the horse transports were prevented from sailing by a contrary wind.

From Dover the expedition sailed on, and disembarked between Walmer and Deal. The landing was violently opposed by British cavalry and chariots, which in a stiff fight were routed; but no pursuit was possible for lack of cavalry. The Britons then treated for peace and agreed to surrender hostages to Caesar.

Four days later the cavalry transports appeared off Caesar's camp, but before the men and horses could be disembarked, the flotilla was caught by a sudden gale and scattered, some of its ships being driven back to Gaul. Worse still, because Caesar had not beached his transports, their anchors dragged and they were driven ashore; twelve were wrecked and many of the remainder seriously damaged. This caused a near panic in the camp, and at the same time so encouraged the Britons that they decided to renew hostilities. 'They thought,' writes Caesar, 'that the best thing to do was . . . to cut off our corn and other supplies, and prolong the business into the winter.'[2] Unsuspicious of what was brewing, when the 7th Legion was on the daily task of cutting corn, it was violently attacked and might have been annihilated had not Caesar promptly come to its rescue.

Of the British chariot tactics Caesar writes:

'First of all they drive in all directions and hurl missiles, and so by the mere terror that the teams inspire and by the noise of the wheels they generally throw ranks into confusion. When they have worked their way in between the troops of cavalry, they leap down from the chariots and fight on foot. Meanwhile the charioteers retire gradually from the combat, and dispose the chariots in such fashion that, if the warriors are hard pressed by the host of the enemy, they may have a ready means of retirement to their own side. Thus they show in action the mobility of cavalry and the stability of infantry.'[3]

When the Britons had been repulsed, they again treated for peace, and this time Caesar doubled the number of hostages demanded of them; and as 'the equinox was close at hand', he took advantage of a

---

[1] In 1066 William the Conqueror sailed from St Valéry, in the estuary of the Somme, at about midnight September 27, and at 9 the following morning landed at Pevensey.

[2] *B.G.*, IV, 30.  [3] *Ibid.*, IV, 33.

spell of fair weather to return to Gaul. There another surprise was in store for him.

Three hundred men aboard two of the now crowded transports, unable to make Boulogne, were landed further down the coast, and on their march to the camp were suddenly attacked by the Morini, who 'were fired by the hope of booty'. For more than four hours they were hemmed in, and, so it would seem, only in the nick of time rescued by the Roman cavalry. The next day Labienus with the 7th and 10th Legions was sent out to punish the Morini; they speedily submitted to him.

Caesar then placed all his legions in winter quarters in Belgic territory. 'Thither', he writes, 'no more than two of the British states sent hostages'; a frank and honest measurement of the value of the campaign, which in Napoleon's estimate was 'a second-class operation'.[1]

Before he left for Italy, Caesar ordered the legion commanders 'to have as many ships as possible built during the winter, and the old fleet repaired.' The new ships were to be of a more suitable construction, built lower than hitherto, 'for speed of loading and for purposes of beaching',[2] and the horse transports were to be broader in beam; all were to be fitted with oars as well as sails, and supplied with improved tackle.

When, in the spring of 54 B.C., Caesar rejoined the army, he found that some 600 of the new design of transports and 28 galleys were nearing completion, and, when ready, he ordered them to assemble at Portus Itius, probably Wissant; then a delay occurred.

During his absence in Italy, the Treveri had been negotiating with the Germans beyond the Rhine, and many of the anti-Roman Gallic chieftains, including his old enemy Dumnorix, had joined them. To leave these malcontents in his rear when in Britain would be to court another rebellion. Therefore, when he learnt of the conspiracy, with four legions and 800 horse he marched into the Ardennes where he discovered that Indutiomarus and Cingetorix, two leading chieftains of the Treveri, were contending for the leadership of that tribe. Because the latter at once came to terms with Caesar, he supported his claim, compelled Indutiomarus to submit to his authority, and as a guarantee of his good behaviour demanded the surrender of 200 hostages. This done, he set out for Portus Itius, and on arrival summoned all suspect Gallic chiefs to assemble there, as he had decided to take them with him as hostages. Thus, unsuspectingly, they were trapped, and when

[1] *Correspondance de Napoléon Ier*, vol. XXXII, p. 26.  [2] *B.G.*, V, 1.

Dumnorix pleaded to be left behind, on Caesar's refusal he took to flight, was pursued by a detachment of cavalry and slain.

Early in July Caesar handed over the command in Gaul to Labienus, and, as the sun was setting, the largest fleet the Channel must have seen until 1944 stood out for Britain[1] with five legions and 2,000 cavalry aboard, and at about noon on the following day the troops disembarked between Sandown and Sandwich. This time the landing was unopposed, because, according to Caesar, the size of the armada – 'eight hundred [ships] had been seen at once'[2] – so terrified the Britons that they fled inland to a stronghold on the high ground. Intent on marching against them, so as to save time, instead of beaching his ships, Caesar left them riding at anchor under the protection of ten cohorts commanded by Quintus Atrius; and on the same day, under cover of night, he set out to attack the stronghold, which the 7th Legion successfully stormed. Three columns were sent in pursuit of the fugitives, and when, after a stiff day's march, their rear guards were sighted, a message was received from Atrius, which informed Caesar that a violent storm had driven the fleet ashore, and nearly all its ships had been damaged in collision with one another.

At once Caesar recalled the three columns and hastened back to the fleet, to find that forty ships had been lost and that most of the others needed extensive repairs. He immediately called up all artificers in the legions, ordered shipwrights from Gaul, and instructed Labienus to build as many ships as possible to replace those wrecked. He then did what he had failed to do on landing, had all ships securely beached and protected by an entrenchment.

Caesar's negligence, which went far to wreck the campaign at its start, is hard to explain. Not only had he suffered an identical disaster the year before, but he had had the bulk of his ships constructed to prevent it. The probable explanation is that instinctively he was a

[1] That in the night the vast number of ships avoided fouling each other must have demanded superb navigation.

[2] Caesar's shipping figures are perplexing. His grand total of 800 ships (*B.G.*, V, 8) is made up of 540 of the 600 new ships, as 60 failed to sail (*B.G.*, V, 5), plus 28 galleys and 232 old and private ships (*B.G.*, V, 8). In his first voyage two legions (say 10,000 men) and (assumed) 300 cavalry were carried in 80 infantry and 18 cavalry transports – that is, 125 infantry or 17 cavalry per transport. Therefore in his second voyage five legions (say 25,000 men) and 2,000 cavalry would require 200 infantry and 118 horse transports, which makes a total of 318, and when 28 galleys and 232 old and private ships are added, a grand total of 578 ships. This leaves over a surplus of 222 ships.

gambler, a man over-apt to chance his luck. On this occasion, it would seem, the unopposed landing had led him to assume that his enemy was so terrified of him that he could finish off the campaign in a gallop. Because his luck was out, the reverse was the case; for when the Britons became aware that their enemy was in retreat, they jumped to the conclusion that Caesar was terrified of them; set aside their tribal feuds, and elected Cassivellaunus, king of the Catuvellauni, beyond the Thames (in Hertfordshire), their leader.

When Caesar learnt that Cassivellaunus was at the head of a far greater force of Britons than hitherto met with, directly the ships had been beached he set out against him.

For a barbarian, Cassivellaunus was a leader of unusual ability; instead of seeking or accepting battle, he resorted to guerrilla warfare, which Caesar says disconcerted his troops. 'It was clear,' he writes, 'that in all such fighting our infantry, by reason of their heavy armament, since they could neither pursue a retiring enemy nor venture far from the standards [*i.e.*, were armed to fight only in formation], were but poorly fitted for an enemy of this kind', because 'the enemy never fought in close array'.[1] To overcome these tactics, the legions of a Sertorius were needed.

Steadily and cautiously Caesar advanced to the Thames, possibly at or near Brentford. There he found a great force of the enemy drawn up on its left bank, which 'was fortified with a fringe of sharp projecting stakes, and stakes of the same kind fixed under water were concealed by the stream.'[2] In spite of these defences and the depth of the river, the far bank was won. But meanwhile Cassivellaunus had thought out a cunning counterstroke; he had sent messengers to the petty kings of Kent to band their warriors together and surprise the Roman naval camp.

From the ford Caesar marched eastward into the country of the Trinobantes, and, in order to win their support, the troops were strictly forbidden to ravage their lands. So it would appear, this unexpected leniency led to deputies being sent to him to announce the willingness of the Trinobantes to surrender to him. From them he learnt that the stronghold of Cassivellaunus was not far off, and in it many of the inhabitants had taken refuge. He marched against it, and stormed it on two of its sides. In the meantime the attack on the naval camp had been beaten off in a sortie by its garrison.

This failure, coupled with the defection of the Trinobantes and five

[1] B.G., V, 16.   [2] *Ibid.*, V, 18.

other tribes, caused Cassivellaunus to lose heart; he sent envoys to the Roman camp to propose surrender. It was speedily arranged, because Caesar had learnt 'of sudden commotions in Gaul', and as the summer was now far advanced, he was eager to end his British campaign. So he made requisition for hostages; fixed the tribute Britain should pay yearly to Rome; bade Cassivellaunus keep peace with the Trinobantes, and led his army back to the sea 'fearing he might be precluded from sailing . . . as the equinox was nigh at hand.'

The return to Gaul was made in two trips, and immediately after it had ended 'a council of the Gauls was held at Samarobriva (Amiens).' The chiefs were in a dangerous mood, and, because of the drought, the corn-crop had been so scanty that the requisitioning of grain was adding to the general discontent. As the Belgic states appeared to be the most restless, Caesar decided to quarter his legions in them for the winter: three, under Marcus Crassus, Lucius Munatius Plancus, and Gaius Trebonius, at Amiens and Beauvais; one, under Gaius Fabius, among the Morini; one under Labienus, among the Remi; one under Quintus Cicero, among the Nervii; one, 'the most recently enrolled', at Aduatuca, in the country of the Eburones, under Titurius Sabinus and Aurunculeius Cotta; and one outside Belgic territory in the Orne, under Lucius Roscius. Because of the unsettled state of Gaul, Caesar decided to remain at Amiens until all the legions were in their stations and their camps entrenched.

Thus ended his escapade in Britain – it cannot be called anything else. Because no garrison was left there, his compact with Cassivellaunus was worthless, and it would seem improbable that any tribute was ever paid. He had gained the fame of being the first Roman general to set foot on a distant and little known island of no political, strategical, or economic value to Rome; and its price was his absence from Gaul. It gave time for the smouldering discontent, ever present there, to gain a firmer grip, until, in 52 B.C., it flamed forth in a national rebellion, which threatened to annul all his successes.

# VI

## Suppression of the Gallic Revolt

### I. PRELUDE TO THE REVOLT

WHILE Caesar was in Britain, Indutiomarus, the discarded Treverian chieftain, had been nursing his grievances, and when it became apparent how isolated Caesar's winter camps were, the idea occurred to him that one or more might be overwhelmed before it could be reinforced. The one occupied by Sabinus and Cotta at Aduatuca was particularly vulnerable. In all probability it lay east of the Meuse in the vicinity of Liège,[1] and the nearest camp to it was Quintus Cicero's,[2] at or near Namur, some 50 miles to the west, while Caesar at Amiens, with three legions near by, was 170 miles away. To effect its capture, Indutiomarus instigated Ambiorix and Catuvolcus, joint chiefs of the Eburones, to attack it, and as the latter was old and decrepit, the project was undertaken by the former.

Ambiorix's plan was a cunning one. He was aware that he lacked the means to besiege the camp, and was unlikely to storm it; therefore, the only way open to him was to induce its garrison to abandon it. To effect this, he first made an abortive assault on the camp, then broke it off, and shouted to the men on its rampart that he wished to parley with their chiefs, as he had something of the greatest importance to convey to them. Two deputies were sent out, and were told by Ambiorix that, as he was greatly indebted to Caesar, he wished to befriend him, and that he had been compelled against his will to carry out the attack. To assure the deputies of his friendly intentions, he divulged to them in a most plausible way that, as no one camp could reinforce the other rapidly, the Gallic chiefs had decided within two days to attack all the camps simultaneously. Further, he informed them that a horde of Germans was on its way to overwhelm Aduatuca, and he urged and entreated them, if they valued their lives, with the utmost

[1] See *The Roman Republic*, vol. II, p. 123.
[2] Brother of M. Tullius Cicero, the orator.

speed to withdraw either to Labienus' or Cicero's camp. All this he confirmed with solemn oaths.

When the deputies returned, and Sabinus and Cotta were informed of this, they at once assembled a council of war to consider Ambiorix's proposal. Cotta vigorously opposed it, and Sabinus as vigorously urged its acceptance. A lengthy argument followed, and although the senior centurions sided with Cotta, the legionaries, most of whom were raw recruits, who had been listening to the dispute, were so thoroughly frightened by what they heard that Sabinus got his way, and it was finally decided to evacuate the camp at dawn on the following morning.

Encumbered by a heavy baggage train, the legion set out for Cicero's camp, and after an hour's march, while descending a forest ravine, it was ambushed. Except for a few men who made their way to Labienus' camp, 60 miles distant, every man was slaughtered. Caesar's account of their end is a highly dramatized one.

Ambiorix immediately exploited his victory. With his horsemen he set off at speed and aroused the Aduatuci. Then he pressed on to the Nervii and urged them to fall on Cicero's camp. Fired by his enthusiasm, they at once set out to do so, and as they had learnt much about their enemy's siegecraft, they laid siege to it in Roman fashion.

Desperately pressed, and after several abortive attempts to communicate with Caesar, Cicero succeeded in getting a slave to carry a message to him. Without a moment's delay, Caesar despatched a messenger to Marcus Crassus to speed to Amiens and take over command there. Another was sent to Fabius bidding him with his legion join Caesar on the line of march; and yet another to Labienus to advance his legion to the borders of the Nervii; but he was unable to comply, because at the time Indutiomarus was threatening his camp. Then, with Trebonius' legion and 400 horse, Caesar set out by forced marches for Cicero's camp. As he neared it he received a despatch from Cicero, which informed him that the Nervii had raised the siege and were on their way to intercept him.

According to Caesar, they numbered 60,000 warriors, and as his two legions numbered barely 7,000 men, when the enemy was caught sight of, he at once halted and entrenched a camp. To persuade the enemy to attack it, he made it as small as possible, bade his horsemen retire without fighting, and instructed his legionaries to simulate confusion as if in panic. Deluded by this show of terror, the Nervii attempted to rush the camp, and, when they were filling in its ditch and tearing down its rampart, 'Caesar caused a sally to be made from all the gates, and sending out the cavalry put the enemy speedily to flight.' Because of the woods and marshes he did not pursue; instead, on the same day he pushed on to Cicero's camp, to find 'that not one-tenth of the soldiers were left unwounded.' And 'he marvelled at the towers erected, the shelters, the fortifications of the enemy.'[1]

When Caesar learnt that the news of his victory had caused Indutiomarus to abandon his projected attack on Labienus, he sent Fabius with his legion back to his old camp, quartered three legions around Amiens, and 'in view of the great disturbances which had arisen in Gaul, he decided to remain with the army in person throughout the winter.'[2]

Meanwhile Indutiomarus sent deputations in all directions to rouse the Gauls against their common enemy. By now his authority was so great that he proclaimed a general call to arms, and, with the exception of the Aedui and Remi, writes Caesar, 'scarcely a single state was free from suspicion on our part.' But Indutiomarus' days were numbered, for when once again he set out to threaten Labienus' camp he was killed in a sortie. The Eburones and Nervii then withdraw their forces and Gaul became somewhat more tranquil.

Caesar was not deluded by this fall in the temperature of revolt, and to be better prepared to meet the uncertain future, he sent an agent to Cisalpine Gaul to raise two new legions and borrow a third from Pompey: all three reported at Headquarters Amiens before the winter was over.

In the meantime Caesar had learnt that the Treveri had gone into alliance with Ambiorix; that the Nervii, Aduatuci, Menapii, and all the Germans west of the Rhine were under arms, and that the Senones and Carnutes were conspiring against him. To assert his authority, before the winter ended he suddenly raided the lands of the Nervii at the head of four legions, captured 'a great number of cattle and human beings', laid waste the fields, and compelled the Nervii to surrender hostages. After which, at the beginning of spring he held his annual convention of Gallic chiefs, this time at Lutetia (Paris). All attended, except those of the Senones, Carnutes, and Treveri. Because this pointed to an armed rebellion, on the same day upon which the convention assembled he set out against the Senones, whose territory adjoined that of the Parisii. When the report of his coming reached Acco, chief of the Senones, he ordered his people to withdraw into

[1] B.G., V, 51–52.    [2] Ibid., V, 53.

their strongholds; but such was the speed of Caesar's advance that they were unable to do so, and, on the intercession of the Aedui, Acco submitted, and was ordered to deliver 100 hostages to them. Next, when the Remi interceded for the Carnutes, the same terms were imposed. The convention was then closed by a requisition of contingents of cavalry made upon these states

Caesar next set out to punish Ambiorix, who had brought such discredit and shame on Roman arms. First, he determined to deprive him of his allies, the Menapii, Treveri, and the Germans. He moved against the first and Labienus against the second, and both tribes were forced to submit. Then, with Labienus, he advanced against the Germans, in order to prevent them from offering asylum to Ambiorix. Again he bridged the Rhine in the territory of the Ubii; advanced against the Suebi, who withdrew to the Thuringian forest and awaited his coming. But as the country was bare of corn, Caesar soon abandoned the advance, and turned toward the Ardennes, as he had learnt that Ambiorix was sheltering in its forests.

When he reached Sabinus' and Cotta's old camp at Aduatuca he left his heavy baggage there with the 14th Legion – a newly raised one – under the command of Quintus Cicero, while Labienus and Gaius Trebonius, each with three legions, respectively devastated the lands of the Menapii and Aduatuci. With the remaining three[1] he marched toward the lower Scheldt, in the territory of the Eburones, in search of Ambiorix, but could effect nothing because its warriors took to guerrilla warfare, which the legions were neither organized nor trained to wage. To overcome this deficit, 'He sent messengers round to the neighbouring states and invited them all, in hope of booty, to join him in pillaging the Eburones, so that he might hazard the lives of the Gauls among the woods, rather than the soldiers of the legions. . . . A great number assembled speedily from every side.'[2]

When news of this reached the Sugambri, with 2,000 horsemen they crossed the Rhine to join in the plundering, and from prisoners captured they learnt that Caesar was afar off, and that Quintus Cicero was isolated at Aduatuca with the Roman baggage. So inviting a prize was too tempting to be resisted, so they set out to emulate Ambiorix.

Cicero had been warned by Caesar that on no account was any man, not even a single camp-follower, to leave the camp during his absence,

---

[1] Besides these ten legions, twelve cohorts had been detailed to garrison the western exit of the Rhine bridge; the eastern half of the bridge was dismantled.
[2] *Ibid.*, VI, 34.

which would be for seven days. But, as on the morning of the seventh day Caesar had not returned, and as Cicero's corn was getting short, and his young soldiers were critical of his inactivity, he sent out five cohorts, 300 convalescents, and a large number of camp-followers and pack-animals to some neighbouring corn-fields. Barely were they out of sight than the Sugambri, who had arrived that same day, burst out of the woods and fell upon the camp, but were repulsed. Meanwhile the corn-gatherers, when on their way back, were surrounded, and while three cohorts cut their way through the enemy and regained the camp, the remaining two, which had sought refuge on some high ground, were exterminated, and with them must have perished many of the convalescents and camp-followers. The Germans then departed with such booty as they could collect, and that night Caesar's advanced guard reached the camp to find its garrison dithering with terror.

'Of these events,' Caesar writes, 'the most remarkable seemed to be that the Germans, who had crossed the Rhine with the definite intention of devastating the territory of Ambiorix, by their descent on the Roman camp rendered Ambiorix the most acceptable service.'[1] What is more remarkable is, that in the ill-fated camp at Aduatuca, haunted by the ghosts of the Roman dead, for a second time Caesar detailed a legion of raw recruits to hold it.

The harassing campaign was then launched, and 'a great host from the neighbouring states was sent in every direction' to harry the lands of the Eburones. Caesar writes:

'Every hamlet, every homestead that anyone could see was set on fire; captured cattle were driven from every spot; the corn-crops were not only being consumed by the vast host of pack-animals and human beings, but were laid flat in addition because of the rainy season, so that, even if any persons succeeded in hiding themselves for the moment, it seemed that they must perish for want of everything when the army was withdrawn.'[2]

All this devastation was in vain, the elusive Ambiorix was never caught; with a few horsemen he got away to disappear from the pages of Caesar's Commentaries.[3]

When the campaign ended, Caesar brought the army to Durocortorum (Rheims); held a convention, and had Acco, who is termed 'the arch-conspirator', executed in Roman fashion – he was flogged to

[1] *Ibid.*, VI, 42.　　　　　　　　　[2] *Ibid.*, VI, 43.
[3] He is again mentioned by Aulus Hirtius in Book VIII, 24, of *The Gallic War*.

death. Two legions then went into winter quarters on the borders of the Treveri; two among the Lingones (about Langres) and the remaining six[1] at Agedincum (Sens) in the territory of the Senones. After that, 'when Gaul was quiet', Caesar set out for Italy.

## 2. VERCINGETORIX, LEADER OF THE REVOLT

The lull in Gaul was the calm before the storm, for Caesar's ferocious campaigns had no more than stunned the Gallic tribes, and the hideous fate of Acco like a Damoclean sword hung over the head of every chieftain. Thus it came about that his systematic devastations and slaughterings, instead of compelling coercion, awakened desperation, and they were to lead to the one thing he feared most – a coalescence of the tribes in a war of liberation.

Soon after his departure, a group of Gallic chieftains met secretly in remote spots in the forests to discuss what should be done to free their countrymen from the Roman yoke. The times seemed propitious; the events leading to the murder of Clodius[2] had thrown Rome into turmoil, and the crushing defeat of Crassus at Carrhae[3] had shown that Roman arms were not invincible. These events might detain Caesar in Italy, and without him his legions would be paralysed. But should they fail to do so, then he must be prevented from rejoining them. Since their cantonments were far away in the north of Gaul, were they to strike at the Province, he would be compelled to go to its assistance, and that would keep him and his legions apart.

As yet there was no question of a general rising throughout Gaul, a number of tribes were still loyal to Rome and many others were neutral. Therefore the initial problem was, how to detonate the revolt by a startling stroke which would swing those tribes over to the rebels?

At what must have been their final conference, it was decided that the Carnutes should strike the first blow. Their lands lay athwart the middle Loire with Cenabum (Orléans) as their chief town. It was the centre of an extensive corn-growing district, which supplied the legions, and a number of Roman corn-brokers and traders had settled in it. Were these men assassinated, it would rock all Gaul.

On the day appointed, the unsuspecting traders were put to the sword by two chieftains, Cotuatus and Conconnetodumnus. The news of it was shouted from village to village, and within a few hours it

---

[1] This accounts for ten legions; therefore the 11th, or its equivalent, must still have been guarding the Rhine bridge.

[2] See *infra*, Chapter VII, p. 173.     [3] See *infra*, Chapter VII, pp. 171–2.

reached the borders of the Arverni 160 Roman miles to the south. It was at once reported to a young Arvernian by name Vercingetorix, son of Celtillus a former king of the Arverni, and, as subsequent events were to show, Vercingetorix was almost certainly one of the leading conspirators, if not their chosen leader. He forthwith summoned his retainers; raised the flag of revolt; was at first opposed by his uncle and other chieftains; and was greeted by his followers as 'King'. Envoys were despatched by him in all directions to demand tribal loyalty.

He requisitioned hostages from the tribes, ordered them to mobilize for war, had arms made and collected, and enforced the strictest discipline. By these means he speedily raised an army, part of which he placed under the command of Lucterius, a Cadurcan, with orders to march into the lands of the Ruteni, a tribe which bordered on the Province, while with the remainder he set out against the Bituriges, who after an unsuccessful attempt to obtain aid from the Aedui, threw in their lot with him.

When this was reported to Caesar, he set out for the Province, and on his arrival 'was confronted with a great difficulty, as to the means whereby he could reach his army.'[1] He feared to order it south, because he did not trust it to fight successfully unless he were in command, and should he seek to join it, he considered it unsafe to entrust his person to the tribes he would meet *en route*. But when he learnt that Lucterius was advancing on Narbo (Narbonne) he set out for that town, and ordered the Provincial levies and the body-guard he had brought with him from Italy to assemble in the territory of the Helvii (30 miles north of Avignon and west of the Rhône) which adjoined the lands of the Arverni. By these and other measures he checked Lucterius, who fell back. Then, in spite of the road over the Cevennes being deep in snow, he cleared his way along it, and by a supreme effort on the part of his soldiers reached the borders of the Arverni, who were dumbfounded at his arrival.

When news of this was brought to Vercingetorix, his soldiers, terrified that their homeland would be devastated, persuaded him against his better judgement to withdraw from the country of the Bituriges and speed homewards. Caesar had anticipated he would do so, and when he learnt that he was on his way, he handed the levies over to Decimus Brutus and instructed him to occupy the enemy's attention by burning his villages. Then, with utmost secrecy, he set out for Vienna (Vienne) on the Rhône, where he found a body of cavalry

[1] *Ibid.*, VII, 6.

awaiting him. With it 'he pressed on through the country of the Aedui into that of the Lingones – where two legions were wintering – so speedily as to forestall even the possibility of any design of the Aedui on his own safety.' Upon his arrival at the cantonments, he sent word to the other legions to concentrate in one place (probably at or near Sens). And when Vercingetorix became aware of this he led his army back into the country of the Bituriges, and prepared to lay siege to Gorgobina, the chief city of the Boii, who were clients of the Aedui and allies of the Romans.[1]

Again Caesar was in a quandary. If he left Gorgobina to its fate, the tribes still loyal would lose faith in him and join the rebels. If, on the other hand, he marched to its succour, owing to the severity of the winter, how was he to supply his army without the aid of the Aedui, and could he trust them? He decided it was better to march than to leave an ally in the lurch, and, after he had parked his baggage at Agedincum (Sens) under the protection of two legions, he set out to relieve the Boii.

The next day he came to Vellaunodunum (? Montargis) and, in order to leave no enemy in his rear, and so 'to expedite the corn-supply', he occupied it after a three days' siege. Next, in order to end his march as soon as possible,[2] he set out for Orléans and reached it in two days, to the consternation of its inhabitants. He took it, plundered it, and burnt it; crossed the Loire by the town bridge,[3] and arrived on the borders of the Bituriges.

As soon as Vercingetorix heard of Caesar's approach, he raised the siege of Gorgobina, and set out to meet him. Meanwhile Caesar had marched to Noviodunum of the Bituriges (? Villate), which surrendered to him. Immediately after, Vercingetorix's vanguard was sighted in the distance; a cavalry engagement followed in which his Gallic horsemen were routed by some 400 German horse that Caesar had kept in his service since his campaign with Ariovistus. He then moved on Avaricum (Bourges), the largest and best fortified town of the Bituriges. It was situated in a fertile district, and Caesar was confident that, could he take it, he would bring the Bituriges again into his power.

---

[1] See *supra*, Chapter V, p. 105.

[2] A perplexing reason, because Orléans would seem to be well out of his direct line of march to Gorgobina, if – as is generally held – that town was near Noviodunum of the Aedui (Nevers). Possibly it may have been because the Loire was bridged at Orléans.

[3] Rendered famous by Joan of Arc in 1428.

## 3. THE SIEGE OF AVARICUM

Vercingetorix's strategy had failed. Because of Caesar's energy, audacity, and astuteness, his threat to the Province had led to the very thing he had set out to prevent – the reunion of Caesar and his army. Since when Vellaunodunum and Cenabum had been lost, and he had been outgeneralled in his attempt to occupy Gorgobina. Aware that he was unable to meet his enemy in the field, and that the defence of fortified towns deprived him of the initiative, he changed his strategy to one of attrition. Henceforth he intended to strike at Caesar's system of supply – at the weakest link in his military organization. For that, the season and the means at his disposal were propitious: forage could not be cut until the grass began to grow, and it would be months before the corn could be harvested; therefore his enemy, in order to subsist, would be compelled to scour the countryside with foraging parties, easy prey to his numerous horsemen.

He assembled his followers, explained to them his intentions, and told them the commonweal demanded that all interests of private property must be disregarded. The countryside was to be scorched, hamlets and homesteads burnt, also all towns which by nature or artifice were not impregnable to the Romans, so that no refuge might be left for those who sought to avoid service, and no centres of supply for the enemy to plunder.

By general consent this was approved, 'and in a single day', writes Caesar, 'more than twenty cities of the Bituriges were set on fire. The same was done in other states, and in every direction fires were to be seen.'[1] But when the destruction of Avaricum was debated, because of its natural strength, the Bituriges pleaded that it should be spared. Although Vercingetorix argued strongly against this, at length he yielded to their supplications out of compassion for its numerous inhabitants, and a garrison was detailed to defend it.

When Caesar set out for Avaricum, Vercingetorix followed in short stages, and went into camp at a spot, 'fenced by marshes and woods', 16 miles distant from it.

By nature Avaricum was well protected; except for a narrow approach in one quarter, it was enclosed by a river and marsh. Opposite the approach, Caesar pitched his camp, and as he was unable to invest the town, he at once began to build a ramp from which to storm it. At the same time Vercingetorix put his policy of attrition into operation,

[1] B.G., VII, 15.

and with immediate effect, for no sooner had the siege opened than Caesar importuned 'the Boii and the Aedui in the matter of the corn-supply.' The former had little corn to offer, and the latter, he says, had 'no zeal for the task', which presumably means that they were losing confidence in him. The situation grew so critical that Caesar told his men 'that if the burden of scarcity were too bitter for them to bear he would raise the siege.'[1] Nevertheless, one and all urged him to press on with it.

In his turn, Vercingetorix soon ran short of forage, and to obtain more he moved his camp nearer to Avaricum, and continued to raid the Roman foragers. When from prisoners Caesar learnt that on one of these *razzias* he was away from his camp, he set out by night to surprise it. But when he found it so strongly posted that an attack on it would be extremely costly, in spite of his men clamouring to be led on, he called off the attempt, and pacified them by saying that he valued their lives more than his own reputation.

Unknown to him at the time, it was not entirely profitless, because it so terrified the Gauls that, on Vercingetorix's return to camp, he found his army bordering on mutiny. He was accused of treachery, because he had not appointed a commander to hold the camp during his absence. He replied, somewhat lamely, that he had not done so because a deputy might have been driven 'by the zeal of the host to an engagement'; and then, more to the point, that it was the fear his men had instilled in the enemy which had led to Caesar's 'disgraceful retreat'. Thereupon the men shouted with one accord, and clashed their arms together in approval.

The Gauls, says Caesar, 'are a nation possessed of remarkable ingenuity, and extremely apt to copy and carry out anything suggested to them.'[2] This became apparent as the siege was pressed. They had learnt much about Roman siegecraft, and they put their knowledge to the test: they dragged aside the besiegers' grappling hooks with nooses worked from windlasses; mined the assault ramp; erected wooden turrets on their rampart in order to gain increased command, and made use of many kinds of obstacles to protect their walls.

By the twenty-fifth day of the siege the ramp was nearly finished, it was 330 feet broad and 80 feet high,[3] and almost touched the enemy's wall. Much of it must have been constructed of timber and tree trunks, because immediately after this is recorded, we are told that, shortly

---

[1] *B.G.* VII, 17.  [2] *Ibid.*, VII, 22.
[3] These figures appear excessive.

before the third watch,[1] smoke began to rise from it, 'for the enemy had set fire to it from a counter-mine.'[2] At the same time a shout was raised and a sortie made from two gates, while pitch and every kind of combustible was hurled from the wall on to the ramp. Caesar was, however, prepared for this, as it was a standing order that two legions should always be in bivouac close to the ramp. They rushed forward, dragged back the towers, cut a gap in the ramp and beat back the sortie. Fighting, nevertheless, continued throughout the night, and on the following morning Caesar notes an incident of military interest.

'A certain Gaul [he writes] before the gate of the town was hurling into the fire over against a turret lumps of grease and pitch that were handed to him. He was pierced by a dart from a 'scorpion' in the right side and fell dead. One of the party next him stepped over his prostrate body and went on with the same work; and when this second man had been killed in the same fashion by a scorpion-shot, a third succeeded, and to the third a fourth; and that spot was not left bare of defenders until the ramp had been extinguished.'[3]

Now that the Gauls had tried every expedient, Vercingetorix decided to withdraw the garrison of Avaricum under cover of night; a feasible operation, because the greater part of the town was not invested. But when this became known to the wives of the soldiers, they begged, prayed, and beseeched them not to abandon them and their children to the mercy of the enemy. When their appeals went unheeded, they rushed to the ramparts and shouted to the Romans what their husbands intended. Terror-struck that the enemy would occupy their lines of retreat before they could gain them, the Gauls abandoned the attempt.

On the next day the towers were advanced, and during a heavy downpour of rain the storming parties secretly made ready under cover of their mantlets. The signal was then given for the assault. Because of the rain, the ramparts were lightly guarded, and the Gauls, taken by surprise, rushed back to the market square and other open places to sell their lives as dearly as they could. But the Romans did not follow them,

[1] The Roman night, from sunset to sunrise, was divided into four equal 'watches'. Therefore the duration of a watch varied with the time of the year.

[2] Rather a gallery, driven from the enemy's side of the wall under the ramp, which ended in a combustion chamber (see *supra*, Chapter IV, p. 93). It was a highly skilled job, and Caesar (*B.G.*, VII, 22) notes that the Gauls were skilful miners, 'because they have large iron-workings in their country, and every kind of mine is known and employed.'

[3] *B.G.*, VII, 25.

instead they poured round the walls to cut off all means of escape. This led to a *sauve qui peut* toward the gates on the river side of the town, and what followed is thus described by Caesar:

'Maddened by the massacre at Cenabum and the toil of the siege-work', the troops 'spared not aged men, nor women, nor children. Eventually of all the number, which was about forty thousand, scarcely eight hundred, who had flung themselves out of the town when they heard the first shout, reached Vercingetorix in safety.'[1]

The next day Vercingetorix summoned a conference. Great leader that he was, he rose above the calamity, and exhorted his followers not to lose heart. He told them that he had never agreed with the defence of Avaricum, and that the disaster had been brought about by the short-sightedness of the Bituriges; that he would bring to his side the states which had failed to join in the revolt, and would unite all Gaul against her oppressor. His speech was well received, and after he had spoken, he at once set about to make good his losses. He recruited soldiers from the states, including a large body of archers, of whom there was a great number in Gaul,[2] and the casualties he had suffered at Avaricum were speedily made good.

## 4. THE SIEGE OF GERGOVIA

For several days Caesar rested his army at Avaricum, replenished his supplies from the immense quantity of corn found there, and, as winter was now almost over, he contemplated a move against his opponent's camp. But before he could do so, a party of Aeduan chiefs came to him to seek his aid. They told him that a dispute had arisen between two of their leading chieftains, Convictolitavis and Cotus, each of whom claimed to have been legally elected Vergobret, and unless Caesar decided which of the two had the better claim, a civil war would result.

Although Caesar was loath to release his hold on Vercingetorix, the loyalty of the Aedui was of such importance to him that he felt that, unless he intervened, the chieftain who was ousted would seek succour from that arch-rebel. To obviate this, he summoned the two parties and the Aeduan Senate to meet him at Decetia (Décize). They did so, and after he had heard what each side had to say, because Convic-tolitavis was supported by the Druids, he decided in his favour. At the same time he ordered all concerned to set aside their private quarrels

[1] *B.G.*, VII, 28.

[2] No mention has so far been made of archers in the Gallic army; therefore the bow must have been used solely for hunting purposes.

and support him in the present campaign, and his fee for the settlement was that they should provide him with 10,000 infantry and all their horsemen to protect his convoys.

When this disturbing incident had been settled, he established his chief magazines at Noviodunum (Nevers), and because the Senones and Parisii had joined in the revolt, he divided his army into two parts, four legions – two already at Agedincum – under Labienus, were to move north and bring them to heel, while the remaining seven, under his personal command, moved down the eastern bank of the Allier to strike at Gergovia (Gergovie), the chief town of the Arverni and the heart of the rebellion. As soon as Vercingetorix became aware of this, he ordered all bridges over the Allier to be broken, and set out down the western bank to follow Caesar.

Because Gergovia lay on the western side of the Allier, which at this time of the year was unfordable, Caesar had to bridge it; this he could not do as long as Vercingetorix faced him on its far bank. By a ruse he overcame the difficulty, and Vercingetorix, when he discovered that Caesar had gained the western bank, set out by forced marches for Gergovia to avoid a clash with him. Five days later Caesar reached it, at once reconnoitred it and was struck by its natural strength.

Gergovia – four miles south of modern Clermont-Ferrand – stood on an oblong plateau which crowned a mountain that rose 1,200 feet above the plain. In Caesar's day, its northern and eastern sides were probably wooded and steeper than they are today.[1] Its southern sloped in a series of terraces toward a 'huge buttress . . . with rocky face on the south and east', now called La Roche Blanche, a mile south of and about 500 feet lower than Gergovia. Immediately beyond it flowed the Auzon river,[2] a tributary of the Allier. To the west of Gergovia lay the heights of Risolles; their summit was about 100 feet below the town, and was connected with it by a col. The town itself was walled, apparently, only on its southern side.

Vercingetorix pitched his camps on the southern side of the town wall, and to protect their outward face he hastily built a six-foot-high wall of loose stones. He garrisoned the Roche Blanche, so that he might

---

[1] Theodore A. Dodge (*Caesar* (1892), vol. I, pp. 254–5), who visited the position, says that 'The northern slope is wont to be described as impossible to capture. It is not so. The slope is not steep, though it is long . . . it is now covered with rich fields and vineyards'.

[2] Not to be confused with the Auzon which flows into the Arroux at Toulon-sur-Arroux (see *supra*, Chapter V, p. 105).

5. Siege of Gergovia

secure contact with the meadow lands of the Auzon, which supplied him with much of his forage; also he picketed the heights of Risolles. It is interesting to read that, each morning at sunrise he assembled his tribal chiefs in conference and allotted them their daily tasks – a modern procedure. They mainly consisted in raids of his horsemen accompanied by archers.

From his reconnaissance it became apparent to Caesar that he could neither besiege nor assault the town; therefore he would have to blockade it. On his return he pitched his camp on a plateau 3,000 yards to its south-east and about half a mile north-west of the modern village of Orcet on the Auzon. A few days later, probably after another reconnaissance, it occurred to him that, were he to occupy the Roche Blanche, he would be in a position to cut his enemy off from part of his water-supply and much of his forage. He had observed that it was weakly held.

'In the silence of the night', he took it by a *coup-de-main* before it could be reinforced from the town; built a lesser camp on it and garrisoned it with two legions. From it he dug two parallel communication trenches, each 12 feet broad, to connect it with the greater camp.

During these operations, Convictolitavis, the Aeduan Vergobret, was bribed by Vercingetorix to desert to him, and in his turn he won over a young Aeduan noble, by name Litaviccus, by sharing the bribe with him. He then placed him in command of the 10,000 soldiers about to be sent to Caesar, and instructed him to proceed to Gergovia and join Vercingetorix.

The column set out and, when about 30 miles from Gergovia, Litaviccus halted it, camped, assembled his men, and harangued them. He told them he had learnt that all the Aeduan cavalry with Caesar, among whom were two noted chiefs, Eporedorix and Viridomarus, had been accused of treason and butchered. To substantiate this, he produced some well-primed stooges, who informed the soldiers how they had escaped the massacre, which they described in detail. Horrified at what they heard, the soldiers appealed to Litaviccus to secure their lives. In reply he urged that the sole course all should take was to join the Arverni. 'Can we doubt,' he added, 'after committing an abominable crime the Romans are already hastening hither to slay us? Wherefore, if we have any spirit in us, let us avenge the death of those who have perished most shamefully, and let us slay these brigands.'[1] He pointed to certain Roman citizens in charge of a large convoy of corn, who

[1] *B.G.*, VII, 38.

accompanied the column; his listeners fell on them and put them to death. Then, to rouse the Aedui against Caesar, he sent out messengers to spread throughout the land news of the fictitious massacre, and to call them to arms.

In Gaul rumours travelled fast, and a few hours after the massacre, Eporedorix and Viridomarus, in the Roman camp, learnt of it, and at midnight the former reported it to Caesar. It caused him such alarm that, 'without a moment's hesitation', he placed Gaius Fabius in command of the two camps with two legions to hold them, while he and the others, as well as all the cavalry, set out to suppress the revolt.

After he had marched 25 miles, he sighted the column, and sent Eporedorix and Viridomarus ahead with the cavalry, but forbade them to put any man to the sword. When the two chieftains, who were supposed to have been slain, were seen among the horsemen, the Aedui realized that they had been hoaxed. They cast down their arms and begged for mercy, while Litaviccus and his retainers slipped away and fled to Gergovia to join Vercingetorix.

Eager to return to Gergovia with the least possible delay, Caesar sent a messenger to the Aeduan Senate to inform its members that, though by right of war he could have put all the rebels to death, he had treated them with forbearance. Then, after he had rested his men for three hours, he set out on his return – in all, a march of 50 Roman miles in a little over twenty-four hours.

When about half-way to Gergovia, he was met by some horsemen sent by Fabius. They reported to him that during his absence the greater camp had been violently attacked; that many men had been wounded by 'swarms of arrows'; but that the artillery had broken the assault. By a supreme effort of his troops, Caesar reached Gergovia before sunrise.

In the meantime, on receipt of the first message sent by Litaviccus, Convictolitavis 'urged the common folk to fury', and, in order to compromise the whole tribe, incited them to massacre the Roman citizens and traders among them. In the midst of the turmoil came the second message: it stated that all the soldiers were prisoners in the power of Caesar. Fury gave way to panic, and deputies were sent to Caesar to clear the Aedui of their crime. No sooner had they departed than, alarmed by the fear of the penalty Caesar would exact, they began to entertain designs of war, and to strengthen their situation they sent out envoys to sound the neighbouring tribes.

Caesar says he was fully aware of all this, and when the deputies arrived he assured them that his good will toward the Aedui as a whole had in no way been influenced by 'the ignorance and inconsequence of the common people'. This he did, because at the time 'He himself was anticipating a greater rising in Gaul; and that he might not be surrounded by all the states, he began to plan how he might withdraw from Gergovia and once more concentrate the whole army without allowing a departure occasioned by fear of the revolt to resemble flight.'[1]

Soon after, a chance to do so presented itself. When on a visit to the lesser camp, Caesar noticed that a hill held by the enemy (the heights of Risolles) which on the previous day had been crowded with men, appeared to be undefended. He questioned some deserters, and they told him that the hill was almost on the level with the town, and because Vercingetorix feared that, should it be lost, he would be cut off from all egress to forage, therefore he was fortifying it. This set Caesar thinking, and as his aim was to win a spectacular, albeit limited, success before he withdrew, he decided by a feint attack on the hill to draw the bulk of his enemy's troops out of the town, and then launch a frontal attack from the lesser camp against Vercingetorix's camps, while his Aeduan contingent advanced from the greater camp and threatened the south-eastern corner of Gergovia. Lastly, when as much damage as possible had been done, to withdraw the attackers before they could be counter-attacked.

At midnight he sent out some troops of cavalry toward the present village of Opme; they were to act noisily, in order to attract the enemy's attention. Next, at daybreak, he sent out a number of baggage-drivers on their mules, equipped to resemble cavalry; their advance would be in view from Vercingetorix's camps, and they were to conceal themselves in the woods about modern Chanonat. To make the feint more realistic, he despatched a legion in the same direction. That, Caesar says, aroused the suspicions of the Gauls, and Vercingetorix brought the bulk of them over to the fortified hill. Caesar then moved his soldiers in the greater camp to the lesser one by way of the two communication trenches, and marshalled them out of sight at the Roche Blanche. He instructed the officers to keep their men well in hand; there was to be no looting; and he urged them to advance with utmost speed, as 'it was a question of surprise, not of battle.'[2] When all was ready, he signalled the advance.

With *élan*, the legions moved forward, how many Caesar does not

[1] *B.G.*, VII, 43.          [2] *Ibid.*, VII, 45.

tell us; but as he held back the 10th as a reserve under his personal command, had detailed one for the feint, and probably another was needed to hold the two camps, there were probably four in front line. They rushed the six-foot camp wall, scrambled over it, and gained possession of three camps so unexpectedly that the king of the Nitiobriges 'in a noonday sleep' in his tent barely escaped from the hands of the plundering soldiers. Then, we read: 'Having thus secured his particular purpose, Caesar ordered the retreat to be sounded and at once halted the Tenth Legion.'[1]

Because of the noise, excitement, and confusion, as well as the lay of the ground, the signal went unheard, and, in spite of the efforts of the officers to hold their men back, intoxicated by their success and the flight of the enemy, they pressed on until they neared the town wall, which by now was crowded with women imploring the Romans to spare them. A few of the attackers actually scaled the wall and entered the town.

When the Gauls on the heights of Risolles heard the hubbub in the distance, which signalled that something untoward had happened, they sped back to Gergovia, fell on the disorganized Romans and drove them out of the camps. Meanwhile Caesar, when his men did not respond to his signal, feared that they might be overwhelmed, and sent an urgent message to Titus Sextius, whom he had left in the lesser camp with some cohorts, to advance them with the utmost speed and post them on the right flank of the enemy's line of advance; at the same time he moved forward the 10th Legion.

When the fighting was at its height, suddenly the Aeduan contingent was seen to be appropaching on 'the exposed flank of the troops', and as its men were similarly armed to the Gauls, they were mistaken for the enemy. Although Caesar does nòt say so, it would seem probable that a panic resulted, and continued until 'any immoderate pursuit on the part of the Gauls' – whatever that may mean – was checked by the 10th Legion and the cohorts of the 13th under Titus Sextius. As soon as the legions 'touched the plain they turned their standard against the enemy and halted.' This unfortunate fiasco cost Caesar 46 centurions and nearly 700 soldiers.

On the next day Caesar paraded his soldiers and reprimanded them; he praised their courage and censured their indiscipline. Then he led them out of camp, and formed them up in line-of-battle; but naturally Vercingetorix did not respond to his challenge. This face-saving ritual

[1] B.G., VII, 47.

was repeated on the following day with the same result; but, apparently, to the great benefit of the troops. Caesar, then, struck camp and moved into the territory of the Aedui. When he came to the Allier, he bridged and crossed it.

There he was greeted by Viridomarus and Eporedorix. They told him that Litaviccus with all his horse was on his way to rouse the Aedui, and that they themselves must head him off if their state was to be kept loyal. Although Caesar suspected their loyalty, he did not detain them, 'lest he might seem to be inflicting an injury [on his allies] or affording some suspicion of fear,'[1] which his code of honour, his *dignitas*, forbade. His suspicions were well-founded, for when they reached Noviodunum and learnt that Convictolitavis had declared for Vercingetorix, they threw in their lot with him.

Noviodunum was Caesar's administrative base. At it were to be found all his hostages, his corn reserve, his war chest, and the greater part of the army baggage, as well as a great number of horses he had obtained from Italy and Spain. Eporedorix and Viridomarus massacred the garrison and the traders gathered there, released the hostages, divided the money, removed or spoilt the corn, and fired the town. Next, they recruited their forces from the neighbouring districts, picketed the Loire, and sent out raids of horsemen in the hope that they might cut off their enemy from his corn-supply, and compel him to retreat into the Province.

The situation Caesar now found himself in was critical in the extreme. His tribal allies had deserted him; the Arverni, elated by their victory, were on his rear; the Bituriges, burning with revenge, on his left flank; and the Aedui barred his front. It was of his own making: he had failed to appreciate that his strategy of annihilation had engendered a spirit of desperation, and that for the first time in the war he was confronted by a general able enough to exploit it. Although the Avaricum campaign had proved Vercingetorix to be a bold and imaginative leader, Caesar opened his Gergovia campaign by dividing his army. His penalty was his repulse; it had revealed to all Gaul that his legions were not invincible. One thing alone saved him – his own invincibility.

Not for a moment did he contemplate a retreat to the security of the Province; instead, he determined to advance, to link up with Labienus, and with a reunited army regain the initiative. By forced marches, day and night, he reached the Loire so speedily that the Aedui were taken off-guard. He crossed it at a deep ford; halted for a brief spell to

---

[1] *Ibid.*, VII, 54.

gather in cattle and corn; and then decided to march into the country of the Senones, presumably, in order to reach Labienus' base at Agedincum (Sens).

When Caesar was at Gergovia, with great difficulty Labienus advanced to Lutetia (Paris), which he found burnt, as also its bridge. When there he received rumours from the countryfolk that Caesar had withdrawn from Gergovia, and that the Aedui were in revolt. Erroneously they affirmed that Caesar had failed to cross the Loire, and that lack of corn had compelled him to make for the Province. When these disasters were reported, the Bellovaci were preparing to join in the war, and with the Parisii in revolt, Labienus decided to fall back as rapidly as he could to his administrative base at Agedincum, pick up his baggage train, and then, as best he could, make his way south until he heard from Caesar. His immediate problem was how to cross the Seine in face of an enemy army on its far side, commanded by an old chieftain by name Camulogenus. By a clever ruse he outwitted him, and in a stubbornly fought battle defeated him. From Agedincum he marched southward, and on the third day rejoined Caesar at an unrecorded spot.

## 5. THE SIEGE OF ALESIA

The revolt of the Aedui brought the rebellion to its climax. Hitherto they had been Rome's oldest and most trusty ally; but now that they had revolted and had captured all of Caesar's hostages, they were in the position to blackmail the recalcitrant tribes and do him great damage by forcing them to join in the rebellion. Thereby their authority was so enhanced that they sought to head the revolt, and they requested Vercingetorix to meet them at Bibracte and discuss with them the future conduct of the war. Accordingly a general assembly was convened there, at which all the tribes, except the Remi and Lingones, who remained faithful to Rome, and the Treveri, who at the time were pressed by the Germans,[1] were represented. At it the Aedui insisted that the supreme command should be assigned to them. Their demand was put to the vote, and much to their exasperation the assembly acclaimed Vercingetorix their commander-in-chief.

As such, he decided to adhere to his original plan: to avoid a pitched battle, and continue his harassing tactics. He had already 80,000 infantry, and required no more; therefore he restricted his demands to

[1] Holmes considers that these three tribes were not the only ones who failed to send representatives (see *The Roman Republic*, vol. II, p. 206).

horsemen, and requested the tribes to raise his cavalry to 15,000 strong. He selected Alesia (Mount Auxois) in the territory of the Mandubii as his stronghold, and to draw Caesar into the Province, he raised two subsidiary forces, the one to attack the Helvii and devastate the borders of the Volcae Arecomici – two Provincial tribes – and the other to make war on the Allobroges, should they refuse to join him.

His plans became immediately known to Caesar, and to frustrate them he appointed Lucius Caesar, a kinsman and ex-consul, his lieutenant-general in the Province, and instructed him to raise twenty-two cohorts to protect its frontier. At the same time he secured the allegiance of the Allobroges, and they strongly picketed the Rhône; but the Helvii were defeated and took to their strongholds. Of his own situation he says: because of the enemy's superiority in mounted troops, 'all the lines of communication were interrupted', which meant that 'he could in no wise be assisted from the Province and from Italy.' To remedy this he sent agents across the Rhine to recruit a force of German horse and their attendant light-armed troops, and on their arrival, when he found their horses unsuitable, he remounted the troopers on those belonging to his tribunes, knights, and re-enlisted veterans (*evocati*) who were privileged to ride when on the march.

Some weeks must have elapsed before both sides were ready to take the field, and while Vercingetorix was assembling his contingents at Alesia, Caesar with his army, now united, was probably encamped in the neighbourhood of Troyes among the friendly Lingones. His aim was to reach the Province, and, when ready to move, he set out 'to the country of the Sequani across the outmost borders of the Lingones'[1] to gain the valley of the Saône, the direct road to the Province.

When Vercingetorix became aware of this, he assembled his cavalry commanders and told them that the enemy was fleeing to the Province, and were he allowed to reach it, he would certainly return with stronger forces than ever. Therefore, in order to prevent this, his plan was to destroy him on his line of march, when he would be encumbered by a heavy baggage train. This was not to abandon his harassing tactics and seek a decision in a pitched battle, because he was aware that his infantry were no match for the legions. Instead, it was to ambush his enemy, as Hannibal had ambushed Flaminius and his legions at Lake Trasimene. The measures he took confirm this.

When Caesar was *en route* toward the upper Saône, Vercingetorix advanced from Alesia to a spot, probably in the vicinity of Dijon,

[1] *Ibid.*, VII, 66.

which lay on his enemy's line of march. There he encamped his army by a stream 10 miles distant from him. On the following day, when the legions were reported to be approaching, he drew up his infantry in order of battle immediately outside their three camps, so as to 'strike terror into the enemy' – that is, surprise him by the sudden appearance of a bold front. Next, under cover of the consternation aroused, his cavalry, divided into three divisions, were to attack the column; one division the front of the leading troops, and the other two their flanks. Obviously, his idea was to throw the head back in confusion on to the troops in rear of it, and thereby detonate a general panic.

Caesar's account of what took place is so sketchy that it is difficult even to conjecture what actually resulted. But one thing is almost certain: again, as on the Sambre, through lack of cavalry reconnaissance he had been caught *flagrante delicto*. Had his enemy's horsemen been worth their salt, he would in all probability have suffered a severe repulse, if not a rout; but, apparently, they failed to close with the column, and did no more than skirmish about it. Thus Caesar was allowed sufficient time to form his cavalry into three groups, which kept the attackers at bay. Under cover of this holding operation the column halted, and each of its legions formed square with its baggage within it. This must have taken a considerable time; yet all we are told is, that at any point where the legionaries 'seemed to be distressed or too hard pressed Caesar' ordered 'the standards to advance and line of battle to be formed. This served to check the enemy in pursuit and to encourage' the legionaries 'by hope of succour' – whatever that may mean. At length Caesar's German cavalry gained the summit of a ridge, and drove a body of Gallic horse headlong back as far as the stream, behind which Vercingetorix's infantry were drawn up, 'and slew not a few'. When the other Gallic horsemen witnessed the rout they took to flight.

When Vercingetorix saw that the surprise had failed, and that the battle he had not intended to get involved in was lost, he withdrew his army to Alesia, and ordered his baggage train to follow it closely. At the same time Caesar ordered his train to park on the nearest hill, under the protection of two legions, and with the rest of his army he pursued the enemy as long as there was daylight; some 3,000 of his rear guard were slain.[1]

[1] B.G., VII, 66–68. There is something 'phoney' about Caesar's account of this battle. For instance, no mention is made of the capture of Vercingetorix's baggage train, which, as it was in rear of the retreating army, must have been the first to be involved in Caesar's pursuit.

The stronghold of Alesia[1] was built on an isolated and elevated plateau, from east to west a mile and a quarter in length and half a mile in width. It rose 500 feet above the surrounding valleys, in the confluence of two small streams, the Ose and the Oserain, which bounded it on the north and the south, and on the west of it joined the river Brenne, which flows through the Plaine des Laumes. On its northern, eastern, and southern sides the town was surrounded by hills, of which the eastern, Mt Pevenel (or Pennevelle), is described by Colonel Dodge as 'a sort of natural siege-mound'[2] that pointed toward the eastern end of the town. Another important feature was Mt Réa, a mile north-west of its western extremity. Of the hill itself, the slopes to the stronghold, though not severe, were in the days of hand-to-hand fighting a serious consideration for the attacker, and what was more so was the natural wall of rock that crowned much of the summit of the plateau.

When, on the day after the battle, Caesar approached Alesia from the east by the Dijon road, he found the Gauls busily engaged on building a six-foot-high wall between the Ose and Oserain across the western extremity of Mt Pevenel, as it was the weakest section in their defences. And after he had reconnoitred the stronghold, he concluded that the only way to take it was to reduce it by blockade, so he decided to enclose it within a line of contravallation.

Barely had the siege-work started than Vercingetorix took the offensive; he sent all, or the greater part, of his cavalry into the plain to the west of the town, and a furious engagement with Caesar's horse resulted. What his intention was can only be guessed at, because Caesar, who so often was aware of his enemy's intentions, on this occasion provides no hint. It is unlikely to have been to cut his way out of Alesia before it was enclosed; more probably it was to cripple his enemy's ability to forage by decimating his horsemen. In the *mêlée* Caesar's Gallic and Spanish horse were worsted, and not until he brought forward his German squadrons were the tables turned. They put the Gauls to flight, and in rout drove them up the hill to the ditch and wall which protected their camps outside the western side of the town. Because the gates in the wall were too narrow to admit the fugitives quickly, they became jammed with struggling horsemen, who in numbers were slaughtered outside them. This started a panic among the Gauls in the camps, who fled up the hillside to seek refuge in the town, and to

[1] The site of Alesia is certain, and has been excavated (see *Caesar's Conquest of Gaul*, pp. 354–63, for particulars).

[2] *Caesar*, vol. I, p. 285.

prevent the camps from being deserted Vercingetorix was obliged to order all gates in the town wall to be shut.

Vercingetorix now committed his fatal blunder: he set aside his harassing tactics and decided to hold Alesia until a relieving army could come to his succour.

We are told that he 'made up his mind to send away all his horsemen by night, before the Romans could complete their entrenchments.'[1] They were to proceed to their respective tribes and urge them to raise an army, come to his relief, and compel Caesar to raise the siege. The tribes were to be told that, unless this were done, 'eighty thousand chosen men were doomed to perish'; also that food-stocks in Alesia would be exhausted in thirty days, or a little more. Because he had between 10,000 and 15,000 horsemen with him, it is understandable that lack of forage compelled him to part with them; but it is not understandable why *all* were needed to recruit the tribes. Surely the right course to have taken was to send out a few hundreds on that task and, while his infantry held Alesia and pinned Caesar to it, to have led out the remainder and impeded the Roman foragers. The reason why he did not do so may have been that he did not trust any of his subordinates to hold Alesia during his absence, nor command his cavalry were he himself to remain there.

When his cavalry departed, he ordered all stocks of food to be collected at his headquarters for daily issue, which was to be 'measured out sparingly'. He distributed the slaughter cattle among the troops, and withdrew all detachments into the stronghold.[2] 'By such measures', we read, 'did he prepare for the conduct of the campaign, in anticipation of the succours from Gaul.'[3]

Caesar soon learnt of this from deserters, and his problem became a threefold one: (1) How to prevent Vercingetorix from breaking out; (2) how to prevent the relieving army from breaking in; and (3) how meanwhile to ration his army.

To effect the first, he strengthened his line of contravallation by adding to it entrenchments and obstacles on a scale unprecedented in classical warfare. Across the eastern border of the Plaine des Laumes,

---

[1] *B.G.*, VII, 71.

[2] Caesar says 'he withdrew into the town all the forces which he had posted in front of it.' This cannot have included the camps immediately outside the town wall, because the town itself could not have accommodated 80,000 men as well as an unknown number of inhabitants.

[3] *Ibid.*, VII, 71.

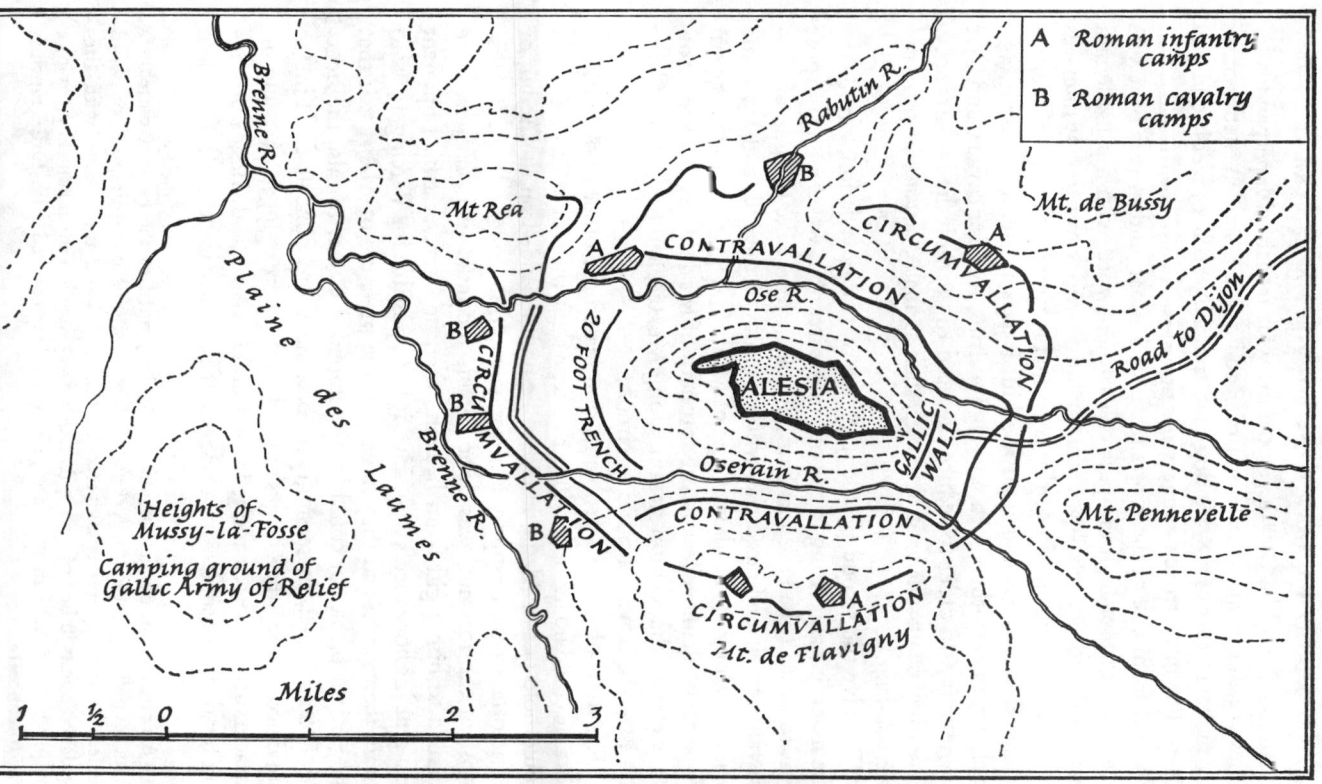

Legend:
- **A** Roman infantry camps
- **B** Roman cavalry camps

Breme R.

Rabutin R.

B

Mt Réa

A CONTRAVALLATION

CIRCUMVALLATION

Mt. de Bussy

A

B CIRCUMVALLATION

Ose R.

ALESIA

GALLIC WALL

Road to Dijon

20 FOOT TRENCH

B CIRCUMVALLATION

B

Plaine des Laumes

Brenne R.

Oserain R.

CONTRAVALLATION

Mt. Penneyelle

Heights of Mussy-la-Fosse

Camping ground of Gallic Army of Relief

A

A

CIRCUMVALLATION

Mt. de Flavigny

Miles

1   ½   0   1   2   3

6. Siege of Alesia

from the Ose to the Oserain, a 20-foot-wide trench with perpendicular sides was dug as an obstacle, in order to impede a sudden enemy onset by night. In rear of it were dug two trenches, both 15 feet broad and deep. The inner trench – that is the nearer of the two to the hill – was flooded from one of the rivers to form a moat, and in rear of it was erected a 12-foot-high rampart of earth crowned with a palisade and provided with 'turrets' – wooden or hurdle-work towers – at intervals of 80 feet. On the flanks of this formidable system, the line of contravallation was extended round the hill; it was 11 miles in circuit, and included twenty-three forts and eight camps, four for cavalry and four for infantry. In order to reduce the need to garrison the line strongly, extensive use was made of obstacles, such as abatis, *chevaux-de-frise*, and *trous-de-loup*.[1]

To solve the second problem, a line of circumvallation, parallel to the inner line and facing in the opposite direction, was dug; its purpose was to protect the besiegers from attack in rear. Like the line of contravallation, it embraced the whole circuit of the hill, and from the plain ran along the northern slope of Mt de Flavigny, across the eastern slope of Mt Pennevelle, and the southern of Mt de Bussy; thence across the valley of the Rabutin stream, along Mt Réa, and back to the Plaine des Laumes. It was 14 miles in circuit.

The third of Caesar's problems dominated the other two. Without corn he could no more continue the siege than without it Vercingetorix could hold fast to Alesia. Hitherto he had depended on the Aedui, or some other tribe, to supply it, now he could no longer do so. Because most of the foraging was done by his mounted men, it must have seemed to him a gift from heaven when he learnt that his opponent had sent his horsemen away. Had it been possible for Vercingetorix to retain them, even had they never left the precincts of Alesia, fear that they might break out could have compelled Caesar to raise the siege. As it lengthened, increasingly it became more difficult for him to obtain corn; soon the villages around Alesia were stripped of it, and his foragers had to search for it farther and farther afield. Beside providing for daily consumption, a reserve of corn was imperative, for when

---

[1] An abatis is an obstacle made of boughs pinned to the ground with their branches pointing outwards. A *cheval-de-frise* consists of long iron spikes, or sword blades, fixed in a horizontal piece of timber; Caesar used stakes with fire-hardened points in lieu of iron spikes. A *trou-de-loup* is a small conical pit with a sharply pointed stake in its centre; normally it is covered with turf, branches, etc., to conceal it.

the army of relief arrived he would be cut off from the countryside. To provide against this, he ordered the legions to lay in thirty days of corn and forage as a reserve. For an army of some 70,000 men or more, this in itself was a formidable task.

On the arrival of Vercingetorix's horsemen, the tribal leaders summoned a council of war, at which his proposal to call up all who could bear arms was rejected, because so vast a host would be unmanageable and impossible to supply. Instead, tribal contingents were mobilized – forty-three are named by Caesar[1] – and together with 8,000 Helvetii an army of 8,000 horsemen and about 250,000 infantry was mustered in the country of the Aedui, under the command of four chieftains – Commius,[2] Viridomarus, Eporedorix, and Vercassivellaunus, a cousin of Vercingetorix. We are told that this enormous array set out in high spirits for Alesia, and that 'there was not a man of them all who thought the mere sight of so vast a host could be withstood, especially in a two-sided engagement.'[3]

By the time this quite impossible *attroupment* was nearing Alesia, its garrison was so desperately short of food that Vercingetorix assembled his chiefs to consider what to do. Some voted for surrender, others for an immediate sortie, and one, an Arvernian, Critognatus by name, proposed that they should do what their forefathers had done during the invasion of the Cimbri and Teutoni – kill their useless old people and resort to cannibalism.[4] In a more civilized way his proposal was adopted. It was decided, rather than eat the old folk or surrender, to evacuate all useless mouths, as well as the Mandubii with their wives and children. But when these unfortunates approached the Roman lines and prayed to be admitted as slaves, very properly Caesar refused to receive them.

Immediately following this tragic episode, the long-awaited army of relief reached the neighbourhood of Alesia and camped on the heights of Mussy-la-Fosse, which rise above the western border of the Plaine des Laumes.

On the day after its arrival, Commius and his three colleagues drew

[1] A notable exception was the Bellovaci, who 'declared that they would wage war with the Romans on their own account.'

[2] In 55 B.C., Caesar had appointed him king of the Atrebates, a tribe in the Arras-Cambrai region.

[3] *B.G.*, VII, 76.

[4] Caesar supplies a detailed summary of this speech; like most of such effusions, much of it is what the writer, posing as the speaker, would in the circumstances have said.

up their masses of infantry on the heights overlooking the plain, and advanced their cavalry into it; it filled its entire length of three miles. The sight of this so heartened the besieged within Alesia that they hastened down the hill, and set to work to fill up the 20-foot trench, so as to facilitate an assault on the defensive works in rear of it.

To meet this dual challenge, Caesar at once manned his lines of contra and circumvallation, so that their defenders faced both ways, and he ordered his cavalry to engage. The Gauls had mingled archers and light-armed among their horsemen, and a considerable number of the Romans were wounded and began to withdraw from the fight. This encouraged the Gauls, who with shouts and yells pressed on, and 'As the action was proceeding in sight of all, no deed, of honour and dishonour, could escape notice.' After this Froissartesque hyperbole, for by now some 12,000 cavalry must have been whirling around in clouds of dust, we are told that 'The fight lasted, and the victory was doubtful, from noon almost to sunset,' when the Germans once again came to the rescue. They massed their troops of horse in one part of the field, charged the Gallic horsemen, routed them and slaughtered the archers. When Vercingetorix's men who, presumably, had meanwhile been engaged on their attempt to force Caesar's line of contravallation, saw the Gallic horse pursued to their camp, in despair they withdrew into the town. So ended the first attempt to relieve Alesia.

After a day's interval, a second attempt was made, this time under cover of darkness. Loaded with hurdles, ladders, and grappling-hooks, at midnight the Gauls silently approached the entrenchments in the plain, raised a sudden shout, as a signal to the besieged, and, under cover of showers of arrows and sling-shot, began to fill in the trench of circumvallation.

When the shout was heard in Alesia, Vercingetorix by trumpet blast assembled his men, and led them down to the plain to assault the entrenchments of the line of contravallation, but they were beaten back by volleys of sling bullets, one-pounder catapults,[1] and stakes[2] set ready in the works. Meanwhile the Gauls from the camp, under a barrage of arrows, struck in the opposite direction; but when they closed in on the entrenchments they were 'caught unawares by the

---

[1] Catapults throwing one-pound stones.

[2] As the Romans had long discarded the spear, these stakes would appear to have been improvised substitutes with fire-hardened points, used to thrust back an opponent should he attempt to scramble up the rampart.

"spurs",[1] or they sank into pits [trous-de loup] and were impaled, or they were shot by artillery pikes[2] from the rampart and the turrets, and so perished on every side.'[3] Nowhere were the entrenchments penetrated. By now the attackers from Alesia had filled in part of the 20-foot trench, but it took up so much time that they were unable to get at the defences on its far side. When daybreak drew near, and they saw that the relieving army was again in retreat, they abandoned their task and withdrew.

Twice beaten at great loss, the four Gallic leaders took counsel and questioned some men who were well acquainted with the locality. From them they learnt that the line of circumvallation had not yet been carried around the camp close to the Ose at the foot of Mt Réa. The camp was occupied by two legions, and was overlooked by the high ground above it.

After it had been reconnoitred, 6,000 picked men, commanded by Vercassivellaunus, set out under cover of night, passed round to the north of Mt Réa, and before dawn concealed themselves behind the heights. There Vercassivellaunus rested his men until midday, when he advanced downhill on the camp. At the same time the Gallic cavalry moved toward the entrenchments on the plain, and the rest of the infantry drew up before their encampments.

Vercingetorix, it would appear, was aware of the project, because he was ready to take part in it. When Vercassivellaunus struck, he led out a body of men, loaded with 'hurdles, poles, mantlets' and 'grappling-hooks', to assault the rampart beyond the 20-foot trench, which in places was now filled up.[4] Also, it would appear – since we are told 'the fighting went on simultaneously in all places' – that he had arranged for demonstrations in other localities, aimed at pinning his enemy to his works.

From his command post Caesar could observe what was proceeding in each quarter, and, therefore, was able to reinforce any severely threatened point. He writes: 'The Gauls utterly despaired of safety unless they could break through the lines; the Romans anticipated an end of all toils if they could hold their own.'[5] In other words, it was to be a fight to the finish.

---

[1] A 'spur' (stimulus) was a short post armed with a sharp hook, like a fishhook; it was driven into the ground and lightly covered over.

[2] As it was night time, aiming must have been at random.     [3] Ibid., VII, 82.

[4] This is conjecture, because Caesar does not mention the point of attack.

[5] Ibid., VII, 85.

At the camp of the two legions, a desperate struggle took place. The downward slope favoured the Gauls, who in dense masses rushed toward it. Some discharged missiles, others advanced under cover of their shields in tortoise (*testudo*) formation; fresh men replaced the exhausted, and large numbers threw earth into the ditch and covered over the obstacles concealed in the ground. The situation grew so critical that, when it was reported to Caesar, he sent forward Labienus with six cohorts to reinforce the camp.

Meanwhile on the plain, 'because of the size of the entrenchments' Vercingetorix's men found it impossible to surmount them, and in desperation 'made an attempt to scale the precipitous parts.' Whereabouts they were is not mentioned; possibly they may have been at the foot of Mt Flavigny. Wherever they were, we are told that 'They dislodged the defenders of the turrets by a swarm of missiles, filled in the trenches with earth and hurdles, tore down rampart and breastwork with grappling-hooks.'[1] Twice Caesar reinforced this point, and not until he had done so for a third time, under his personal command, was the assault repulsed.

Immediately after this he set out to join Labienus with four cohorts and a body of cavalry. He ordered part of the latter to follow him, and the other part 'to go round the outer entrenchments and attack the enemy in rear.' In the meantime Labienus, when he found that neither the trenches nor the ramparts could much longer withstand the onrushes of the enemy, collected together forty cohorts and sent back to Caesar for instructions.

On receipt of his message, Caesar hastened on, and when, as he neared the camp, its exhausted defenders saw his scarlet cloak,[2] they raised a great shout, which was answered by a shout from the enemy. Heartened by his presence, the men dropped their *pila* and got to work with their swords. Then, suddenly, the cavalry Caesar had sent forward appeared in rear of the Gauls. 'There is a moment in engagements', wrote Napoleon, 'when the least manœuvre is decisive and gives victory; it is the one drop of water which makes the vessel run over.' That moment had arrived. The suddenness of this unlooked-for attack detonated a panic: 'The enemy turned to flee; the cavalry met them in flight, and a great slaughter ensued.' Vercassivellaunus was captured in the rout, seventy-four standards were taken, and 'of the vast host few returned safe to camp.' All this was seen from Alesia, and, when it was,

[1] *B.G.*, VII, 86.
[2] Worn by a commander-in-chief.

Vercingetorix recalled his forces from the plain, and directly the Gauls on Mt Mussy-la-Fosse witnessed the *débâcle*, they abandoned their camp. At midnight the cavalry were sent out to pursue them; 'a great number were taken and slain, and the rest fled away into their different states.'

Thus this remarkable siege was brought to an end by the simultaneous defeat of two armies by a single army, no greater than the one and incomparably smaller than the other. An army which not only was the besieger but itself was besieged, and which had to hold 25 miles of entrenchments in order, at one and the same time, to achieve its aim and secure itself against defeat. In spite of the paucity and frequent vagueness of details provided by Caesar, and the consequent difficulty in reconstructing some of the incidents, the siege of Alesia remains one of the most extraordinary operations recorded in military history.

On the following day Vercingetorix summoned a council of chieftains, and offered himself to them, either 'to give satisfaction to the Romans by his death or to deliver him alive.' Deputies were sent to Caesar, and he ordered all arms to be delivered up and all chiefs to be brought to him. This was done, and when he was seated in front of one of the camps, Vercingetorix surrendered to him. The captured Aedui and Arverni were set apart by Caesar 'to see if through them he could recover their states;' and he 'distributed the rest of the prisoners, one apiece to each man throughout the army, by way of plunder.'[1]

According to Suetonius, 'excepting only the nations in alliance with the Republic, and such as had merited his favour', by which is presumably meant the Remi, Lingones, Aedui, and Arverni, Caesar grouped the rest of the tribes 'into the form of a province', and imposed upon 'the new organization an annual tribute of 40 millions of sesterces.'[2] This moderate sum he authorized the tribes to collect and pay without the interference of the grasping Roman tax collectors. Further, what must have been equally pleasing to them, he reverted to the earlier Roman practice toward conquered peoples by accepting whatever form of government prevailed among them.[3]

After this he set out for the country of the Aedui, who submitted to him, as also did the Arverni, from whom he demanded a great number of hostages, and restored to both tribes some 20,000 prisoners, apparently in order to win their favour, and thereby build up a powerful group of allies loyal to the Republic, that would act as a counterpoise

---

[1] *B.G.*, VII, 89.    [2] *Div. Iul.*, XXV.
[3] See *Roman Imperialism*, Tenny Frank (1914), pp. 340–1.

to the numerous lesser tribes which, once he had departed from Gaul, he would no longer be able to control. He then placed the legions in winter quarters: Labienus with two in the country of the Sequani; Fabius with two in that of the Remi; one each in the territories of the Ambivariti (about Bourg), the Bituriges and the Ruteni (on the river Tarn); two under Quintus Cicero and Publius Sulpicius, respectively at Cabillonum (Châlons-sur-Saône) and Matisco (Mâcon) to secure the corn-supply. With the remaining two he decided to winter at Bibracte. In Rome he was granted a public thanksgiving of twenty days.

## 6. END OF THE REVOLT

Barely had the legions occupied their cantonments than further troubles arose. Hirtius, who now takes up the story in Book VIII of *The Gallic War*, mentions a concerted plan; but it would seem more probable that it was nothing other than the backwash of Alesia: actions of disbanded men turned brigands, of certain disgruntled and ambitious chiefs, and a return to inter-tribal jealousies. These had to be suppressed as rapidly as possible, because in the spring of 49 B.C. Caesar's term of office would expire, and it was imperative for him to leave Gaul at peace.

The first dissension occurred among the Bituriges in December, 52 B.C., and as a single legion stationed among them was insufficient to cope with it, Caesar marched from Bibracte to its assistance with another legion. Swiftly he suppressed the malcontents, showed un-accustomed leniency toward them – a distinct change in policy – and took hostages from them.

Soon after his return to Bibracte, the Bituriges sought his aid against the Carnutes, who were raiding their lands. With two legions he set out for Cenabum (Orléans), camped there and sent his cavalry after the raiders, who soon were so distressed by the wintry weather that many of them died of cold, and the survivors dispersed.

When on this punitive expedition, Caesar had received repeated reports from the Remi that the Bellovaci, the most important tribe to hold aloof in the Alesia campaign, were mustering an army, under their chieftain Correus and Commius of the Atrebates, to attack the Suessiones, who were tributaries of the Remi. Because it was repugnant to Caesar to leave a faithful ally in the lurch, and therefore was a question of honour as well as of necessity, he led four legions into the country of the Bellovaci, encamped there and sent out his cavalry to capture prisoners, from whom he might ascertain his enemy's plans. They told him that the Bellovaci and their allies were encamped on

Mt St Marc[1] in the forest of Compiègne, a hill protected by a marsh, that Correus was holding it, and that Commius was temporarily away in search of German aid. Further, that Correus intended to accept battle should Caesar bring with him no more than three legions; otherwise he would remain in camp and harry the Roman foragers, as Vercingetorix had done. On this information Caesar arranged his column of march to resemble three legions, then rapidly moved forward and encamped on Mt St Pierre, which faced Mt St Marc, and was separated from it by a deep and narrow valley, or ravine.

The camp was of a novel kind. It was surrounded by a 12-foot-high rampart protected by two 15-foot-wide trenches, both with perpendicular sides, and on, or immediately in rear of, the rampart was a line of turrets linked together by a covered gangway protected by a wattle breastwork, so as to obtain two tiers from which missiles could be shot or hurled.

Skirmishes occurred between the two camps, and became more frequent when Commius returned with 500 German horse. To put a stop to them, as it was not possible to storm the camp, Caesar decided to invest it, and as he required more troops for this, he ordered Trebonius to reinforce him with three additional legions, and join him by forced marches.

When the Bellovaci learnt of this, they feared that they would suffer the fate of Alesia, so they decided to send away by night all non-combatants and their baggage train, and when they had got safely away to evacuate the camp. But the withdrawal of the train was carried out in such confusion that, when day broke, only part of it had cleared the camp. When Caesar saw what was taking place, he rapidly bridged the marsh,[2] led his legions across it, and occupied a ridge which stretched almost to his enemy's camp; on it he mounted his artillery. He then built a new camp which faced his enemy's, and kept the army in a state of immediate readiness to meet a sudden emergency. It came, but not in the way he could have expected.

Presumably by now the train and non-combatants were well on their way; therefore Correus' problem was how to evacuate the camp without the risk of being attacked while he did so. He solved it by a

[1] The position has been located and excavated. See Holmes's *Caesar's Conquest of Gaul*, pp. 826–30, and *The Roman Republic*, vol. II, pp. 287–91.

[2] Probably by means of a corduroy causeway (a road surfaced with facines and logs laid side to side and pinned together). If the material was ready at hand, it could rapidly be built.

ruse which does him credit. In the camp there happened to be a large number of bales of straw and faggots. These the Bellovaci 'piled up in front of their line, and at the end of the day fired them at a given signal. So a continuous flame suddenly covered the whole force from the sight of the Romans.'[1] Then they 'fled away at a most furious speed.'

Caesar, who could see nothing of the enemy 'through the screen of fire', sent forward his cavalry and advanced the legions slowly in their rear. But the cavalry were afraid to enter the cloud of smoke, which was so dense that the troopers 'scarce could make out the front part of their horses,' and, because they feared an ambuscade, the Bellovaci got away without the loss of a man. They occupied another camp 'in a strongly fenced place' 10 miles away on the river Oise. From it, so we are told, 'they wrought great havoc upon the Roman foraging parties.'[2]

At length Caesar learnt from prisoners that Correus intended to place 6,000 foot and 1,000 horse in ambush in the woods which adjoined a plain bordering the river, which was frequented by Roman foragers. So he decided to turn this information to his advantage. He sent out the foragers under a strong escort of cavalry and light-armed auxiliaries, and in support followed them with a body of infantry kept out of view of the enemy. When the escort entered the plain, Correus emerged from the woods and, instead of the easy victory he had expected, was so violently opposed that his horsemen were virtually beaten by the time the Roman infantry came up. When they did, the Bellovaci were panic-stricken, and fled by way of the woods and the river side. Half of them were slain.

Caesar then advanced on his enemy's camp. Thereupon Commius fled to the Germans, and the remaining chieftains surrendered and sued for peace. He treated them leniently, as he had the Bituriges, and the immediate result was that those states that had been 'watching to see how the Bellovaci fared', on learning of Caesar's clemency at once submitted, 'gave hostages and did as commanded.'

'So,' writes Hirtius, 'the most warlike nations were subdued,' and Caesar divided the army in order to sweep up the few remaining mal-

[1] B.G., VIII, 15. To effect this, naval searchlights were used at the Battle of Santiago Bay in 1898; at the siege of Port Arthur in 1904; and in the attempts to force the Narrows in the Gallipoli campaign of 1915. In the Second World War, tanks fitted with searchlights (code-named C.D.L.s) were designed for an identical purpose.

[2] Ibid., VIII, 16.

contents. Labienus with two legions was sent to the land of the Treveri; Fabius with twenty-five cohorts to 'several states' in the west; Caninius, who had been wintering with two legions near Rodez, was transferred to Poitou, and the 15th Legion was ordered to Cisalpine Gaul to repel an incursion of Illyrian brigands.

The sole operation distinct from these was conducted by Caesar in person. Seemingly, Ambiorix was again on the warpath, and to vindicate his own prestige and make Ambiorix's name hated by his subjects[1] 'who might chance to survive', Caesar determined to exterminate the Eburones. He stripped their country 'of citizens, buildings, and cattle', and devastated it by 'slaughter, fire, and pillage.'[2] This uncalled-for act of ferocity shows that, in spite of all his greatness, there was a streak of demoniacal malevolence in his nature. The next and last incident in the war again reveals this.

A rebel chieftain, by name Dumnacus, with a band of several thousand desperadoes, laid siege to Lemonum (Poitiers) and when Caninius with two weak legions came to its relief, he found he had not sufficient men, and Fabius set out to reinforce him. When Dumnacus learnt of his approach, he raised the siege, was pursued and routed. Some 2,000 of the fugitives were rallied by a chief called Drappes and Lucterius, Vercingetorix's old ally, and marched south to plunder the Province. While Fabius set out after a body of Carnutes, which had assisted Dumnacus, Caninius followed the fugitives, who sought refuge in Uxellodunum (Puy d'Issolu).[3]

The town of Uxellodunum stood on a plateau of some 200 acres, which crowned the summit of a rocky hill with precipitous sides that rose 600 feet above a plain bordering the northern bank of the Dordogne. Its eastern flank fell sharply to the plain and its western as sharply to a small affluent of the Dordogne – the Tourmente – which flowed through a narrow valley, and beyond it lay hilly country. North of Uxellodunum rose a smaller hill, now known as the Pech Demont.

On his arrival, Caninius built three camps, one on the Pech Demont and two on the hills west of the Tourmente. Next, he set his two legions to work to construct a line of contravallation.

When Lucterius gauged his intention, to avoid the fate of Alesia he set out with Drappes to collect supplies before the town was enclosed,

[1] Surely, Hirtius should have written 'Caesar's name'.

[2] *Ibid.*, VIII, 25.

[3] See Holmes, *The Roman Republic*, vol. II, pp. 291–2, and *Caesar's Conquest of Gaul*, pp. 483–93.

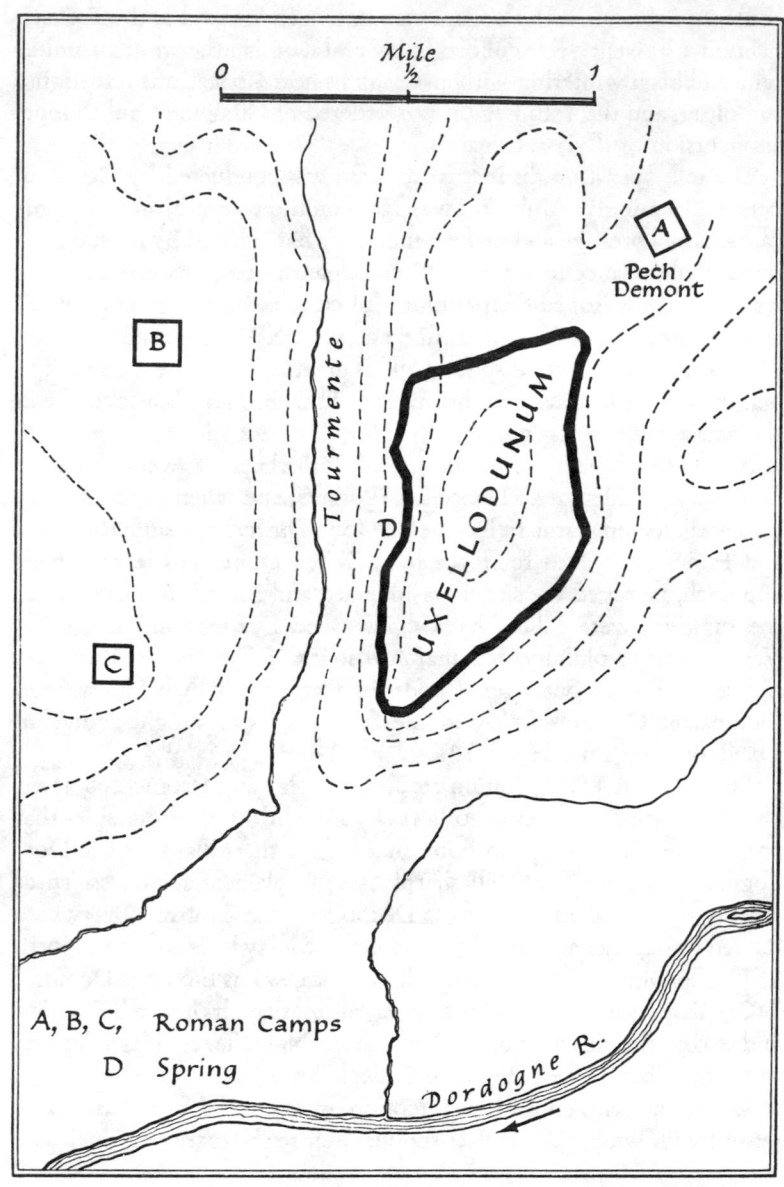

7. Siege of Uxellodunum

while its garrison raided the Roman working parties  When they had collected a great quantity of grain, they massed it in a camp 10 miles from the town, and while Drappes took charge of the camp, by night Lucterius convoyed the corn in consignments to Uxellodunum. How many trips he made is not stated; but as later we are informed that the town was well supplied, it was probably several. On one of them, the noise it occasioned led Caninius to suspect what was afoot, and just before dawn he surprised a convoy. Lucterius with a few followers escaped capture, but did not return to Uxellodunum.[1] Next, from the prisoners taken, Caninius learnt of the whereabouts of Drappes; he surprised his camp and captured him.[2] Who was then left in command of Uxellodunum is not recorded.

The day after this twofold success, Caninius was reinforced by Fabius. Meanwhile Caesar, who had been visiting the various states on a mission of conciliation, had moved to Cenabum to avenge the massacre of the corn-brokers that had detonated the great revolt. He demanded the surrender of Cotuatus, the chief culprit, and the townsmen eager to win his forgiveness hunted him down. He was flogged until he was insensible and then beheaded. When at Cenabum Caesar received despatches from Caninius. Anxious to bring the siege to a speedy end, lest it might encourage the outbreak of similar incidents, he proceeded to Uxellodunum with the cavalry and ordered Quintus Calenus to follow him with the legions.

When he reached Uxellodunum he at once saw that the problem was neither to storm it nor to starve out its garrison. Instead, it was to cut the town off from its water-supply. There were two sources, the Tourmente stream and a spring close under the centre of the western edge of the plateau. To deprive the garrison of the first offered little difficulty; all that was necessary was to block the approaches to it with archers, slingers and catapults; this was done. The second was more difficult, and the solution Caesar adopted was to besiege the spring instead of the town. He pushed forward his mantlets, and under their cover built a ramp which led up to it, and at the same time he ordered a tunnel to be driven from nearby the ramp to the source of the spring. When the ramp had been built, he had a ten-storied tower erected on it; it must have been at least 60 feet high, and its purpose was to gain command of the spring by mounting catapults on it.

[1] Soon after the siege Lucterius was betrayed to Caesar, and what his fate was can only be guessed.
[2] Drappes wisely committed suicide by starving himself to death.

To meet this threat, the townsfolk rolled down against the ramp barrels filled with blazing grease and pitch, and when the tower caught fire they attacked 'with the utmost ferocity' in order to prevent the conflagration from being extinguished. Caesar then ordered a series of feint attacks from various quarters to be made, so as to draw the Gauls away from the spring and facilitate the fire being quenched. Actually this was unnecessary, for meanwhile the tunnel had reached the underground source of the spring, and all the sappers had to do was to divert its water, presumably, down the tunnel, which made it impossible for the garrison to obtain water on the surface. The town then surrendered.

To put a stop to any further designs of this kind, Caesar decided to inflict an exemplary punishment. While he granted the garrison – some 2,000 in all – their lives, 'he cut off the hands of all who had borne arms, to testify the more openly the penalty of evildoers.'[1] This atrocity brought the conquest of Gaul to its end.

After this inhuman act, he spent the remainder of the summer in visiting the tribes of Aquitania, and then despatched his legions to their winter quarters: four to the lands of the Belgae; two to the country of the Aedui; two among the Turoni (about Tours); and two to the country of the Lemovices (Limousin). This done, he established his winter headquarters at Nemetocenna (Arras).

During the winter, Hirtius writes:

'Caesar had one definite purpose in view – to keep the states friendly, and to give hope or occasion of armed action to none. There was nothing, in fact, which he desired less than to have the definite necessity of a campaign imposed on him on the eve of his quitting his province, for fear that, when he was about to lead his army south, he might leave behind a war which all Gaul could readily take up without immediate danger. Accordingly, by addressing the states in terms of honour, by bestowing ample presents upon the chiefs, by imposing no new burdens, he easily kept Gaul at peace after the exhaustion of so many defeats, under improved conditions of obedience.'[2]

Of defeats, certainly there had been an abundance. Plutarch records that, in less than ten years, Caesar 'had taken by storm above eight hundred towns, subdued three hundred states, and of the three millions of men, who made up the gross sum of those with whom at several times he engaged, he had killed one million and taken captive a

---

[1] B.G., VIII, 44.    [2] Ibid., VIII, 49.

second.'[1] Whatever this may be worth, the fact remains that by now Gaul was so devastated and her tribes so decimated that for years to come they were incapable of waging war against the Romans. Therefore, in spite of his barbarities, it must be acknowledged that Caesar gained his end – the conquest and pacification of Gaul. Yet, had he heeded a maxim to be found in a book obtainable in his day, might not he have accomplished all he did more speedily, at lesser cost, and at greater advantage? The maxim reads:

'But he who acts in a harsh and savage manner, immediately after becoming master of a city ... makes other cities hostile, so that the war becomes laborious for him and victory difficult to attain. ... For nothing makes men so brave as the fear of what ill they will suffer if they surrender.'[2]

[1] *Caesar*, XV, 3. According to Velleius Paterculus (II, xlvii, 1) in Gaul Caesar slew 'more than 400,000 of the enemy'.

[2] Aeneas Tacticus, XXXVIII, 1–5. Themistocles (Herodotus, VIII, 109) and Jason of Pherae (Xenophon, *Hellenics*, VI, iv, 23) said much the same.

# VII

## Prelude to the Civil War

### I. THE CONFERENCE AT LUCA, 56 B.C.

ALTHOUGH the conquest of Gaul was the greatest of Caesar's achievements, at the time it was little other than a stepping-stone in his struggle for power, and, as we have seen, that was why at the close of each campaigning season he wintered in Cisalpine Gaul. There he could regain touch with political events, and during the two years which followed his departure from Rome conditions in Italy had progressively worsened. Pompey and Crassus had renewed their quarrel, and because the former had no troops to overawe the rabble, law and order were at a discount. Pompey's one aim was to obtain them, not to enforce his authority, but to render himself independent of his colleagues, and because the Senate was equally determined to deny them to him, real power passed into the hands of the armed bands raised by the antagonistic demagogues Publius Clodius and Titus Annius Milo[1] – the 'Blues' and the 'Greens' of the Forum. The first was the creature of Caesar and the second of Pompey.

In order to arrest the activities of Clodius, Lentulus Spinther, a devoted friend of Cicero and one of the consuls elected in 58 B.C., supported by Milo and Publius Sestius, who had been elected tribunes, advocated Cicero's recall. And no sooner had Lentulus entered office than, with Pompey's approval, he brought the question before the Senate. Finally, on August 4, 57 B.C., a bill sanctioning Cicero's return was passed in the Assembly, the voters being protected by Milo and his band from Clodius and his ruffians. Exactly a month later Cicero was back in Rome.

On the day of his arrival the price of corn suddenly rose, and two days later Cicero carried a motion that Pompey should be invited to control it. To Atticus he wrote: 'The consuls drew up a law by which complete control over the corn-supply for five years throughout the

---

[1] He assumed the name of Milo in honour of the athlete Milo of Crotona.

whole world was given to Pompey. A second law is drawn up ... granting him power over all money, and adding a fleet and an army, and an *imperium* in the provinces superior to that of their governors.'[1] It was tabled by the tribune Gaius Messius, and though rejected was a significant straw in the political wind.

From then on rioting became more and more violent, and in February, 56 B.C., in his attempt to dispose of Milo, Clodius suborned one of his followers to bring an action for riot against Sestius, who called upon Cicero to defend him. Willingly he did so, and when Vatinius, author of the Vatinian Law of 59 B.C., gave evidence against Sestius, Cicero smothered him with his invective, and, as he told his brother Quintus, 'made mincemeat' of him.[2]

Sestius' acquittal so completely turned Cicero's head that he contemplated the dissolution of the Triumvirate by widening the breach between Pompey and Caesar. In April he moved that the question of Caesar's Campanian land law should be referred to a full Senate.[3] Although this would not affect Pompey, because his veterans had already been provided for, should the law be repealed it would preclude Caesar from using the remaining land for his own veterans. In addition to Cicero's onset on Caesar, Lucius Domitius Ahenobarbus – Cato's brother-in-law – who had opposed Caesar in 59 and 58 B.C., and was standing for the consulship of 55, announced that, should he be returned, he would deprive Caesar of his armies.[4] There can be little doubt that Cicero expected Pompey to favour his proposal, but without an army to back him, he was too wary to do so. At the time Caesar was at Ravenna, and in haste Crassus posted to him and informed him of what Cicero had done.

Caesar at once decided to stop the rot; the Triumvirate would have to be reconstructed. He set out for Luca, the southernmost town of Cisalpine Gaul, and sent a message to Pompey to meet him and Crassus there.

The meeting attracted a vast number of notables, and so many were present that, at one time, 120 lictors were to be seen around Caesar.

[1] Cicero, *Letters to Atticus*, IV, i. Subsequently referred to as *Ad. Att.*

[2] Cicero, *Letters to Quintus*, II, iv, i.

[3] In a letter to Lentulus, dated December, 54 B.C., Cicero writes: 'Could I have more uncompromisingly invaded the very stronghold of the triumvirs' party, or more completely forgotten the days of my trouble and recalled the days of my power?' (*Letters to his Friends*, I, ix, 8. Subsequently referred to as *Ad. Fam.*)

[4] Suetonius, *Div. Iul.*, XXIV.

Also 200 senators attended, 'some returning thanks for what they had received, others asking for money or seeking some other advantage'. Therefore 'all things were now possible to Caesar by reason of his large army, his great riches, and his readiness to oblige everybody'.[1]

The Triumvirs met in secret; they agreed that Pompey and Crassus should hold consulships in 55 B.C., and at the conclusion of their term of office receive important proconsular provinces: Pompey was to be assigned the two Spains with an army, and Crassus Syria, also with an army, each for a term of five years. In exchange, Pompey and Crassus agreed to procure the enactment of a law which would prolong Caesar's governorships for a second period of five years. Also, Holmes suggests, 'there is reason to believe that Caesar stipulated that the question of appointing his successor should not be raised before the 1st of March, 704 (50 B.C.), and that he should be enabled to pass direct from his province to a second consulship'.[2]

After the meeting Pompey invited Cicero through his brother Quintus[3] to cease his attacks on Caesar and withdraw his motion on the Campanian land. Awake now to the danger his vanity had placed him in, not only did he comply, but to blazon his recantation he persuaded the Senate to decree a thanksgiving service in honour of Caesar's victories, and in his speech *On the Consular Provinces* he delivered a panegyric on Caesar's achievements. In April, or May, he wrote to Atticus: 'I was a bit ashamed of my palinode ... and at last have come to my senses. ... Since those who have no influence refuse me their affection, I may as well try to win that of those who have some influence. You will say you wish I had before. I know you wished it, and I was a downright ass.'[4]

Although the new compact armed Caesar's partners in the event of a clash between him and either of them, he adhered to his principle of first things first. He knew that their mutual antagonism would never permit them to unite their forces against him, and that he himself could always link up with Crassus should Pompey make a bid for supremacy.

[1] Appian, *The Civil Wars*, II, 17.

[2] *The Roman Republic*, vol. II, pp. 74 and 301–2. See also *A History of the Roman World from 146 to 30 B.C.*, Frank Burr Marsh (2nd edit., 1957), Appendix 7, and *Ad. Fam.*, VIII, 8, 9.

[3] *Ad. Fam.*, I, ix, 9.

[4] *Add. Att.*, IV, v. Thirteen years later in his *Philippics* against Antony he committed a similar folly, but with less happy results, as it led to his name being added to Octavian's proscription and to his death on December 7, 43 B.C.

The sole danger was that, before the five years were up, one of them might die.

## 2. THE DEATH OF CRASSUS

When, after the conference at Luca, Pompey and Crassus became aware that their candidature for consulship of 55 would be opposed, they bought over the tribune Gaius Cato, hitherto one of Pompey's bitterest enemies, to stop the elections by his veto, and the year passed by without any being held. Accordingly, on January 1, 55 B.C., an *interrex* was appointed, and, except for Pompey and Crassus, the sole candidate to come forward was Domitius Ahenobarbus. As they were now supported by a party of soldiers, under Crassus' son Publius, whom Caesar had sent to Rome, nominally as voters but actually to overawe opposition, on the morning of the elections Domitius and his supporters were attacked and routed, and Pompey and Crassus returned. Then, by bribery and violence, they secured most of the magistracies for their friends, and put up one of the tribunes, Gaius Trebonius, to give effect to the secret compact concerning the consular provinces. This he did, and after rioting and bloodshed his bill was passed. When they had gained what they wanted for themselves, they carried a bill which prolonged Caesar's tenure of his provinces for five years.

Notwithstanding their extensive powers, the triumvirs were unable to stifle opposition, and the consuls elected for 54 were Domitius Ahenobarbus and Appius Claudius; the one an implacable enemy of Caesar and the other no friend of Pompey. But due to corruption, intrigue, and violence they were impotent.

On the termination of his consulship, Pompey sent legates to govern his Spanish provinces and command the seven legions stationed in them, while he himself remained in Italy to superintend the corn-supply. This enabled him to recruit troops, ostensibly for service in Spain but actually to overawe the Senate. His aim was to paralyse government and persuade the Senate to call upon him as dictator.[1] This became apparent in the consular elections held in July, 54 B.C., in which there were four candidates, Gaius Memmius, Valerius Messalla, Domitius Calvinus, and Aemilius Scaurus; Memmius and Messalla were backed by Caesar, and Scaurus by Pompey. The enormous sums paid to the electors provoked violent debates in the Senate, and led to repeated postponement of the elections. To add to the confusion, in September the death of Pompey's

[1] Appian, *Civil Wars*, II, 19.

wife Julia broke the family link between him and Caesar.[1] From then on the chaos in Rome is vividly depicted by Cicero in his letters to his brother Quintus:

October 11: 'All who are candidates for the consulship have been indicted for bribery.'

October 21: 'One date after another for holding the elections is being daily cancelled by the announcement of adverse omens.'

October 24: 'Alarming rumour ... of a dictatorship. ... But you can see that there is really no Republic in existence, no Senate, no law-courts, no position of authority held by any one of us.'

Early in November: 'All business has been postponed, and the elections so long deferred that there must be an interregnum.'

December: 'For anything more corrupt than the men and the times of today cannot be conceived.'

At length, in July, 53 B.C., exactly twelve months after the date upon which the elections should have been held, Domitius Calvinus and Messalla were elected consuls for what remained of the year.

Meanwhile, in November, 54 B.C., Crassus had left Rome for Syria. His intention was to provoke a war with Parthia, emulate Alexander the Great, and gain fame and popular applause which would put him on a level with Pompey and Caesar. 'Now being altogether exalted and out of his senses,' writes Plutarch, 'he would not consider Syria nor even Parthia as the boundaries of his success, but thought to make the campaign of Lucullus against Tigranes and those of Pompey against Mithridates seem child's play, and flew on the wings of his hopes as far as Bactria and India and the Outer Sea.'[2] Early in 53 B.C., he arrived in Syria, and there was joined by his son and 1,000 Gallic cavalry sent to him by Caesar.

Though his eventual defeat at Carrhae (Harran) alone directly concerns Caesar, it is of some interest briefly to describe his campaign, as it is an outstanding example of the weakness of the Roman tactical organization when confronted by a highly trained mounted enemy, a foe Caesar never encountered, but might well have had he not been assassinated.

The army Crassus was to meet was commanded by Surenas, a young

[1] Some time in 53 B.C., Caesar offered to renew the family alliance by divorcing his wife Calpurnia and marrying Pompey's daughter should Pompey agree to marry Octavia, a grand-daughter of Caesar's sister Julia. Pompey declined to do so.

[2] Plutarch, *Crassus*, XVI, 2.

man of under thirty, less than half Crassus' age. He was a leader of imagination, and of him Sir William Tarn writes: 'he feared nothing and had an idea, a dangerous combination.' The idea, which 'does not seem to have occurred to anyone before,' was 'that archers were useless without arrows.'[1] To meet their demand he attached to his army, which consisted of 10,000 professional horse-archers, a corps of 1,000 camels laden with a huge reserve of arrows, and to it he added a division of 1,000 mailed lancers. Thus his army combined the two tactical essentials – projectile power and shock.[2]

When·he had marshalled his army, apparently in order to establish an advanced base, Crassus invaded Western Mesopotamia, occupied and garrisoned the towns along the western bank of the river Belik (Qarainuch), an affluent of the Euphrates, and then withdrew his army into winter-quarters. Soon after, Surenas occupied the eastern bank between Carrhae and Ichnae, which lay a few miles north of Nicephorium (Rakka), with a line of observation, and kept the bulk of his army out of sight. In the spring of 53 B.C., Crassus set out from Syria to occupy Seleuceia, close by Ctesiphon, on the Tigris. Besides his garrison troops, his field army comprised 28,000 infantry, 4,000 light-armed, and 4,000 cavalry. He crossed the Euphrates below Zeugma (Birejik), came to the desert track before the Belik, and, on May 6, reached that river between Carrhae and Ichnae. As no enemy had been sighted, his staff advised him to form camp; but his one concern was that his enemy might escape him, so he pushed on southward toward Ichnae. Soon after, when his scouts reported that the Parthians were advancing upon them, he ordered his army to form square, and sent forward his son, Publius, with eight cohorts, 1,300 cavalry and 400 light-armed, to check them. A charge of Surenas' mailed lancers scattered Publius' light-armed; then the lancers withdrew behind the horse-archers, who advanced and smothered the cohorts with their arrows. To gain time for his father to complete the square, Publius, at the head of his cavalry, charged the horse-archers, who took to their heels and drew him on, then wheeled round, ringed him in, and annihilated him and his men.

The square was next attacked, and despite the heavy losses it sustained from the showers of arrows poured upon it, it held its ground until nightfall, when Crassus abandoned his wounded and withdrew his now demoralized men to the fortress of Carrhae. But, as it was not

[1] *C.A.H.*, vol. IX, pp. 606–7.
[2] For Parthian tactics see Dio, XL, 15, 2–5.

provisioned, he decided on a night withdrawal to Sinnaca (Vodena) at the foot of the Armenian mountains, where the remnants of his army would be safe. Unfortunately for him he was misled by his guide and again surrounded; nevertheless, he struggled on, and when Surenas saw that he might escape him, he rode forward and proposed terms of honourable surrender. Crassus rightly suspected that it was a trick to capture him; but by now his men had lost all discipline, and when they threatened to take his life he rode forward with some of his officers to parley. They were at once seized and butchered.

Thus ended the worst defeat Roman arms had suffered since Cannae. Of Crassus' 44,000 men, including his garrisons, some 10,000 ultimately reached Syria, another 10,000 were made prisoners, and the rest perished.

Carrhae virtually spelt the end of the Triumvirate. It upset the balance between Caesar and Pompey, and meant that from now on they would drift apart. But for the time being it was apparent to the latter that he could not resist Caesar without the support of the Senate, and the first step he took toward gaining it was to marry Cornelia, the widow of Publius Crassus and the daughter of Caecilus Metellus Scipio, an alliance which brought him close to the aristocratic party in the Senate.

### 3. POMPEY'S THIRD CONSULSHIP

The belated elections of July, 53 B.C., in which Calvinus and Messalla were returned for the remainder of the year, were followed by a prolonged struggle over the choice of their successors. The candidates were Metellus Scipio, Pompey's father-in-law, and Plautius Hypsaeus, who had served under Pompey in the East, opposed by the formidable Milo who, by his costly games during his aedileship, had won the favour of the populace and now was overwhelmed with debt. Further to exacerbate the issue, Milo's deadly enemy Clodius was standing for the praetorship, and while Pompey supported Scipio and Hypsaeus, Cicero, in pursuit of his vendetta with Clodius, backed Milo. Unprecedented scenes of violence occurred: armed bands fought each other on the Sacred Way, the consul Calvinus was wounded in a riot, and Cicero narrowly escaped with his life. Due to bribery and violence the elections were repeatedly postponed throughout the remainder of the year. Then, on January 18, 52 B.C., an unexpected event decided the issue.

That day Milo and his band of ruffians, when proceeding down the Appian Way, collided head-on with Clodius and his band coming in the opposite direction. An affray resulted, in which Clodius was wounded and then killed. His body was conveyed to Rome and carried by an exasperated mob into the Senate House, where it was burnt on a funeral pile of senators' benches and chairs. The house itself and several adjacent buildings were burnt down. Pandemonium followed, and the situation grew so tense that the Senate passed the ultimate decree, elected an *interrex*, armed him, the tribunes, and Pompey with extraordinary powers to save the city,[1] and authorized Pompey to raise troops throughout Italy. But to avoid making him dictator, at Cato's suggestion, Bibulus carried a motion which appointed him sole consul. A series of trials next followed, and Milo was convicted of murder and exiled to Massilia (Marseilles).

While these events were agitating Rome, Caesar was engaged in bringing his conquest of Gaul to a victorious conclusion, and the nearer it was approached the more real became his political danger. Well aware that, as soon as he relinquished his command and reverted to private citizenship, he would be prosecuted for illegal acts committed by him during and since his first consulship, it was imperative for him to secure his election to a second consulship while still proconsul of Gaul, and to retain the command of his army until the time came to enter upon it.

This was one half of the question which was fated to precipitate yet another civil war. According to Asinius Pollio: 'When Caesar at the battle of Pharsalus saw his enemies slain or in flight, he said, word for word: "They would have it so. Even I, Gaius Caesar, after so many great deeds, should have been found guilty, if I had not turned to my army for help." '[2] And its complementary half is clearly defined by Cicero in his letter of August 2, 50 B.C., to M. Caelius Rufus: 'Cn. Pompeius,' he wrote, 'is determined not to allow C. Caesar to be elected consul, unless he has handed over his army and his provinces; Caesar on the other hand is convinced that there is no safety for him, if he once quits his army.'[3]

Because Caesar's aim involved a serious menace both to the Senate and Pompey, their aim was to find some means whereby Caesar might be superseded in Gaul before he assumed his second consulship.[4] As

---

[1] Dio, XL, 49, 5.      [2] Cited by Suetonius, *Div. Iul.*, XXX, 4.
[3] *Ad. Fam.*, VIII, xiv, 2.
[4] The wrangle between them revolved round the terminal date of Caesar's Gallic command, on which there is an extensive literature. Some scholars hold that Caesar could be succeeded in Gaul shortly after March 1, 50 B.C., and others

consul, should he have no soldiers at call, while Pompey, as proconsul of Spain, continued to head a considerable army, he could be compelled to toe the line. Obviously Caesar could not accept a second consulship on those terms; besides, he was morally bound to see that his soldiers, who had served him so devotedly, received the rewards he had promised them: he had no intention to repeat Pompey's error of 62 B.C. In brief, not only his own future but also that of his legionaries compelled him to insist on holding his second consulship on his own terms, cost what they might.

At the time, Pompey's reconciliation with the Senate was still too recent and uncertain to permit of him brusquely breaking with Caesar, and, under pressure of Caesar's partisans, he set out to mollify him; or, as Holmes suggests, honour a secret pledge he had given him at Luca.[1] He authorized a bill which granted Caesar the privilege to stand for the consulship *in absentia*, and because it was passed by the whole college of tribunes, it was known as the Law of the Ten Tribunes. Actually, it was no great surrender, and would be of little value to Caesar should he be superseded before he took over his consulship. Next, because his term in Spain and Caesar's in Gaul would expire at about the same time, in order to strengthen his position Pompey persuaded the Senate to prolong his proconsulship of Spain.[2] That secured, he brought his sole consulship to an end, by taking as his colleague his father-in-law Metellus Scipio.

Although Pompey's prolongation of command upset the parity arranged at Luca, Caesar had no desire to prolong his own, except in so far as it would cover him until after the elections of 49 B.C., when he intended to be a candidate *in absentia*, and to secure this prolongation he needed Pompey's support. But Pompey, who was ever ready to procrastinate, was neither willing to give nor to refuse it. Further, both he and Caesar were aware that not only the bulk of the people but also many members of the Senate dreaded civil war as the worst of all possible evils, and were ready to accept any compromise to avoid one. This meant that the one who appeared responsible for its outbreak would lose the support of public opinion; therefore both endeavoured

---

that he was safe until at least January, 49 B.C. (See *The Journal of Roman Studies*, vol. XXIX, 1939, 'Consular Provinces under the Late Republic', J. P. V. D. Balsdon; and *American Journal of Philology*, vol. LIX, 1938, 'The Terminal Date of Caesar's Command', C. E. Stevens.)

[1] *The Roman Republic*, vol. II, p. 236. See *supra*, p. 168.

[2] Dio (XL, 56, 2) says for five years, and Plutarch (*Pompey*, LV, 7) says four.

to throw the odium of a resort to arms on the other, and thereby morally justify himself.

## 4. THE FINAL CRISIS

The stage was now set for the last round, and it was opened by the election of Marcus Claudius Marcellus and Servius Sulpicius Rufus as consuls for 51 B.C. The former was a bitter opponent of Caesar, and when Caesar asked the Senate to grant him a brief extension of his command in Gaul, he forbade it, and proposed that successors be sent 'to take command of Caesar's provinces before his time had expired'. Although Pompey objected to this, 'he made it plain that Caesar's command must come to an end immediately on its expiration. For this reason the bitterest enemies of Caesar were chosen consuls for the ensuing year'[1] – for 50 B.C. They were Lucius Aemilius Paullus and Gaius Claudius Marcellus, a first cousin of Marcus Marcellus; and among the tribunes elected – most of whom were Caesar's partisans – was an ardent supporter of Pompey and a bitter enemy of Caesar – Gaius Scribonius Curio. He was a young noble of keen intellect and audacity, popular with the masses, upon whom he lavished his money and was now deep in debt.

To meet this new combination and prepare for the rapidly approaching show-down, Caesar set out to purchase the support of everyone who could serve him, even of slaves who might influence their masters, with the enormous wealth he had acquired in Gaul. Among them was the consul Aemilius Paullus, whose neutrality he bought for 1,500 talents (£360,000), and more important, Curio, for whose active support he paid an even larger sum.[2] The price was high, but the money could not have been more profitably invested, because without Curio's proficiency in political intrigue, it would have been almost impossible for Caesar to have cornered his enemies without being the first to resort to arms, which of all things he wished to avoid.

So that his change of sides might not be detected, when Gaius Marcellus proposed to send successors to take over Caesar's provinces on the expiration of his term of office, Curio praised the motion, 'but added that Pompey ought to resign his provinces and army just like Caesar, for in that way the commonwealth would be made free and be relieved from fear in all directions.' When this was opposed, he came

---

[1] Appian, *Civil Wars*, II, 26. See also Dio, XL, 58 and 59.

[2] *Ibid.* See also Holmes (*The Roman Republic*, vol. II, p. 321) who treats these figures with caution.

out more openly against appointing successors to Caesar unless Pompey also should lay down his command, because 'there could be no lasting peace in the commonwealth unless both were reduced to the status of private citizens.' He said this, because he knew that Pompey would not surrender his command. In this he was not mistaken, and when Pompey addressed the Senate and promised to lay down his command *after* Caesar had laid down his, Curio replied that 'promises were not sufficient,' and moved that, 'unless they both obeyed, both should be voted public enemies and military forces be levied against them. In this way he concealed the fact that he had been bought by Caesar.'[1]

Because the Senate persisted in adhering to the resolution that Pompey should not be deprived of his command until Caesar had laid his own down, Curio resorted to the veto, and the sole decree voted before the session ended was, because of the defeat suffered by Crassus, that Pompey and Caesar should each send a legion to Syria. Pompey nominated the one he had loaned to Caesar after the Aduatuca disaster in 54 B.C. Caesar complied with this, and on his own account sent the newly raised 15th Legion. When they arrived in Italy they were quartered at Capua, and remained there until the outbreak the of Civil War. Therefore, the object of the decree was not to strengthen Syria but Pompey at Caesar's expense.

Nevertheless, it proved to be a boomerang, because it enabled Caesar to resort to the ruse of the Trojan Horse. Before the two legions set out, he awarded each soldier 250 drachmas, and placed in command of them leaders whom he had instructed on their arrival in Italy to spread reports derogatory to himself and his men. This they did: 'They said that Caesar's army was wasted by protracted service, that the soldiers longed for their homes and would change to the side of Pompey as soon as they should cross the Alps.'[2] According to Appian, Pompey believed these reports, and instead of accelerating his recruiting relied on diplomatic action to see him through. Plutarch's version corroborates this: 'When some were saying that if Caesar should march against the city,' he writes, 'they could not see what forces there were to resist him, he [Pompey] replied with a smile, bidding them be in no concern, "for," said he, "whenever I stamp with my foot in any part of Italy there will rise up forces enough in an instant, both horse and foot." '[3]

---

[1] Appian, *Civil Wars*, II, 27–28. For additional detail see Caelius' letters to Cicero, *Ad. Fam.*, VIII, vi–xiv.     [2] Appian, *Civil Wars*, II, 30.

[3] *Pompey*, LVII, 5. Holmes (*The Roman Republic*, vol. III, p. 2) suggests that Pompey was too thorough a soldier to believe these rumours; nevertheless, he

Early in September Caesar left Labienus with the 13th Legion in Cisalpine Gaul and returned to Nemetocenna (Arras). There he reviewed his army, and then quartered four legions, under Gaius Fabius, at Matisco (Mâcon); four, under Trebonius, among the Belgae, and a recently recruited legion of Gauls, the *Alaudae* ('Larks'), probably in the Province. He then left for Ravenna, where he arrived early in December.

On December 1 Gaius Marcellus brought two motions before the Senate: the one was – 'Shall successors be sent to Caesar?' and the other – 'Shall Pompey be deprived of his command?' When the majority voted against the latter, it was decided that successors to Caesar should be sent. Thereupon Curio moved that, in order to avoid civil discord, 'both should lay down their commands.' It was carried by 370 votes to 22; thereupon, in a rage, Marcellus dismissed the Senate and exclaimed: 'Enjoy your victory and have Caesar for master!'[1]

A few days later a rumour was current in Rome that Caesar had crossed the Alps and was marching on the city. Forthwith Marcellus assembled the Senate, moved that Caesar be proclaimed a public enemy, and that the two legions at Capua be sent against him. Curio insisted that the rumour was false – which it was – and vetoed the motion. Marcellus then proposed a vote of censure against Curio,[2] and, when it was rejected, he rushed from the Senate to Pompey's house outside the city, presented a sword to him, and called upon him to lead the two legions at Capua against Caesar; also he authorized him to raise additional levies. Pompey accepted the commission, but at once put it into cold-storage by exclaiming: 'Unless we can do better.'

Because, as a tribune, Curio had no power beyond the city walls, and because his term of office was about to expire (on December 10), when his inviolability would cease, he hastily left Rome for Ravenna, where Caesar had concentrated the 13th Legion, about 5,000 infantry and 300 cavalry, and had summoned from Gaul the 8th and 12th.

When he arrived, he urged Caesar to assemble his whole army and march on Rome. But Caesar, still anxious not to be the first to provoke war, decided on yet another effort to come to terms with his opponents. He sent a messenger to his supporters in Rome to propose on his behalf that, should he be allowed to retain two legions and his provinces of

---

thought it expedient to broadcast them in order to reassure his hearers. If so, it was an unsoldierlike thing to do, because they would put a damper on recruiting, and should they be proved false, might lead to panic.

1 Appian, *Civil Wars*, II, 30.   2 Dio, XL, 64, 1.

Cisalpine Gaul and Illyricum until he entered upon his consulship, he was willing to surrender Gaul and the legions stationed there. Although Pompey was agreeable, the consuls rejected the proposal, and when Caesar learnt of it, he despatched Curio with yet another message – virtually an ultimatum. According to Appian, 'The letter embraced a calm recital of all Caesar had done from the beginning of his career and a proposal that he would lay down his command at the same time as Pompey, but that if Pompey should retain his command he would not lay down his own, but would come quickly and avenge his country's wrongs and his own.'[1]

Curio set out, travelled at top speed and reached Rome on the night of December 31. The next day he delivered Caesar's letter to the newly elected consuls, Lucius Cornelius Lentulus and Gaius Claudius Marcellus, brother of Marcus Marcellus, who declined to bring it before the Senate. Caesar, however, was prepared to meet their obstruction, for when, on December 10, Curio's term as tribune expired, he had replaced him by two others, Mark Antony and Quintus Cassius, and they vehemently insisted that the letter should be read before the Senate. This the consuls refused to do, because they were afraid that those senators who were inclined toward peace would vote in its favour. Therefore, instead of permitting a vote on Caesar's offer, they raised a debate on the general political situation. Lentulus spoke first, and said: if the senators supported him, he would adopt strong measures; if not, he would consider his own interests. ' "I too," said he, "can shelter myself under the favour and friendship of Caesar," ' and Scipio expressed himself in similar terms.[2]

On the following day, intimidated by Lentulus, the senators adopted Scipio's resolution 'that Caesar should disband his army before a fixed date [March 1] and that, if he failed to do so, he should be considered to be meditating treason against the republic.'[3] The resolution was passed, and at once vetoed by Antony and Cassius.

Because the 3rd and 4th of January were days on which the Senate could not legally meet, the debate was renewed on the 5th, when Caesar's father-in-law, Lucius Calpurnius Piso, and Lucius Roscius, one of the praetors, pleaded it was only right that Caesar should be informed of how his proposal had been received, and they volunteered to go to Ravenna and inform him. This was rejected, and, on the 7th, the consuls

---

[1] Appian, *Civil Wars*, II, 32. See also Dio, XLI, 1, 3-4.

[2] *Caesar – The Civil Wars* (Loeb Classical Library, 1957), I, 1. Subsequently referred to as *B.C.*                 [3] *Ibid.*, I, 2.

warned Antony and Cassius to quit the House if they wished to escape violence. Antony and Cassius protested, but as Pompey had stationed soldiers outside it, no course was left them but to comply. The ultimate decree was then passed, and 'the consuls, the praetors, the tribunes, and all the proconsulars' were empowered to 'take measures that the state incur no harm.'[1] Also a resolution was passed that Italy should be divided into recruiting districts, each under the supervision of a senator, and that Lucius Domitius Ahenobarbus should succeed Caesar in Gaul.

Disguised as slaves, Antony and Cassius, accompanied by Curio and Marcus Caelius Rufus, sped in a hired carriage to Ariminum (Rimini), and when a few hours later the news reached Ravenna, Caesar paraded his legionaries, 'whom he excited by saying that his soldiers, after all their great deeds, had been stigmatized as public enemies and that distinguished men like these [Antony and Cassius] who had dared to speak out for them, had been driven with ignominy from the city.'[2] His words were answered by a shout of anger and a declaration that his officers and men were ready 'to repel the wrongs of their commander and of the tribunes.'

After the ultimate decree was passed, the Senate expected Caesar would await the arrival of his legions from Gaul before he marched southward. But, as Appian says: 'As he was accustomed to rely upon the terror caused by the celerity and audacity of his movements, rather than on the magnitude of his preparations, he decided to take the aggressive in this great war with his 5,000 men and to anticipate the enemy by seizing the advantageous positions in Italy.'[3]

On the 10th, Caesar sent forward a party of picked men to occupy Ariminum, the first town in Italy, and toward evening he set out by carriage, escorted by his 300 cavalry. When his course brought him to the river Rubicon (Fiumincio) 12 miles north of Ariminum, which divided Cisalpine Gaul from Roman Italy, according to Appian, he halted and said to those present: 'My friends, stopping here will be the beginning of sorrow for me; crossing over will be such for all mankind.' He then exclaimed: 'Let the die be cast,'[4] crossed the river and entered Ariminum at daybreak January 11, 49 B.C.[5] The Civil War had begun.

[1] B.C., I, 5.          [2] Appian, Civil Wars, II, 33. See also B.C., I, 7.
[3] Appian, Civil Wars, II, 34.
[4] Ibid., II, 35. Suetonius' version is: 'Even yet we may draw back; but cross yon little bridge, and the whole issue is with the sword' (Div. Iul., XXXI).
[5] November 23, 50 B.C., of the Julian Calendar.

# VIII

## The Civil War in Italy

### I. THE STRATEGICAL SITUATION

THE theatre of war embraced the entire empire, and geographically was divided into three sub-theatres: Italy in the centre; Gaul and Spain on her western flank, and Illyricum, Greece, the greater part of Asia Minor and Syria on her eastern, to which, as an appendix, may be added the provinces of Cyrenaica and Africa. Of Rome's inhabitants, the aristocracy and landowners feared Caesar, while the city proletariate and the majority of the common people favoured or tolerated him.[1] Spain was Pompey's stronghold; Gaul, Caesar's recruiting ground, and in the East most of the client kings were loyal to the Senate-Pompey coalition.

At the outset of the war, besides the 13th Legion at Ravenna, Caesar had eight legions in Gaul,[2] of which the 8th and 12th were on the march to join him. In all, Pompey had ten:[3] seven in Spain and three in Italy: of the latter, his two veteran legions, the 1st and 15th, were at Capua, and the third was presumably composed of recently enrolled recruits. Besides these, he had at call scattered divisions of troops in the provinces of Syria, Asia, Africa, etc. In a long war his greatest strategical asset was his undisputed command of the sea. According to Plutarch, his fleet comprised 500 warships and a vast number of light galleys,[4] and, in March, 49 B.C., Cicero heard that the fleets of Alexandria, Colchis, Tyre, Sidon, Aradus, Cyprus, Pamphyllia, Lycia, Rhodes, Chios, Byzantium, Lesbos, Smyrna, Miletus, and Cos were 'being got ready

[1] On December 17, 50 B.C., Cicero wrote to Atticus: 'My fears as to the political situation are great. And so far I have found hardly a man who would not yield to Caesar's demand sooner than fight' (*Ad. Att.*, VII, 6).

[2] Omitting the *Alaudae*, apparently not yet organized (see *The Roman Legions*, H. M. D. Parker (1958), p. 57). The eight legions were the 6th, 7th, 8th, 9th, 10th, 11th, 12th and 14th.

[3] *B.C.*, I, 6.

[4] Plutarch, *Pompey*, LXIV, 1.

to cut off the supplies of Italy and to blockade the grain-producing provinces'.[1]

Although in fighting forces, both actual and potential, Caesar was inferior to Pompey, morally he was vastly superior to him. His conquest of Gaul had endowed him with enormous prestige; his singleness of command enabled him to come to rapid and unfettered decisions, and the devotion of his men imbued him with complete confidence in their loyalty.

Compared with him, Pompey was at a serious discount. He had last seen active service in 62 B.C., since when his prestige had slumped. And he was the servant of the Senate, and, therefore, lacked absolute command; added to this, he was encumbered by two indifferent consuls.[2] Shortly before the outbreak of war he told the Senate that Caesar's troops were disaffected and would not obey his orders; but no sooner did it break out than he doubted whether his two veteran legions could be trusted to fight against their old commander: lack of faith in his men was the missing linch-pin in his strategy. His sole moral asset was that Caesar's second in command, Labienus, had deserted to him, which was somewhat discounted when, on learning of his defection, Caesar contemptuously sent his personal baggage after him.[3] A laugh or two must have been raised in Rome when the pack-animals arrived.

Even more important than his moral superiority was Caesar's intellectual grasp of the nature of war. Two thousand years before Clausewitz, he had appreciated that war 'belongs to the province of social life', and that policy demands that 'at the commencement of every war its character shall be defined according to what the political conditions and relations lead us to anticipate as probable.'[4] From the outset he grasped that he was faced with a civil war and not a foreign war, and that each demanded a technique of its own. He saw that the type of war he had fought in Gaul was out of place in Italy. He realized that in a civil war it was as important to win the goodwill of the civil population as to impose his own will on his adversary, and more profitable to subvert his adversary's fighting forces than destroy them. When the first

---

[1] *Ad. Att.*, IX, 9.

[2] In *The Oxford Classical Dictionary* Lentulus is described by 'all authors, including Cicero . . . as lazy, luxurious and pretentious'; and of his colleague Cicero wrote: 'Only one man, C. Marcellus, have I known to be more timid, and he is sorry he was ever a consul' (*Ad. Att.*, X, 15).

[3] Plutarch, *Caesar*, XXXIV, 3.

[4] *On War* (English edit., 1908), vol. I, p. 6, and vol. III, p. 87.

was won, intelligence of his enemy's movements, security of his own communications, and ability to supply his legions would be vastly facilitated; and when the loyalty of his enemy's soldiers was undermined, not only would they desert their leaders but, in order to secure their eventual rewards – grants of land, donatives, etc. – they would throw in their lot with him. In brief, his two dominant aims were: to convince the people, the property owners, and the capitalists, that his cause was the more desirable one, and to convert his enemy's legions into a profitable recruiting ground.

This is not conjecture, because a letter has survived in which Caesar revealed the secret of his civil war technique. It was written early in March, 49 B.C., and was addressed to his agents Gaius Oppius and Lucius Cornelius Balbus. In it he wrote:

'Let us see if by moderation we can win all hearts and secure a lasting victory, since by cruelty others have been unable to escape from hatred and to maintain their victory for any length of time except L. Sulla, whose example I do not intend to follow. This is a new way of conquering, to strengthen one's position by kindness and generosity.'[1]

Whether Caesar was temperamentally cruel or not is beside the mark. The fact to note is, that he was master of his emotions and, in consequence, of his actions. Cruelty and moderation were but means toward gaining specific ends, and not ends in themselves. This was noted by Curio in a conversation with Cicero less than a month after the above letter was written. On April 14, 49 B.C., he said: 'Caesar himself was not by nature and inclination averse to cruelty, but he thought mild measures would win popularity. But, if he lost popular favour, he would be cruel.'[2]

In other words, he fitted his means to his end: he was neither a devil nor an angel, he was a craftsman.

The Senate had no policy other than the negative one of maintaining their authority, and such evidence as we have of Pompey's outlook and intentions is recorded by Cicero in two interviews with him immediately before the outbreak of war, the one on December 10 and the other on December 25, 50 B.C. Of the first, Cicero informed Atticus

---

[1] *Ad. Att.*, IX, 7c. When proconsul of Cilicia, Cicero also discovered this. In a letter to M. Cato, dated January, 50 B.C., he wrote: 'I found my strongest safeguard against the threat of a most serious war in my fair dealing and moderation. With these forces to aid me, I succeeded, where no legions could have enabled me to succeed, in converting the most disaffected allies into the most devoted' (*Ad. Fam.*, XV, iv, 14). [2] *Ad. Att.*, X, 4.

that 'He [Pompey] hinted at certain war, without hope of agreement,'[1] and of the second he wrote:

'Pompey thinks that the constitution will be subverted even if Caesar is elected consul without an army; and he fancies that when Caesar hears of the energetic preparations against him, he will give up the idea of the consulship this year, and prefer to keep his army and his province. Still, if Caesar should play the fool, Pompey has an utter contempt for him, and firm confidence in his own and the state's resources. ... In a word, he appeared not only not to seek peace but even to fear it. But I fancy the idea of leaving the city shakes his resolution.'[2]

That hints that, little more than a fortnight before war was unleashed, Pompey's intention was to abandon Rome. The reason for this may be surmised: he could not trust his two veteran legions to hold the capital. Should they desert to Caesar, the war would be lost at its inception; therefore, as events proved, his plan was to avoid battle, evacuate Italy, withdraw into Macedonia and, as Ronald Syme says, leave Caesar 'entrapped between the legions of Spain and the hosts of the East, and then to return, like Sulla, to victory and power.'[3] It was a grandiose scheme, but at the start it surrendered the initiative to Caesar, and because Caesar was not going to emulate Sulla, as we shall see, it was in the first two months of the war that the foundations of Pompey's ruin were laid.

## 2. THE CORFINIUM CAMPAIGN

When the news that Caesar had occupied Ariminum reached Rome, the Senate immediately assembled, and while Cato urged that Pompey be appointed commander-in-chief with absolute powers, Cicero proposed that envoys be sent to Caesar to treat for peace. Both suggestions were ignored; nevertheless, Lucius Caesar[4] and Lucius Roscius were despatched to Caesar to inform him of the decree which had deprived him of his province, and the latter carried with him a private message from Pompey, in which he asked Caesar not to reproach him for what

[1] *Ibid.*, VII, 4.

[2] *Ibid.*, VII, 8. Already on October 1, 50 B.C., when on the point of sailing from Epirus, in a letter to Atticus Cicero had mentioned that he had been told 'Pompey thinks of leaving Rome' (*Ad. Att.*, VI, viii).

[3] *The Roman Revolution*, p. 49.

[4] Son of Lucius Caesar, Caesar's legate in Gaul. In addition, Dio (XLI, 10, 4) points out: Spain was 'wholly devoted' to Pompey; therefore he could rely on its loyalty when he went to Greece.

he had done 'for the sake of the state', and begged him not to be 'so bitterly angry with his enemies as to injure the commonwealth in hope that he is injuring them'. It suggests that Pompey's aim was, either to come to a compact with Caesar, by which a diarchy, on the lines of the old triumvirate, might be established, or else to gain time to further his preparations. The envoys arrived at Ariminum on January 17, and Caesar's reply was:

'Let Pompeius go to his own provinces, let us disband our armies, let everyone in Italy lay down his arms, let fear be banished from the state . . . let Pompeius himself come nearer or allow me to approach him. In this way a conference will settle all disputes.'[1]

When the mission was on its way, Caesar advanced southward. First he seized Pisaurum (Pesaro), Fanum (Fano), and Ancona on the coastal road, and despatched Antony with five cohorts to occupy Arretium (Arezzo) on the Via Cassia – the direct road to Rome. Next, he sent Curio with three cohorts to Iguvium (Gubbio) on the Via Flaminia. On his approach the Pompeian garrison at once deserted to him, and when Caesar was informed of it and that the inhabitants had received Curio with 'the utmost goodwill', he ordered all detachments of the 13th Legion to rendezvous at Ancona, which they did by January 29.

When Caesar's advance became known in Rome, the city was thrown into an uproar: while 'those who dwelt outside the city came rushing in . . . those who dwelt in Rome were rushing out.'[2] Everyone, according to his fancy, was pressing and urging Pompey to adopt his own particular plan. At length, in order to put an end to the clamour, Pompey ordered Rome to be abandoned, and, on the 17th, he instructed the Senate and the consuls to follow him to Capua. At the same time he declared that all who failed to do so would be held to be enemies of the State. Of this decision Cicero wrote to Atticus:

On January 17: 'What, in heaven's name, do you think of his plan? I mean his desertion of Rome. I don't know what to make of it . . . nothing could be more ridiculous.'[3]

---

[1] B.C., I, 9. See also Ad. Fam., XVI, 12, 3.

[2] Plutarch, Pompey, LXI, 2.

[3] Ad. Att., VII, 11. Cicero was too emotional a witness to be consistent; nevertheless, he probably voiced the popular temper in Rome. On December 25, 50 B.C., Pompey had hinted to him that he intended to abandon Rome. On February 27, 49 B.C., Cicero wrote to Atticus: 'Pompey has not abandoned Rome because it was impossible to defend . . . but it was his idea from the first. . . . A sort of Sulla's reign has long been his object' (ibid., VIII, 11).

On January 21: 'As to your request for information on Pompey's policy, I don't think he knows himself; certainly none of us know. . . . Everywhere there is panic, and confusion. . . . No one knows whether he will make a stand anywhere or cross the sea. If he remains in Italy, I fear it is impossible for him to have a reliable army. . . . I imagine that Caesar, whom you fear may be a Phalaris, will stick at no abominations.'[1]

On January 22: 'Rome is delivered to him [Caesar] stripped of defenders, stocked with supplies: one may fear anything from a man who regards her temples and her homes . . . as his loot. . . . We depend entirely on two legions that were kept here by a trick, and are practically disloyal. For so far the levy has found unwilling recruits, afraid of war. . . . As for Tullia and Terentia [Cicero's daughter and wife] when I picture the approach of the barbarians on Rome, I am terrified.'[2]

These emotional outbursts are of significance when related to Caesar's policy of moderation. In Gaul his atrocities had earned for him the reputation of a ruthless general; now in Italy it was assumed that he would be equally ruthless, and memories of Sulla were awakened. Hence the terror and the panic, born of their anticipation, not only facilitated his advance, but, when he implemented his policy, it came as the anticlimax of all their expectations.

When they had received Caesar's reply, Lucius Caesar and Roscius set out on their return, and, on January 23, submitted it to Pompey and the consuls at Capua. According to Cicero, 'His conditions were accepted with the reservation that he should withdraw his garrisons from the towns he had occupied outside his own province,'[3] and Pompey refused to meet him. Caesar's version is more detailed;[4] but, obviously, it was out of the question to expect him to withdraw beyond the Rubicon while Pompey continued to raise his levies. Therefore Caesar rejected the terms, and, now that Antony and Curio had rejoined him at Ancona, he set out for Auximum (Osimo), garrisoned by three Pompeian cohorts, under Publius Attius Varus.

Caesar's objective was not Rome, as Cicero and others surmised; for since it had been abandoned, it had lost its military and political significance. Instead it was Corfinium (Pentima), held by Domitius Ahenobarbus with a large group of levies. It lay close by the direct road to Brundisium, Pompey's main port of escape, and Caesar had

---

[1] *Ibid.*, VII, 12. Phalaris, tyrant of Acragas, was notorious for his cruelty. He roasted his victims in a hollow brazen bull.

[2] *Ibid.*, VII, 13.     [3] *Ibid.*, VII, 14.     [4] *B.C.*. I, 11.

determined, if possible, to bring him to battle before he could cross the Adriatic.

When Varus became aware of Caesar's approach, he started to withdraw from Auximum; but no sooner had he done so than his men began to desert him; some returned to their homes and others joined Caesar, who next overran Picenum. Everywhere he was welcomed by the inhabitants, and all the prefectures of those parts received him gladly and furnished him with supplies.

Now that the 12th Legion was approaching, he pressed on to Asculum (Ascoli), held by Lentulus Spinther and ten cohorts. As he neared the town, the bulk of Lentulus' troops also deserted, and when with the remainder he was on the road to Corfinium, he was met by Vibullius Rufus, who had been sent by Pompey into Picenum to inquire into the loyalty of its inhabitants. Vibullius took command of Lentulus' followers; he gathered in the local levies, in all thirteen cohorts, and by forced marches he fell back on Corfinium, where Domitius had assembled twenty cohorts.

At Firmum (Fermo) Caesar halted for a day to forage, and then pressed on to Corfinium. As he neared it he surprised five cohorts Domitius had sent out to demolish the bridge over the Aternus (Pescara); secured it, and with his two legions – the 12th by now had joined him – and the Pompeian cohorts that had deserted to him, he crossed the river, and, on February 15, encamped outside the walls of Corfinium.

At the time, Pompey with his two veteran legions was at Luceria (Lucera), 130 miles to the south of Corfinium, and Domitius, who had been appointed to succeed Caesar in Gaul, as a proconsul was not under Pompey's authority. But, instead of going to Gaul, he had established himself at Corfinium, and had taken command of the levies which were being raised there. When he learnt from Vibullius that Caesar was advancing on him, on February 9 he decided to evacuate Corfinium,[1] then, a few hours later, he changed his mind, and determined to hold the town.

When, on February 11 or 12, Pompey learnt of this from Vibullius, he wrote to Domitius:

'With divided forces we cannot hope to cope with the enemy. . . . Wherefore, as you had arranged, according to Vibullius' letter, to start with your army from Corfinium on the 9th of February and to

[1] *Ad. Att.*, VIII, 11a.

come to me, I wonder what reason there has been for your change of plan. . . . Wherefore again and again I entreat and exhort you . . . to come to Luceria on the first possible day, before the forces which Caesar has begun to collect can concentrate and divide us.'[1]

Next, when on the 15th Caesar surprised him, Domitius sent an urgent message to Pompey to come to his rescue, otherwise 'he himself and more than thirty cohorts and a great number of senators and Roman knights will be imperilled.'[2]

This appeal was received by Pompey on the 16th. He replied to it at once, and after he had outlined the general situation he wrote:

'I beg you earnestly to come here on the first opportunity with all your forces . . . do not be disturbed if you hear of my retreat in face of Caesar's possible advance, for I consider that I must take every step to avoid being trapped. . . . Again and again I beg you to come to me as soon as possible. . . . Division means weakness . . . I cannot comply with your requests for assistance, because I do not put much trust in these legions.'[3]

Again, on the 17th, he wrote to Domitius in similar terms, and added: 'So do your best, if any tactics can extricate you even now, to join me as soon as possible before our enemy can concentrate all his forces.'[4] On the same day, or the next, he informed the consuls of his despatch to Domitius, and said: 'My fears have been realized, Domitius has been trapped and is not strong enough to pitch a camp [come into the field] because he has my nineteen and his own twelve cohorts scattered in three towns (for some he has stationed at Alba and some at Sulmo), and he is unable to free himself [cut his way out] even if he wished. . . . I am resolved to lead my present forces to Brundisium.'[5]

On February 15, when Caesar was encamping at Corfinium, news was brought to him that the inhabitants of Sulmo (Sulmona), seven miles distant, were eager to surrender to him, but were prevented by Domitius' garrison of seven cohorts. So he immediately sent Antony with five cohorts to their assistance. The outcome was the mutiny of the garrison, who delivered to Antony their commander, Attius the Pelignian. Antony then set out on his return, and when he got back to Corfinium the seven cohorts were embodied in Caesar's army and Attius freed.

[1] *Ibid.*, VIII, 12b.  [2] *B.C.*, I, 17.
[3] *Ad. Att.*, VIII, 12c.
[4] *Ibid.*, VIII, 12d.  [5] *Ibid.*, VIII, 12a.

On the 17th, the 8th Legion, accompanied by twenty-two cohorts of newly raised Gallic levies and some 300 Noric horse, joined Caesar, a reinforcement which enabled him to build a second camp and surround Corfinium.

Completely invested as Domitius now was, while he encouraged his men in the belief that Pompey was on his way to succour them, he secretly plotted his own escape and that of some of his friends. But his demeanour belied his words, and certain of his men grew suspicious, seized him, and sent envoys to Caesar to inform him that they were willing to surrender the town to him that night. Although Caesar recognized the importance of its immediate occupation, lest the mutineers be bribed to change their minds, to avoid the possibility of the town being plundered by his men 'under the licence of night', he ordered the envoys to return and instruct their comrades to keep the gates and walls carefully guarded. Then he drew a close line of outposts round the town to guard against sallies and to prevent individuals secretly escaping.

Toward dawn, February 21, Lentulus Spinther shouted from the town wall to one of Caesar's sentries that he wished to speak to Caesar. His request was granted, and when brought before him he pleaded for his life. When Caesar assured him that no injury would be done him, he asked to return to the town, so that his own safety might be proof to those within it of Caesar's clemency. He was allowed to do so, and at daybreak the garrison of Corfinium surrendered.

Among those brought before Caesar, all of whom he protected 'from the clamour and insolence of the troops', were fifty of the senatorial order, including Domitius, Vibullius, Lentulus, and Attius Varus, a large number of knights and many municipal councillors. He addressed them in a few words; complained that 'no gratitude had been shown him on their part for his signal acts of kindness', and then freed them unconditionally. The 6 million sesterces seized in the town he returned to Domitius, so that, as he writes, he himself might 'not be thought more self-controlled in dealing with men's lives than with their property, although there was no doubt that this money belonged to the state and had been assigned by Pompeius for military pay.'[1] Lastly, Domitius' soldiers were ordered to take the oath of allegiance to Caesar; the camps were then struck and the army set out by forced marches for Apulia.

Thus, within six weeks after crossing the Rubicon, the first phase of

[1] B.C., I, 23.

the conquest of Italy was accomplished without bloodshed: a trium-phant vindication of Caesar's policy, concisely summed up by Caelius Rufus who, on March 9, in a letter to Cicero wrote: '. . . did you ever read of anyone more vigorous in action than our Caesar, and more moderate in victory.'[1]

Cicero, who flattered himself on his 'imaginative insight', thought otherwise, and the day before Caelius wrote to him, he had written to Atticus: '. . . how can Caesar keep himself from a destructive policy? It is forbidden by his character, his previous career, the nature of his present enterprise, his associates.'[2] At one moment he predicted that Caesar would be a second Cinna,[3] at another that Pompey would be a second Sulla,[4] and that Atticus would see '. . . poor Italy trodden down next summer or in the hands of their slaves drawn from every quarter of the globe. . . . That is my prophecy.'[5] The truth is, his strategical insight was so imaginative that he failed to see that the only sound course open to Pompey was to evacuate Italy, and that, in consequence, the most profitable course Caesar could adopt was to pacify Italy before Pompey could return, or he himself could cross the Adriatic and challenge him in Greece. From now on Italy was to be Caesar's base of operations, and it was his policy rather than his legions which rendered and kept it loyal to him.

### 3. THE SIEGE OF BRUNDISIUM

Two days before Corfinium surrendered, Pompey quitted Luceria and set out for Brundisium, which he reached on February 25. There he mustered his forces, in all two veteran legions, thirty cohorts of levies,[6] and 800 horse raised from the slaves on his own estates. Transports had already been assembled, but sufficient only to convey half his forces at one time. Preparations were in hand to blockade Italy, and Domitius, in spite of Caesar's clemency, had collected seven ships at the Tuscan port of Cosa (Orbetello), manned by his slaves and retainers, ready to proceed to Massilia as proconsul of Gaul.

Meanwhile Caesar was pressing after Pompey in the hope of reach-ing Brundisium ahead of him and compelling him to accept battle. When, en route, Pompey's chief engineer, Numerius Magius, was cap-tured, Caesar at once freed him and sent him to Pompey with a request that they meet to consider proposals of peace.

[1] *Ad. Fam.*, VIII, 15.     [2] *Ad. Att.*, IX, 2a.
[3] *Ibid.*, VIII, 9.     [4] *Ibid.*, VIII, 11.
[5] *Ibid.*, VIII, 11.     [6] The equivalent of three legions.

On March 1, Cicero wrote to Atticus:

'... if Pompey has crossed the sea, we must look for war and massacre. Do you see the kind of man into whose hands the state has fallen? What foresight, what energy, what readiness! Upon my word, if he refrain from murder and rapine, he will be the darling of those who dreaded him most.'[1]

And again on March 4:

'The country towns are treating him as a god. . . . What ovations . . . what honour paid him! In fright I dare say, but they are more afraid of Pompey. They are delighted with the cunning kindness of Caesar, and afraid of the anger of his rival.'[2]

On March 9, Caesar arrived at Brundisium with six legions – three veteran and three of levies fully equipped – to find that the consuls with the greater part of the Pompeian army had already sailed, but that Pompey with twenty cohorts was still in the port. He immediately invested the town on its landward side, and because he had no fleet to blockade it, he decided to block the narrow entrance of the harbour with two moles, one on each side of it in the shallow water, and in the deeper mid-channel link the moles together by a chain of anchored rafts. The rafts were 30 feet square, and on each was erected a two-storied turret armed with catapults. To counter these, Pompey fitted out a number of large merchant ships, which carried three-storied turrets manned by archers and equipped with catapults.

When the rafts were being made, as no response had come from Magius' mission, Caesar again attempted to persuade Pompey to agree to an interview, but nothing came of it. The aim of these numerous attempts to meet him may have been that Caesar genuinely wished to come to terms with him, but that is unlikely. Also it may have been to gain time. Yet what would seem more probable is that, because Caesar was the aggressor, he wished to justify himself in the eyes of the people at large, and if so, when coupled with his policy of moderation, this is understandable. All along he must have realized that, as there was no longer a counterpoise between Pompey and himself, their argument would have to be settled by force of arms.

Before the entrance of the harbour was more than half blocked, Pompey's transports returned from Dyrrachium, and perturbed by the progress of the blockade, he decided on the earliest possible embarkation of the remainder of his army. To cover its withdrawal, he ordered the town gates to be strengthened, and the streets to be entrenched,

[1] *Ad. Att.*, VIII, 13.    [2] *Ibid.*, VIII, 16.

barricaded and blocked with obstacles, so as to assist the defenders in street fighting. He detailed a small force of light-armed troops to hold the walls and fight a delaying action in the streets until they received a signal to withdraw to ships set apart for their escape. On the night of March 17 the embarkation began.

Embittered by the bad behaviour of the Pompeian soldiery, the inhabitants of Brundisium favoured Caesar, and, when the embarkation was under way, they signalled to his outposts what was taking place. Scaling-ladders were rushed to the walls, and guided by the townsfolk along unblocked byways, the storming parties reached the harbour, manned some boats, and captured two transports which had fouled one of the moles. The others escaped.

On March 18, Caesar entered Brundisium. It was the sixty-sixth day since he had crossed the Rubicon. Few campaigns of comparable importance can have been fought in so brief a time with such little bloodshed. Italy was his, and Italy was the hub of the Civil War.

Caesar's problem now became a maritime one: to create a fleet to carry his army across the Adriatic, and meanwhile to prevent Pompey's fleet from starving out Italy. To solve the first, he ordered two fleets to be assembled and built by the Adriatic and Tyrrhenian coastal towns; and to assure the Italian corn-supply, he instructed Quintus Valerius with one legion to occupy Sardinia, and Curio with two to seize Sicily and, when he had done so, to occupy Africa. These three legions were formed out of the Domitian cohorts that had surrendered to Caesar.

At the time, Sardinia was held by the Pompeian governor Aurelius Cotta; but no sooner did its inhabitants learn that Valerius was to be sent out than of their own accord they ejected Cotta, who fled to Africa. Cato was in command of Sicily; but when he learnt of Curio's approach, he declared that he was utterly unprepared to hold the island because Pompey had left him in the lurch. He also fled and joined Pompey at Dyrrachium.

When these arrangements had been made, Caesar left Brundisium for Rome, and on his arrival 'he found the people shuddering with recollection of the horrors of Marius and Sulla, and he cheered them with the prospect and promise of clemency.'[1] He forthwith called the Senate together – that is, all senators who had not followed Pompey – and addressed them. He explained that 'he had sought no extraordinary office,' and had been 'waiting for the legitimate time of his consulship, [and] had been content with privileges open to all citizens.'[2] Next, he

---

[1] Appian, *Civil Wars*, II, 41.  [2] *B.C.*, I, 32.

proposed that envoys be sent to Pompey to effect a settlement, not that he feared him, but because 'his own wish was to be superior to others in justice and equity as he had striven to surpass them in action.'[1]

Although the Senate approved his proposal, no senator came forward to go on the mission, because Pompey had declared that all senators who failed to follow him would be declared public enemies. Caesar then requested the Senate's permission to draw on the public treasury, and when a tribune vetoed it, he ordered the treasury door to be burst open, and seized 15,000 bars of gold, 30,000 bars of silver, and 30,000,000 sesterces. Further, he ordered all existing galleys to be grouped into two squadrons, one under Quintus Hortensius to patrol the Tuscan Sea, and the other, under Cornelius Dolabella, the Adriatic. Lastly, he appointed Aemilius Lepidus prefect of the city and Antony governor of Italy.

[1] B.C., I, 32.

# IX

# *The Civil War in Spain*

## I. THE SIEGE OF MASSILIA

Now that Italy was his, Caesar was faced with three alternatives: To wait until his fleet was ready, and then pursue Pompey; to march by way of Illyricum and challenge Pompey in Macedonia; or to carry the war into Spain, and liquidate Pompey's seven legions.

To so dynamic a soldier, the first course is unthinkable; therefore we are left with the remaining two, and of them Colonel Dodge considers that he should have adopted the first – that is, to have advanced through Illyricum[1] – for were he to proceed to Spain, Italy would be left at Pompey's mercy; it was but a day's sail from Dyrrachium, and in Spain Caesar would be several hundred miles away. This is to misconceive not only the strategical situation but also the character of the war.

Dodge trips up when he writes that 'the keystone of war is preparation',[2] and that Pompey had been driven out of Italy because he was militarily unprepared. Though this is valid in a foreign war, in a civil war neither side can be prepared, because the slightest inclination toward any worthwhile preparation at once condemns the party concerned to be the aggressor, and thereby deprives him of his moral basis – the justice of his cause – which in a civil war, and incomparably more so than in a foreign, is the keystone.[3] The first problem of a would-be civil war leader is to secure the support not only of his faction but of the majority of the people, who must be brought to feel that his cause is just. As we have seen, this was the secret of Caesar's success, not that his cause was legally or morally just, but because the peace-loving

---

[1] *Caesar*, vol. II, pp. 431–2.    [2] *Ibid.*, p. 429.
[3] It is strange that Dodge failed to appreciate this, if only because he had fought in the American Civil War, a war in which both sides, and for identical reasons, were as unprepared as Pompey and Caesar were in January, 49 B.C.

Italians *felt* it to be to their advantage. Particularly in time of stress, 'justice' and 'self-interest' are synonymous in the mind of the emotional masses.

Caesar, therefore, decided to liquidate Pompey's army in Spain, a decision guaranteed, not so much by Pompey's hebetude, as by the goodwill of the inhabitants of Italy. Further, while Caesar was raising a fleet, Pompey would be raising an army; therefore for the latter to return to Italy before he had done so – that is, with his demoralized troops at Dyrrachium – would have been an act of madness. The crucial factor was, therefore, time: could Caesar deprive Pompey of his seven legions in Spain, and thereby secure his rear – his base in Italy – by the time his fleet was ready to convey his army across the Adriatic and before Pompey could raise a reliable army to invade Italy? To advance through Illyricum, a wild and roadless country inhabited by barbaric tribes, without a fleet to supply him *en route* must have appeared to Caesar, if he ever contemplated it, to be impracticable.[1] Instead, as we shall see, in spite of a series of initial misfortunes, he solved his problem in yet another bloodless campaign. Incidentally, it was to be a perfect example of the limited warfare campaigns of the eighteenth century, and would have rejoiced the hearts of Marshal Saxe and the Duke of Brunswick.

When no senator had come forward to convey Caesar's request to Pompey, and after several days had been wasted in futile discussion with the Senate, rather than squander his time in talk, Caesar left Rome for Massilia, where he arrived on about April 19. There he learnt that Vibullius, whom he had released at Corfinium, had been sent by Pompey to warn the Massiliots and the legions in Spain that Domitius was on his way to Massilia. On Caesar's arrival the Massiliots closed their gates against him; called to their aid the Albici, a Ligurian tribe, augmented their food stocks, repaired their town walls, and began to manufacture arms. At Caesar's request, they sent fifteen of their leading men to discuss the situation with him, and they informed him that the one desire of the citizens was to remain neutral. This was no more than a pretence, for when, during the conference, Domitius arrived, he was immediately put in command of the city.

Because Massilia lay on Caesar's line of communications between Italy and Spain, he had no intention of tolerating this. At once he decided to lay siege to the town, and he ordered Gaius Trebonius to

[1] As late as the first quarter of the third century A.D., Dio Cassius (XLIX, 36), at one time governor of Dalmatia, describes that country as completely barbarous.

leave his legions, now at Matisco, hasten to Italy, take command of three newly raised legions, bring them to Massilia and invest it. At the same time he ordered twelve war galleys to be built at Arelate (Arles) on the Rhône delta – which they were within thirty days – and he appointed Decimus Brutus to command them. Also he ordered Gaius Fabius with his three legions now at Narbo (Narbonne) to clear the Pyrennian passes, and then advance into Spain, and the three legions at Matisco were instructed to follow him.

## 2. THE ILERDA OPERATIONS

When Vibullius arrived in Spain, Pompey's seven legions were commanded and distributed as follows: three, under Lucius Afranius, in Nearer Spain, north of the Iberus (Ebro); two, under Terentius Varro, in Further Spain; and two, under Marcus Petreius, in and about Lusitania. Petreius was ordered to join his senior Afranius, and together they decided to concentrate their combined forces, five legions, 5,000 cavalry, and some cohorts of native levies, at Ilerda (Lerida), 30 miles north of the Ebro. Against them Caesar could muster six legions the 6th, 7th, 9th, 10th, 11th and 14th – 5,000 auxiliary light-armed troops, and 6,000 cavalry, excluding his bodyguard of 900 horsemen. The cavalry consisted of 3,000 he had with him 'during all his former wars, and an equal number from Gaul'.[1]

When Caesar was at Massilia, rumours were current that Pompey was marching through Mauritania (Morocco) to the support of his legions in Spain. Probably they were circulated by his legates in order to encourage, or overawe, the Spanish tribes. Although it is unlikely that Caesar put much trust in them, it would seem that they were taken seriously by some of his officers and men. To allay their fears he resorted to a trick: '. . . he borrowed sums of money from the tribunes and centurions and distributed them among the soldiers. By this proceeding,' he writes, 'he gained two results: he established a lien on the loyalty of the centurions and purchased by the bounty the goodwill of the troops.'[2]

The town of Ilerda is dominated by a rocky hill, upon which a medieval castle now stands. It rises abruptly on the right bank of the Sicoris (Segre), an unfordable, torrential river, spanned at the town in Caesar's day by a stone bridge. About a mile south of Ilerda is a long low eminence, now called the Hill of Gardeny, on which Afranius encamped his infantry, with his cavalry between it and the river, and

[1] B.C., I, 39.　　　　　　　　　　[2] Ibid., I, 39.

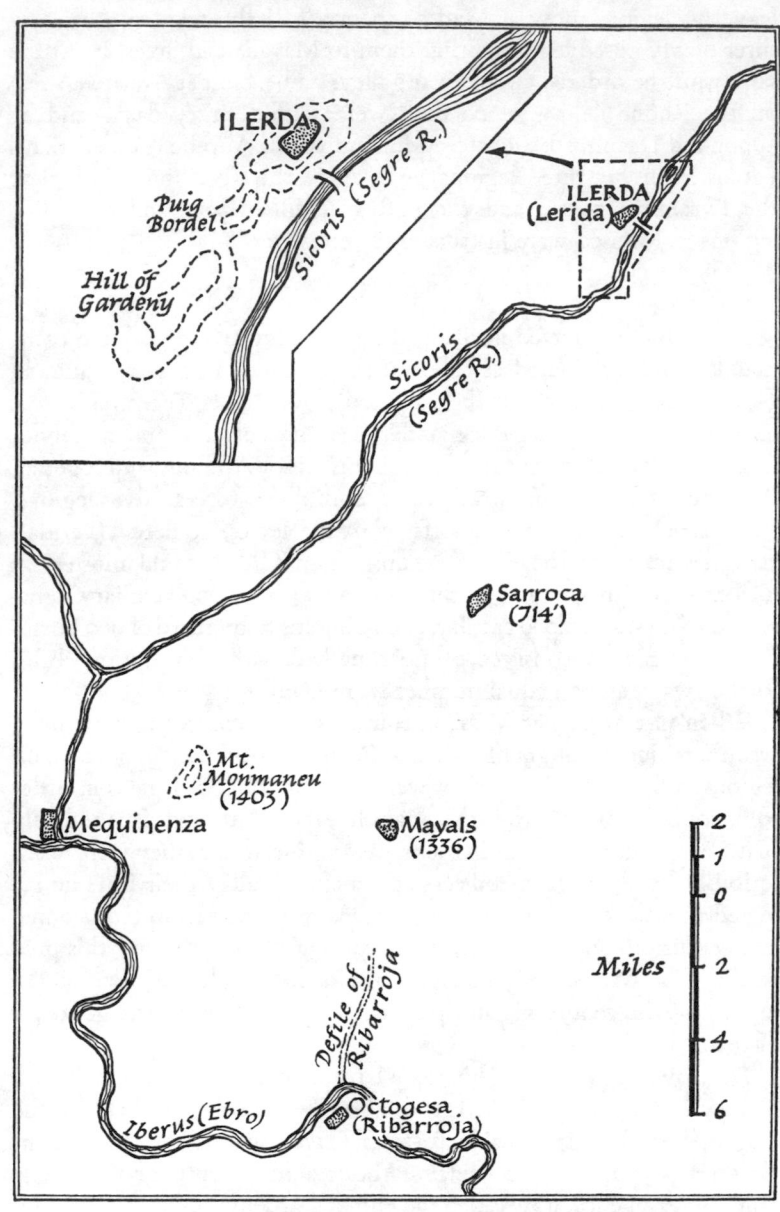

8. Ilerda and Ebro Campaign

between this eminence and the town rises a low knoll (the Puig Bordel). It is conjectured that, when he arrived, Fabius pitched his camp on the southern slopes of a hill, since named Larrala, some three miles north of Afranius' camp, and in order to gain access for his foragers to the land east of the Sicoris, he bridged the river in two places; one nearly opposite the eastern wall of his camp, some two miles above Ilerda, and the other four miles higher up the Sicoris.

When, on June 23,[1] Caesar and his bodyguard arrived at Ilerda, he found Fabius engaged on rebuilding the lower of his two bridges. It had been swept away in a violent storm, which had converted the Sicoris into a raging torrent, and had placed his foragers and their escort of two legions in a precarious situation. From Fabius he must have learnt that the neighbouring villages were deserted, their granaries bare of corn, and that Afranius had stored it in Ilerda. Therefore the enemy was well supplied, whereas he himself was at his wit's end how to feed his men, and soon would be unable to do so. Caesar had already arranged for a large convoy to come to his relief; but the situation was so alarming that, because Ilerda could not be stormed, and to reduce it by siege would take too long, the only course open to him was to cut Afranius' camp off from the town and the stone bridge.

At once, he writes, he 'made himself acquainted with the character of the country,'[2] and noticed that the knoll of Puig Bordel, which linked Afranius' camp with Ilerda, was not held, and if he could occupy and fortify it 'he would cut off his adversaries from the town and the bridge and from all the stores which they had brought into the town.'[3] To achieve this, on the day after his arrival he advanced Fabius' legions from their camp to close by Afranius', offered battle and was refused. Next, as he was so close to his enemy and overlooked by him, instead of building a formal camp, under cover of the first and second lines of the legions, the third line was ordered to dig 'secretly' a 15-foot-wide trench facing the enemy, to which no rampart was to be added, so that it might not be seen from the enemy's camp.[4]

Toward evening, Caesar bivouacked his legions behind the ditch, and on the following morning three similar ditches were dug on the

[1] All dates in this chapter are those of Holmes in *The Roman Republic*, vol. III, p. 408. June 23 was May 6 by the Julian calendar.
[2] *B.C.*, I, 41.   [3] *Ibid.*, I, 43.
[4] Presumably the ditch was dug in a shallow dip in the ground, and had a rampart been added the dip would not have been deep enough to hide it from the enemy's camp.

sides and to the rear of the first one, so as to form an entrenched quadrilateral. This work was noticed by Afranius, who unsuccessfully attempted to impede it. Then, on the next day, Caesar strengthened his entrenchments with a rampart, and transferred the baggage train from Fabius' camp to the new one. This done, he drew out three legions, and ordered the first line of the 14th, which was on the left, 'to charge and occupy the mount'.[1] But Afranius, who had drawn his forces up in front of his camp, was closer to the knoll than the 14th Legion, and he was able to occupy it as his enemy was advancing up it and drive him back.

Immediately following the description of this repulse, Caesar excuses it by attributing it to the loose-order tactics his enemy had adopted. They had advanced, so he writes, in small groups, and because they kept on charging in succession, the men of the first line 'thought that they were being surrounded on their exposed flank',[2] and were thrown into confusion. This caused a panic in the second and third lines in rear – 'an event as unusual as it was unexpected'. To check it, Caesar advanced the 9th Legion, and drove the enemy back to the walls of Ilerda. Carried away by their success, the men of the 9th Legion got out of hand; they rushed after their flying enemy and got jammed up in a confused mass in the ravine through which the road west of the Sicoris led into the town. Nevertheless, for five hours they held their own, and when their missiles were spent, they charged with their swords, and then beat as rapid a retreat as they could to the plain below, where the pursuing enemy was halted by the cavalry.

Caesar records that his losses were 70 men killed and 600 wounded, that more than 200 of the enemy were slain, and that 'the commonly received view of the day's event was that each side thought it had come off superior.' This may be doubted, so far as Caesar himself was concerned, because a few lines farther on he writes: 'The enemy fortified the hill [Puig Bordel] for the possession of which they had fought, with great works, and placed a garrison on it.'[3]

Two days after the fight for the knoll, Caesar suffered a serious disaster; both his bridges were swept away in a storm, and he found himself cut off from all foraging east of the river. Worse still, the large

---

[1] B.C., I, 43. Prior to the Marian reforms, the first of the three lines was composed of *hastati*, the most active men (see *supra*, p. 78). Subsequently they were renamed *antesignani*, chosen men who fought before the standards. They were the cutting-edge of the legion.

[2] *Ibid.*, I, 44.  [3] *Ibid.*, I, 47.

convoy from Gaul, now approaching, was also cut off by the swollen river, and could not reach him until one of the bridges was rebuilt, an impossible task until the flood waters subsided. The convoy comprised not only a long train of wagons, but also a mixed multitude of some 6,000 souls – drivers, slaves, Roman citizens, women, and children – escorted by a body of archers and some Gallic cavalry. We are told that no one was in 'fixed authority, each following his own devices'.

When, from his scouts, Afranius learnt of its approach, according to Caesar, he set out by night 'with all his cavalry and three legions', and attacked the convoy when off its guard.[1] Although few in number, the Gallic cavalry repelled Afranius' horsemen, gained time for the convoy to seek refuge on 'higher ground', and when the Gauls saw the enemy's legions approaching they withdrew to some neighbouring hills.

The account of this action is unsatisfactory. How came it that the convoy escaped destruction? Holmes suggests that 3,000 of the 6,000 persons in the convoy may have been Caesar's Gallic cavalry on their way to join him.[2] But this is improbable, because Caesar mentions that they were 'few' in number. Even should the surmise be correct, because the Gallic cavalry withdrew to some nearby hills, and not to the 'higher ground' on which the convoy had sought refuge, and as the convoy had no means of defending itself other than a body of tribal archers, why did not the three Afranian legions assault and exterminate it? The ascent to the higher ground cannot have been abnormally difficult, because it had been negotiated by loaded wagons. The whole account savours of propaganda aimed at discrediting Afranius, who had bested Caesar in the fight for the knoll. The losses recorded by Caesar of some 200 archers, 'a few horsemen, and a small number of camp followers and beasts of burden'[3] would seem to bear this out.

Although the convoy had been saved, because it could not cross the Sicoris, Caesar's supply position grew more and more precarious, and the bridges could not be rebuilt because the Afranians held the eastern bank of the river. Then Caesar bethought himself of a solution: he had a number of coracles built of light timber and wattle covered with hides, such as he had seen in Britain, but of greater size. These he transported on 'coupled wagons'[4] some 22 miles up-stream from his camp, and by means of them he ferried a party of men across the river, occupied an adjoining hill and fortified it. Next, he ferried over a legion to establish a bridgehead, and when two days later a bridge had been

[1] *Ibid.*, I, 51.  
[2] *The Roman Republic*, vol. III, p. 389.  
[3] *B.C.*, I, 51.  
[4] *Ibid.*, I, 54.

built, he brought the greater part of his cavalry over, attacked his enemy's foragers, and cut off great numbers of them and their pack animals.

When these things were under way, news was brought to Caesar from Massilia that Decimus Brutus had defeated Domitius' fleet, a victory which must have heartened his sorely-tried men, and, so it would seem, was made much of by him in order to impress the natives. When coupled with the slaughter of the Afranian foragers, it must greatly have added to his prestige, because immediately after a number of towns and tribes – Osca, Calagurris and Tarraco,[1] the Iacetani, Ausetani and Illurgavonenses – sent envoys to him and agreed to supply him with corn. Next, we are told that 'a great change of fortune rapidly followed'; five important states came over to him. Further, that the rumoured approach of Pompey through Mauritania was 'suppressed', and that a number of distant communities deserted Afranius and threw in their lot with Caesar.[2] As so often happens in a civil war, a sudden change of fortune leads to an immediate shift of public opinion from one side to the other. Whatever their political views may be, and generally they are nebulous, the urge of the masses is to be on the winning side, because the winner will be their eventual master, and it is to their advantage to propitiate him.

To overcome the loss of time in sending his cavalry over the bridge 22 miles up-stream from Ilerda, Caesar decided to make an artificial ford a short distance above the town, where the Sicoris flowed in three channels, as it still does. To reduce the depth of the streams, he had a number of 30-foot-wide trenches dug to carry off sufficient of their water into the river below as to render them wadeable. It must have been a tremendous task. Why Caesar did not resort to bridging he does not say, but he probably had a good reason for not doing so.

When Afranius and Petreius fathomed what Caesar's intention was, and that the ford would put a stop to all foraging east of the river, they decided to abandon Ilerda and transfer operations to the south side of the Ebro, where the native tribes favoured Pompey and knew little or nothing of Caesar. Among them they hoped to recruit large reinforcements of cavalry and light-armed troops; with them prolong the war into the winter, and thereby gain time for Pompey. When they had

---

[1] Osca (Huesca) lay north-west of Ilerda; Calagurris (Calahorra) on the upper Ebro; and Tarraco (Tarragona) on the Mediterranean, north of the mouth of the Ebro.

[2] *Ibid.*, I, 60.

decided on this, they instructed the tribes along the Ebro to collect all obtainable barges and boats at the town of Octogesa[1] and bridge the river. To prepare for the withdrawal, two legions were sent over the stone bridge at Ilerda to build a fortified camp on the eastern bank of the Sicoris.

### 3. THE EBRO MANŒUVRE

The town of Octogesa lay 27 miles to the south of Ilerda, and for marching troops was considerably more. For the first 12 miles, as far as the present village of Sarroca, the country is either level or rolling; the next seven, to the present village of Mayals, are broken and hilly; and the last eight to the Ebro are rugged and mountainous land. A few miles south of Mayals there is a defile which leads to Octogesa, and six miles to the west of Mayals rises Mt Monmaneu to a height of 1,403 feet; it dominates the surrounding country. Because of the superiority of Caesar's cavalry, the aim of Afranius and Petreius – from now on the latter would appear to have taken the lead – was to gain cover of the mountainous area, and then make for the Ebro at Octogesa.

When, through his scouts, Caesar learnt that a bridge was to be built at Octogesa, he pressed on, day and night, with the work on the ford. He had begun it on July 19, and by the 25th the depth of the river had sufficiently fallen to enable his cavalry to cross it; but foot-soldiers could only do so submerged to their shoulders, and the current was so strong that Caesar feared they would lose their foothold. Nevertheless, when his men clamoured to be led across, not to disappoint them, he decided to attempt it, and to break the force of the current and prevent his men being swept away he formed up in the stream two lines of transport animals, one above and one below the point of crossing. Between them the infantry waded over without loss, and on the far bank formed order of battle.

Instead of beginning to withdraw when they first became aware of what Caesar was about, Petreius and Afranius foolishly waited until July 25 before they did so, and were soon after harried by their enemy's cavalry. When they caught sight of his approaching infantry they were dismayed, and pressed on with all speed toward the hilly country, where they hoped to pitch a camp which, by blocking its approaches, would be reasonably secure. But before they could reach it, worn by the day's fighting, they decided to encamp short of it and resume their

1 Holmes (vol. III, pp. 399–404) identifies its site as that of the present village of Ribarroja.

withdrawal under cover of night. When Caesar caught up with them, he pitched his camp on a nearby hill.

About midnight, some of the Afranians, who had left their camp in search of water, were captured by Caesar's cavalry, and from them he learnt that his enemy was beginning to withdraw. At once he ordered the fall-in to be sounded, and when it was heard in the Afranian camp, to avoid a night engagement when encumbered with a baggage train, Petreius and Afranius countermanded the withdrawal. Next morning Petreius reconnoitred the neighbouring country, and reported that for five miles it was level, after which it became rugged and hilly, and that whoever gained the hills first would be able to hold up the other by occupying the defiles. At the same time Caesar also sent out a reconnoitring patrol, and it brought back a similar report.

On the 26th, both sides remained in their respective camps, and to decide on what next to do, Petreius and Afranius assembled a council of war to consider whether to continue their withdrawal by night or by day. Finally the latter course was agreed, and timed to begin on the following morning.

Because the tracks which led to the Ebro at Octogesa were blocked by his enemy's camp, Caesar reconnoitred the country in its vicinity in order to find a way round it. When he had decided on his route, shortly before dawn on July 27 he set out without his baggage train. He relates that the army had to cross a number of large and difficult valleys, in places so steep that his men had to pass their arms from hand to hand when scrambling up their sides. When, from their camp, the Afranian soldiers noticed what was in progress they were overjoyed, because they thought that Caesar was on his way back to Ilerda to replenish his supplies. Then, when a little later they saw his column wheel to the right, and its vanguard on the point of outflanking their camp, they fathomed the danger they were in, and except for a few cohorts left to guard the camp, Petreius and Afranius hurriedly set out 'on a straight course for the Ebro.'

As Caesar writes: 'The whole contest turned on speed.' Whichever side could first 'seize the defiles and the hills would escape peril'. He won the race, and when, 'after crossing the great rocks', he emerged on a level plain, he drew up his line opposite his enemy. When Petreius and Afranius found him in front of them, while their rear was harassed by his cavalry, they made for a nearby hill and halted on it. Next, they despatched four cohorts of light-armed 'to a mountain which was the loftiest of all in sight' (? Monmaneu), but before they could reach it, they were surrounded by Caesar's cavalry 'and slain in the sight of both armies'.[1]

'There was now an opportunity', says Caesar, 'for a successful action', because his enemy was demoralized and surrounded on every side by cavalry. His legates, centurions, and tribunes urged him to battle, but he rejected their pleas because 'Afranius was certainly bound to come down from his position, and could not continue to hold it without water.'

We now come to Caesar's most interesting decision, and we will leave it to him to describe it:

'Caesar had entertained the hope that, having cut off his adversaries from their food supply, he would be able to finish the business without exposing his men to fighting or bloodshed. Why should he lose any of his men even in a successful battle? Why should he suffer soldiers who had served him so well to be wounded? Why, in a word, should he make trial of fortune? Especially as it was as much the duty of a commander to win by policy as by the sword. He was moved, moreover, by compassion for his fellow-citizens whose slaughter he saw to be inevitable. He preferred to gain his object without loss or harm to them. This policy of his did not commend itself to the majority; in fact, the soldiers said openly among themselves that, since such an opportunity of victory was being let slip, they would not fight even when Caesar wished them to.'[2]

In spite of their insubordination, he adhered to his intention, and after posting outposts on the hills, he shut off every route to the Ebro, and entrenched his camp as close as possible to his enemy's.

The two camps were now so close together that a situation, common in wars of the past, arose.[3] The men of both armies began to fraternize and visit each other's camp. The Afranians expressed their gratitude for not having been attacked on the previous day. ' "To your kindness", they said, "we owe our life." ' Then some inquired whether, were they to commit themselves to Caesar, would he spare them? And on being told of his clemency, they said they would be willing to do so, were the lives of Petreius and Afranius spared. Things went so far that Afranius' youthful son, through an envoy, pleaded with Caesar for his own and his father's safety. We read:

'The whole place was full of rejoicing and congratulation, on the

[1] *B.C.*, I, 70.    [2] *Ibid.*, I, 72.
[3] *E.g.*, the Peninsular War in Spain, the American Civil War, and more recently on one occasion in the First World War.

one hand of those who were deemed to have avoided such perils, and on the other of those who were seen to have wrought such achievements without bloodshed; and Caesar in the general estimation reaped a great advantage from his traditional leniency, and his policy met with the approval of all.'[1]

It would appear that Afranius was willing to come to terms, but Petreius most certainly was not. When he learnt of what was taking place, he ordered his body-guard to seize and slaughter all Caesarian soldiers discovered in his camp, and when he had established his authority, he demanded an oath of loyalty from his officers and men. First, he took the oath himself, then compelled Afranius to do so, and after him the centurions, tribunes, and the rank and file. Caesar's response was in accordance with his policy, for when he heard of the massacre of his men, instead of retaliating, he released all Afranians found in his camp and returned them to their own. An amazing example of self-control, which must have put his enemy to the blush.

By now the Afranians were in desperate straits; their legionaries still had some corn left – they had taken twenty-two days' supply[2] with them when they left Ilerda – but their auxiliaries had none and were starving; daily they were deserting in large numbers to the enemy. Worse still, difficulty in obtaining water made it impossible for them to remain where they were, and, on July 29, Petreius and Afranius, after they had considered a retreat to Tarraco, decided to cut their way back to Ilerda. When on the following day they set out, they were immediately attacked by Caesar's horse, and by now their own were so cowed that they sought refuge in the centre of the infantry column which, presumably, was retiring in square formation. So it came about that, after they had covered four miles, to free themselves from cavalry attack they occupied a hill, entrenched a camp, and kept their baggage animals loaded, so as to be in immediate readiness to resume the retreat. Soon after, Caesar encamped near by them, and when they saw his foragers and their escort leave camp, they quickly set out again, in the hope that they might cover another lap before the pursuit could catch them up.

As they moved off, Caesar recalled his foragers and cavalry, and after he had rested his legions for a few hours, the pursuit was pushed again,

---

[1] B.C., I, 74. Whether fact or fiction, it is first-class propaganda; it hints that Caesar would make an ideal head of state.

[2] Much by now must have been lost, or left behind in their camp of July 27.

and so fiercely that time was insufficient for the Afranians to seek a suitable spot for a camp, and they were compelled to occupy a position 'far from water and in a place unfavourable by nature'. Caesar then called in his cavalry and forbade his men to pitch their tents, so that they might be in instant readiness to move against the enemy should he again attempt to slip away.

To strengthen their position, the Afranians pushed forward 'out-works' during the night, and continued to do so on July 31. 'But,' we are told, 'the more they advanced with their work and pushed forward their camp, the further they were from water.'[1] Presumably this means that their camp was on the lower slope of a rise, and the more they pushed up it, the farther they were away from such water as was to be found near its foot. To add to their danger, in order to guard against a sudden attempt on their part to break out, Caesar began to hem their camp in with a contravallation.

When, on August 1, Petreius and Afranius realized that, should the contravallation be completed, they would be trapped, they determined on a desperate expedient – to decide their fate by battle. They led out their legions and formed them into line immediately outside their camp, and as they began to do so, Caesar recalled his working parties and followed suit. That he could have annihilated his enemy in battle is beyond doubt, but he was too knowing a soldier not to see that, in the circumstances in which his enemy was placed, 'a victory could not greatly promote his [own] final success.'[2] Therefore he decided to refuse battle, unless he was attacked, and the Afranians refrained from doing so, because they feared to lose contact with their camp. Thus it came about that the opposing armies faced each other until sunset, and then withdrew into their respective camps.

On the next day, August 2, work on the contravallation was resumed, and the Afranians were blockaded on every side. For four days their baggage animals had been without fodder, and water had now become unobtainable. Therefore there was but one thing Petreius and Afranius could do – surrender. They sent an envoy to Caesar to beg an interview with him, 'if possible, in a place out of reach of the soldiers'. He approved, provided it was held in public – that is, within earshot of the soldiers of both armies. He was too astute a diplomatist to miss so dramatic an opportunity to publicize his policy of moderation and reap its political harvest.

Afranius spoke first. He pleaded his loyalty to Pompey; confessed his

<hr />

[1] *Ibid.*, I, 81.  [2] *Ibid.*, I, 82.

army beaten, and besought Caesar not 'to proceed to the extreme of punishment.' To which Caesar replied that he had been 'unwilling to fight even when conditions were favourable . . . that there might be absolutely nothing to prejudice the chances of peace.' That when his men had been butchered he had not retaliated; that it was not his object to retain an army taken from his enemy, although that would not be difficult to do; but instead to deprive his enemy of one he could use against him. Finally, he announced his terms: that Afranius' army be disbanded. 'This,' he declared, 'is my one and final condition of peace.'[1]

Amazed at Caesar's generosity, by voice and hand the Afranian soldiers signified their approval and gratitude. Those domiciled in Spain were forthwith discharged, and the remainder were to withdraw from Spain and be disbanded when they reached the river Varus (Var). Pledges were given by Caesar that no wrong should be done to them *en route*, and that no one would be compelled against his will to swear allegiance to him. Further, he promised to provide them with corn on the way, and that whatever any one of them had lost due to war would either be restored to him or paid for.

Because Varro was still holding Further Spain, Caesar despatched two legions there under Quintus Cassius Longinus. He next issued an edict that all communities should send representatives to Corduba (Cordova) to attend a general assembly. When news of this was received, the province declared for Caesar; its chief towns closed their gates against Varro, and when Caesar arrived at Corduba he learnt that Varro had submitted. At the assembly Caesar remitted all burdens imposed by Varro, distributed rewards and assigned Cassius as governor of the province with four legions to hold it. Then he went to Gades (Cadiz), took ship to Tarraco, and thence proceeded overland to Massilia, where he arrived in late September.

Thus, in three months, by avoiding battle and relying on manœuvre, in an almost bloodless campaign he deprived Pompey of his stronghold, and thereby secured both Italy and Gaul against a rear attack when the time came for him to cross the Adriatic.

[1] *B.C.*, I, 84–85.

# X

## The Civil War in Greece

### I. CAESAR'S FIRST DICTATORSHIP

WHILE Caesar was in Spain, Trebonius pressed the siege of Massilia, and Curio, when he had occupied Sicily, crossed to Africa, then held by Attius Varus, who had opposed Caesar at Auximum, and who was supported by Juba, king of Numidia. The campaign which followed opened with a victory for Curio, and ended with a disastrous defeat, in which he perished and his legionaries were butchered.[1]

Both these operations are fully described by Caesar, but as he played no part in the first, other than to announce his terms of surrender, which were exceedingly moderate, and was not present at the second, both fall outside the subject of this book. Nevertheless, it is pertinent to mention that his appointment of Curio was an unfortunate one; he was young, headstrong, and inexperienced in war; equally ill-advised was it to place him in command of an army recently recruited from Domitius' raw levies which, indirectly, is noted by Caesar himself.

At Massilia, Caesar learnt that the instructions he had recently sent Aemilius Lepidus to nominate him dictator[2] – an unconstitutional act – had been complied with. And when he learnt that some of his soldiers at Placentia had mutinied, either because they had not received a donative previously promised them,[3] or because they had not been allowed 'to plunder the country'[4] – presumably when in Spain – he set out from Massilia. At Placentia he discovered that the 9th Legion was the chief culprit, and he ordered it to be decimated – that is, one man out of every 10 was to be executed. This, the maximum penalty, led to the mutineers throwing themselves at his feet in supplication. Little by

[1] B.C., II, 42.  [2] Dio, XLI, 36, 1.
[3] Appian, Civil Wars, II, 47.
[4] Dio, XLI, 26, 1.

little he relented, and in the end, out of 120 who had taken the lead, 12 were chosen by lot and put to death.

From Placentia Caesar hastened to Rome, and on his way learnt of a disaster which was seriously to handicap him *vis-à-vis* Pompey. Scribonius Libo and Marcus Octavius, in command of a Pompeian squadron in the Adriatic, had driven Dolabella and his fleet on to the Dalmatian coast, and had sunk or captured forty of his ships.

On Caesar's arrival in Rome, he forthwith held the consular elections, and as he considered it inexpedient to retain the dictatorship, he had himself elected consul, and chose as his colleague Publius Servilius. Next, by virtue of his dictatorial power, to allay a financial crisis due to the war, he regulated the position between debtors and creditors; recalled most of those exiled by Pompey, and restored civic rights to the descendants of those who had been proscribed by Sulla. Also he appointed the magistrates and provincial governors for the following year. All these measures were crowded into eleven days; at the conclusion of them he resigned his dictatorship, quitted the city and sped to Brundisium, to where he had ordered twelve legions and all the cavalry to assemble.

Meanwhile Pompey had gained nine months in which to prepare, and during them he had gathered together a large fleet from Asia, the Cyclades, Corcyra, Athens, Pontus, Bithynia, Syria, Cilicia, Phoenicia, and Egypt. He had requisitioned large sums of money from the kings, potentates and communities of Asia, Syria, and Achaia, and had compelled the tax-farmers to disgorge further sums. He had recruited an army of nine legions of Roman citizens, five from Italy – those he had brought overseas – and four legions of veterans raised in Cilicia, Crete, Macedonia, and Asia. Further, he had distributed among these legions a large number of men from Thessaly, Boeotia, Achaia, and Epirus to bring them up to strength, and besides these legions he had two under his father-in-law, Scipio, in Syria. From Crete and other states he had recruited 3,000 archers and 1,200 slingers, and had raised 7,000 cavalry. From Thessaly, Asia, Egypt, and other localities he had amassed a large quantity of corn, and at the time Caesar arrived at Brundisium had distributed the greater part of his fleet in five squadrons along the eastern shore of the Adriatic and Ionian Seas, under command of Caesar's old opponent Marcus Bibulus.[1]

When Caesar arrived at Brundisium, he found only sufficient ships to embark seven legions and 500 cavalry, lightly equipped and closely

[1] B.C., III, 3–5.

packed. The remainder, all of whom had not yet arrived at Brundisium, were left under Antony, who was to hold them in readiness to join him immediately the transports returned. Caesar mentions that he took with him 15,000 legionary soldiers, therefore the average strength of his legions was but a little over 2,000 men each. Further, he says that, when he harangued his troops before they boarded their ships, he instructed, or begged, them 'to leave with a quiet mind their slaves and baggage in Italy . . . so that a larger number of men could be put on board.'[1] Should this mean anything more than their personal effects, it is difficult to see how a successful campaign could be undertaken; therefore it may be assumed that the normal baggage train accompanied the legions.

Because, at the time, Caesar must have been aware that Pompey had garrisoned the eastern Adriatic and Ionian ports, had an immense fleet of war galleys, and had recruited an army considerably greater than his own, well may it be asked: was he justified to risk a winter crossing and challenge Pompey?

Throughout classical times and for long after, because of stormy weather naval operations were avoided during the winter months. 'Pompey,' writes Dio, '. . . did not suppose that Caesar had yet arrived in Italy from Spain . . . he did not suspect that he would venture to cross the Ionian Gulf in the winter.'[2] Appian says much the same: 'Pompey thought that as the weather was bad and the sea boisterous Caesar would not attempt to cross till the end of winter, but would be occupied in the meantime with his duties as consul. . . . So heedlessly did Pompey form his judgement of what was about to take place.'[3] Pompey was not heedless, his misfortune was that he was Pompey; he measured Caesar in terms of himself.

Caesar must have suspected this, and appreciated that, were he to wait until spring, when his conventional adversary expected him, he would be faced by an equal danger – Bibulus would be on the alert, and under no conceivable circumstances could Caesar hope to wrest from him the command of the sea. Further, because there were occasional spells of fair weather during winter, since the coast of Epirus was but a day's sail from Brundisium, a single calm day would be sufficient for him to slip across. Therefore, great soldier that he was, he pocketed his fears and decided to surprise Pompey. This is corroborated by Appian in the speech he records that Caesar made to his soldiers,

[1] *Ibid.*, III, 6.  [2] Dio, XLI, 44, 1.
[3] Appian, *Civil Wars*, II, 52.

which in part is based on Caesar's own words, and even should Appian's elaborations be apocryphal, they are patently Caesarian:

'Fellow-soldiers – you are joined with me in the greatest of undertakings – neither the winter weather, nor the delay of our comrades, nor the want of suitable preparations shall check my onset. I consider rapidity of movement the best substitute for all these things. . . . Let us oppose our good fortune to the winter weather, our courage to the smallness of our numbers, and to our want of supplies the abundance of the enemy, which will be ours to take as soon as we touch the land. . . . Let us go while Pompey thinks that I am spending my time in winter quarters also, or in processions and sacrifices appertaining to my consulship. It is needless to tell you that the most potent thing in war is the unexpected. . . . For my part I would rather be sailing than talking, so that I may come to Pompey's sight while he thinks me engaged in my official duties at Rome.'[1]

## 2. CAESAR'S ADVANCE ON DYRRACHIUM

Because Pompey held command of the sea — actually, Caesar had available no more than twelve galleys to escort his transports – and because Caesar suspected that the ports of Illyricum and Epirus were garrisoned, to avoid them and the enemy squadrons based on them, he selected 'a quiet harbourage among the Ceraunian rocks' at a place called Palaeste (Palissa)[2] about 25 miles south of the Gulf of Valona, to disembark at, and on January 4,[3] 48 B.C., the wind being favourable, he weighed anchor and stood out to sea.

At the time, Bibulus with 110 ships lay off Corcyra (Corfu) some 50 miles to the south of Palaeste; and about 25 miles to its north his two lieutenants, Lucretius Vespillo and Minucius Rufus, were in command of 18 at Oricum, at the southern extremity of the Gulf of Valona. Fortunately for Caesar they had failed to scout the seas and suspected nothing, and, on the 5th, he disembarked his troops 'without damage to a single one of his ships.'

That same night the transports, under the legate Fufius Calenus, stood out on their return to Brundisium; but unfortunately they missed the night breeze, and Bibulus, now awake to what was happening, was able to capture thirty of them, and to vent his rage 'caused by the vexa-

---

[1] Appian, *Civil Wars*, II, 53. The speech is reminiscent of Bonaparte's address to his soldiers before invading Italy in 1796.

[2] *B.C.*, III, 6.

[3] November 6 by the Julian calendar.

tion of his own slackness', he set fire to them and burnt their crews alive, in order to strike terror into those who escaped. It was a purblind thing to do, and more likely to stimulate revenge than terror.

Coincidental with this insensate act, was an irrational decision made by Caesar. In face of overwhelming odds and with an audacity seldom

9. Northern Greece

equalled in war, he had brought half his army safely to Epirus; nevertheless, not until the remaining half joined him could he hope to meet Pompey on favourable terms. Therefore it was imperative to keep Pompey in ignorance of his landing and weakness as long as he possibly could. The haste with which he ordered his transports to return to Brundisium proves he was fully aware of that. Notwithstanding, within a few hours of landing, he decided to send an envoy post-haste to Pompey to consider terms of peace, an act so irrational that it would seem only explicable on the grounds, held by some psychologists, that genius and madness are separated by no more than a hair's breadth.

To make matters worse, instead of selecting a discreet and trustworthy envoy, he entrusted the mission to Vibullius Rufus, who had surrendered to him in Spain for a second time, and since then had been kept under surveillance. He did so, he says, 'in consideration of the benefits that he had conferred on him' – namely, to pardon him twice – and therefore held him to be 'a suitable person'.[1] Because Vibullius was Pompey's chief engineer and was loyal to him, it would have been hard to have found a less suitable one. He was briefed to inform Pompey that 'Conditions of peace should now be sought at Rome from the Senate and the people, since it had not been possible to agree on them before. Meanwhile it ought to satisfy the republic and themselves if each should swear in a public assembly that he would disband his army within the next three days.'[2] Had he not been obsessed by his peace-seeking, he could not have believed for a moment that Pompey would accept such terms. Instead, he would have realized that Vibullius, a skilled and educated soldier, would inform Pompey of the precarious position he was in, with half his army in Epirus, half still at Brundisium, and Bibulus in between. Nothing Caesar could have done was more likely to lose or prolong the war than to send Vibullius to Pompey. Nevertheless, the most inexplicable thing of all is that, although his decision eventually placed him in a critical situation, he naïvely records it in his *Commentaries* as if it redounded to his credit.

When Vibullius had been briefed, Caesar set out for Oricum, apparently on the evening of January 5. It was held by Manlius Torquatus and a garrison of tribesmen, but on Caesar's approach they refused to fight against a Roman consul, and Torquatus was compelled to surrender the town. At Oricum Caesar left Marcus Acilius and one legion to hold it, and next, 'with no interval of delay', he pressed on to Apollonia, held by L. Staberius; but the inhabitants refused to shut their gates against Caesar, and sent to him envoys to surrender the town.

---

[1] *B.C.*, III, 10.

[2] *Ibid.* There was no operative Senate, part was in Rome and part with Pompey, and neither part possessed the slightest authority. Further, it was as complex a problem in the first century B.C., to disband approximately 100,000 soldiers before providing them with a means of livelihood, as it is today to dismiss 100,000 armament workers without doing the same. To suggest three days is meaningless.

The neighbouring communities followed suit, and the whole of Epirus, so Caesar tells us, sent envoys to him who promised to do his bidding. Caesar then advanced at top speed to seize Dyrrachium, Pompey's main depot and arsenal.

Meanwhile Vibullius had set out to warn Pompey of Caesar's 'sudden approach . . . that he might be able to take counsel thereon before they should begin to discuss the instructions.'[1] He travelled night and day, changed horse 'at every town to gain speed', and hurried to Pompey to announce Caesar's arrival.

He caught up with him as he was leisurely marching along the Egnatian Way, somewhere east of Scampa (Elbassan), to take up winter quarters in Apollonia and Dyrrachium. Astounded by the news, Pompey set out by forced marches for Apollonia, and soon after, when he learnt that Oricum and Apollonia were in Caesar's hands, fearful that he might occupy Dyrrachium ahead of him, he pressed on night and day at so high a speed that his peace-soft troops were reduced to a rabble of stragglers. At length he halted near Dyrrachium, probably at Asparagium (near Rogozina) where he could block the southern branch of the Egnatian Way, which led to Apollonia, and along which Caesar was approaching. It would appear that it was only then that Vibullius broached the subject of his mission. Pompey rejected the terms.

In the meantime Caesar was pressing on at speed from Apollonia, but when he found himself forestalled in his attempt to reach Dyrrachium, he fell back to the river Apsus (Semani) and pitched his camp on its southern bank. There he decided to await the arrival of his legions from Italy and to winter in tents. Pompey then moved southward from Asparagium and went into camp on the northern bank of the Apsus, opposite Caesar, 'who must have reflected,' as Holmes comments, 'that by prematurely despatching Vibullius on a futile errand he had lost the chance of ending the war.'[2]

The chance was, now that Caesar was in possession of Oricum and Apollonia, that had he occupied Dyrrachium ahead of Pompey, he would have deprived Bibulus of all his naval bases between Lissus (Alesso) and Corcyra, and have opened a 160 miles wide gap for Antony to exploit.

Bibulus was alive to this danger, therefore he ordered his fleet to keep at sea and watch all ports from Salonae (Split) to Oricum, in case Antony should attempt a landing. And when Caesar became aware of this, he sent a despatch boat to Brundisium to warn Antony and

[1] *Ibid.*, III, 11.  [2] *The Roman Republic*, vol. III, p. 123.

Calenus not to sail because all the coast of Illyricum and Epirus was watched. Next, he picketed the shore-line in order to prevent Bibulus from procuring wood and water, or moorings for his ships. The result was, their crews were placed in such straits that supplies of wood, water, and other stores had to be brought to them in merchant ships from Corcyra, and at times they were reduced to collecting the night dew on skins in order to quench their thirst. At length the rough weather and the strain of watching proved too much for Bibulus, and before the winter ended he sickened and died. For some reason, which is not recorded, Pompey did not replace him, and the command of his squadrons was left to the initiative of their respective commanders.

The two armies now faced each other across the Apsus and were so close together that their men frequently engaged in conversations. This offered Caesar an unsolicited opportunity to resume his peace negotations, and he instructed one of his legates, P. Vatinius, to go to the bank of the river and propose that Caesar and Pompey should come to terms.

It would appear that a considerable number of Pompeian soldiers listened favourably to him, and in reply Vatinius was told that Aulus Varro, from the opposite bank, would on the following day discuss with him proposals for a conference. When they met, 'a great multitude came together from both sides . . . and the minds of all seemed earnestly turned towards peace.' Not quite all, because, when Labienus stepped forward, a dispute between him and Vatinius was interrupted by a 'shower of missiles from every quarter', and several notables and some centurions and soldiers were wounded. Protected by the shields of his soldiers, Labienus both appropriately and prophetically wound up Caesar's attempt to discuss peace; he roared out: 'Cease then to talk about a settlement, for there can be no peace for us till Caesar's head is brought in.'[1] That was the heart of the quarrel, only one of two severed heads could bring peace to the Roman world, and it was not Caesar's that was writ in the Book of Fate.

After Bibulus' death, Pompey continued to follow his policy of watching the ports of Illyricum and Epirus, in order to deny them to Antony. Because it was an exceedingly onerous and dangerous task for galleys, on his own initiative Libo decided to substitute for it a more positive one, to sail his fifty galleys to Brundisium and destroy Calenus' transports.

His raid found Antony wholly unprepared, and after Libo had suc-

[1] B.C., III, 19.

ceeded in burning several merchantmen, in towing away another laden with corn, and in dispersing a cavalry outpost in a night landing, he was so elated that he sent a despatch to Pompey in which he said 'that, if he liked, he might order the rest of his ships to be beached and repaired, and that with his own fleet he would keep off Caesar's reinforcements.'[1]

He had counted his chickens before they were hatched, for when Antony recovered from his surprise, he manned sixty row-boats, by a ruse enticed five of Libo's quadriremes into the harbour, captured one and drove the others out. What proved more effective was, that he picketed the shore-line with his cavalry, and prevented Libo from watering his ships. 'Moved by this need and by his disgrace,'[2] writes Caesar, Libo abandoned the enterprise.

The disgrace was rather Pompey's, because long before he should have appreciated that Libo's idea was the soundest one to prevent Antony from linking-up with Caesar, and that had the expedition, which probably was no more than a hastily organized raid, been carried out with a larger force and in accordance with a carefully thought-out plan, it might have deprived Caesar of his entire fleet of transports. Later, as we shall see, and when it was too late to prove decisive, a kindred operation was successfully carried out by Pompey's son Gnaeus.

The winter was now nearly over, and with approaching spring the crews of the Pompeian ships became increasingly more vigilant and active, and Caesar more and more pressing in urging Antony to put to sea and join him. At length the weather became favourable and Antony embarked his army, three veteran legions, one legion of recruits and 800 cavalry, and weighed anchor.

The wind was blowing from the south, and on the following day the fleet sailed past Apollonia on a northerly course. Soon after it was sighted by the Rhodian squadron at Dyrrachium, which put to sea to intercept it. An exciting stern chase followed, but a change of wind enabled Calenus to make for Nymphaeum (San Giovanni di Medua) three miles beyond Lissus. 'An incredible piece of luck,' Caesar writes, because sheltered by the shore, Antony was able to land in safety, while the wind, rising to a gale, drove sixteen of the Rhodian galleys on to the rocks and wrecked them. Those of their rowers and fighting men who succeeded in gaining the shore were captured; 'all these,' we are told, 'Caesar saved and sent back home.'[3] Only one of Antony's transports was lost with 220 recruits; she had lagged behind during the night,

[1] *Ibid.*, III, 23.      [2] *Ibid.*, III, 24.      [3] *Ibid.*, III, 27.

and surrendered on a solemn pledge that all lives would be spared; nevertheless, subsequently, all were massacred.

After he had landed, Antony was well received by the citizens of Lissus, who assisted him in every possible way. First, he sent a message to Caesar to inform him of his disembarkation and of the troops he had brought with him. Next, he instructed Calenus to station at Lissus thirty Gallic merchantmen, and then return with the remaining transports to Italy and bring over the rest of the horse and foot.[1] No mention is made by what route Antony intended to join Caesar; but as the coastal road was in enemy hands, the only other he could follow led from Lissus up the Mali river to Bassania, and thence by way of modern Tirana to Scampa on the Egnatian Way.

Pompey, who by road was closer to Lissus than Caesar, must have been the first to have received news of Antony's landing. Secretly he set out by night to ambush Antony on his southward march, and when his approach was reported, he halted at a suitable spot, and, in order to keep his forces hidden, he forbade camp-fires to be lit. Unfortunately for Pompey, Antony learnt of this through some Greeks, and at once went into camp and sent a messenger to Caesar to warn him of Pompey's intention. Meanwhile Caesar, who had received the news of the landing some hours after Pompey, set out on the following morning, and as the Apsus opposite his camp was unfordable, he marched up-stream, crossed by a ford, and then followed Pompey. When the latter became aware that Caesar was in rear of him, 'to escape being shut in by two armies', he abandoned his enterprise and withdrew his army to Asparagium. This opened the road for Caesar, who forthwith joined Antony.

Now that he was strongly reinforced, Caesar sent Domitius Calvinus with two legions – the 11th and 12th – and some 500 cavalry to intercept Scipio, who had left Syria and at the time was advancing through Macedonia to join Pompey. Also, because Thessalian and Aetolian envoys had arrived to solicit his protection, he sent L. Cassius Longinus (brother of Quintus) with the 27th Legion and 200 horse into Thessaly and Calvinus Sabinus with five cohorts and a few horsemen into Aetolia, to procure supplies of corn. To find troops for Sabinus, he took them from the legion under Acilius at Oricum, who was then left with three cohorts to hold it and guard the galleys Caesar had brought with him from Italy. To secure them, Acilius withdrew them into the inner harbour, sank a merchantman at the mouth of the chan-

[1] It is not mentioned that he did so.

nel which led into it, and anchored to her another, fitted with a turret of artillery, to ride above her. In spite of this, when Pompey's elder son Gnaeus, who commanded the Egyptian squadron, learnt that Acilius had been deprived of the greater part of his command, he determined to seize the galleys. First, he overwhelmed the floating blockship; next, by means of a windlass, he shifted the submerged one; then he stormed the town wall, and on rollers hauled four biremes[1] into the inner harbour, removed four of the galleys and burnt the others.

Not content with this remarkable feat, he next sailed to Lissus and burnt the thirty Gallic transports Antony had left there. Thus Caesar's entire fleet in Grecian waters was destroyed; not a single ship was left him even to communicate with Italy.

When Caesar learnt that Pompey was at Asparagium, he marched down the left bank of the river Genusus (Skumbi) and pitched his camp close to him. Next, he drew up his legions in order of battle, and when Pompey refused his challenge, he decided to move on Dyrrachium. Because Pompey barred his way, in full view of his camp Caesar marched up the valley of the Genusus, then took 'a wide circuit by a difficult and narrow route, in the hope that Pompeius could be either driven to Dyrrachium or cut off from it.'[2] Pompey inferred that Caesar had been compelled to abandon his camp through lack of supplies, and not until evening, when his scouts reported that he had turned northward, did he grasp Caesar's intention. Early on the following morning he set out at utmost speed for Dyrrachium.

Meanwhile Caesar, who suspected that this would happen, stayed 'his march only for a short period during the night', and then pushed on to the river Arzen, followed it some miles down-stream, then struck across the hills westward toward Dyrrachium, and pitched his camp on the northern side of a torrent, the Shimmihl. As he did so, to the south of him he saw Pompey's advanced guard marching northward along the Egnatian Way. He had short-headed his rival by, perhaps, an hour.

When Pompey found his road to Dyrrachium blocked, he entrenched his camp at a spot called Petra (Sasso Blanco) immediately to the south of the Shimmihl torrent, and as it had a moderately good roadstead he ordered a squadron of warships to proceed there. The advance on Dyrrachium had ended.

---

[1] A small two-banked galley.
[2] *Ibid.*, III, 41. Why 'driven to Dyrrachium' is not explained.

## 3. CAESAR'S BLOCKADE OF POMPEY

The situation in which the opposing armies were now placed, if not unique,[1] was an exceptional one. Both were cut off from their bases; Caesar's from Italy by Pompey's fleet, and Pompey's from Dyrrachium by Caesar's army. Of the two, Caesar's was at the greater disadvantage: not only had his army to be sustained in an enemy's country, but its inferiority in cavalry severely restricted foraging, whereas Pompey's, because of his command of the sea, could be supplied from Dyrrachium, which was well stocked with all warlike supplies. Time, therefore, favoured the latter, as also did the site of Dyrrachium. It occupied the southern extremity of a mountainous peninsula, some six miles in length, separated from the mainland by a lagoon, spanned at its southern extremity by a bridge, and at its northern end linked to the peninsula by a narrow sand bank. *Vis-à-vis* Caesar, the town was unattackable, for not only did he lack the necessary siege equipment, but even had he possessed it, because his army was half the strength of Pompey's, he could not simultaneously have held it at arm's length and laid siege to the town.

Because Pompey was unwilling either to risk a pitched battle, or relinquish his hold on Dyrrachium, in which 'his whole war material' was stored,[2] Caesar foresaw that the campaign was likely to be a lengthy one; therefore, at its outset, he sent one of his legates into Epirus to gather in supplies of corn and convey them to Lissus. But only a very small amount could be obtained, because little was grown in that mountainous country, and most of it had been carried away to Petra by Pompey's horsemen. When this was reported to Caesar, in spite of his numerical inferiority, he decided to blockade his enemy's army with three objectives in view: first, to secure his foragers by confining Pompey's cavalry to the coastal lands; next, to restrict its grazing, in order to render the horses 'useless for active operations'; and, lastly, 'that he might diminish the moral influence on which Pompey seemed chiefly to rely among foreign nations, when the report should be spread throughout the world that he was being beleaguered by Caesar and did not dare to fight a pitched battle.'[3]

Between Petra and the river Lesnikia (Gesnike) – five miles to the south – the bay of Dyrrachium was occupied by Pompey. It is shaped

---

[1] At the battle of Valmy, 1792, both Dumouriez and Brunswick fought facing their respective bases.

[2] *Ibid.*, III, 44.      [3] *Ibid.*, III, 43.

like a bow, the cord of which runs north-west and south-east, and east-ward of it lies a mountainous region, which forms the watershed of the streams that flow into the Arzen river or descend to the sea. Caesar's plan was to push southward from his camp a line of contravallation

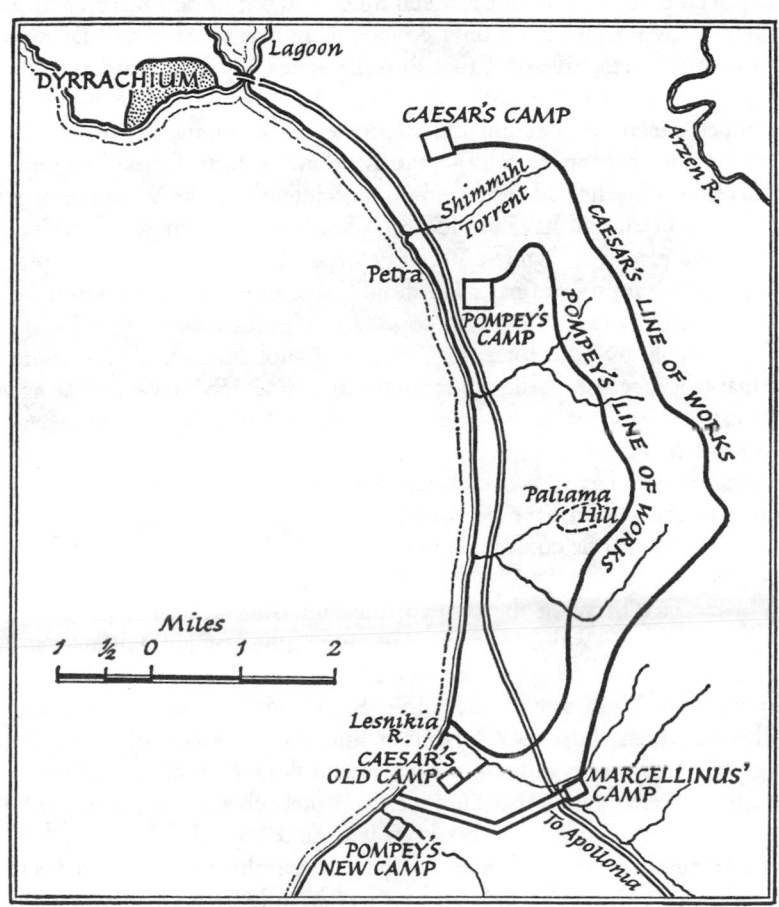

10. Blockade of Dyrrachium

along an irregular chain of heights; firstly, to fortify the hill tops in succession, and secondly, to link them together by groups of entrench-ments, until the whole area occupied by Pompey was enclosed.

To counter this, we are told that, because Pompey did not choose to fight a pitched battle, his 'only remaining course' was to occupy 'as many hills as possible', and enclose 'the widest extent of land possible', so as to compel Caesar to over-extend his chain of works, and at the same time gain the greatest extent of land on which to graze his horses. In all, he built a counter-line, reinforced with twenty-four redoubts, which embraced 'a circuit of fifteen miles, and within this he foraged.'[1]

It was by no means his only course, there was another and far and away a more effective one; that Pompey failed to adopt it is inexplicable. Because he did not intend to fight a pitched battle, in order to compel Caesar to abandon the blockade, his obvious course was to attack Caesar economically – that is, prevent him from foraging. Therefore, once he had fathomed Caesar's intention, like Vercingetorix at Alesia, he should have cut loose his vastly more numerous cavalry, and have placed it – which Vercingetorix failed to do – under command of a bold subordinate. He should have instructed him, while he himself held Caesar to his task, to wage a vigorous *guerre de course* on Caesar's convoys and foragers. That he did not do so is all the more remarkable because, in the mountainous area in which he was operating, his cavalry was not only virtually useless for battle but a serious encumbrance. Had he adopted this course, there can be little doubt that Caesar would have been compelled to abandon the blockade; that Dyrrachium would have been occupied by Pompey without need of a battle, and that he could then have decided whether to pursue Caesar or invade Italy.

In the race between the two fortified lines, Pompey was favoured by his interior position and the greater number of his workers; together they enabled him to prevent Caesar from closing in, and thereby compelled him to extend his line. In the daily engagements on the hills, in which the heavy legionary infantry were out of place, he rightly relied on his numerous archers and slingers, who wounded so many of Caesar's men that, in order to protect themselves, they made 'jerkins and other protections out of felt, quilt, or hide.'[2]

The most important of these engagements would appear to have been fought when Caesar had advanced some six miles from his camp. We are told that the 9th Legion, under Antony, 'occupied a certain post and had begun to fortify it.'[3] From Caesar's description of it, it would seem to have been the hill of Paliama. If so, it may be conjectured that,

---

[1] *B.C.*, III, 44. Caesar (III, 63) mentions 17 miles as the final length of his contravallation. According to Dodge's calculations (*Caesar*, vol. II, p. 518) Pompey enclosed about 16 square miles and Caesar about 20.

[2] *Ibid.*, III, 44.  [3] *Ibid.*, III, 45.

once it had been fortified, Caesar's intention was to push his contravallation to the coast, a little over a mile to the west of it. It was, therefore, imperative for Pompey to wrest the hill from Caesar. A stiff fight ensued, which is described by Caesar in considerable detail, and as it includes a disaparaging reference to Pompey as 'a worthless commander', in part at least it would appear to be an apology for Antony's failure to retain the hill. Because it is the first Pompeian success recorded since the campaign opened, it is probably referred to by Cicero in a letter he addressed from Dyrrachium to Atticus in the middle of June, in which he says that Pompey was 'in high hopes.'[1] Well might he be, for had Caesar succeeded in linking the hill with the coast, he would have shortened his eventual contravallation by more than a third of its length.

At the time, Caesar's supply situation must have been critical, because his account of his failure to hold the hill is immediately followed by a comment on it. While the enemy, he writes, has an 'abundance of all necessaries', and 'every day a large number of ships was gathering from every quarter to bring up stores, nor could any wind blow without their having a favourable course from some direction', he himself 'was in extreme straits'.[2] All the corn far and wide had been exhausted, and his men were reduced to making a kind of bread out of a root called *chara* (kelkâss) which is still eaten in Albania. We are told that when the Pompeians, in conversations across the trenches, taunted Caesar's men with hunger, the latter threw at them loaves made of this root, so as to show that they were not starving. And Appian mentions that, when some of these loaves were brought to Pompey, he was by no means pleased, and exclaimed: 'What kind of wild beasts are we fighting with?'[3]

These straits, borne by Caesar's men with great fortitude, were considerably allayed when they learnt from deserters that, although Pompey's cavalry horses were still being fed, great numbers of his baggage animals were perishing from starvation. Added to this, although Caesar could not hope to feed his army adequately until the corn ripened, he was not a man to be nonplussed by any difficulty, and since he was unable to prevent Pompey from supplying his army, he set out to deprive it of its water. This he did by damming and diverting the small streams which flowed from the mountains to the sea. To meet this unexpected danger, the Pompeians dug wells in the low land along the coast, but due to the hot weather they quickly dried

[1] *Ad. Att.*, XI, iv a.    [2] *B.C.*, III, 47.    [3] Appian, *Civil Wars*, II, 61.

up. Thus it came about that shortage of water, when added to lack of fodder, compelled Pompey to transfer his cavalry by sea to Dyrrachium,[1] where it could be readily fed, and was well placed to sally out in rear of Caesar's camp and attack his foragers.

The next incident, a most interesting one, is obscure, because of a missing passage in the *Commentaries*, as well as a gap in Appian's history. All the latter states is: 'A certain man of Dyrrachium having offered to betray the town to him, Caesar went by agreement with a small force by night to the gates of the temple of Artemis. . . .'[2] Then follows the gap, which in part is filled by Dio. He writes: 'Upon Dyrrachium itself Caesar made an attempt by night, between the marshes [lagoon] and the sea, in the expectation that it would be betrayed by its defenders. He got inside the narrows [? the bridge at the southern end of the lagoon] but at that point was attacked both in front and in the rear by large forces which had been conveyed along the shore in boats and suddenly fell upon him; thus he lost many men and very nearly perished himself.'[3]

From these tenuous excerpts it would appear that the alleged betrayal was a stratagem on the part of Pompey to draw Caesar away from his camp, so as to facilitate three attacks on his contravallation, with the aim of penetrating it and breaking the blockade.

Before Caesar set out, as he himself states, he placed Publius Sulla in command of the army during his absence. And when Caesar's narrative is resumed, we are told that, when Sulla was informed of an attack on one of the redoubts, held by a single cohort, he rushed to its support with two legions, and repulsed it, and when his men set out in pursuit, he recalled them and was blamed for doing so. But, when Caesar returned, he judged Sulla to have acted rightly, as it was not the part of a legate in temporary command to bring on a pitched battle in the absence of his commander. Of the other two attacks, one was made by a Pompeian legion against a redoubt held by three cohorts and was driven back; and the other was repulsed by Caesar's German cavalry, presumably dismounted.

Thus, writes Caesar, six battles were fought in one day, 'three at Dyrrachium and three at the outworks.'[4] In them, he says, 2,000 Pompeians fell and no more than 20 of his own men were lost. This

---

[1] As he had some 7,000 cavalry horses, this must have been a vast undertaking.
[2] *Ibid.*, II, 60. Holmes (vol. III, p. 480) conjectures that the date was July 1, 48 B.C.    [3] Dio, XLI, 50, 3–4.
[4] *B.C.*, III, 53. Of the three at Dyrrachium, nothing is known of two of them.

is hard to believe, because we are told that 30,000 arrows, discharged at one of the redoubts, were gathered up and counted, and that the shield of a centurion, by name Scaeva, was found to have 120 arrow holes in it. To have suffered such a paucity of casualties for such a multiplicity of arrows discharged at only one of several redoubts, must have been most gratifying to Caesar, because he presented Scaeva with 200,000 sesterces, promoted him to the post of first centurion of the first cohort, and rewarded the garrison of the redoubt – all of whom had been wounded – 'with double pay, grain, clothing, bounties, and military gifts.'[1] The profusion of these rewards clearly shows that the point of attack was an exceptionally important one.

For five days Pompey maintained his forward position, and then withdrew to his original line; whereupon Caesar advanced to a little short of catapult range of him, and challenged him to battle. As nothing came of the gesture, he made his final attempt to arrive at a peaceful settlement, and because he knew that it was useless to approach Pompey he sent an envoy to Scipio to discuss terms of peace. Once again nothing came of the mission.

At the same time he did something more profitable. To prevent Pompey's cavalry at Dyrrachium from foraging, by means of two forts he blocked its two narrow approaches. The result was that Pompey was compelled to bring back his cavalry by sea to his entrenched area, and supply it with fodder brought by sea from Corcyra and Acarnania – the district south of the gulf of Arta. Because this put a severe strain on his shipping, he decided to attempt another sortie, and as his objective he wisely selected the extreme left of Caesar's contravallation on the Lesnikia, 17 miles from his headquarters' camp north of the Shimmihl torrent.

At the time, in order to complete his line of contravallation, Caesar was carrying his entrenchments across the plain south of the Lesnikia, and to protect the rear of its garrisons he was also building a line of circumvallation parallel with it (see Plan No. 11). The two lines were 200 paces apart; the first consisted of a ditch 15 feet wide with a 10-foot rampart, and the second was of lesser proportions. These works were unfinished, because Caesar states that 'he had not yet completed the cross stockade facing the sea to join these two lines.'[2] By this he means that no transverse rampart linked the two lines of entrenchments together at their coastal end. This fact became known to Pompey through a stroke of unexpected good luck.

[1] *Ibid.*, III, 53.        [2] *Ibid.*, III, 63.

There were in Caesar's camp among his horsemen two Allobrogian officers, brothers, by name Raucillus and Egus, who had served with him in Gaul, and had been highly rewarded by him. Not content with the wealth they had accumulated, they embezzled the pay of their men and plotted to assassinate their brigade commander. When these things were discovered, they and a band of their intimates deserted to Pompey, and, as they were fully acquainted with the state of Caesar's fortifications, they informed Pompey of their weak points, including the absence of the 'cross-stockade' on the sea front.

So as to face Caesar's line of contravallation over the plain, Pompey had swung the right of his own line of entrenchments westward along the right bank of the Lesnikia, and to the south of the river, some 300 paces from the sea, he occupied a camp which had been built by Caesar's 9th Legion, but soon after was abandoned. As he expected to post several legions in it, he built around it a larger camp, and, in order to secure its water supply, he had an entrenchment, or rampart, of 400 paces in length, dug from its north-eastern corner to the river. But at the time he did not garrison the camp.

When he had gathered all the information he could from the two deserters, Pompey decided to carry out a combined land and sea attack on Caesar's left. While sixty cohorts advanced against his entrenchments close to the coast, a force of light-armed soldiers and archers was to move by sea and land in two parties: the one south of the wall of circumvallation to assault it from the south, and the other on the coast between the two lines – that is, where the transverse rampart had not yet been built. In brief, Caesar's left was simultaneously to be attacked in front, in rear, and in flank. In every way it was an admirably planned operation.

On July 9,[1] the attack was launched under cover of night, and the light troops were landed a little before daybreak. At the time, Lentulus Marcellinus, in command of the 9th Legion, was in camp on Caesar's contravallation about two miles from the coast, and two of his cohorts were relieving the guard at its seaward end. Although they at once manned the defences, the sudden landing on the coast between the two lines – the weak point indicated by the deserters – enabled the Pompeians to attack the defenders of both lines in flank. Under cover of a great number of archers, the light infantry gained a footing in the unwalled gap. They were met by volleys of stones, which did them little harm because visors made of osiers had been fitted to their

[1] See Holmes, vol. III, p. 480.

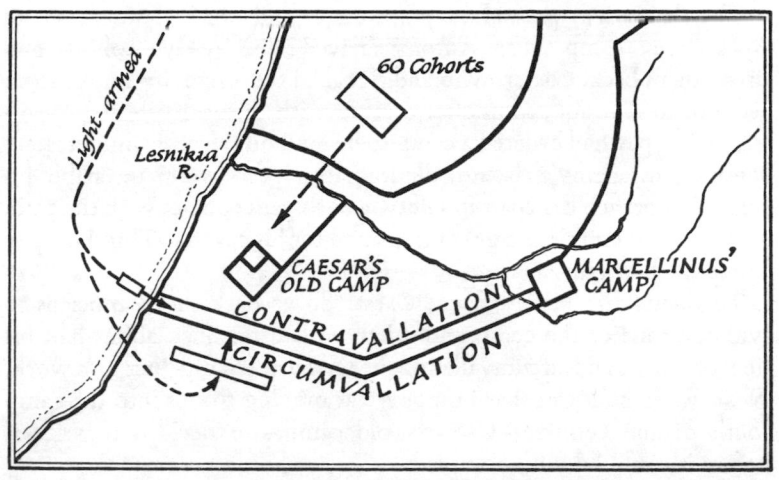

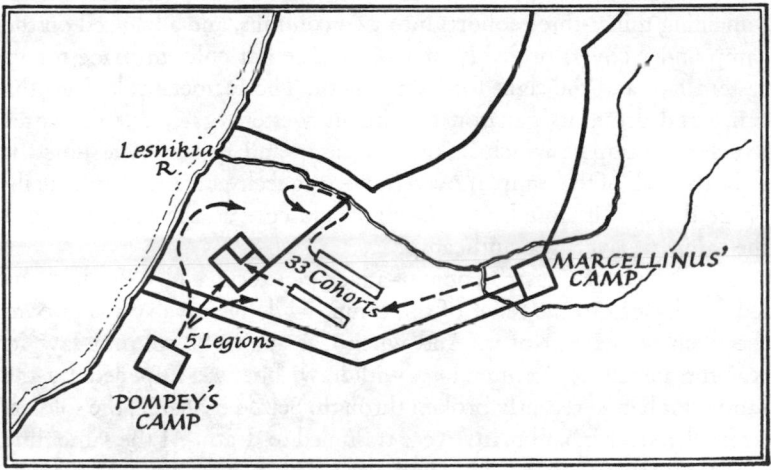

11. Battle of the Lesnikia

helmets.[1] Panic then seized on the defenders, who fled inland between the lines and impeded the advance of the reinforcements Marcellinus had despatched to their aid.

[1] In classical warfare, stones hurled by hand were common projectiles, and as the soldier's body was protected by his large shield, his face alone was vulnerable. Therefore, previous to the attack, Pompey had ordered his men 'to make protective coverings of osier for their helmets' (B.C., III, 62). It is interesting to note

The Pompeians pressed on after them, and were about to storm Marcellinus' camp when Antony arrived with twelve cohorts and drove them back. Caesar, who had signalled the alarm 'by smoke from redoubt to redoubt', soon after arrived with thirteen cohorts. Meanwhile Pompey had ordered a camp to be built on the coast immediately south of his enemy's circumvallation. Its objects were: to enable his ships to approach the coast in safety, and to gain contact with the plain south of the Lesnikia as a grazing ground for his cavalry. Thus Pompey broke the blockade.

To re-establish his left flank, Caesar drove back the Pompeians to within a mile of the coast, and when he had regained about half his lines of contra and circumvallation, he linked them together by a work. Next, when he learnt that Pompey was moving troops into the camp south of the Lesnikia – Caesar's old camp – he decided to seize it before it could be fully occupied.

He left two cohorts to hold the work he had built, then formed his remaining thirty-three cohorts into two columns, and advanced on the camp under cover, probably of woods. The left column made for its eastern face and the right for its northern. The former broke into the camp and drove its garrison toward its western gate, but the latter struck the rampart which linked the camp and the river, assumed it to be the wall of the camp, moved down it to seek a gate, and eventually broke through it close by the Lesnikia and entered the plain between the rampart, river, sea, and camp.

When news of Caesar's counter-attack was received by Pompey, he led five legions to the relief of the camp, while his cavalry swept over the plain to the east of it. And when Caesar's right column saw its rear threatened, it attempted to withdraw, but was impeded by the rampart it had so recently broken through. Seized by panic, the soldiers scrambled over it, and many were trampled to death. At the same time the Pompeian garrison, who had been driven back by Caesar's left column, when they saw Pompey advancing, turned about and charged it. But when the left column descried the right column in rout, its men were also swept by panic and a general *émeute* followed. 'Every place,' writes Caesar, 'was full of disorder, panic, and flight, so much so that when [he] grasped the standards of the fugitives and bade them

---

that in the First World War, visors of wire mesh were introduced to protect the eyes of British tankmen from 'splash', fragments of molten metal which frequently penetrated the joints in the tank's armour.

halt, some without slackening speed fled at full gallop, others in their fear even let go their colours, nor did a single one of them halt.'[1]

Fortunately for Caesar, Pompey did not pursue. Probably his men were in great disorder; but whatever the cause, it saved the routed army, and when at length Caesar restored order, he found that he had lost 32 tribunes and centurions, 960 rank and file, and 32 standards. We are told that many of these men perished without wound, having been trampled to death in the panic and flight of their comrades.

The losses sustained by Pompey are not recorded. All Caesar tells us is, that Pompey was hailed *Imperator*; that Labienus put the captives to death; and that 'the Pompeians gained so much confidence and spirit that, instead of forming a plan of campaign, they regarded themselves as having already conquered.' Finally, he adds: 'They did not re-flect that the cause of their success had been the small number of our troops'; that they had not won a pitched battle; and that their victory had been due not to valour but to fortune. Nevertheless, it was a notable success, and the Pompeians had every justification 'by reports and despatches ... to celebrate throughout the world the victory of that day.'[2]

## 4. CAESAR'S WITHDRAWAL INTO THESSALY

Now that Pompey had broken the blockade, and had solved his cavalry problem by gaining ingress to the grasslands south of the Lesnikia, Caesar's numerical inferiority, both in infantry and cavalry, rendered it impossible for him either to re-establish the blockade or supply his army. And, until the morale of his troops had been restored, it was out of the question to contemplate bringing Pompey to battle. There-fore the only course open to him was to withdraw his army to some other locality, or, as he writes: 'Driven from his former plans [he] came to the conclusion that he must alter his whole method of cam-paign.'[3] In other words, seek an area in which he could feed his army, revive its morale, and resume operations in more favourable conditions. This was complicated by his oversea bases at Apollonia and Oricum; which he could not relinquish because he was expecting reinforce-ments from Italy. Also, he was now encumbered with a large number of sick and wounded, and, unlike Bonaparte in Syria, in 1799, he valued his men too highly to leave them to a merciless enemy, which would further have reduced the morale of the army. He decided,

[1] *B.C.*, III, 69.    [2] *Ibid.*, III, 72.    [3] *Ibid.*, III, 73.

therefore, to convey them to Apollonia, and there consider what next to do.

First, he called in the garrisons of the redoubts and ordered a general assembly of the army, probably in the vicinity of Marcellinus' camp. There he harangued his men, praised some and publicly disgraced others, and 'inflamed' them with an eager desire to fight.[1] At nightfall on the day following the battle he sent ahead his baggage train, his sick and wounded, escorted by one legion, to Apollonia, and he 'forbade them to stop for rest till the journey was finished.' Some hours later four legions followed, and when they were on their way, with the two remaining ones as rear guard he evacuated his camp. As he departed, in order to comply with the military etiquette of the times, he had the signal for breaking-camp sounded, so 'that his departure might be known as late as possible' by the enemy – a gesture of defiance that he was not sneaking away.

Warned by the signal, with the utmost haste Pompey set out in pursuit, and at the river Genusus, the crossing of which delayed Caesar, his cavalry caught up with his enemy's rear guard, but was kept at bay by it and 400 'light-armed front-rank men' detailed to reinforce it. Under their cover, the retreat continued, and when Asparagium was reached, Caesar reoccupied his old camp. Soon after Pompey's army came up and also manned its former camp.

Then occurred an example of the bad discipline of Pompey's men. Because the camp fortifications were intact, they had little work to occupy them, and because in the hasty departure from the Lesnikia camp, the greater part of the baggage train had been left behind, without orders numbers of them returned to it to fetch their belongings. When Ceasar became aware of the confusion in Pompey's camp, he again signalled his departure, and gained a march of eight miles on his adversary. Only on the following morning was the latter able to resume the pursuit, which he pressed for four days and then abandoned.

At Apollonia Caesar housed his sick and wounded, and detailed four cohorts to garrison it and three to hold Oricum.[2] Then he considered the courses open to Pompey and himself.

---

[1] B.C., III, 73–74. It is characteristic of him that he said: 'The loss that had been sustained should be attributed to the fault of anyone rather than himself.' Caesar must be above reproach, and to have acknowledged his responsibility would have lowered his authority. According to Appian (Civil Wars, II, 64) in private he confessed to some friends that the blockade had been a mistake.

[2] One cohort at Lissus is also mentioned, but it must have been already there.

(1) Should Pompey move against Domitius Calvinus, he would compel him, when he was separated from his base at Dyrrachium, to accept battle.

(2) Should Pompey cross into Italy, he would unite with Domitius, and by way of Illyricum march to Italy's rescue.

(3) Should Pompey, in order to exclude him from the coast, lay siege to Apollonia and Oricum, he would join Domitius, and then advance against Scipio to compel Pompey to come to his support.[1]

To join Domitius was therefore imperative, in order to frustrate whichever course Pompey might adopt.

It will be remembered that, when Caesar had been reinforced by Antony, he had detached Domitius with two legions to hold back Metellus Scipio in Macedonia. Now he set out to join him, probably by advancing up the valley of the Aous river (Osum) which flowed from the western slopes of the Pindus range into the sea near Apollonia. It would lead him by way of the Metzovo pass into Thessaly, a country rich in corn, where he could solve his supply problem. Ahead of him he sent couriers to warn Domitius of his coming, and, presumably, named a *rendezvous*.

When he abandoned his pursuit, Pompey returned to the Egnatian Way, most likely at Asparagium. Already he had sent letters to the provincial governors and city magnates announcing his victory in glowing terms, with the result that those who had favoured Caesar forthwith turned their political coats and pronounced for Pompey. Beset by his rabble of self-seeking senators, knights and notables, whom he should have left at Dyrrachium, where he had posted Cato with fifteen cohorts, he assembled a council of war in order to pacify them, instead of sending them to Dyrrachium and acting on his own initiative

Some urged that he should invade Italy, others that he should pursue Caesar and bring him to battle. Neither course appealed to him. He thought it impolitic to carry the war into Italy, and dishonourable 'to fly a second time before Caesar, and be pursued'. Also that it would be disgraceful to abandon Scipio.[2] His own plan, which in the circumstances he was placed in was undoubtedly the right one, was 'to avoid a battle', and 'keep Caesar under siege and harass him with lack of supplies by following close upon him.'[3] Abused, criticized

---

[1] *Ibid.*, III, 78.

[2] Plutarch, *Pompey*, LXVI, 5. See also Dio, XLI, 52, 3.

[3] Plutarch, *Pompey*, LVII, 1. See also his *Caesar*, XL, 1, and Appian, *Civil Wars*, II, 66.

and insulted, according to Plutarch, he gave way. 'They forced him to forsake his own prudent resolution:'[1] to march to the support of Scipio in order to prevent his defeat, but not in order to defeat Caesar.

Caesar's version would seem to bear this out. It is that Pompey decided, should Caesar advance against Scipio, to march to Scipio's support; but should Caesar remain in 'the district of Oricum, waiting for his legions and cavalry from Italy,' he would attack Domitius 'in full force.'[2] He adopted the first alternative, which suggests that he was aware that Caesar had left the coast to join Domitius, when Scipio would be placed in extreme peril.

Meanwhile none of Caesar's couriers succeeded in reaching Domitius, who had been manœuvring against Scipio, and, in order to forage his two legions, had moved to Heraclia (Zervokhori) on the Egnatian Way. He was unaware that Pompey was advancing along it through Candavia until one day, when Pompey's cavalry van was within four hours' march of Heraclia, his own cavalry scouts bumped into a party of Allobrogian horsemen, 'friends of Raucillus and Egus.' As it happened, both parties had been acquainted with each other in Gaul, and were friendly. From the Allobrogians the Domitian scouts learnt that Pompey's army was only a few miles in rear of them. When this was reported to Domitius, he instantly struck camp, and with haste made for the valley of the Aliacmon (Vistritza) to his south. In the meantime Caesar had crossed the pass of Metzovo, and, so it would seem, by chance the two armies met at Aeginium (Kelambaka).

From Aeginium Caesar advanced to Gomphi (Paleo-Episkopi), 20 miles to its south, and as the report of Pompey's victory had led its governor to assume that Caesar had lost the war, he closed the town gates against him, and sent messengers to Pompey and Scipio – now at Larissa – to come to his aid. Forthwith Caesar stormed the town, and as a warning to all who had changed sides, he 'gave it over to his men for plunder.'[3] Next, he advanced on Metropolis (Palaeo-Kastro), 30 miles to the south-east, and because the news of Gomphi's fate had

---

[1] Plutarch, *Pompey*, XLVII, 4. Appian, *Civil Wars* (II, 67), says: 'he prepared for battle against his will, to his own hurt and that of the men who had persuaded him to it.'

[2] *B.C.*, III, 78.

[3] *Ibid.*, III, 80. Appian (II, 64) states that: 'The soldiers, who had suffered much from hunger, stuffed themselves immoderately and drank wine to excess;' the worst offenders were the Germans.

reached it, its inhabitants surrendered to him, and in recompense 'were most carefully preserved from harm.' After this, with the exception of Larissa, 'there was no state of Thessaly ... that did not obey Caesar and submit to his authority.' Then, we are suddenly told that Caesar found 'a suitable place in the country district, where the crops were now nearly ripe,' and there 'he determined ... to await the arrival of Pompeius and to transfer thither all his military operations.'[1] A few days later Pompey marched into Larissa and joined Scipio. The withdrawal into Thessaly had ended.

## 5. THE BATTLE OF PHARSALUS

Where was the 'suitable place' mentioned by Caesar? He gives no inkling, which is all the more remarkable because Thessaly, since 148 B.C., had been absorbed by the Roman province of Macedonia, and many of its place-names were household words in the days of Homer.[2]

Appian says that it was near Pharsalus (Férsala), also Plutarch, Polyaenus, and Suetonius; and Hirtius says near Palaepharsalus, Old Pharsalus, now called Mt Koutouri; with him Frontinus, Eutropius, and Orosius agree. Both cities are located south of the Enipeus river (Kutchuk Tchanarli), and the latter lies some seven miles west of the former. Because recent criticism tends to favour the latter, and because Dr Holmes and Sir Frank Adcock accept the locality of the battlefield as conjectured by F. L. Lucas,[3] it is accepted here. According to Lucas, Caesar pitched his camp on the right bank of the Enipeus to the north of Palaepharsalus, and when Pompey came down from Larissa, he pitched his on the eastern slopes of Mt Dogandzis to face Caesar's, which probably lay about three and a half miles east of it. The Enipeus was fordable, and in places its banks were steep. The date of the battle was August 9, 48 B.C., June 6 of the Julian calendar.

At Larissa Pompey paraded his army, and harangued it. He thanked his own men for their past deeds, and promised Scipio's that, when victory was won, they would share in the plunder. But while he was encouraging them, his quarrelling and self-seeking subordinates were undermining his authority by openly taunting him and contending among themselves for the prizes of victory. 'In a word,' writes Caesar,

[1] B.C., III, 81.

[2] An example of how slipshod the *Commentaries* frequently are, which at times makes them so exasperating to a military student.

[3] See 'The Battle-Field of Pharsalos', *Annual of the British School of Athens*, vol. XXIV (1919–21).

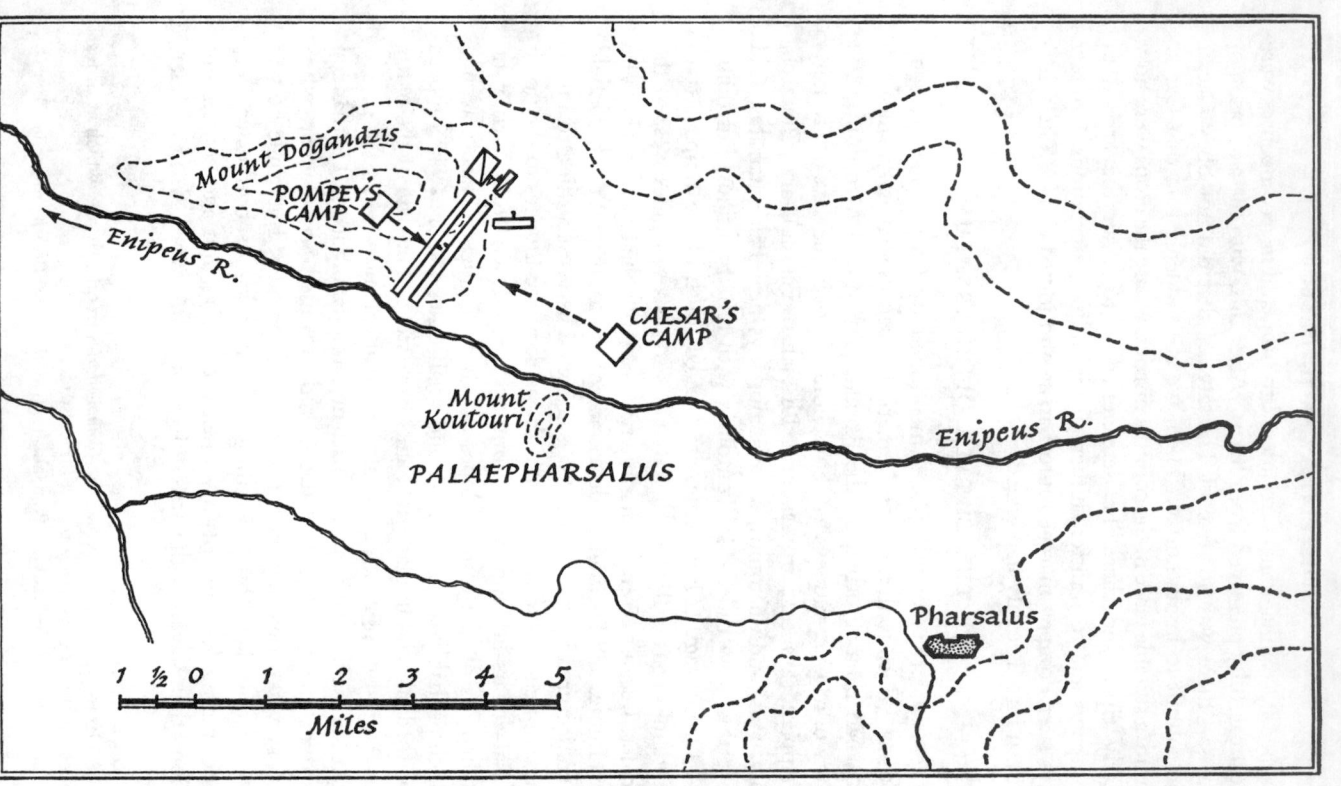

12. The Battle of Pharsalus

'all were agitating about honours for themselves, or about prizes of money, or about the prosecution of their private quarrels, nor were their reflections concerned with the means by which they could gain the upper hand, but with the way in which they ought to use their victory.'[1] Nor did they cease their wrangles and clamour even when Pompey had camped on Mt Dogandzis and faced his redoubtable antagonist.

Meanwhile Caesar had replenished his supplies, and when Pompey arrived he led his army out of camp to 'a position favourable to himself' and challenged him to battle. This he did daily, and on each occasion he approached closer to Pompey's camp; but with the exception of some cavalry skirmishes, in which one of the two Allobrogian deserters was killed, he failed to induce Pompey to do more than draw up his line on the spurs of the mountain – that is, on ground unfavourable for his enemy to attack over. This led Caesar to assume that Pompey could not be enticed to accept battle, and, as his supplies were nearly exhausted, he decided to move from his camp, first revictual, and then manoeuvre Pompey out of each strong position he might occupy and compel him to accept battle on more favourable ground, or else wear out his army by constant marching.

On the day of departure, when the tents had already been struck, and the troops were about to fall in, it was noticed that Pompey had advanced his line considerably further from his camp, 'so that it seemed [to Caesar] possible for a battle to be fought in no disadvantageous position.' He cancelled the withdrawal, and said to his officers: 'We must put off our march . . . and think of giving battle, as we have always demanded. Let us be prepared in heart for a conflict; we shall not easily hereafter find an opportunity.'[2] Then he led out his troops in fighting order.

What had induced Pompey to abandon his defensive position? The reason may be conjectured with tolerable certainty. It was that his daily refusals to accept Caesar's challenge had brought his generalship into such contempt that, to put an end to his intolerable position, he decided to substitute for his Fabian policy an offensive plan. To discuss it, he assembled a council of war, and to the consternation of those present, announced that his plan was to defeat Caesar's army before the opposing lines could meet. 'I have induced my cavalry,' he said, '. . . as soon as the two armies have drawn nearer, to attack Caesar's right wing on his open flank, and by surrounding his column from the rear to

[1] B.C., III, 83.          [2] Ibid., III, 85.

drive his army in confused rout before a weapon is cast at the foe by us. So we shall finish the war without imperilling the legions and almost without a wound. And this is not difficult, considering that we are so strong in cavalry.'[1]

Labienus next spoke. He extolled 'to the utmost the strategy of Pompeius', and scoffed at Caesar's army. It was no longer the army that had subdued Gaul and Germany; only a small part of that army had survived; many of its men had perished of fever, and its flower had fallen in the Dyrrachium battles. All then swore that they would not return to their camp except as victors.

The cavalry plan was an admirable one, reminiscent of Alexander's at the battle of the Hydaspes, and, as in the days of Achaemenides, Pompey's cavalry consisted of national contingents, some good and some no doubt indifferent – normally the Oriental horse were considerably superior to the Oriental foot. His 6,700 were made up of: 600 Galatians, 500 Cappadocians, 500 Thracians, 200 Macedonians, 500 Gauls and Germans from Alexandria, 200 Syrians – mostly mounted archers – and 800 of Pompey's slaves and herdsmen. To these were added 3,400 Dardani, Bessi, Thessalians, and men of other nations. Whatever the defects of this gathering of chivalry may have been, if skilfully led, its very numbers rendered it formidable.

According to Caesar, he deployed on the battlefield eighty cohorts (8 legions)[2] and Pompey deployed 110 (11 legions); their respective strengths were 22,000 and 45,000 men. In addition to them, each detailed seven cohorts to garrison his camp.

Pompey's order of battle was as follows: On the left, under his personal command, the two legions Caesar had sent him before the war, now numbered 1st and 3rd; under Scipio, in the centre, his two Syrian legions, and in the right wing, under Lentulus, the Cilician legion with some cohorts under Afranius.[3] The remaining six were posted between the centre and the wings. The right wing rested on the Enipeus, 'a stream with difficult banks', and 'the whole of the cavalry and all his archers and slingers' were posted, under Labienus, 'on the left

[1] B.C., III, 86.

[2] After Antony had reinforced him, Caesar had eleven legions; where were the remaining three? Presumably, in part, they are accounted for by the eight cohorts at Apollonia, etc.; the five with Calvinus Sabinus in Aetolia, and the seven which garrisoned Caesar's camp. According to Dio (XLII, 14, 1) Caesar sent Fufius Calenus to capture the Piraeus; this may have accounted for another ten cohorts.

[3] When he joined Pompey is not recorded.

of the left wing'.[1] The legions were marshalled in three lines, each ten ranks deep.[2]

As usual, in his order of battle, Caesar posted the 10th Legion on the right of his line, and the 9th on its left, and as the latter had suffered heavy casualties in the Dyrrachium battles, he brigaded it with the 8th Legion; his remaining five legions he distributed in between them. Antony commanded the left wing, Domitius Calvinus the centre, and Publius Sulla the right wing, in rear of which Caesar took post. Like Pompey's army, Caesar's was organized in three lines, but as it was vital that its front should not be overlapped, and as it was half the strength of Pompey's, the ranks of each line are unlikely to have numbered more than six; therefore, theoretically, Pompey's army had the greater staying power. Nevertheless, it was a mistake on Pompey's part not to have adopted a less dense order, because it would have enabled him to prolong his front, and have compelled Caesar to over-extend his, as he had been forced to do during the blockade, but it may have been due to the lay of the ground.

When Caesar noticed that his enemy's cavalry was massing on Pompey's left, he immediately divined that its purpose was to envelop his right flank, and that his 1,000 horsemen,[3] whom he had posted on the right of it, would, unless supported, be overwhelmed. Therefore, in order to reinforce them, he adopted Xenophon's suggestion,[4] withdrew six cohorts from his third line,[5] and posted them out of sight obliquely behind his right wing cavalry and infantry – that is, *en crochet*. He reminded them that 'the day's victory depended on the valour of

[1] Frontinus (*Stratagems*, II, 3, 22) says that Pompey posted 600 cavalry on his right wing; Eutropius (VI, 20) says 500. It is unlikely, because on the right there was no room to manoeuvre.

[2] Frontinus, II, 3, 22.

[3] *B.C.*, III, 84.

[4] In his *The Cavalry Commander* (V, 13 and VIII, 19) he pointed out that, because mounted men stood higher than those on foot, it was possible to hide infantry in rear of cavalry, and if on a sudden 'they came out and went for the enemy . . . they would prove an important factor in making the victory more decisive'.

[5] *B.C.*, III, 89 and 91. Both Appian (*Civil Wars*, II, 76) and Plutarch (*Pompey*, LXXI) agree that Caesar detached six cohorts, and that they numbered 3,000 men. Holmes (vol. III, pp. 168 and 469) objects, and says that Caesar meant eight when he wrote six – that is, one from each legion, because the average strength of his cohorts was 275 and not 500 men. But eight cohorts of 275 men each make a total of 2,200 and not 3,000. Obviously Appian and Plutarch, unaware of the average strength of Caesar's cohorts, quoted the establishment figure – a common makeshift in military history.

these cohorts',[1] and at the same time 'he commanded the third line and the whole army not to join battle without orders from himself,' which would be signalled by flag.[2] This done, he addressed his troops.

When the two opposing lines were within charging distance – that is, about 150 paces apart – in order to stimulate the ardour of Caesar's men, an Homeric incident opened the battle. A centurion of the right wing rushed out of the ranks, and, presumably, was engaged by an opposing champion. During this display of defiance, or immediately following it, Caesar ordered his line to advance, while Pompey ordered his to stand fast, so that its ranks would not be disordered, and, when the two lines clashed, his men would not be breathless. These tactics are condemned by Caesar as 'irrational' on the part of Pompey, 'because there is a certain keenness of spirit and impetuosity implanted by nature in all men which is kindled by the ardour of battle.'[3] Although this is true enough from one point of view, Pompey's decision to stand his ground is no less so from another, and in the history of war there are to be found many examples which confirm this. For instance, at the battle of Taginae, in 522, Justinian's army, under his eunuch general Narses, stood to its ground, accepted the Gothic assault, and utterly defeated it. The same tactics were adopted by Edward III at Crécy, in 1346, with overwhelming success, and again by Wolfe at Quebec and by Wellington at Waterloo. Which of the two is to be preferred depends, like most things in war, on circumstances.

Because Pompey stood his ground, when Caesar's line had advanced half-way across the interval between the two armies, he halted it in order to allow his men to regain their breath, and after the pause they advanced at the double, hurled their *pila* and charged home. 'Nor, indeed,' writes Caesar, 'did the Pompeians fail to meet the emergency:' they parried the shower of missiles with their shields, and 'had recourse to their swords'. In other words, they stood their ground and vindicated Pompey's tactics.

[1] B.C., III, 89. Appian (II, 76) says that Caesar ordered them, 'When they should see the enemy trying to flank him, to rise, dart forward and thrust their spears [they had none, only *pila*] directly in the faces of the men because . . . still in the bloom of youth, they could not endure injury to their faces.' Plutarch and others repeat this rubbish; but that he told them to use their *pila* like spears is probable. Pompey adopted a somewhat similar tactical order in the battle on the Abas river against the Albanians under Oroeses (Dio, XXXVII, 4, 2).

[2] B.C., III, 89.
[3] Ibid., III, 92.

At the same time Labienus charged Caesar's right wing, and Caesar's description of what happened is as follows:

The Pompeian cavalry 'charged in a body and the whole multitude of archers poured forth.' Thereupon Caesar's cavalry fell back, and as they did so, the Pompeians pressed eagerly forward and began to surround Caesar's exposed flank. Caesar then gave the signal to his fourth line, 'composed of six cohorts'. It advanced rapidly and 'attacked Pompeius' horse with such fury that not one of them stood his ground, and all wheeling round, not only quitted the position but forthwith in hurried flight made for the highest hills.' Next, we read: 'all the archers and slingers, left defenceless, without support, were slain.'[1]

What does this amount to? That some 1,600 legionaries, armed with the *pilum* – an indifferent anti-cavalry weapon – routed some 6,700 cavalry, and slew some 3,000 archers and 1,200 slingers – very agile troops. This is pure Munchausen, and really will not do.

Instead, what seems more probable is, that Labienus never made any use of his archers and slingers; never allotted specific objectives to his squadrons, and did not think to lead in person those he should have detailed to carry out the decisive assault, whether aimed at the front, flank, or rear of his enemy's right wing. It would seem that throughout, like the Duke of Plaza-Toro, he led his charge from behind!

What he should have done – which at least is sensible – is to have organized his cavalry into five divisions. With one have driven back his enemy's cavalry; then advanced his archers and slingers, closely supported by another division; have smothered the enemy right wing with missiles,[2] and when its ranks were in confusion, with two other divisions, as well as the one with the archers, have charged them in front, flank, and rear, while he held the fifth division in reserve.

Instead, it is suggested that what he actually did was to assemble his entire force of cavalry on a narrow frontage – that is, marshalled in great depth – and then ordered the whole to charge Caesar's right wing cavalry.[3] It did so, and when its leading squadrons suddenly saw ahead of them the serried ranks of Caesar's fourth line with *pila* at the charge,

---

[1] *Ibid.*, III, 93.

[2] *Cf.* William the Conqueror at Hastings.

[3] Or it may have been due to a not uncommon occurrence, that in cavalry engagements the excitement of man and horse is frequently so over-mastering that, when a body is ordered to charge, neighbouring bodies either join in, or are unable to hold back their horses. A classical example is the twice repeated un-authorized charge of Lefebvre-Desnouettes' and Guyot's cavalry divisions at Waterloo. The antidote is to keep the several bodies of cavalry well spaced.

they swerved aside to avoid it. This caused a panic in rear of them, and in the *sauve qui peut* which followed, the archers and slingers were ridden down. Panic, rather than the furious attack of the six cohorts,[1] would seem the more probable cause of Labienus' ignominious failure, which cost Pompey the battle.

When Labienus' horsemen were in wild retreat, the fourth line cohorts wheeled inward and fell upon the now exposed flank of Pompey's left wing, and as they did so Caesar signalled his third line – his reserve – to reinforce his first and second lines, at the time hotly engaged. To be simultaneously attacked in flank and in front was too much for the Pompeians, who broke and in rout fled to their camp.

It was staunchly defended by its garrison, supported by a contingent of Thracians and other auxiliaries; yet, in spite of their resistance, it was stormed, and the fugitives sought refuge on an adjoining height. Although there was much valuable loot in the camp, Caesar urged his men 'not to let slip an opportunity of completing their task' by plundering it. They pressed on and began to enclose the height the Pompeians had occupied with an earthwork; but because the position lacked water, the fugitives withdrew from it to a hill some four miles distant, at the foot of which flowed a stream. In spite of his troops being by now 'worn out by the continuous toil of a whole day,' Caesar continued the pursuit with four legions, and cut the fugitives off from the stream by an entrenchment. The game was now up, and the Pompeians sent a deputation to him to treat of surrender. At early dawn on the following day they came down from the hill and piled their arms before their conqueror. Caesar addressed a few words to them 'about his own lenity . . . and commended them to his soldiers, urging that none of them should be injured.'[2] Then he ordered all his legions to join him, and with them he marched to Larissa.

What of Pompey? He remained in his camp until its rampart fell. Then he discarded his insignia as *Imperator*, mounted a horse and sped to Larissa, from where with 30 horsemen he rode to the coast and boarded a corn-ship, which carried him to Amphipolis (Yeni Keui). There he procured money, and then sailed to Mytilene, where his

---

[1] When charged by cavalry, the natural impulse of infantry is either to stand fast and meet it, or break and scatter; it most certainly is not to attack. Pompey's suspicion that the disaster was due to betrayal (*B.C.*, III, 96) is unlikely, because Labienus hated Caesar.

[2] *B.C.*, III, 98.

wife Cornelia and his younger son Sextus had been living during the war.

According to Caesar, his losses were 200 men and about 30 centurions killed, and of Pompey's he states that 15,000 'appeared to have fallen,' more than 24,000 surrendered, and that 180 military standards and nine eagles were brought to him. Also he mentions that, in the pursuit, Domitius Ahenobarbus was slain.

## 6. POMPEY'S GENERALSHIP

Throughout the campaign, Pompey had proved himself to be no unworthy opponent, and, like Hannibal, no friendly contemporary hand has recorded his deeds. When it is borne in mind that his army was largely a mosaic of hastily raised levies; that the loyalty of his best troops was suspect; that, unlike Caesar, he was not absolute master of his policy, was consistently frustrated by a junta of self-seeking senators; and, above all, was faced by one of the most renowned captains of antiquity, he did not do so badly.

His strategy of attrition was excellent, and his tactics able. During the blockade he worsted Caesar at Dyrrachium by ruse; on the hill of Paliama by driving Antony off it; and in his final break-through by a well-conceived amphibious operation. The position he took up on Mt Dogandzis was well chosen; it fitted his strategy, and compelled Caesar either to attack him uphill and risk defeat, or retire through lack of supplies. And in the battle of Pharsalus his tactical plan to overwhelm Caesar's right with his vastly superior cavalry was an admirable one, and it probably would have succeeded had he had at call, not necessarily a Cromwell, a Seydlitz, or a Murat, to command it, but nothing more than a normally efficient cavalry general. His failure was not due to lack of ability, or skill, but to lack of resolution, which Napoleon acclaimed 'the essential quality of a general'. He allowed himself to be hectored, badgered, and pushed into battle against his better judgement, and the result was an unnecessary and totally disastrous defeat.

# XI

# The Alexandrian and Pontic Wars

## 1. CAESAR'S STRATEGICAL SOMERSAULT

AFTER Pompey's defeat, the war might have been brought to an end had Caesar put his policy of moderation to its final test and declared a general amnesty. This is what Cicero considered he should have done, and he outlined his proposal in a letter addressed to Gaius Cassius in August, 47 B.C. – that is, a year after Pharsalus. In it he wrote:

'I thought that after the great battle . . . had been fought, the victors would desire measures to be taken in the interests of the community, and the vanquished in their own [*i.e.*, the former by offering lenient terms, the latter by laying down their arms]; but I held that both the former and the latter depended upon the promptitude with which the victor acted.'[1]

Why Caesar did not adopt this policy we do not know: it may never have occurred to him, or, if it did, he may have considered it too chimerical. He was more of a soldier than a statesman – a man of action than a man of thought – and time and again he placed himself in a critical predicament by rushing his problems head down.

When Cicero's policy is set aside, and Caesar's military problem is alone considered, what should his answer have been? Should he pursue Pompey and eliminate him for good and all; or should he return to Italy, consolidate his victory, and then eliminate Pompey's surviving adherents?

The choice depended on the correct appreciation of the change in the strategical conditions arising out of the battle. Although some were obscure, the following were either conjectural or apparent:

(1) That in the eastern provinces and client kingdoms Pompey's prestige, like Hannibal's after Zama, was likely to be reduced to ghostly form, and that it would rematerialize was highly improbable.

---

[1] *Ad. Fam.*, XV, xv, 2.

(2) That many of Pompey's subordinates – Scipio, Labienus, Afranius, Gnaeus Pompey, and others – had escaped capture, had joined Cato at Corcyra, and because their nearest secure refuge was the province of Africa, which remained Pompeian, they were likely to go there.

(3) That, since the Ebro campaign, the Pompeian cause in Spain had revived and was increasingly gaining popular support. In Numidia King Juba was still as anti-Caesarian as in the days of Curio. And although many of the provincial and client naval contingents had abandoned the Pompeians, their fleet remained a formidable one.

(4) That during Caesar's withdrawal into Thessaly, the Pompeian admirals, Decimus, Laelius and Gaius Cassius, had struck at Brundisium and Messana (Messina), and though their expeditions were unsuccessful, they showed that Italy was still open to attack.

With hindsight at our disposal, these strategical conditions suggest that Caesar's most profitable course was to leave Pompey to his Hannibalic doom, and eliminate his followers before they could recover from the shock of defeat. But Caesar was not endowed with second sight; therefore there is little to quibble at when he tells us that he 'thought it right to put aside everything and follow Pompeius, into whatever parts he should have betaken himself in his flight, that he might not be able again to collect other forces and to renew the war.'[1]

When that had been accomplished, should he act with his customary speed, he would be in a position to eliminate Pompey's adherents before they could raise and train an army of sufficient power to resist him.

At Larissa he paused for a bare twenty-four hours, during which he appointed Antony to govern Italy, and take with him such legions as could be spared, and he instructed Domitius Calvinus to form three new legions out of Pompey's surrendered troops, and proceed with them to the province of Asia. Then he ordered the 6th Legion to follow him, while he himself with 800 cavalry rode to Sestus (Kilid Bahr) on the Hellespont. From Sestus he sailed to Ephesus, and there, when he learnt that Pompey had been in Cyprus, he rightly concluded he was *en route* for Egypt. So he sailed on to Rhodes and then for Alexandria with the 6th Legion and another, under Fufius Calenus, he had summoned from Achaia, as well as his 800 cavalry, escorted by 'ten warships from Rhodes and a few from Asia'.[2] Together the two legions numbered no more than 3,200 men.

---

[1] *B.C.*, III, 102.

[2] *Ibid.*, III, 106. Actually ten Rhodian, eight Pontic, five Lycian, and twelve from Asia. According to Holmes (vol. III, p. 180) 'he embarked with the 6th and

He considered this minute force sufficient, because his victory had so raised his prestige 'that every place would be equally safe for him'.[1] This *folie de grandeur* led him to commit what Napoleon held to be a crucial error in generalship: '*Un général,*' he said, '*ne doit jamais se faire de tableaux, c'est le pire de tout.*' In other words, a general should never base an actual situation on an imaginary one – he should found his actions on facts and not on fancies. But Caesar imagined that his fame was so great that no one would dare to resist him.

Meanwhile from Mytilene Pompey sailed to Rhodes, and on being refused entry proceeded to Attalia (Antalya) in Pamphylia and thence to Cyprus. On his way he took aboard some 2,000 troops and 60 fugitive senators, and on about September 24, when he neared Pelusium, close by the eastern branch of the Nile, he noticed a large army encamped, and rightly judged it to be that of King Ptolemy XIII, a boy of about thirteen years of age. He sent to him a message to request asylum.

At the time, Ptolemy was at war with his sister Cleopatra VII, who had been associated with him in the sovereignty. Recently he had defeated her, and she had fled to Syria. There she raised a new army, had returned, and, when Pompey arrived, was encamped not far from her brother's position. Because the king was a minor, Pompey's message was considered by his chief ministers: the eunuch Pothinus, his treasurer; Achillas, his commander-in-chief; and Theodotus, his tutor. Should they agree with Pompey's request, they feared that he might intrigue with Cleopatra; besides, like all Egyptian armies, the king's was a mercenary one, and in its ranks were many old soldiers who had served under Gabinius and Pompey. Therefore they also feared that, should Pompey be allowed to land, he might foment a revolution and make himself master of Egypt. So they decided to lure him ashore and assassinate him.

Their plan was, that Achillas, accompanied by two of Pompey's former officers, Salvius and Septimius, bribed or hostile to him, should be rowed out to Pompey and hand him a friendly message from the king. This they set out to do, and when they came alongside Pompey's galley, Cornelia at once suspected treason and entreated her husband not to go ashore. Nevertheless, he agreed to do so, and was accompanied

---

part of the cavalry alone, leaving the rest of the cavalry and the legion of Calenus to follow.'

[1] *Ibid.,* III, 106.

by his freedman Philippus and three other servants. The skiff then pulled away and made for the shore, and as it reached it, in full view of the king and his army, Septimius stabbed Pompey in the back, cut his head off and presented it to Ptolemy, who ordered it to be embalmed.

Thus, on September 28, 48 B.C., perished Pompey the Great. It was the anniversary of the day on which he had entered Rome to celebrate his triumph for his subjection of the pirates and his conquest of the East, and, as Plutarch records, he was 'in the fifty-ninth year of his age, the very next day after [? before] the day of his birth.'

Within a few days of his death, Caesar cast anchor outside Alexandria, and when his arrival became known, Theodotus put off in a boat, and, in order to propitiate him, proffered him the embalmed head of his great antagonist. From it Caesar turned away in abhorrence, and by Plutarch is said to have shed tears.

The conflict between him and Pompey was at an end; the purpose for which he had come to Egypt was accomplished. All that now remained to be done was to send a friendly envoy ashore, revictual his ships, stand out for Italy, and bring the Civil War to its conclusion. Instead, he did nothing of the sort, and decided to land his minute army and impose his will on the Egyptians! Was it because he was so infatuated by his success that he took it for granted that no man would dare to oppose him? Should the apologies for this will-o'-the-wisp decision, as suggested by Holmes, be valid: that it was legally incumbent on him to settle the dispute between Ptolemy and his sister, and to extract from the former the money his father had promised to pay the Roman people for their assistance in restoring him to his throne, they are quite secondary to his task of bringing the Civil War to a rapid end. Further, to suggest that 'above all it was essential to secure Egypt with its great resources against an enemy who might use it as a base,'[1] is fantastic. Should Caesar have ever contemplated so considerable a task, surely he would have brought with him more than a strong body-guard.

As suggested, it would seem far more likely that he assumed his fame alone was sufficient to warrant the immediate submission of the citizenry of Alexandria, and to impress them with his authority, he committed once again a totally irrational blunder: he stepped ashore preceded by his consular lictors with their fasces – that is, as a Roman general empowered to impose marshal law on Egypt. This act of blind arrogance caused the greatest indignation, first among the garrison of the city,

1 *The Roman Republic*, vol. III, pp. 181-2.

and then among the citizenry. 'The whole multitude,' Caesar naïvely writes, 'asserted that the royal authority was being infringed,' as it most certainly was. When the tumult subsided, it broke out again on successive days, 'and many soldiers' – presumably his own – 'were killed in all parts of this town.'[1] Thus, writes Suetonius, was started 'a war . . . of great difficulty, convenient neither to time nor place . . . carried on . . . within the walls of a well-provisioned and crafty foeman, while Caesar himself was without supplies of any kind and ill-prepared.'[2]

To secure his little army from annihilation, he occupied the royal palace, which abutted on the Great Harbour, and fortified it. Now awake to the desperate position he had placed himself in, he sent a courier to Domitius to instruct him to send two of his legions to Alexandria; another to Mithridates of Pergamum to hasten to his aid with all the troops he could raise: also he 'summoned every fleet from Rhodes and Syria and Cilicia; from Crete he raised archers, and cavalry from Malchus, king of the Nabataeans, and ordered artillery to be procured, corn despatched, and auxiliary troops mustered from every quarter.'[3] These frantic calls for aid are a just measure of his strategic blunder; nevertheless, in no way did they abate his arrogance, and he sent an envoy to Ptolemy, still at Pelusium, to inform him it was 'his pleasure that King Ptolomaeus and his sister Cleopatra should disband their armies . . . and should settle their disputes by process of law before himself rather than by armed force between themselves.'[4]

Although by treaty he was justified to act as arbiter,[5] in the circumstances in which he had placed himself he lacked power to back his mandate; therefore it appeared to be little more than an insult to the free and hitherto friendly Egyptians. Further, as he was in need of money to pay his troops, when Ptolemy came to the palace, he demanded that 10 million drachmas be paid to him. This demand was replied to by Pothinus, who accompanied Ptolemy, and, according to Plutarch, he bade Caesar 'go away now and attend to his great affairs, assuring him that later he would get his money with thanks.' To this somewhat insolent remark 'Caesar replied that he had no need whatever of Egyptians as advisers, and secretly sent for Cleopatra.'[6] She

---

[1] B.C., III, 106.                              [2] Div. Iul., XXXV.

[3] The Alexandrian War, 1 (vol. III of the Loeb translation of Caesar's Commentaries, by an anonymous author); subsequently referred to as Bell. Alex. We are not told whether any of the last mentioned reinforcements ever arrived.

[4] B.C., III, 107.                     [5] See supra, Chapter III, p. 72, footnote 2.

[6] Plutarch, Caesar, XLVIII, 4–5.

had a right to be heard if Caesar was to adjudicate between her and her brother.

By descent Cleopatra was half Macedonian and half Greek, and at the time was in her twenty-second year. Not remarkably beautiful, she possessed that seductive attractiveness which appeals to passionate men. She was intensely alive and quite fearless, highly intelligent, conversant with several languages, and, what was unique among monarchs of Macedonian blood, she could speak to her people in the vernacular. The key-note of her character was not sex, but ambition, and 'the essence of her nature', writes Sir William Tarn, 'was the combination of the charm of a woman with the brains of a man, both remorselessly bent to the pursuit of . . . power.' Alone of Alexander's successors she became a legend: she was the daughter of Re, as he was the son of Ammon, and like him she dreamt of becoming a world ruler. For this the Romans looked upon her as a deadly rival; they feared her, hated her, and accused her of the vilest vices. They called her a wanton and a sorceress, a traitor, a coward, a worshipper of beast-gods, and a queen of eunuchs. Yet all these many calumnies only built up, as Sir William Tarn says, 'the monument which still witnesses to the greatness in her. For Rome, who had never condescended to fear any nation or people, did in her time fear two human beings: the one was Hannibal, and the other was a woman.'[1]

From Pelusium Cleopatra contrived to make her way to Alexandria, and there, with her friend Apollodorus the Sicilian, under cover of night she embarked in a small boat and landed near the palace. To enter it unobserved, she stretched herself at full length on some bedding, was rolled up in it, and carried on Apollodorus' back through the palace gates to Caesar's apartment. No disguise could have fitted the occasion more appropriately, and it is to be hoped that no papyrus will be discovered which refutes its suggestive appeal, for history will then be deprived of one of its most fascinating erotic moments.

When the bedding was unrolled and Cleopatra arose from it like Aphrodite from the ocean foam to make love to the god of war, Caesar was captivated 'by the proof of [her] bold wit', and soon was 'so overcome by the charm of her society that he made a reconciliation between her and her brother, on condition that she should rule as his colleague.'[2] But it would appear that Pothinus soon became aware

[1] Précised from Sir William Tarn's sections in the *C.A.H.*, vol. X, pp. 35, 36, and 111.

[2] Plutarch, *Caesar*, XLIX, 2.

that Caesar was Cleopatra's lover and no impartial judge, and to strike at her he plotted against Caesar. According to Plutarch, during a banquet held in celebration of the reconciliation, the plot was hatched by him and Achillas; they were overheard by a slave, who reported it to Caesar, and Pothinus was put to death,[1] but Achillas escaped.

As Achillas took no part in the reconciliation, it would seem more likely that, when Caesar was dallying with Cleopatra, Pothinus sent a message to Achillas to march on Alexandria and take Caesar unawares, because immediately following Caesar's words, 'When these matters were being dealt with' by him – namely the will of Ptolemy Auletes – 'and he was particularly desirous of settling the disputes of the princes,' he writes: 'word is suddenly brought that the royal army and all the cavalry are on their way to Alexandria,' and that his own 'forces were by no means so large that he could trust them if they had to fight outside the town [? palace].'[2] All he could do with his tiny army was to hold the palace walls and wait to see what Achillas would do. At the same time he ordered Ptolemy and Pothinus to be detained.

Thus started the Alexandrian War, which had nothing whatsoever to do with the Civil War. It was an affair of heart and not of head, of Lancelot and Guinevere, and not unlike that of Nelson and Lady Hamilton. 'As for the war in Egypt,' writes Plutarch, 'some say it was not necessary, but due to Caesar's passion for Cleopatra, and that it was inglorious and full of peril for him.'[3] What 'some say' is undoubtedly correct.

## 2. THE STRUGGLE FOR ALEXANDRIA

Alexandria was built on a narrow neck of land between Lake Mareotis and the sea, opposite the island of Pharos, on the eastern extremity of which stood the famous lighthouse – one of the Seven Wonders of the World.[4] The island was linked to the city by a mole, the Heptastadium ('Seven Furlongs'), which provided a double harbour, the Great Harbour on its eastern side, and the Harbour of Eunostus on its western. The mole was pierced by two bridged archways, one at either end, to permit of ships passing from one harbour into the other, and on their

[1] An error.  [2] B.C., III, 109.
[3] Plutarch, Caesar, XLVIII, 3.
[4] The lighthouse was built of white limestone. It consisted of a square tower 60 metres high, above which rose a smaller octagonal structure of 30 metres, surmounted by one of cylindrical form. From sea level to its apex it was 110 metres in height – 360 feet.

landward side each was shielded by a redoubt. The chief edifices stood on the south side of the Great Harbour, they included the Emporium, Royal Palace, and Theatre, probably also the Museum and Library. The streets were laid out in grid fashion, as in many American towns, and

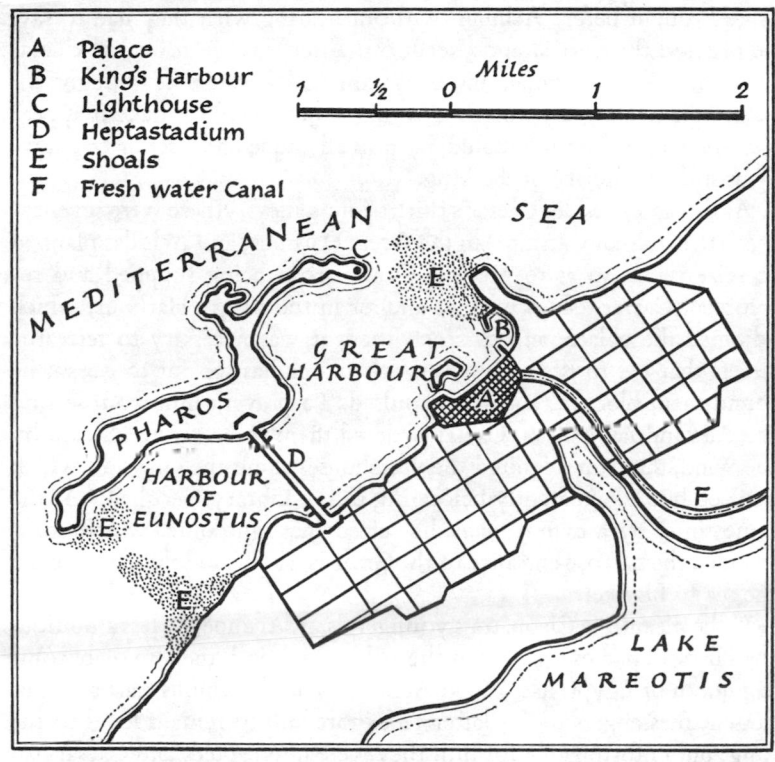

A Palace
B King's Harbour
C Lighthouse
D Heptastadium
E Shoals
F Fresh water Canal

13. Alexandria

on the southern side of the city a canal supplied it with fresh water. Its inhabitants numbered some 300,000 souls, and consisted of a mixture of many races notorious for their turbulence.[1]

Marooned in the Royal Palace of this restless city, Caesar awaited the arrival of Achillas and his 20,000 mercenaries and 2,000 cavalry. Many were old soldiers of Gabinius who had married native women and settled in Egypt; others had been freebooters and brigands from Syria

[1] See Polybius (XXXIV, 14). He includes mercenary soldiers, 'who have learnt to rule rather than obey.'

and Cilicia, and not a few condemned criminals, fugitive slaves, and exiles.

When these armed ruffians were still on the march, Caesar exhorted Ptolemy to send two envoys to Achillas to explain to him his friendly intentions. The boy king complied, but with no success, for when they were brought before Achillas, without hearing what they had to say, he ordered their arrest and execution. After this we read that Caesar brought the king 'under his own control,' because he thought his sovereignty had great weight with his subjects, and to make it appear that the war had been initiated 'by a small clique and a set of brigands' against the authority of the king.[1]

At the time, besides Caesar's thirty-four galleys,[2] there were seventy-two Alexandrian warships[3] in the Great Harbour, and Achillas planned to seize them, so as to prevent Caesar from being supplied and re-inforced. Caesar's ships were at anchor in the King's Harbour, which adjoined the palace, and to reach them it was necessary to seize the streets that led to the quays. But when Achillas set out to do so, he found them blocked, and was repulsed. To prevent him from seizing the Alexandrian galleys, Caesar ordered them to be burnt.[4] Swept by the wind, the flames ignited the warehouses along the quays, in which 400,000 books, apparently belonging to the Library, perished.[5] At the same time, by a *coup de main* he seized the lighthouse, which commanded the narrow entrance to the Great Harbour, and thereby opened the sea to his fleet.

In the meantime Cleopatra's younger sister, Arsinoë, no less ambitious than herself, had escaped from the palace, and with the aim of becoming queen of Egypt, had joined Achillas. When Pothinus learnt of this, he sent messengers to the latter to exhort him to remain loyal to the king; but unfortunately for him they were intercepted; and Caesar had him put to death. Soon after this a quarrel arose between Arsinoë and Achillas over who should command the army, and as the latter refused to give way, through her eunuch Ganymedes she had him murdered, and appointed Ganymedes in his stead.

[1] *B.C.*, III, 109.    [2] One Rhodian had been lost on the coast of Egypt.

[3] They consisted of fifty galleys lent to Pompey that had now returned, and twenty-two guard-ships which normally were on duty at Alexandria.

[4] It would appear that the twenty-two guard-ships were not involved, because (see *infra*, p. 250) later they were withdrawn by Ganymedes into the Eunostus harbour.

[5] The Library was destroyed by Amrou, lieutenant of the Caliph Omar, in A.D. 651.

This change in command in no way advantaged Caesar, because Ganymedes was the abler man of the two. Instead of pitting his unreliable mercenaries against Caesar's legionaries, he decided to force their surrender by depriving them of their water, which by means of conduits was distributed from the fresh-water canal to cisterns within the city. He sealed off the conduits which supplied the region he occupied from those which fed the palace area, and then, 'by means of mechanical water-wheels,'[1] raised water from the sea into the higher part of the city, whence it flowed through the unsealed conduits into the cisterns which supplied Caesar's troops.

When the water was found to be undrinkable, the soldiers were thrown into panic, and demanded to be embarked. But Caesar was no shunner of difficulties; besides he now had Cleopatra to consider, and he had no intention of abandoning her, nor could he risk an embarkation in face of overwhelming opposition. Therefore, to allay their fears, he ordered them to sink wells along the low-lying land near the sea. It was done, and 'a great quantity of sweet water was discovered.'

Most fortunately for him, on the following day, Domitius' 37th Legion arrived, but because of the east wind the transports were compelled to anchor eight miles west of the Great Harbour, and as they had exhausted their water, a despatch boat was sent to Caesar to re-supply them.

To meet this call, Caesar put to sea with his whole fleet; but as he had not sufficient soldiers to man the ships as well as the palace defences, he ordered his captains to sail with oarsmen alone. When off the promontory of Chersonesus, some eight miles west of Alexandria, he cast anchor and sent oarsmen ashore to search for water.[2] Some of these men, bent on plunder, advanced too far inland and were captured by enemy cavalry, who reported to Ganymedes where Caesar's fleet lay, and that it had no soldiers aboard. He at once set out from the Eunostus Harbour to intercept Caesar who, as he had no soldiers with him and because evening was closing in, avoided battle. Nevertheless, one of the Rhodian galleys got into trouble, so Caesar went in his own to her rescue, and in the engagement which followed one Alexandrian ship

---

[1] *Bell. Alex.*, 6. Probably what is termed the 'Persian Wheel', a rude water-wheel, with earthen pots on an endless chain running round it, and worked by oxen. Still in use in Egypt, and called the *sakya*.

[2] Why the 37th Legion had not already done so, is not recorded. Nor is it, why Caesar did not bring with him some of 'the great quantity of sweet water' obtained from the wells.

was captured and another sunk. Caesar then took the transports in tow, and brought them safely into the Great Harbour.

In no way dismayed by his failure, Ganymedes next decided to prevent supplies from reaching Caesar, and to do so he patched up his damaged ships, repaired some old ones, and withdrew from the Great Harbour the guard-ships through the archways in the Heptastadium into the Eunostus Harbour. Within a few days he had twenty-two quadriremes, five quinqueremes, and a considerable number of smaller vessels ready for sea. Caesar was confident he could meet his challenge, so he sailed his galleys round Pharos, and formed line of battle facing his enemy. Because a bank of dangerous shoals, the passage through which was narrow, separated the two fleets, each side paused for the other to negotiate it first. At length the Rhodian admiral, Euphranor, in command of the flagship, turned to Caesar and said: 'It seems to me, Caesar, that you are afraid that, if you once sail into these shoals . . . you may be forced to fight before you can deploy the rest of your fleet. Leave it to us: we shall bear the brunt of the fighting.'[1] Caesar left it to him, and Euphranor was as good as his word. In a masterly way, he brought the Rhodian squadron through the shoals, formed line, and in spite of his enemy's superiority, rammed three of their ships and forced the surrender of two others. The rest then wore about and rowed at speed to shelter under the engines and archers on the Heptastadium.

To put a stop to further naval sorties, Caesar decided to gain command of the Heptastadium: firstly, to occupy the whole of Pharos, and secondly, gain a footing on the northern end of the mole. To effect this, he detailed ten cohorts, some light-armed troops and a party of dismounted Gallic cavalry, conveyed in small craft, to land on the eastern side of the island. At the same time, in order to distract the enemy, he arranged for several galleys to row round to its northern side and threaten it from that direction.

At first the Alexandrians put up a stout resistance, but when they found themselves attacked in front and threatened in rear, a panic occurred among them: they abandoned the defences of the harbour, and fled to their ships on the water-front and along the mole. As they did so, many were cut down and, according to the author of *The Alexandrian War*, 6,000 were captured, which would appear to be an exaggerated figure. Caesar, then, ordered the buildings on the water-front to be demolished, and to reward his men he granted them leave to plunder; not a wise thing to do, because plundering always led to disorganiza-

[1] *Bell. Alex.*, 15.

tion. More pertinently, he occupied and then strengthened the abandoned redoubt which protected the northern of the two bridged archways. But as the southern one and its redoubt were still occupied by
the enemy, in order to put a stop to 'the sallies and sudden forays of
the enemies' ships',[1] he determined to seize it on the following day.

To carry the southern end of the mole he landed three cohorts near
the bridge, under cover of discharges of arrows and catapult bolts,
while the main body of his assault troops remained in the galleys. The
bridge was carried, and to secure it Caesar ordered it to be blocked by
a rampart on its landward side; also, to block the entrances of the archway under the bridge, large stones were cast into the sea. But before the
rampart could be completed, Ganymedes launched a violent counter-
attack. He brought his ships in the Eunostus Harbour into line with the
mole, and from them opened discharges of artillery on it, while a body
of his men 'burst out of the town' against the unfinished rampart. 'And
so,' writes the historian, 'the battle proceeded, with us fighting from
the bridge and the mole, and with them fighting from the area facing
the bridge and from their ships opposite the mole.'[2]

While, in full view of his galleys alongside the mole, Caesar was
urging his men on, the troops on board them got so excited and eager
to join in the fray that, without orders, some of them succeeded in
landing on the mole, and from it, with volleys of sling stones and other
missiles, they drove back the enemy's galleys on its far side. Their
success was short-lived, for while they were engaged, a small number
of Alexandrians landed on the mole 'on their unprotected flank' – that
is, to the north of them. This sudden and unexpected counter-attack
sparked off a panic, and the over-eager attackers made in confusion for
their ships. At the same time, in order to prevent the enemy from gaining possession of them, their crews seized gang-planks to ease them
away from the mole. This retrograde movement and the clamour on
the mole so alarmed the three cohorts on and about the bridge that,
terrified of being attacked in flank and their retreat cut off by the departure of their ships, they abandoned their posts and rushed frantically
back to embark on them. Then, we are told, 'Some of them gained the
nearest ships, only to be capsized by the weight of so many men; some
were killed by the Alexandrians . . . and some . . . swam off to ships
near by.'[3]

In this wild struggle Caesar was himself involved, and as it was
impossible to restore any semblance of order, he hastened to board

[1] *Ibid.*, 19.         [2] *Ibid.*, 19.         [3] *Ibid.*, 20.

his galley, and was followed by a multitude of men who struggled to do the same. But when it became apparent to him that they were likely to capsize her – which happened – he leapt into the sea. According to Dio, while divesting himself, because his clothing weighed him down, and when 'pelted by the Egyptians (for his garments, being of purple, offered a good mark)'[1] in a series of aquatic acrobatics – which must have severely taxed his *dignitas* – he succeeded in avoiding their missiles, swam to a nearby skiff, and, when he had boarded her, he sent out pinnaces to rescue from drowning such men as they could. Surely, with the possible exception of some of the predicaments Charles XII of Sweden got himself into,[2] this is one of the most extraordinary any commander-in-chief has placed himself in.

So ended this disastrous day. It cost Caesar 'approximately 400' legionaries and 'a slightly larger number of seamen and rowers'[3] – that is, four times the casualties he had sustained at Pharsalus! No Alexandrian losses are mentioned, and when the fighting ceased, Ganymedes had the redoubt at the southern end of the mole strengthened and furnished with artillery, and ordered the obstructions which blocked the archway to be removed.

Caesar was now too crippled to risk another attack until reinforced, and the morale of the Alexandrians was too badly shaken to risk another battle until it was restored. To revive it a plot was hatched.

The story of the author of *The Alexandrian War* is that the king's friends, either in the palace or in the city, sent envoys to Caesar to persuade him to release Ptolemy. Their plea was, that the inhabitants of Alexandria were tired of Arsinoë and the remorseless tyranny of Ganymedes, and were ready to do the king's bidding. If, at his instance, 'they were to enter into a loyal friendship with Caesar,' the war would end.[4]

Although Caesar was well aware that the Egyptians were 'a deceitful people', he decided to chance his release. Should Ptolemy prove loyal, well and good; if not, then Caesar thought it would be 'greater honour

[1] Dio, XLII, 40, 4.

[2] At Bender, in 1713, with 40 of his men, he defended himself in an unfortified house against 12,000 Turks and 12 guns, and killed some 200 – 10 fell to his own sword – before he was overpowered.

[3] *Bell. Alex.*, 21.

[4] It would seem as probable that it was the priesthood who were behind the plot. Like all the pharaohs, Ptolemy was a divinity – 'the living image of Re'. Again in their hands, they could use him as a spiritual charm to revive the morale of the people.

and distinction for him' to wage war 'against a king than against a motley collection of refugees.' So he sent Ptolemy back to his people, and no sooner had he done so than, 'Like a horse released from the starting-gate and given his head, the king proceeded to wage war against Caesar.'[1] What happened to Ganymedes, whether he became Ptolemy's commander-in-chief, or was assassinated, is not recorded; nothing further is heard of him.

At the time of the king's return, rumours were current in Alexandria that large reinforcements were on their way from Cilicia and Syria to join Caesar. Next, and before Caesar heard of it, the Alexandrians learnt that a convoy of supplies was on its way by sea to Caesar, and to intercept it, they stationed a squadron of galleys near Canopus.

When Caesar was informed of this, he ordered his entire fleet, under Tiberius Nero – father of the emperor Tiberius – to put to sea. In the engagement which followed, Euphranor and his Rhodian squadron were in the van, and when his galley had sunk one of the enemy's, because Nero failed to support him, she was surrounded, rammed, and foundered. Thus 'the one and only man who was successful in that battle perished alone along with his victorious quadrireme.'[2]

## 3. THE BATTLE OF THE NILE

The rumours were true. The army reported to be approaching through Syria was that of Mithridates of Pergamum, who loyally had answered Caesar's summons. It consisted of Cilician, Syrian, and Arabian levies, and at Ascalon it was joined by Antipater, father of Herod the Great, with 3,000 Jews.[3] From there Mithridates marched on Pelusium, occupied it after a day's fighting, and because the innumerable canals and water-courses of the Nile delta rendered it impracticable to proceed westward to Alexandria, he advanced up the Pelusian branch of the river toward modern Cairo, from where he would have to march down the Canopic branch to reach it; in all a distance of about 250 miles. Thanks to Antipater, the army was welcomed by the large Jewish peasant population of the Delta.

When Ptolemy and his regents learnt of the loss of Pelusium they despatched a force to intercept Mithridates.[4] It caught up with him at a spot, some 17 miles north of modern Cairo, called the Encampment of the Jews, attacked, was counter-attacked, and routed. Mithridates

[1] Ibid., 24.  [2] Ibid., 25.  [3] See Josephus, Antiquities, XIV, viii.
[4] The timings of this campaign are beyond conjecture. Possibly this force set out from Memphis, 12 miles south of Cairo.

then sent a messenger to Caesar to notify him of his success, and at the same time that Caesar received the welcome news, Ptolemy learnt of the defeat of his advanced troops. Both then acted simultaneously. Ptolemy embarked his army and set out by way of the Canopic branch to crush Mithridates before Caesar could join him, and Caesar set out to join him before he could be crushed. To mislead Ptolemy, and persuade him to believe he was pursuing him, he sent some ships by night with lanterns lit toward Canopus, and when off it he withdrew them with their lanterns extinguished. In the meantime he ferried his army over to Chersonesus, and from there, with Lake Mareotis on his left flank, marched toward the Nile. Whether Ptolemy was misled by Caesar's ruse we are not told; but the advance by Chersonesus was the only practical one by land, and although it was considerably longer than Ptolemy's by river, in terms of time it was shorter, because in all probability some of the king's ships had to be towed up-stream. The result was that Caesar was able to gain the lead, and – so it would appear – unite with Mithridates before Ptolemy could attack him.

When Ptolemy became aware of this, he 'encamped . . . in a naturally strong position,' and it has been conjectured that it may have been at Abu-el-Khazr, or at El Teiria, two villages on the Canopic branch; the former is about 30 miles from Alexandria, and the latter about 70.

Wherever it was, it was a strong defensive position. The camp occupied an isolated rise, or hillock, and of its four sides, one 'abutted on the river Nile', another 'ran along very high ground', the third was 'encircled by a marsh',[1] and presumably the fourth, which is not mentioned, was the easiest of approach. In advance of the camp was a hamlet, which the king fortified.

When Caesar caught up with Mithridates, who is completely ignored by the historian of *The Alexandrian War*, he halted at a 'narrow river' – probably a canal – with high banks, some seven miles from his enemy's camp, and along which the king had posted his cavalry and a force of light-armed troops. It would appear to have been a formidable obstacle, and not until a party of Caesar's German cavalry, in search of a ford, succeeded in swimming it at a point where its banks were low, was it crossed. Apparently they attacked the defenders in flank, and as they did so the legionaries felled some trees of sufficient height to span the canal, and by means of these extemporized bridges crossed it. The defenders then withdrew to the king's camp.

Directly his men were over the canal, Caesar advanced against the

---

[1] *Bell. Alex.*, 28.

camp, but on nearing it, he noticed how strongly entrenched it was, and rather than risk an assault with exhausted troops, he went into camp opposite the fortified hamlet.

On the day following he stormed the hamlet, advanced on the camp, and after some preliminary skirmishing drove the Alexandrian outposts into it. He then decided to assault the camp on two of its sides, on the easiest of approach and on the one facing the Nile. The first was held by the king's picked troops, who successfully repulsed their attackers, and the attack on the second had to be abandoned because of the missiles discharged by his archers and slingers from the ships in the river.

While both these assaults were making no headway, Caesar observed that the highest sector of the camp was not only weakly held, but that numbers of its defenders were deserting it, either to join in the fighting, or to watch it. To take advantage of this, he ordered 'some cohorts' to skirt the camp, presumably by way of the marsh and hidden by its reeds, and assault that sector. This they successfully did, and when the Alexandrians engaged in the battle heard shouts and yells in their rear, they were stricken with panic and fled to the river to gain their ships; or, as the historian writes, 'hurled themselves *en masse* from the rampart into the area adjoining the river.'[1] There vast numbers were slaughtered and drowned, and the unfortunate boy king's galley, on which he had taken refuge, became so over-crowded that she capsized and sank, and with her he perished.

So confident was Caesar that this dramatic climax was the end of the Alexandrian war, that he left his legions to follow him, and with his cavalry hastened back to Alexandria, and entered the city 'by that quarter ... which was held by the enemy garrison.'[2] His confidence was fully justified, for no sooner did the soldiers and the townsfolk learn of the defeat and the death of the king than they abandoned their fortifications, threw down their arms and pleaded for mercy. He then proceeded to the palace area to be cheered by the troops he had left to hold it.

Now master of Egypt, he 'appointed as kings those whose names Ptolemaeus [Auletes] had written down in his will,'[3] and no doubt enforced the settlement of the royal debt due to Rome by treaty. As the boy king was dead, he assigned the kingdom to a younger brother and to Cleopatra to rule as joint sovereigns. Arsinoë he removed from the realm and sent her to Italy.

[1] *Ibid.*, 31.   [2] *Ibid.*, 32.   [3] *Ibid.*, 33.

So ended this unnecessary war. It had opened in early October, 48 B.C., and it ended in March the following year. During those six months Scipio, Labienus, and Pompey's sons had been left at large to prepare for a renewal of the Civil War. At times, as Mommsen says, it 'brought him [Caesar] within a hair's breadth of destruction;'[1] from which he had been saved by the skill of Euphranor, the prompt support of Domitius, and the loyalty of Mithridates, coupled with his own unconquerable spirit.

Yet this loss of time would seem to have been of no consequence to him; for instead of setting out at top speed to catch up with the Civil War and extinguish it, no sooner had he placed his mistress on the throne than he spent the following two months in a honeymoon with her on the Nile.

> So turn up thy face to the stars!
> In their peace be at peace for awhile!
> Let us pass in their luminous cars
> As a sob, as a sigh, as a smile!
> Love me and laze
> Through the languorous days
> On the breast of the beautiful Nile![2]

Appian says that the lovers were accompanied by 400 ships;[3] an obvious exaggeration, because there could not have been sufficient time to assemble and organize so vast a fleet. And Suetonius records that 'he [Caesar] would have gone with her . . . in dalliance, as far as Ethiopia . . . had not the army refused to follow him,'[4] which on the face of it is absurd. Although the author of *The Alexandrian War* has not a word to say about this passionate adventure, and barely mentions Cleopatra by name in his history – which is significant – there can be little doubt that this pleasure cruise took place.

On his return to Alexandria, Caesar handed over to Cleopatra three of his legions, because 'he thought that the interests of the Empire demanded that if kings were set up they should be supported, and that if they rebelled, the means of coercion should be at hand.'[5] Although

[1] *The History of Rome*, vol. IV, p. 406.

[2] A. Crowley, 'Said' (*Gargoyles*, 1906).

[3] Appian, *Civil Wars*, II, 90. He also mentions that details of the trip were recorded in his lost *History of Egypt*.

[4] Suetonius, *Div. Iul.*, LII.

[5] *Bell. Alex.*, 33. W. Warde Fowler's translation, *Julius Caesar* (1935 edit.), pp. 313–14.

her lover, he was nevertheless a practical one; by now he knew his Cleopatra, and he was not inclined to take any risks.

## 4. THE PONTIC WAR

The Alexandrian War had kept Caesar occupied for slightly longer than had either his conquest of Italy and Spain, or his campaign against Pompey in Greece. Eight months had been squandered on the execution of the will of a foreign monarch instead of on the liquidation of the Civil War, and during them, so it would seem, Caesar lost all contact with Italy. On June 14, 47 B.C., Cicero wrote to Atticus: 'There is no news that Caesar has left Alexandria; and it is well known that no one at all has left that place since the 15th of March, and that he has despatched no letters since the 13th of December.'[1] Two months later he wrote to Gaius Cassius:

'But those days of vital importance [when Caesar was in Alexandria], especially in civil wars, having been wasted, the year that intervened tempted some [i.e., the Pompeians in Africa] to hope for victory, others to think lightly of defeat itself. And the blame for all these evils is on the shoulders of fortune. For who would imagine that the war would be protracted or cause so long a delay as that caused by the Alexandrian War, or that this Pharnaces, whoever he may be, would intimidate Asia.'[2]

Exactly a week before Cicero wrote the first of these letters, Caesar had bade *au revoir* to his mistress, then with child,[3] and accompanied by the 6th Legion, now reduced to less than 1,000 men,[4] had left Alexandria. Not for Italy, where his presence was urgently needed, but by sea for Syria, on his way to chastise the man who was to Cicero so unimportant that he knew nothing about him.

At Ace (Acre) in Syria, Caesar found despatches awaiting him, and from them he learnt of the situation in Italy: no department of the government was efficient; rivalries between the tribunes were producing dangerous rifts, and the 'flattering indulgence' shown to the troops by their commanders was leading to gross insubordination. All this, we read, urgently demanded Caesar's presence in Italy; 'yet, for all that, he thought it more important to leave all the provinces and districts [he was about to visit] organized in such a way that they would be immune from internal disagreements. . . . This he was confident he

---

[1] *Ad. Att.*, XI, xvii a.    [2] *Ad. Fam.*, XV, xv.
[3] Plutarch, *Caesar*, XLIX, 5.    [4] *Bell. Alex.*, 69.

would speedily achieve in Syria, Cilicia and Asia'; but in Bithynia and Pontus he saw a 'heavier task'.[1]

During the winter, Pharnaces, self-appointed king of Pontus and son of Mithridates the Great, had seized the opportunity offered by Caesar's absence in Alexandria to overrun Lesser Armenia and Cappadocia, and their rulers, Deiotarus and Ariobarzanes, appealed to Domitius Calvinus for aid. Although Domitius had but one of his original three legions left, when reinforced by Deiotarus and Ariobarzanes, he advanced against Pharnaces and was defeated by him near Nicopolis in Lesser Armenia. He then withdrew his shattered army to his province, and Pharnaces invaded Pontus; there he indiscriminately murdered and plundered its Roman and native inhabitants, and emasculated a number of Roman youths. Unquestionably these barbarities demanded punishment, but for Caesar to decide that this comparatively small affair had priority over rectifying the chaotic conditions in Italy is beyond understanding, unless it be assumed that, because he had deprived Domitius of two-thirds of his army, he felt himself to be responsible for his defeat.

In Syria he spent several weeks in visiting its more important communities and in settling their disputes. He then handed the province over to Sextus Caesar, and set out by sea for Cilicia. At Tarsus he did the same, and, because the prosecution of the war 'admitted of no further delay,' he advanced by forced marches through Cappadocia, and on the boundary of Galatia was met by Deiotarus. Because he had sided with Pompey, he came as a supplicant, and was forgiven by Caesar for his lack of foresight in not having foreseen that he and not Pompey would be 'master of Rome and Italy'. Caesar borrowed from him his one and only legion together with all his cavalry, and to these he added Domitius' 36th Legion and another he had recruited in Pontus.[2]

He next crossed into Pontus, and was met by envoys from Pharnaces, who entreated him not to approach their country in a hostile spirit, because the king would carry out all his instructions. In reply, after he had recounted the wrongs Pharnaces had committed, he forgave him on the understanding that he withdrew forthwith from Pontus, released the prisoners he had captured, and made good the cost of the damage he had done.

[1] *Bell. Alex.*, 65.
[2] Their province was Asia, 400 miles to the west. How they managed to join him is not mentioned.

Because Pharnaces was aware that 'there were many reasons demanding Caesar's return to Rome,'[1] he accepted these terms with the full intention of ignoring them directly Caesar had left for Italy. He began, therefore, to prevaricate and ask for more time to withdraw in. 'Realizing the fellow's cunning,' Caesar's reply was to advance on the town of Zela (Zilleh) near by which Pharnaces' army lay encamped.

Zela was built on a hill situated in a plain surrounded by hills; on one of which, Mt Scotius, about three miles to the north of the town, Mithridates the Great had encamped prior to his defeat of Lucullus' lieutenant Valerius Triarius in 67 B.C.[2] Pharnaces had occupied it, and when Caesar came up he pitched his camp two miles south of the town. From his scouts he learnt that immediately south of Pharnaces' camp was another hill, separated from it by a deep ravine which rendered it virtually impregnable on its southern side. Therefore, were he to occupy that hill, his camp would be as impregnable on its northern side.

When it is borne in mind that Caesar was now in a hurry to settle with Pharnaces, on the evidence supplied by the author of *The Alexandrian War* it is by no means clear why he should seek to occupy a position which, although it would secure his own camp, would prevent him from assaulting his enemy's. Nevertheless, he decided to do so, and because it was 'not more than a mile' from the unoccupied hill, and his own camp was five miles distant from it, his problem was how to do so before Pharnaces could anticipate him. To solve it, he decided to seize the hill under cover of night, and because, once he had occupied it, he might have little time to entrench a camp, he ordered all necessary materials for its rampart to be collected and ready to be carried forward.

When at dawn, on August 2, Pharnaces became aware that Caesar had occupied the hill, he drew up his army in front of his camp, and because of the ravine Caesar assumed that it was no more than a gesture of defiance. Next, his army began to descend into the ravine, and 'for some little time,' we are told, 'Caesar laughed contemptuously at this empty bravado on the part of the king,' because he did not believe that any enemy in his senses would attack over such ground. Nevertheless, 'Pharnaces with his forces in battle array proceeded to climb the steep hill-side.'[3]

'This incredible foolhardiness or confidence on the part of the king

1 *Ibid.*, 71.
2 See *supra*, Chapter II, p. 41.  3 *Ibid.*, 74.

disconcerted Caesar, who was not expecting it and was caught un-prepared.'[1] He at once recalled his working parties, ordered the stand to arms, and began to form line of battle. But the confusion was so great that, before a regular line could be formed, 'the king's chariots armed with scythes'[2] threw it it into confusion; but 'were speedily overwhelmed by a mass of missiles.' In their wake came the king's foot, and 'heavy and bitter hand-to-hand fighting took place.' At length the 6th Legion on the right of Caesar's line thrust the enemy back down the slope, and more slowly the legions in the centre and on the left did the same. Soon the king's whole army was in rout, hotly pursued by Caesar's legionaries, who swarmed up the far side of the ravine and stormed the king's camp. Pharnaces' entire army, we are told, was either killed or captured; but he and a few horsemen escaped.

Caesar, writes the anonymous historian, was transported 'with incredible delight' by his victory. His elation is summed up in his words '*Veni, vidi, vici*', which were inscribed on a tablet carried before him at the triumph held to commemorate his victory.[3]

Immediately after the victory, Caesar ordered the 6th Legion to return to Italy; the Galatian legion he sent back to Deiotarus, and the remaining two he left to garrison Pontus. Then he set out by way of Galatia and Bithynia for the province of Asia; settled disputes and assigned prerogatives to the kings and states; appointed Mithridates king of Bosporus, and also tetrarch of Galatia: 'and when he had accomplished his tasks with the greatest success and expedition, he arrived in Italy more quickly than anyone expected.'[4] Nevertheless, a full year since the battle of Pharsalus had been squandered in two campaigns not even remotely related to the Civil War.

1 *Bell. Alex.*, 75.
2 How the chariots were able to negotiate the steep hill-side is not explained.
3 Suetonius, *Div. Iul.*, XXXVII.
4 *Bell. Alex.*, 78.

# XII

## The Civil War in Africa

### I. PRELUDE TO THE WAR

ACCORDING to Dio, until the news of Pompey's death was received in Rome, the people, hitherto uncertain which of the two rivals to placate, 'openly praised the victor and abused the vanquished and proposed that everything in the world they could devise should be given to Caesar.'[1] Among these gifts was the dictatorship, and as dictator for the second time he landed at Tarentum (Taranto) on about September 24, 47 B.C. (July 10 of the Julian calendar).

In Rome, he found that Antony, now Master of the Horse,[2] had with some difficulty suppressed the agitation fomented by Caelius Rufus, Cicero's friend, and Dolabella, Cicero's son-in-law. Both were overwhelmed with debts and demanded their general cancellation, had expected harsh reprisals against the defeated Pompeians, and were disgusted by Caesar's leniency. To allay further unrest, Caesar conceded some measures of relief to those in financial distress; bestowed privileges on many of the senators; appointed a number of military knights and centurions to fill vacancies in the Senate, and held the consular elections, at which Calenus and Vatinius were returned for the few remaining weeks of the year. Also he raised large sums of money to meet the expenses of his forthcoming campaign. These were but secondary tasks compared with the restoration of discipline in the army.

It was now over a year since the battle of Pharsalus had been fought, and the promises Caesar had made to his soldiers had not been kept: they had not been paid their prize-money, were still enrolled, and many agitated to be discharged. Most were quartered in Campania, and Caesar sent Sallust, the historian, to them with a promise to pay each

---

[1] Dio, XLII, 19, 1, and 20, 3. See also Plutarch, *Caesar*, LI, 1.

[2] A *Magister Equitum* was appointed by every dictator to represent him either on the field of battle or in Rome; he held derivatory *imperium* from the dictator, and ranked with the praetors.

soldier 1,000 *denarii* when the campaign in Africa had been fought. But the soldiers wanted cash and not promises, and when offered the latter they stoned Sallust, who barely escaped with his life. They then marched to the Field of Mars to browbeat their commander, and encamped outside the walls of Rome.

When Caesar learnt of this, perturbed that they might be bent on plunder, he ordered Antony's legion to protect his own house and hold the city gates. Then, disregarding the entreaties of his friends, and without announcing his intentions, he proceeded to the Field of Mars, and mounted the tribunal. Startled by his sudden appearance the mutineers gathered around him and saluted him. Then he did a thing they least expected; he said to them: 'What do you want?' Aware that they were indispensable to him, they anticipated that he would offer to pay them their long overdue prize-money, so they replied that they wished to be disbanded. Without a moment's hesitation Caesar responded: 'I discharge you,' and, after a pause, added: 'And I will give you all that I have promised you when I have conquered with others.' At this they were aghast, for it meant they would be deprived of their share in the African booty. Silence then prevailed until some of Caesar's friends urged him to say a few kind words to the men who had served him in so many campaigns. He spoke again, and addressed the now cowed mutineers, not as 'fellow-soldiers' but as '*Quirites*' ('citizens')[1] which implied that he considered them already discharged. Stung to the quick, they cried out that 'they were his soldiers,' repented of what they had done, and besought him to keep them in his service. He turned away and began to descend the steps of the tribunal, and as he did so they appealed to him to punish them for their misdeeds. For a moment he paused, then remounted the tribunal and said: Because the 10th Legion, to which he had always given the place of honour, had joined in the mutiny, he would disband it alone.[2] But when he returned from Africa he would honour all the promises he had made to it, and would bestow land on all his soldiers when the war ended. This was greeted by loud cheers and clapping of hands; but the men of the 10th Legion implored him to decimate them rather than discharge them.[3] By now,

[1] A term of reproach when applied to soldiers.

[2] In the mutiny of eleven years earlier, he announced that he would march with the 10th Legion alone (see *supra*, Chapter V, p. 108).

[3] The main authorities for the mutiny are Appian, *Civil Wars*, II, 92–94, and Dio, XLII, 52–55. It is no coincidence that in his day Alexander the Great, when faced with his mutinous army at Opis, acted in a similar manner. Also Oliver Cromwell, when confronted by John Lilburne's mutinous regiment.

assured of their repentance, he said no more and became reconciled with his men for the time being, as he was in a hurry to proceed to Africa. But because he held that mutiny was an unforgivable crime, according to Dio, when in Africa, 'he took great satisfaction in using them up ... on various pretexts, since at the same time he was destroying his foes through their efforts he was also ridding himself of them.'[1]

By November Caesar had restored order in Rome and discipline in the army; nevertheless, the time occupied on it was to cost him dear, for it meant that he would have to start his new campaign in the winter, when all sailings between Sicily and Africa would be at the mercy of the weather. Toward the end of the month he left Rome, and on December 17 (September 30 of the Julian calendar) arrived at his port of embarkation, Lilybaeum (Marsala) in Sicily.

The sixteen months lost by Caesar since the battle of Pharsalus were now to take their revenge on him. 'Had he proceeded to Africa immediately after the death of Pompeius,' writes Theodor Mommsen, 'he would have found there a weak, disorganized, and frightened army and utter anarchy among its leaders, whereas there was now in Africa ... an army equal in number to that defeated at Pharsalus.'[2]

Soon after that battle, Scipio, Labienus, and Afranius had sailed to Utica (Sidi-Bou-Shater), the chief town of the province of Africa, (Tunisia) and a dispute had at once arisen between its governor, Attius Varus, and Scipio over who should win the favour of King Juba of Numidia (Algeria). When they were joined by Cato, Petreius, Octavius, and Pompey's two sons, Gnaeus and Sextus, Cato's first action was to put a check on Juba's arrogance and reconcile Scipio and Varus. They offered him the supreme command, but he refused it, because Scipio was a proconsul, and 'the greater part of the army was emboldened by his name.'[3] Scipio then assumed command, and because the inhabitants of Utica favoured Caesar's cause, in order to gratify Juba, he decided to put them to death and demolish the town. But Cato indignantly protested, and on the understanding that he would see 'it might not, either willingly or unwillingly attach itself to Caesar,' the town was spared and Cato appointed its governor.[4]

When Caesar arrived at Lilybaeum he was opposed by the following forces in Africa: besides Juba's four legions, 18,000 horsemen, countless light-armed troops and 120 elephants; Scipio commanded 10 legions –

---

[1] Dio, XLII, 53, 3.      [2] *History of Rome*, vol. IV, p. 412.
[3] Refers to Scipio Africanus, the conqueror of Hannibal.
[4] Plutarch, *Cato the Younger*, LVII, 3, and LVIII, 2.

the bulk encamped at Utica – 1,600 Gallic and German cavalry, brought by Labienus from Greece, and a large number of Numidian mounted levies, archers, and slingers. Many of the coastal towns had been fortified, garrisoned, and stocked with grain; and the fleet, some 50 war galleys, organized in squadrons, was stationed at Utica and other ports. Two contingencies, however, favoured Caesar: the one was that many of the provincials, who had been antagonized by Scipio's harsh requisitionings, were secretly ready to welcome him; and the other, that Bocchus and Bogud, kings of Mauritania (Morocco) – the former had allied himself with Publius Sittius,[1] a Roman soldier of fortune – were at daggers drawn with Juba.

Because the army was of doubtful quality and uninured to war, Cato advised Scipio 'not to give battle to a man who was versed in war and of formidable ability, but to trust to time, which withers away all the vigour which is the strength of tyranny.' He further suggested that 'he was ready to take the legionaries and horsemen whom he himself had brought to Libya and cross the sea with them to Italy, thus forcing Caesar to change his plan of campaign, and turning him away from Scipio and Varus against himself.'[2] Also he proposed that Scipio should adopt a Fabian strategy; draw Caesar away from the coastal towns and his supply ships into the interior, and avoid battles while constantly harassing him by marches, counter-marches, and ambuscades. He was indubitably right, and it was exceedingly fortunate for Caesar that Scipio rejected his common-sense plan.

## 2. THE RUSPINA OPERATIONS

A lesson Caesar should have learnt from his Alexandrian adventure was that prestige, unless backed by adequate force, is unlikely to terrify an enemy. Strange to relate it was not, and this is made clear by the anonymous historian in the opening chapter of his *The African War*. He informs us that, when Caesar arrived at Lilybaeum, although no more than a single legion of recruits and barely 600 cavalry had by then assembled there, had it not been for an unfavourable wind, he would have forthwith embarked them and sailed for Africa. So eager was he to make a start, he had his tent pitched on the beach 'that none should think he had time to delay.' Also he kept the rowers and troops on board the ships, so as not to lose a minute when the wind changed. Even when detailed reports of the immensity of his enemy's forces were

---

1 For him see Appian, *Civil Wars*, IV, 54.
2 Plutarch, *Cato the Younger*, LVIII, 4–5.

handed to him, he was in no way alarmed. From every angle, this elephantine confidence in his prestige – Olympic conceit – whatever his means might be, borders on paranoia. Once again it was to lead him into critical situations of his own making.[1]

It may be urged that, all he aimed at with his single legion and 600 horse was to gain a footing on his enemy's shore, establish a bridgehead, and then land his army. But it was not so, because he surmised that all the African ports were garrisoned, and, therefore, he chose to rely entirely upon fortune and land where occasion offered.[2] That being so, then surely the sane thing to do was, directly he had effected a landing, to send a cutter back to his fleet at Lilybaeum with instructions as to where to sail.

Within a few days of his arrival, six legions – two of veterans and four of recruits – and some 2,000 cavalry reached Lilybaeum, and the greater part was immediately embarked. The fleet was then mustered at the island of Aponiana, 10 miles south of Lilybaeum, and the praetor Aulus Alienus was appointed governor of Sicily, and strictly enjoined promptly to embark the rest of the army on return of the transports. On December 25 the fleet stood out to sea, and when, three days later, Caesar with the van sighted the African coast off Hadrumentum (Susa) the rest of the fleet, scattered by a storm, was nowhere to be seen.

He cast anchor in front of the town, which was held by Considius Longus with two legions and a large force of cavalry, and awaited the arrival of his missing ships. But as he had not briefed their captains on what point of the coast they should make for, none turned up.[3] He then landed the troops he had with him, 3,000 infantry and barely 150 cavalry, and camped close to the town. There he rested his men for a night and a day, and then decided to push on to Leptis Minor (Lemta). As he set out he was worried by a large force of Numidian horse, and we are told that 'an incredible thing took place:' less than 30 of his Gallic cavalry drove back 2,000 Numidian horsemen. Actually, as Caesar soon discovered, there was nothing incredible about that, for no sooner were the Numidians driven away than they wheeled about and repeated their threat, and continued to do so until he posted in rear of

[1] How unlike his uncle Marius who, before he sailed for Africa, loaded his ships with 'provisions, money, arms and other necessities', and took with him 'a considerably greater contingent than had been authorized'. (Sallust, *The War with Jurgurtha*, LXXXVI.)

[2] *Bell. Afr.*, 3.    [3] *Ibid.*, 3.

his column the few veteran cohorts he had with him and part of his cavalry. It was Caesar's first taste of Numidian tactics: of threatening attack, of avoiding counter-attack and of gradually reducing an enemy's power of resistance by exhausting him. At length the column arrived at Ruspina (Monastir) and was welcomed by the inhabitants.

On January 1 Caesar moved on to Leptis, which was found to be ungarrisoned, and again its inhabitants were friendly. There, it so chanced, some of his missing transports turned up, and by their

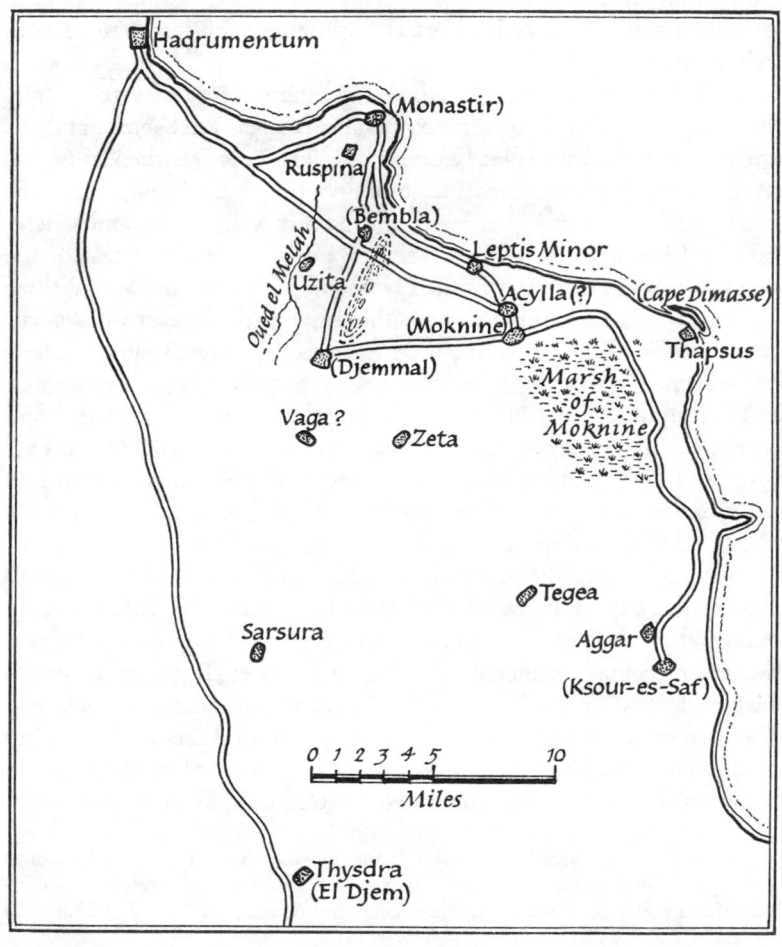

14. African Theatre of War

captains he was told it was rumoured that the rest of the fleet was last seen making for Utica. The rumour was unfounded, and had it sailed into Utica, it would never have sailed out again.

The rumour, so it would seem, opened Caesar's eyes to the situation his impetuosity had placed him in. He sent messengers to Sardinia and other provinces with urgent instructions to send him reinforcements, supplies, and corn; he unloaded some ships and sent them to Sicily to bring over more troops; he ordered Vatinius to take ten warships and search for the missing transports, and keep the sea safe from enemy raiders; and he ordered Sallust to proceed with a detachment of ships to the island of Cercina (Kerkenna) because he had heard that a great quantity of corn was to be found there. 'These orders and instructions,' we read, 'he issued to each individual in such terms as to rule out any excuses as to whether or not they could be carried out.'[1] In brief, he attempted to set right what his insensate eagerness to close with his enemy had set wrong.

At Leptis he left a garrison of six cohorts, and then returned to Ruspina with the intention of putting to sea in search of his missing transports. But when he was on the point of sailing they appeared, and the troops conveyed in them were at once disembarked. Now that practically the whole of his expeditionary forces were reunited, Caesar decided to make Ruspina his oversea base of operations. To provision it, he would have to depend on foraging, until supplies were received from Sicily and elsewhere. This was doubly difficult: not only had most of the surrounding farms been stripped of their corn, but because of the ubiquitous Numidian horsemen the foragers would have to be powerfully protected.

On the first of these expeditions Caesar took with him 30 cohorts and a small force of cavalry, and when he had advanced about three miles from his camp, his mounted patrols reported that they had sighted the enemy. Soon after, when a great cloud of dust was seen in the distance, Caesar sent back for the whole of his cavalry to join him,[2] as well as his small contingent of 150 archers, and then rode ahead with a patrol.

The enemy forces were commanded by Labienus who, immediately after Caesar's landing was reported at Utica, had been sent out to overwhelm him. His army consisted of 1,600 Gallic and German

---

[1] *Bell. Afr.*, 8.

[2] The writer of *Bell. Afr.* says (Chapter 12) that it numbered 400 in all. This may be an error for 2,000 (see Chapter 2).

cavalry, 8,000 Numidian horse, and an immense number of light-armed Numidian foot, archers, mounted archers, and slingers.

This motley gathering was no match against Caesar's 30 cohorts and 400 cavalry in a pitched battle; but Labienus had no intention of fighting one. He was well aware that his Numidian foot, however numerous, were no match for Caesar's legionaries. Therefore he wisely decided to fight a battle on Numidian and not on Roman lines. Or, as we read, his intention was to try out 'new and unfamiliar battle tactics upon Caesar's legionaries', tactics similar to those which had led to Curio's catastrophic defeat: to encircle his enemy, to avoid hand-to-hand fighting, to smother him with missiles, and prevent him from regaining the security of his camp. His hopes were high, because he knew that many of Caesar's soldiers were raw recruits, and from rumours he believed that his veteran legions were mutinous.

To carry out these encircling tactics, Labienus marshalled his Numidian cavalry in a closely packed line, intermingled with light-armed Numidian infantry and unmounted archers, and posted on its flanks strong bodies of cavalry, presumably his Gallic and German horsemen. His idea, it would seem, was to pin Caesar down with his centre, while his flanking cavalry swung round him until he was enclosed, and then to worry his army to death.

To guard, so far as his numerical inferiority permitted, against being enveloped, Caesar deployed his army in a single line, instead of the customary threefold one; posted his cavalry on its wings, and his archers on its front. He instructed his officers 'to take care they were not enveloped by the mass of the enemy's cavalry; for he supposed that he would be engaging infantry troops in the set battle line.'[1] This would seem to show that he had not grasped his enemy's intentions, which were to avoid a 'set battle,' and encircle his army rather than envelop its flanks.

The battle was opened by Labienus' flanking cavalry, who extended outwardly and forced Caesar's cavalry back. Next, when the centres of the two lines came within charging distance of each other, Labienus' groups of horsemen and light-armed infantry rushed forward, and hurled their javelins. 'Hereupon,' we read, 'Caesar's men launched an attack upon them and their cavalry took to flight; but the infantry stood their ground meantime, until the cavalry should renew their charge and return to succour their own infantry.'[2] Presumably this means that the cavalry moved ahead, cast their javelins, then fell back

[1] *Bell. Afr.*, 13.    [2] *Ibid.*, 14.

in rear of the light troops who, if attacked, cast theirs; after which the cavalry returned and repeated the operation.

These repeated tip-and-run missile attacks caused so much disorganization in Caesar's line that he forbade his men to advance more than four feet from the standards. Although the order may have steadied the centre, it could not prevent Labienus' cavalry wings from compressing his line into a circle, so that 'they were all compelled to fight penned behind bars as it were'[1] – in a huddled mass.

Elated by the sight, Labienus rode forward and jeered at his enemy until a heavy *pilum* struck his horse, and he was thrown and carried out of the battle by his attendants.[2] He had every reason to be jubilant, for Caesar's soldiers were becoming more and more demoralized by the showers of missiles hurled at them.

Caesar's situation was now so critical that, unless he could establish some semblance of tactical order, his army would rapidly dissolve into a mob. How he actually did it is by no means clear; for all we are told is that he 'gave orders for the line to be extended to its maximum length'. Presumably that means, somehow or other, he got the mob back into line. Next, he formed the line into a double front – into two lines, that is one facing to the front of the standards, while the other had its back to them. By means of this double front he pushed his enemy, both in front and in rear of him, back, and gained sufficient room between the two fronts to assemble toward their flanks two counter-attacking forces. Then he launched these forces against the encircling enemy, broke through, and under cover of the confusion this created, withdrew his army toward the hilly region to the east of him.

There are two descriptions of how the battle ended, one by the historian of *The African War* and the other by Appian. The former's is:[3] While Caesar was retreating, Marcus Petreius and Calpurnius Piso arrived on the battlefield with 1,600 picked Numidian cavalry. Their appearance so encouraged Labienus' troops that, while Caesar was still in the middle of the plain, they set upon him, but avoided closing with him. It was now nightfall, and although Caesar's cavalry were worn out, he urged them and his weary cohorts to make one more 'vigorous thrust'. They nobly did so, and the enemy was thrown back in confusion, and the high ground gained. A pause followed; after which Caesar's undefeatable soldiers 'retired slowly in battle formation to their . . . fortifications' at Ruspina.

Appian's account is: When Labienus was carried off the field,

[1] *Ibid.*, 15.   [2] *Ibid.*, 16, and Appian, *Civil Wars*, II, 95.   [3] *Bell. Afr.*, 18.

269

'Petreius, thinking that he had made a thorough test of the army and that he could conquer whenever he liked, drew off his forces, saying to those around him, "Let us not deprive our general, Scipio, of the victory." In one part of the day's work did Caesar's luck show itself, in that the victorious enemy seems to have abandoned the field at the very moment of success.'[1]

On the face of it this appears to be a tall story; nevertheless, there may be some truth in it. At the time Scipio was on his way with eight legions and 3,000 cavalry to join Labienus, and it is possible, since contentions among its leaders were a characteristic of the Pompeian army, that Petreius was jealous of Labienus, and wished to deprive him of the glory of rounding up Caesar, which he was certain Scipio could do as soon as he arrived.

Which of these stories is true is of secondary importance when compared with the outcome of the battle: Caesar only escaped annihilation by the skin of his teeth. Never before had he been placed in such a plight, not even when he fought in the ranks against the Nervii on the Sambre, or when he leapt from the Heptastadium into the Great Harbour at Alexandria. He recognized it, and resolved to take no further risks until he was reinforced. With frantic energy he set about making his entrenched camp impregnable. He linked the town of Ruspina to the sea by two entrenchments; armed numbers of his rowers and marines; established smithies to make arrows and missiles; sent to Sicily for hurdles and timber and recruited local inhabitants as light-armed troops, so that they might be mingled with his cavalry 'on the same principle which his opponents had employed'. Had he only foreseen the need for some of these things when he sat in his tent on the beach of Lilybaeum, it is highly unlikely that he would have been in the precarious situation he now found himself in.

When Scipio arrived he pitched his camp alongside those of Labienus and Petreius, 'three miles distant from Caesar'. Its location is unknown, but because proximity to water takes priority over all other camp requirements, it was probably pitched on the wadi Oued-el-Melah, about a mile and a half to the north of a fortified town called Uzita,[2] three miles south-west of the modern village of Bembla. From it, groups of cavalry were sent out daily to restrict Caesar from foraging, and to add to the seriousness of his position, which now closely resembled Pompey's at Dyrrachium, Caesar learnt that Juba with large forces of cavalry and infantry was on his way to join Scipio.

[1] Appian, *Civil Wars*, II, 95.   [2] See *The Roman Republic*, vol. III, pp. 519–20.

Actually Juba's approach was the turn in the tide of Caesar's misfortunes; for when not far from Scipio's camp, news was brought to Juba that Sittius and Bocchus had seized on the opportunity his absence afforded them to storm the city of Cirta (Constantine), the richest in Numidia, and plunder two other towns. Alarmed by it, he turned back to protect his kingdom, and withdrew from Scipio the auxiliary forces he had lent him.

In the meantime Caesar sent an urgent despatch to Alienus in Sicily to ship reinforcements to him as quickly as possible. 'There must be no delay,' we read, 'and no excuses on the ground of wintry weather or adverse winds.'[1] His anxiety is as fully described by the historian as his eagerness was at the opening of the campaign. He writes:

'Caesar himself was in such a ferment of impatient expectancy that on the day after he sent the messenger to Sicily . . . he kept saying that the fleet and army [*i.e.*, the reinforcements] were dallying; and day and night he kept his eyes and attention bent and riveted upon the sea. And no wonder; for he perceived that farms were being burned to the ground, fields stripped, herds plundered or butchered, towns and strongholds destroyed and abandoned, and the principal citizens either murdered or held in chains, and their children haled off to slavery on the pretext of being hostages: yet to these folk, who in their misery implored his protection, he could give no assistance because his forces were so few.'[2]

While the scorched earth policy was perplexing Caesar, Labienus made an abortive attempt to seize Leptis, and practically every day Scipio drew his army into line of battle and challenged Caesar. Nevertheless, in spite of his scant forces, on receipt of an appeal from the townsfolk of Acylla that they would gladly supply Caesar with corn were he to send them a garrison, he despatched three cohorts to them, presumably by sea, because it is conjectured that the town lay on the coast some 30 miles south of Thapsus.

At length, toward the end of January, 46 B.C., the tide turned in full. A fleet of merchant ships from Cercina, freighted with corn, sailed into the harbour of Ruspina, and was followed by a convoy of transports from Sicily bringing with it two veteran legions – the 13th and 14th – 800 Gallic cavalry, and 1,000 archers and slingers. With them Caesar felt strong enough to emerge from his lair.

[1] *Bell. Afr.*, 26.     [2] *Ibid.*, 26.

## 3. THE UZITA OPERATIONS

Of Caesar's plan of action, all we are told is that it was known to no one but himself. Nevertheless, from his subsequent operations it may be conjectured with some assurance. It was to break the deadlock without jeopardizing his army a second time, and the nature of the country between him and Scipio rendered it difficult to avoid.

Three miles to the south of Caesar's entrenched camp at Ruspina rose the northern end of a ridge which stretched southward for some seven miles toward the modern village of Djemmal, and from it rose a number of hill-tops. Westward of the ridge extended a plain traversed from north to south by the wadi Oued-el-Melah, distant between two and three miles from the ridge. To reach Uzita, Caesar would have to cross the plain, and his problem was how to do so without risking encirclement.

Early on the night of January 25–26 he set out along the coastal road which ran southward of Ruspina, ascended the ridge, occupied the first three hill-tops and fortified them. On the third he became aware that the right flank of his advance – that is, the flank which faced westward toward Uzita – was open to cavalry attack, and to provide against it he ordered an entrenchment to be dug from near the third hill 'up to the point from where he had started,' which presumably means where he had turned off the coastal road. If so, it must have been over three miles in length. When Scipio and Labienus perceived this, they led their entire force of cavalry out of camp, deployed it in line of battle, and drew up their infantry in second line 400 paces in advance of their camps.

When Scipio had approached to within a mile and a half of the ridge, Caesar called in his working parties, formed line of battle, and at the same time sent out a squadron of Spanish horse and some light-armed troops to drive a Numidian picket off 'the adjacent hill' on the ridge. This was speedily done, and when Labienus saw the Numidians in retreat, he advanced a considerable force of cavalry to their assistance, was suddenly set upon by Caesar's cavalry, who had been hidden from view 'behind a very large farm building', and routed. This sparked off a panic among Scipio's infantry, who fled back to their camps.

The next day Scipio sent an urgent appeal to Juba to come to his assistance. He agreed to do so, and about a fortnight later, when it was rumoured that he was approaching, Caesar's men took alarm.[1] At the time incessant rain and lack of tents had lowered their spirits, and when

1 See Suetonius, *Div. Iul.*, LXVI.

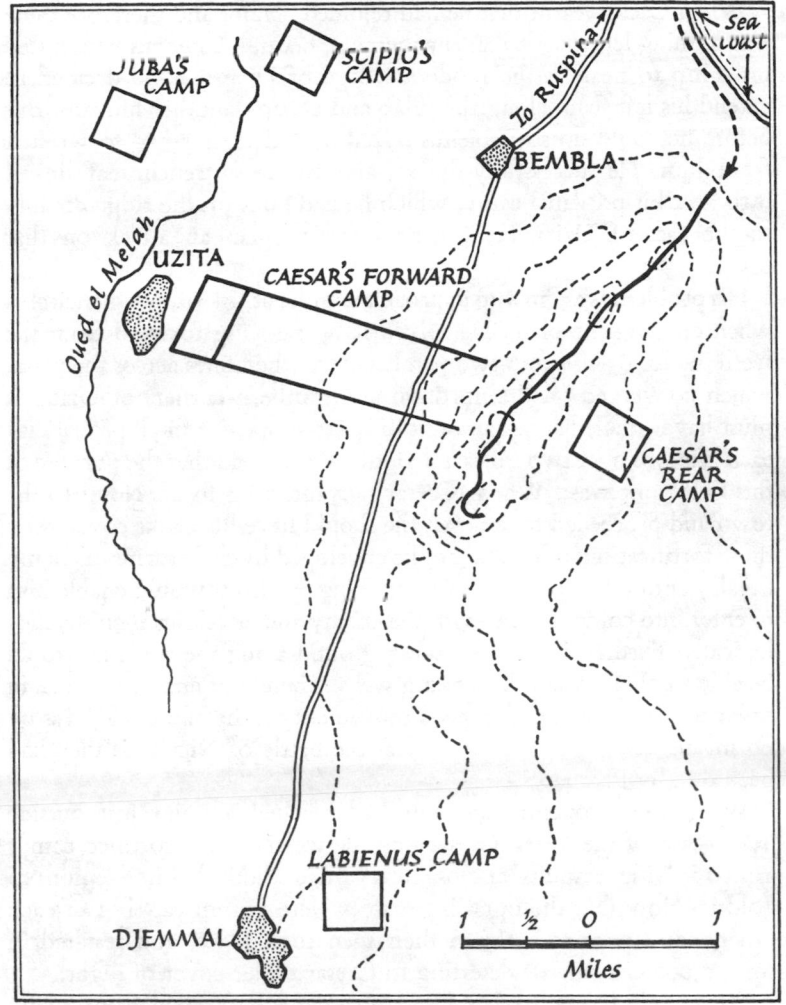

15. Uzita Operations

the 'spears' points [*pila*-heads] of the men of the 15th Legion spontaneously caught fire,'[1] they looked upon it as an evil omen.

About the middle of February Juba arrived and pitched his camp close by Scipio's. He brought with him three legions, 800 Gallic and Spanish cavalry, large contingents of Numidian horse and light-armed troops, and 30 elephants.

[1] *Bell. Afr.*, 47. Probably St Elmo's fire.

When Caesar learnt that he had rejoined Scipio, and therefore there was nothing left to delay an engagement, because Labienus had shifted his camp to near by the modern village of Djemmal, he decided to extend his left flank along the ridge and occupy another hill-top. But before he could do so Labienus seized it, and Caesar had to wrest it from him. He successfully did so, and by an entrenchment linked it to near his principal camp, which he had built on the ridge directly to the east of Uzita. He was now free to plan an attack on that town.

His problem was, how to approach it without risk of being encircled when crossing the plain. He solved it by carrying forward from the western face of his camp two parallel entrenched lines across the plain, which converged on the northern and southern corners of Uzita. It must have entailed a vast amount of spade-work, for in all probability each line was over two miles in length. We are told that the purpose of this fieldwork was: 'When [Caesar] advanced his forces closer to the town and proceeded to attack it, he should have his flanks covered by those fortifications of his and not be enveloped by the swarms of enemy cavalry and so be deterred from attacking.'[1] Also it would enable him to enter into conversations with the enemy and attack his men psychologically. Further, in the low-lying ground along the wadi he would be able to obtain water by sinking wells. The use of entrenchments, in order to gain security or impede movement on the battlefield, was by no means a new idea; as recently as the battle of Nicopolis they had been dug by Pharnaces.[2]

When the two entrenchments had reached a point just outside 'spear-cast' of the town, Caesar built between them a fortified camp; armed it with catapults 'at close intervals', and detailed five legions to hold it. Now that the opposing armies were within ear-shot of each other, conversations between their men took place, and resulted in some 1,000 Gaetulians[3] deserting to Caesar under cover of night.

Meanwhile Caesar's second reinforcements had sailed from Sicily, and when Varus at Utica learnt that they were on their way, he put to sea with fifty-five galleys to intercept them. Of this, Caesar knew nothing, but as he was expecting the transports, to secure their approach he had sent out two squadrons, one of twenty-seven galleys, under Lucius Cispius, to coast off Thapsus, and the other of thirteen, under Quintus Aquila, to do the same off Hadrumentum. Cispius reached his

---

[1] *Bell. Afr.*, 51.    [2] See *Bell. Alex.*, 38.
[3] A Libyan people who inhabited the region south of Mauretania and Numidia.

destination, but a storm prevented Aquila from rounding the promontory of Monastir. When from a deserter Varus learnt that the rest of Caesar's fleet was at anchor off Leptis with crews ashore, he sailed for that port, burnt five transports and captured two galleys. At the time Caesar was inspecting his defences, and when he received the news of Varus' raid on Leptis, he at once mounted his horse, galloped there and ordered the crews to man their galleys and follow him. Next, he boarded a small cutter, sailed north along the coast, took command of Aquila's squadron, and pursued Varus, who was so disconcerted by his audacity that he immediately wore about and with haste made for Hadrumentum. After a four miles' chase Caesar overtook his rear, recovered one of the captured galleys and captured one of the enemy's. Off Hadrumentum he set fire to some transports, and then sailed back to Leptis.

This incident is an illuminating example of Caesar's impulsiveness. Although it was accountable for many remarkable successes, at times it placed him in situations of extreme peril. He was a man who seldom paused to reckon the odds either against him or in his favour. In the present instance, whatever the strength of Varus' fleet might be made no difference to him. His task was not to count his enemy's ships, but to secure his own at Leptis and prevent his incoming transports from being intercepted. To achieve it, without a second thought, he boards a cutter, sets out to join Aquila, whose squadron may not have been in sight, finds it, takes command of its thirteen galleys, and, like a bull with head down, charges after Varus. In these impulsive actions it may be said that, when they were successful, Caesar won them single-handed by élan and audacity alone. Equally astonishing is it that, when they failed and landed him in a desperate situation, with few exceptions, the faith of his men in his invincibility pulled him through.

Soon after Caesar's return to Leptis the transports arrived, and brought with them the 9th and 10th Legions. When added to those he had, the strength of his army was raised to nine legions,[1] the highest number he had commanded since his conquest of Gaul. So it would seem, they were at once hurried to his camp opposite Uzita, because on the day following the desertion of Juba's Gaetulians, when Scipio drew out his army in line of battle in rear of the Oued-el-Melah, and Caesar followed suit in front of it, the 9th and 10th Legions are mentioned as forming his left wing. On this occasion the opposing armies were separated by no more than 300 paces; 'a situation,' we read, 'which had

[1] The 5th, 9th, 10th, 13th, 14th, 25th, 26th, 28th and 29th (*Bell. Afr.*, 60).

never, perhaps, arisen before without leading to an engagement.'[1] The reason is obvious: neither side chose to risk an advance over the difficult wadi. For several hours they faced each other, then, after some skirmishing, withdrew to their respective camps.

The operations around Uzita had now lasted some six weeks, and Caesar was finding it increasingly difficult to supply his army. When he was told that it was a custom of the natives to store their corn in concealed pits, he sent two legions to a village 10 miles from his camp, where a large store was found. When this was reported to Labienus, he concluded that, as much still remained in the village, Caesar would send out again to bring it in, so he laid an ambush to trap his foragers. Unfortunately for him Caesar learnt of it from some deserters, and it was Labienus who was surprised at a cost of some 500 of his light-armed troops.

When no more buried corn could be discovered, Caesar decided to transfer operations to a fertile district around the town of Aggar. It has been conjectured to have been situated close to the coast, a little more than a mile north of Ksour-es-Saf, which is 15 Roman miles south of Thapsus.[2] In preparation for the move, he strengthened the garrisons of Leptis and Ruspina, and instructed his admirals, Cispius and Aquila, to keep Hadrumentum and Thapsus under blockade. Then he set out for Aggar, and encamped near by it. When Scipio and Juba discovered his departure, they followed in his track, and entrenched their armies in three camps to the west of a town named Tegea, which lay six miles westward of Caesar's camp.

## 4. THE THAPSUS OPERATIONS

The first operation in this phase of the campaign was initiated by Caesar, and it shows how capricious he could at times be. In the Ruspina phase he had risked annihilation, and in the Uzita phase he had been ultra-cautious; now, forgetful of his escape in the former, he again tempted fortune. Further, unlike at Ruspina, there was no need for him to do so, because before Scipio caught up with him he had foraged the Aggar district, and gathered in 'a large quantity of barley, oil, wine and figs, and a little wheat.'[3] Nevertheless, after Scipio's arrival, when he learnt that he had sent out two legions to forage in the vicinity of a town called Zeta (Beni Hassan) he decided to intercept them with his entire army, less its camp garrison.

[1] *Bell. Afr.*, 61.
[2] See Holmes, vol. III, pp. 524-5.        [3] *Bell. Afr.*, 67.

Zeta was situated 10 miles north of Scipio's camp and 14 from his own; it could only be approached from the latter by a flank march past the former. Caesar made it and occupied Zeta without opposition. He found that Scipio's legions were foraging further afield, and as he was on the point of advancing against them, he observed enemy forces hastening to their support. He then left a garrison at Zeta, and set out on his return.[1] When not far from Scipio's camp, 'which of necessity he had to pass', suddenly 'from behind the nearby hills where they had been lurking in ambush', Labienus and Afranius with all their cavalry and light-armed troops fell upon his rear-guard. Caesar at once counter-attacked, drove them back, and though by now he should have realized what they were up to, he imagined that they would 'stop their harrying.' But no sooner was the march resumed than they returned, and again and again repeated the same manœuvre – 'chasing the Julians as they marched and taking to flight when their opponents turned to attack them.' Next, we read: 'Caesar realized that what they were trying to do was no less than force him to pitch camp at a spot where there was not a drop of water, so that his famished army . . . should die of thirst.' Thus the fighting went on until close on sundown, 'and less than a hundred paces had been covered all told in four hours, when Caesar withdrew his cavalry – in view of casualites among their horses – from the rear-guard, and called on the legions to replace them.' Then he advanced at a slow pace while 'detachments of the Numidian cavalry kept charging ahead along the high ground to his right and left and availing themselves of their superior numbers to surround Caesar's forces with a kind of continuous circle of troops.' Nevertheless, 'now advancing, now pausing to fight back', Caesar completed his march, 'albeit somewhat slowly', and in 'the first hour of the night . . . brought all his men back to camp, with not a single man lost and ten wounded.' At the same time Labienus 'retired to his lines with roughly three hundred men missing, many wounded, and all his troops exhausted by their continuous offensive.'[2]

Once again Caesar had narrowly escaped disaster, and, we are told, was seriously perturbed, since as often as an engagement had occurred 'he had been quite unable to be a match with his own cavalry, un-supported by legionary troops, for the enemy cavalry and their light-armed units.' Further, so far he had been unable to test the worth of the enemy's legions, 'and how, he wondered, could he cope with their

[1] Why he did not attack the approaching enemy is not recorded.
[2] *Ibid.*, 69–70.

cavalry and amazing light-armed troops if they were backed up by their legions.'[1] To meet this emergency he proceeded to train his men 'as a gladiatorial instructor trains his recruits' – that is, how to fight individually in loose order.[2] Also he issued 'instructions that three hundred men out of each legion should be in light order', so that they might co-operate with the cavalry.[3]

Soon after, the new corps proved its worth. On March 23, Caesar set out to seize a town called Sarsura, which had been occupied by Scipio and was stocked with grain, and when Labienus resorted to his Numidian tactics and cut off the sutler's baggage train, he was suddenly attacked by Caesar's cavalry, supported by the new corps, and repulsed with considerable loss. Sarsura was then captured, and its garrison massacred, while from a distance Labienus passively looked on.

Soon after this, a convoy arrived from Sicily with 400 cavalry, 4,000 infantry, and 1,000 slingers and archers. According to Holmes, apart from garrisons in various towns, Caesar now had at his command a field army of, perhaps, 35,000 legionaries, 4,000 cavalry with their auxiliaries, and 2,000 archers and slingers.[4]

Now that he was in command of so formidable a force, it must have appeared to him more unlikely than ever that Scipio would respond to his frequent challenges to fight it out; therefore he decided to change his strategy. Hitherto it had been to strike at Scipio's foragers, in order to induce him to come to their rescue. In this the main disadvantage was that, in face of Scipio's and Juba's masses of Numidian horse, it presented them with the opportunity to develop to the full their main tactical asset – encirclement. To overcome this, and simultaneously compel his adversaries to accept battle, Caesar selected an area of operations in which the tactics of the Numidians would be severely circumscribed, and in which lay an objective Scipio could not abandon without so great a loss of prestige that he would be discredited as a general. This objective Caesar found in the Pompeian camp at Thapsus, held by a considerable garrison under the praetor C. Vergilius.

Thapsus was located on a promontory (Cape Dimasse) 16 miles to the north of Aggar, and could only be approached by way of two narrow necks, or corridors, of land, one between the sea and the northern margin of an extensive shallow lake, now called the Marsh of Moknine, and the other between the sea and its eastern margin. Because both corridors varied from as little as a mile and a half to three miles

[1] *Bell. Afr.*, 72.     [2] *Ibid.*, 71.     [3] *Ibid.*, 75 and 78.
[4] *The Roman Republic*, vol. III, p. 265.

278

in breadth, neither provided sufficient room for the Numidians to develop to the full their tactics of encirclement.

At about midnight on the night of April 4 Caesar struck camp and set out for Thapsus by way of the eastern corridor, and when he reached its southern entrance, in order to block it, he ordered a fort to be built and garrisoned by three cohorts. Then he continued his advance on Thapsus, pitched his camp close by its walls, and began to invest it with a ring of siege works.

When Scipio learnt of Caesar's departure, not willing to abandon Vergilius, he followed on his heels, and when he found his advance blocked by the fort, he and Juba went into two camps to the south of it – it was eight miles from Thapsus. Next, they decided to hem Caesar in by blocking the two corridors: Juba and Afranius were to remain where they were, while Scipio marched round the western side of the marsh and blocked the northern corridor. This he did, and 'at the first pale light of dawn' on the day after he parted from Juba he built a camp to the west of Caesar's.

When this became known to Caesar, he withdrew his working parties from the fortifications they were engaged on; appointed the proconsul L. Nonius Asprenas to hold the camp with two legions; and instructed part of his fleet to continue the blockade of Thapsus, and part to be prepared at a given signal to sail close inshore to a point in rear of Scipio's camp and cause confusion in his army. Next, he advanced against Scipio, and found him in line of battle in front of his camp, with sixty-four elephants in two groups on the wings of his legions. Caesar deployed his army in the normal three lines; the 10th and 9th Legions formed its right wing and the 13th and 14th its left.[1] Five cohorts of the 5th Legion, covered by archers and slingers, were posted as a fourth line obliquely – as at Pharsalus – in rear of each wing to deal with the elephants, and the cavalry, intermingled with the newly trained light-armed troops, were deployed on the extreme right and left.

When the line of battle was being formed, Caesar hurriedly inspected his legions, and in particular harangued those composed of recruits, who as yet had not taken part in a pitched battle. As he did so, considerable confusion was noticed in the enemy's ranks, and it caused so much excitement in Caesar's that some of the officers and veterans

[1] In *Bell. Afr.*, 81, the 10th and 7th Legions are placed on the right wing and the 8th and 9th on the left. As this has been disputed, the numeration adopted by Holmes (vol. III, p. 267) is followed.

CISPIUS

Thapsus

El Djezira

CAESAR'S CAMP

SCIPIO'S CAMP

*Miles*

1    ½    0    1    2

N

Sidi Massoud

JUBA'S CAMP

ROMAN FORT

AFRANIUS' CAMP

M·A·R·S·H   O·F   M·O·K·N·I·N·E

16. The Battle of Thapsus

of his body-guard urged him to signal the attack. He refused to do so until he had made certain that his line was fully formed. Then, 'suddenly on the right wing, without orders from Caesar but under coercion of the troops, a trumpeter began to sound the charge. Whereupon every cohort began to attack the enemy, despite the resistance of the centurions.'[1]

On the right wing the archers and slingers discharged their missiles at the elephants, who wheeled about and 'trampled under foot masses . . . of their own supporting troops'. The Numidian cavalry then took panic, and within a few minutes Scipio's entire army was in flight. As Holmes sums it up: 'There was no battle; only terror and butchery.'

While part of Caesar's army apparently kept up the pursuit, with the other part[2] Caesar advanced down the eastern corridor and appeared before the camps of Afranius and Juba. The news of Scipio's defeat had already reached them; Afranius and Juba had fled, and the camps were in pandemonium. Intoxicated by their victory, nothing could restrain Caesar's men; no quarter was given to the terrified enemy, and when they 'implored Caesar's protection, they were massacred to a man, despite the fact that Caesar himself was looking on and entreating his troops to spare them.'[3]

In the battle, 10,000 of Scipio's and Juba's men are said to have perished, at a cost to Caesar of 'fifty soldiers missing and a few wounded'.[4]

With Scipio's defeat only two Pompeian forces remained defiant: the garrisons of Thapsus and Thysdra (El Djem), the one commanded by Vergilius, the other by Considius. To the first Caesar addressed a personal appeal to surrender, which was ignored. On the following day he paraded his army in full view of the town; detailed the proconsul Caninius Rebilius with three legions to blockade it, and sent Domitius Calvinus with two to reduce Thysdra.

Meanwhile the remnants of Scipio's cavalry had reached Utica. They burst into the town, massacred many of its inhabitants, looted its houses, and would have destroyed it utterly had not Cato bribed them to depart. Then, philosophically, Cato arranged his private affairs, entrusted his children to his quaestor, Lucius Caesar, retired to his bedroom, read Plato's *Phaedo*, and committed suicide.

---

[1] *Bell. Afr.*, 82.
[2] It is not clear from the text what troops Caesar took with him.
[3] *Bell. Afr.*, 85.
[4] *Ibid.*, 86.

From Thapsus Caesar marched westward, occupied Uzita and Hadrumentum, and pardoned all Pompeians who appealed to his compassion. At Utica he assembled the citizens, spared the lives of the 300 capitalists who had financed Scipio, and imposed on them a fine of 200 million sesterces, to be paid in six half-yearly instalments. Meanwhile Juba and Petreius had fled to Zama (? Jama), and when refused admittance by its inhabitants, as they expected no mercy from Caesar, they fought a duel in which one killed the other and then killed himself. Afranius was captured by Sittius, who delivered him to Caesar, who put him to death for his perfidy; and Scipio, who attempted to escape by sea, was run down by one of Sittius' ships and drowned. While these tragedies were being enacted, Considius abandoned Thysdra and was murdered by his followers, and Vergilius surrendered Thapsus.

From Utica Caesar proceeded to Zama. There he incorporated the kingdom of Juba in the province of Africa, recompensed Bocchus and Sittius, and then returned to Utica. On June 13 he took ship for Sardinia, where he weeded out 'the older men among his soldiers for fear that they might mutiny again', and despatched them under Gaius Didius to Spain,[1] where Pompey's two sons were in revolt. Detained in Sardinia by foul weather, he did not arrive in Rome until July 25 – that is, close on two years after his victory at Pharsalus.

The best that can be said of the African campaign is that, in spite of difficulties which would have overwhelmed a lesser general, Caesar won it; the worst that, because of his Alexandrian escapade, it was fought over a year too late. . . . 'The advantage of time and place in all martial actions is half a victory; which being lost is irrecoverable. . . .'[2] It is strange that Caesar, who was possessed by a fanatical faith in speed – that is, strategic time – should have failed to relate it to place – that is, tactical locality.

[1] Dio, XLIII, 14, 1–2.
[2] Sir Francis Drake to Queen Elizabeth I on April 13, 1588 (*State Papers, Relating to the Defeat of the Spanish Armada* (1894), vol. I, p. 148).

# XIII

## The End of the Civil War

### I. CAESAR'S HONOURS AND TRIUMPHS

WHEN the news of Thapsus was received in Rome, unprecedented honours were showered upon Caesar. The Senate elected that his victory should be celebrated by a thanksgiving of forty days, twice the number granted him after the defeat of Vercingetorix; that he be appointed Prefect of Morals,[1] and that his dictatorship be prolonged to ten years. In addition it was decreed that his triumphal chariot be placed on the Capital opposite to Jupiter's, and that a bronze statue of him should be set up on a monument representing the world, 'with an inscription to the effect that he was a demigod'.[2]

It would appear that Caesar was not deceived by these lavish awards, for we are told that, when he entered Rome, he became aware that the people 'were afraid of his power,' and 'that it was on this account that they had voted him extravagant honours through flattery and not through good-will.'[3] Therefore it is strange that – unlike Pompey[4] – in order to allay their fears, he did not reject or modify the Senate's decrees; for they went far to confirm popular apprehensions. Instead he accepted them, and in a speech addressed to the Senate endeavoured to cast oil on the troubled political waters by saying that it was not his intention to emulate Marius, Cinna, or Sulla, and that he was more eager than ever to be the champion and not the master of the people – their leader and not their tyrant. 'Why should I put any one of you to death,' he is reported to have said, '. . . when I have taken pity on all those who withstood me but once and in many cases have spared even those who fought against me a second time?'[5] He addressed the people

---

[1] Holmes (vol. III, p. 276) remarks: 'a title more sonorous and more ironical than that of Censor'.

[2] Dio, XLIII, 14, 6.

[3] *Ibid.*, XLIII, 15, 1–2.

[4] See *supra*, Chapter I, p. 47.

[5] *Ibid.*, XLIII, 17, 2–4.

in similar terms, and 'relieved them to some extent of their fears, but was not able to persuade them altogether to be of good courage until he confirmed his promises by his deeds.'[1]

On successive days he celebrated four triumphs: over the Gauls, the Egyptians, Pharnaces, and Juba, and although Appian states that 'he took care not to inscribe any Roman names' on the pictures and effigies carried in the processions, the misfortunes of his Roman victims were vividly represented, and the people, in spite of being restrained by fear, 'groaned . . . when they saw the picture of Lucius Scipio . . . casting himself into the sea, and Petreius committing self-destruction . . . and Cato torn open by himself like a wild beast.'[2] Also the sight of Arsinoë, a former queen of Egypt, led in chains among the captives – 'a spectacle which had never yet been seen at least in Rome – aroused very great pity'. Though out of consideration for her brothers, she was released, 'others, including Vercingetorix, were put to death.'[3]

Nor were his soldiers over respectful; in his Gallic triumph they shouted:

> 'Home we bring our bald whoremonger;
> Romans, lock your wives away
> All the bags of gold you lent him
> When his Gallic tarts to pay.'[4]

They also 'jeered at those of their own number who had been appointed to the senate . . . and in particular jested about his love for Cleopatra. . . . Finally . . . they all shouted out together that if you do right, you will be punished, but if wrong, you will be king.'[5]

In rear of the victims and the effigies came wagons laden with the spoils of war.[6] Among them were 60,500 talents of silver, 2,822 crowns of gold weighing 20,414 pounds, from which the legions were to receive their long promised prize-money: to each private soldier 20,000 sesterces, twice as much to each centurion, and four times to each tribune. In addition, each member of the rabble of Rome was to be given 300 sesterces, 10 pecks of grain, and 10 pounds of oil.

When the last triumph had been celebrated, the populace were

[1] Dio, XLIII, 18, 6.   [2] Appian, *Civil Wars*, II, 101.
[3] Dio, XLIII, 19, 3-4.   [4] Suetonius, *Div. Iul.*, LI.
[5] Dio, XLIII, 20, 1-2.
[6] According to Velleius (II, LVI, 2) 'The money borne in his triumph, realized from the sale of spoils, amounted to a little more than 300,000,000 sesterces (£6,000,000).'

entertained at a feast for which 22,000 tables were laid, and after it Caesar was escorted to his house by the people and 20 elephants carrying torch-bearers.

On the following days the populace were amused with spectacles of every kind. Four hundred lions were hunted to death in the Circus, and not only did gladiators fight each other individually, but also in groups. A naval battle was staged on a tract of the Campus Martius, flooded for the occasion; and, as a grand finale, in the Circus Maximus two armies composed of war captives and condemned criminals – 1,000 foot, 200 horse, and 20 elephants on either side – fought each other to the death.

This horrifying and wanton display of power exceeded anything as yet seen in Rome, and it revealed a side of Caesar's character which did him little credit. It unmasked his arrogance and his dominance, and according to Dio, the people sensed it and were frightened.

'He was blamed [he writes] for the great number of those slain, on the ground that he himself had not become sated with bloodshed and was further exhibiting to the populace symbols of their own miseries; but much more fault was found because he had expended countless sums on all that array. In consequence a clamour was raised against him . . . that he had collected most of the funds unjustly . . . that he had squandered them for such purposes.[1] [Also] the soldiers raised a disturbance, not because they cared about the reckless squandering of the money, but because they themselves did not receive the citizens' wealth too. In fact they did not cease their rioting until Caesar suddenly came upon them, and seizing one man with his own hands, delivered him up to punishment . . . and two others were slain as a sort of ritual observance . . . they were sacrificed in the Campus Martius by the pontifices and the priest of Mars, and their heads were set up near the Regia.'[2]

If true, a portentous ending of the most notable and probably the most bloody of triumphs ever witnessed in Rome.

## 2. CAESAR'S LEGISLATION

When the games and contests had ended, Caesar enacted various laws and reforms, the more important of which were: (1) A census of the

[1] Dio, XLIII, 24, 1.
[2] *Ibid.*, XLIII, 24, 3-4. The Regia was the office and dwelling of the *Pontifex Maximus* (Caesar).

paupers in Rome, who since the time of Clodius had received gratuitous doles of grain, and their reduction from 320,000 to 150,000. (2) The provision of land for the discharged veterans without the eviction of legitimate occupants. (3) The restriction of jurors to the equestrian and senatorial orders. (4) The issue of a sumptuary law by which the purchase of certain luxuries was restricted or forbidden. (5) The offer of prizes for large families to make good the fall in population. (6) The dissolution of all guilds, except those of ancient foundation, many of which were subversive political clubs. (7) The limitation of the terms of office of propraetors to one year, and of proconsuls to two consecutive years. (8) A decree whereby 'debtors should satisfy their creditors according to a valuation of their possessions at the price they had paid for them before the civil war, deducting from the principal whatever interest had been paid . . . or pledged . . . which wiped out about a fourth part of their indebtedness.'[1] (9) More permanent than any of these measures was the reform of the calendar.

To put an end to the disorders arising out of the calendar based on the lunar year, Caesar replaced it by the Egyptian calendar regulated by the sun. With the assistance of the Alexandrian astronomer Sosigenes, he fixed the mean length of the year at $365\frac{1}{4}$ days, and decreed that every fourth year should have 366 days and the others 365. In order to restore the vernal equinox to March 25, he ordered two extraordinary months of 33 and 34 days to be inserted between November and December of the current year – 46 B.C. – as well as the intercalary month of 23 days which fell in the year, and that the first Julian year should open on January 1, 45 B.C. Further, he ordered that the months January, March, May, July, September, and November should each have 31 days, and the other months 30, with the exception of February, which should have 29 days in the common year and 30 days every fourth year.[2]

Although, normally, Caesar consulted the Senate before he gave effect to his measures, consultation was purely formal, and at times the consent of the senators was registered without their knowledge. Cicero

[1] For the above see: (1) Suetonius, *Div. Iul.*, XLI, 3; (2) *ibid.*, XXXVIII, 1; (3) *ibid.*, XLI, 3; (4) *ibid.*, XLIII, 2; (5) Dio, XLIII, 25, 2; (6) Suetonius, *Div. Iul.*, XLII, 3; (7) Dio, XLIII, 25, 3; (8) Suetonius, *Div. Iul.*, XLII, 2.

[2] In order to gratify his vanity, Augustus gave the month which bears his name as many days as July, named after Caesar. He took the additional day from February and added it to August. Also he reduced September and November to 30 days and added an extra day to October and December.

refers to this in a letter to Papirius Paetus, dated the middle of October, 46 B.C.:

'Here am I at Rome,' he writes, 'and all the while decrees of the Senate are being drafted at the house of my dear friend. . . .[1] Indeed, whenever it occurs to him, my name is put down as a witness to the drafting, and I am informed that some decree of the Senate alleged to have been passed in accordance with my vote has found its way to Armenia and Syria, before the matter has ever been mentioned at all.'[2]

When Caesar was engaged on these legislative tasks, Cleopatra with a large suite, her boy husband and infant son, Caesarion, arrived in Rome, and was installed by him in his suburban mansion on the Janiculan Hill beyond the Tiber.[3] That he should keep a mistress was no great scandal, but that she was an alien queen 'incurred the greatest censure'.[4] But he cared nothing for public opinion, and his arrogance was such that he enrolled her name among the friends and allies of the Roman people, and placed a statue of her next to the image of the goddess in the temple of Venus Genetrix.[5]

Meanwhile alarming despatches were arriving from Spain.

### 3. CHAOS IN SPAIN

It will be remembered that, before Caesar's departure from Spain in September, 49 B.C., he appointed Quintus Cassius governor of the province of Further Spain and allotted him four legions to hold it; to them Cassius added a fifth, locally recruited. It was an unfortunate appointment, because Cassius was everything a governor should not be – corrupt, avaricious, weak, and brutal. His exactions antagonized the people, and by pandering to his troops he undermined their discipline.

To impede Juba from reinforcing Pompey in Macedonia, Caesar ordered Cassius to invade Numidia by way of Mauretania,[6] and when he was making ready to do so, an attempt was made on his life. When the conspirators were rounded up, he turned their treachery to his profit. He offered them torture and death, or in lieu the payment of a heavy ransom; thereby he put a premium on treason.[7] Soon after this he heard of Pompey's defeat at Pharsalus, and the news, it would appear, led to the mutiny of the two legions which formerly had

---

[1] Probably Balbus, Caesar's agent.     [2] *Ad. Fam.*, IX, xv, 4.
[3] Holmes, vol. III, p. 287.     [4] Dio. XLIII, 27, 3.
[5] Appian, *Civil Wars*, II, 102. Appian, who wrote in the reign of Antoninus Pius (A.D. 138–61), mentions that Cleopatra's statue was 'standing there to this day.'
[6] *Bell. Alex.*, 51.     [7] *Ibid.*, 55.

served under Varro and were still Pompeian at heart. Next, the inhabitants and garrison of Corduba (Cordova) revolted, and when he sent his quaestor, Marcus Marcellus, to restore order in the town, Marcellus associated himself with the rebels who were loyal Caesarians. Thereupon Cassius appealed to Bogud, king of Mauretania, and to Marcus Lepidus, governor of Nearer Spain, to come to his aid. Next, Marcellus blockaded him in Ulia (Monte Mayor), a town some 15 miles to the south of Corduba, and when Bogud came to the rescue he was unable to dislodge Marcellus. Soon after Lepidus arrived with a considerable army, and, in concert with Marcellus, an arrangement with Cassius was made which permitted Cassius to leave his camp and go to Carmo (Carmona). But when he learnt that Trebonius was on his way to supersede him, he hastened to Malaca (Malaga) where he embarked with 'the proceeds of innumerable robberies,' and perished in a storm off the mouth of the Ebro. Peace was then restored for a while.

When the news of Caesar's victory at Thapsus was received in Spain, trouble again broke out. The legions which had mutinied, afraid that Caesar would punish them, revolted and elected as their leaders two Roman knights, Quinctius Scapula and Quintus Aponius, who expelled Trebonius. At the time Gnaeus Pompey was in the Balearic Isles, and when he heard of the revolt he sailed to Spain, and Scapula's followers elected him their commander-in-chief. Soon he was joined by his brother Sextus, Labienus, Varus, and other fugitives from Africa. Elated by the multitudes who flocked to him, 'he proceeded fearlessly through the country . . . and seemed to surpass even his father in power.'[1] Whatever that may actually mean, it was sufficiently threatening to overawe Caesar's legates, Quintus Pedius and Fabius Maximus, who sent an urgent request to Rome for aid. At first Caesar discounted the rising and despatched some reinforcements to assist his two legates; but when more urgent appeals were received, early in November, 46 B.C., he appointed Lepidus his Master of the Horse, and set out for Spain. In 27 days he reached Obulco (Porcuna), 35 miles east of Corduba.[2]

[1] Dio, XLIII 30, 5.

[2] Strabo, III, 4, 9; and Appian, Civil Wars, II, 103. If Caesar travelled overland, from Rome the distance must have been at the least 1,500 miles. Therefore in 27 days he must have averaged between 50 and 60 miles a day, an astonishing feat of physical endurance in a springless reda.

## 4. THE MUNDA CAMPAIGN

The sole contemporary account of the Munda campaign is the *De Bello Hispaniensi*,[1] by an unknown author, possibly a centurion who took part in it, and in Holmes's estimation it 'is the worst book in Latin literature. . . . Trivialities and puerilities abound. Indispensable information is frequently sought in vain. How Gnaeus contrived to defray the cost of the war, how Caesar fed his army, what were the numbers of the troops engaged, why sundry operations were undertaken, we are not told and cannot conjecture.'[2] Therefore, out of justice to Caesar, the account of the campaign will be uncritical. Nevertheless, because prior to his departure from Rome he relied on his legates in Spain to settle accounts with Gnaeus, and when he decided to join them he travelled at such a speed that 'he appeared to both his adherents and opponents before they had even heard that he was in Spain,'[3] it may safely be assumed, as in all his campaigns since Pharsalus, few if any preparations were made to win this last one.

We are told that Caesar could put into the field eight legions and 8,000 cavalry, and Gnaeus thirteen legions, of which only four were worth the name. Obviously, Caesar's aim was to conclude the campaign as rapidly as possible, because at the time he was eager to make war on Parthia, which he had decided on during his Pontic campaign.[4] Obviously, because of his lack of trained troops, Gnaeus' aim should have been to prolong the war indefinitely. This he might have done had he resorted to guerrilla warfare, but he was no Sertorius, and instead he relied on avoiding battle. Further, at the outset of the campaign he locked up two legions in Corduba, and they might have turned the scales in his favour when finally he changed his mind and accepted battle.

When Caesar reached Obulco he found that Gnaeus was besieging Ulia, a town firmly attached to Caesar, and that his brother Sextus was holding Corduba with two legions. No sooner had he arrived than he was met by envoys from Ulia who sought his aid, and he sent to it six cohorts and some cavalry who, in a violent storm, which darkened the sky and obscured their approach, succeeded in passing safely through the besiegers' lines and entering the town. Next, he decided that the

---

[1] The translation used is that of A. G. Way (Loeb edit.) and is referred to as *Bell. Hisp.*
[2] Vol. III, p. 298.
[3] Dio, XLIII, 32, 1.      [4] *Ibid.*, XLIV, 46, 3.

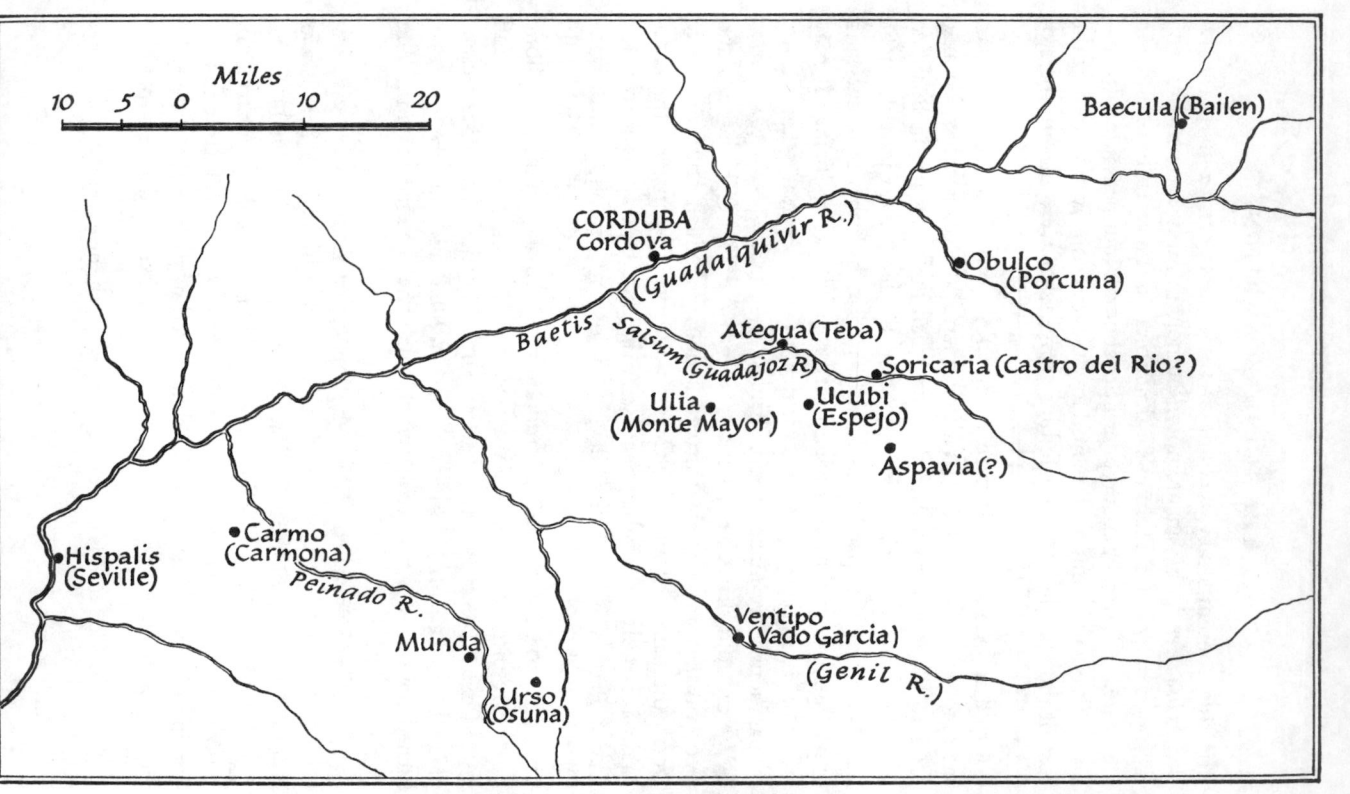

17. Theatre of the Munda Campaign

best way to relieve Ulia was to advance on Corduba and compel Gnaeus to come to his brother's assistance. As always, he relied on speed, and rushed forward a picked force of infantry and cavalry who, when they neared the city, by a ruse[1] induced the Pompeians to attack them. The stratagem was successful; the Pompeians were so roughly handled that Sextus took alarm and sent an urgent message to his brother to aid him. Gnaeus at once complied; but before he could reach Corduba, where a bridge spanned the river Baetis (Guadalquiver), Caesar arrived ahead of him, and as the bridge was held by Sextus, he moved a short distance down stream, and bridged the river by sinking baskets filled with stones to form extemporized piles over which to lay a roadway. Then he went into three camps and invested the town.

When Gnaeus came up, he pitched his camp on the high ground on the southern side of the river, immediately south of Corduba – that is, opposite the town bridge. For some reason, not mentioned, it would appear that he was unable to cross it, and, in order to cut him off from it, Caesar constructed an entrenchment from the *tête de pont* of the temporary bridge toward it; whereupon Gnaeus responded by constructing a counter-entrenchment.[2] Meanwhile frequent skirmishes took place between the covering forces, and when Caesar found that he could not attain his aim, he attempted to provoke Gnaeus to come down from his camp on to the level ground by the river and accept battle. Wisely Gnaeus refused to do so, and Caesar, who by now – so it would appear – was running short of supplies, decided to quit Corduba and move against Ategua (Teba),[3] a fortress which lay slightly to the north of the river Salsum (Guadajoz) and some 20 miles southeast of Corduba. It was strongly garrisoned, and in it Caesar had learnt there was an abundance of grain.[4]

Because Gnaeus' camp flanked Caesar's line of withdrawal, in order to conceal his departure Caesar ordered the camp-fires to be kept burning, and under cover of their deceptive glimmer he slipped away by night, and when on the following morning he reached Ategua he forthwith laid siege to it.

Gnaeus, who relied on the strength of Ategua, and because of the

[1] See *Bell. Hisp.*, 4.

[2] *Ibid.*, 5. The text is obscure.

[3] The localities of towns mentioned in *Bell. Hisp.*, are those determined or conjectured by Holmes, vol. III, pp. 543–7.

[4] Dio, XLIII, 33, 2.

winter thought that Caesar would soon abandon the siege, did not immediately follow him. But when he learnt that the town was being encircled by a contravallation, 'he grew afraid and came with assistance.'[1] There then followed a series of minor operations, which would be tedious to describe. Their marked characteristic was that, as the siege lengthened, fighting became more brutal, and we are told that the besiegers slaughtered their prisoners and cut off the hands of intercepted enemy messengers.[2] Meanwhile dissensions broke out between the townsfolk and the garrison; the former urged surrender, the latter feared Caesar's vengeance and determined to resist. At length the quarrelling became so acute that Munatius Plancus, the garrison commander, arrested all citizens suspected of favouring the Caesarians; butchered them in full view of his enemy's camp, and flung their corpses over the town wall.[3]

The day on which that atrocity was perpetrated, Gnaeus succeeded in passing a courier into the town with an order to the garrison to cut its way out. The attempt was made, and although the besiegers were surprised, it was repulsed. A few days later two Lusitanian deserters reported to Caesar that in a speech Gnaeus had said: Since he was unable to relieve the town, he intended to withdraw by night 'out of sight of his opponents in the direction of the sea'.[4] Caesar at once informed the townsfolk of this, and after the garrison had made another abortive attempt to cut its way out, Mutatius recognized that the game was up. He sent an envoy to Caesar with a letter in which he offered to surrender the town should his life be spared. At the same time envoys from the townsfolk came to Caesar and said that, 'if he would spare their lives, they would surrender the town on the following day. His reply to them ran thus: "I am Caesar and I will be as good as my word." Accordingly, on February 19th he took possession of the town.'[5]

As soon as Gnaeus was informed of the surrender he withdrew toward Ucubi (Espejo), and Caesar followed and encamped close by him. Next, further atrocities are recorded; after which Gnaeus withdrew to Soricaria (? Castro del Rio), six miles south-east of Ategua. Caesar followed him and threatened to cut him off from a fort called Aspavia. It would appear to have been of sufficient importance to induce Gnaeus to fight a minor battle, in which he lost nearly 500 men.

---

[1] Dio, XLIII, 33, 3.
[2] *Bell. Hisp.*, 12.
[3] *Ibid.*, 15.
[4] *Ibid.*, 18.
[5] *Ibid.*, 19.

Followed by Caesar, he retreated to Urso (Osuna) which lay 40 miles south-west of Ucubi, and on his way he burnt the town of Carruca (site unknown) because its inhabitants had shut its gates against him. On March 16 he reached the fortress of Munda, the site of which has led to much speculation, but Holmes is almost certain that it stood on 'a hill or group of closely connected heights . . . about 9 kilometres, or 6 Roman miles, west by north of Osuna'.[1] When Caesar caught up with him, he encamped his army in the plain to the east of Munda, through which ran a rivulet, now named the Peinado.

Early on the following morning, when Caesar was about to strike camp and take the road, scouts reported to him that Gnaeus 'had been in battle formation since the third watch'. He decided on an immediate attack, and deployed his eight legions: the 10th on the right and the 3rd and 5th on the left, the latter flanked by his auxiliaries and 8,000 cavalry,[2] including a corps of Moorish horsemen, commanded by King Bogud. The advance was then sounded, and the army began to cross the plain toward its adversary's thirteen,[3] or – more probably – eleven legions,[4] deployed on the high ground and flanked by cavalry and 6,000 light-armed auxiliaries, besides whom Gnaeus had nearly as many auxiliary troops again, presumably posted in rear.[5] When the rivulet was reached, because of the marshy ground some delay occurred in crossing it.

The author of *The Spanish War* states that, when Gnaeus' line of battle came into sight, Caesar 'had no doubt that his opponents would advance to the level ground to do battle in the middle of the plain'.[6] That is highly improbable, because by now Caesar was fully aware that it was the last thing Gnaeus was likely to do. A better reason is, that Caesar was eager to wind up the campaign, and that he relied on the superior skill and discipline of his men to compensate for his adversary's advantageous position. Further, his men were eager to fight, and he did not want to damp their ardour. Incidentally, the truth may have been that he did not dare to do so.

Nevertheless, the over-eagerness that had prematurely precipitated the battle of Thapsus, if repeated at Munda, might easily spell ruin.

[1] Vol. III, p. 547.

[2] *Bell. Hisp.*, 30. It would be of interest to know how Caesar had been able to keep alive so vast a number of horses during the winter.

[3] *Ibid.*, 30.

[4] *Ad. Fam.*, VI, xviii, 2.

[5] *Bell. Hisp.*, 30.          [6] *Ibid.*, 29.

Therefore, when the battle line 'reached the unfavourable ground at the farthest limit of the plain,' and 'the enemy were ready on higher ground . . . to avoid any blunder being perpetrated owing to rashness or faulty judgement,' Caesar 'began to restrict the operational area.' This would appear to mean that either he reduced the speed of the advance up the slope, or, what is more likely, called a halt in order to rectify the dressing of the battle front. Whatever it may have been, it was bitterly resented by his men, 'as they took it to mean that their chance of deciding the conflict was being hampered.' Also we are told that the 'delay made the enemy keener,' because it led him to assume that Caesar was afraid to join battle. Next, we are told that 'by displaying themselves they gave our men the opportunity of engaging them.' This may mean that Gnaeus advanced his line a short distance down the slope, either to gain a fuller view of his enemy, or to induce him to attack. Nevertheless, we read that 'it was only at great risk that Caesar could approach them.' The advance was resumed; a 'shout was raised, and the battle joined.'[1]

When the opposing lines were about to clinch, each discharged a volley of heavy javelins, and we are told that the Pompeians 'fell in heaps.' No doubt a figure of speech, because most of the javelins must have become transfixed in the soldiers' shields; their object, be it remembered, was to render them difficult to handle by weighing them down, and so facilitate the sword attack. On this occasion, the advantage lay with the Pompeians, because their discharge was delivered down-hill, and the anonymous historian notes that 'so furious [was] the charging with its attendant volley of missiles, that our men well nigh lost their confidence in victory.'[2]

When the opposing legions were fiercely engaged in the wearing fight – the cut and thrust and the replacement of killed, wounded, and exhausted – the battle was decided on the left flank of the Pompeian line. How it actually was brought about is a matter of conjecture, because the various accounts are difficult to square.

The author of *The Spanish War* relates what he saw. In brief, he says that the 10th Legion pressed the enemy back, and Gnaeus, growing anxious, transferred a legion from his right wing to support his left wing and prevent it from being outflanked. But as soon as it set out, 'Caesar's cavalry began to exert pressure on the enemy's left wing,' and in consequence the enemy 'was afforded no opportunity of reinforcing his line'.[3]

[1] *Bell. Hisp.*, 30.    [2] *Ibid.*, 31.    [3] *Ibid.*, 31.

Appian makes no mention of cavalry; the gist of his account is: When the battle was joined, fear seized on Caesar's men, and Caesar rushed forward, removed his helmet,[1] and exhorted and shamed them to face up to the enemy. As this did not abate their fear, he seized a shield from a soldier and shouted: 'This shall be the end of my life and of your military service.' Then 'the whole army rushed forward,' and 'toward evening Caesar with difficulty won the victory.'[2]

Dio mentions the cavalry, and states that the struggle between the two armies was so equal that 'All would have perished or at nightfall they would have parted with honours even, had not Bogud, who was somewhere outside the conflict, set out for Pompey's camp, when Labienus, observing this, left his station and proceeded against him. Pompey's men, then supposing him to be in flight, lost heart; and though later, of course, they learned the truth, they could no longer recover themselves.'[3]

Florus mentions that an incident occurred in the battle which was unparalleled in living memory:

'When the two armies . . . had long been . . . cutting one another down . . . an unaccustomed disgrace presented itself to Caesar's eyes: his tired veterans . . . gave ground, and though they had not gone so far as to flee, yet it was obvious that shame rather than valour made them resist. Sending away his horse, Caesar rushed forward like a madman to the forefront of the battle, where he seized hold of those who were fleeing, heartened the standard-bearers . . . in a word dashed this way and that through the ranks with glances, gestures, and shouts. In the turmoil he is even said to have meditated making an end of himself[4] . . . only, at that moment, five cohorts of the enemy, which had been sent by Labienus to protect the camp, which was in danger,[5] crossed the battle-field and suggested an appearance of flight. Caesar either actually believed that the enemy was fleeing or else craftily made use of the incident and gave them [his men] heart against an enemy, who they thought was fleeing and already conquered, while he discouraged the foe. His men, thinking that they were winning the day, followed more

[1] At a critical moment in the battle of Hastings William the Conqueror did the same.

[2] Appian, Civil Wars, II, 104. See also Plutarch, Caesar, LVI, 2.

[3] Dio, XLIII, 38, 2.

[4] See also Suetonius, Div. Iul., XXXVI.

[5] Although no mention is made of cavalry, no other force could have endangered it.

boldly, while the Pompeians, thinking that their own side was in flight, began to flee.'[1]

Piecing these various accounts together, Holmes's reading is: When the two lines were in clinch, Caesar noticed that some of his cohorts were losing ground. He rushed forward and urged them to make a supreme effort. The 10th Legion responded to his appeal, and bore down on the enemy's left with such energy that Gnaeus, fearing he would be outflanked, ordered Labienus, on his right wing, to support his left wing with a legion. 'But Caesar had already seen how the battle could be won . . . and before Labienus moved he had ordered Bogud . . . to attack the enemy's left flank and rear.[2] Labienus tried in vain to stop him. The Pompeians in the line of battle, fancying that Labienus was retreating, lost heart, and before they could discover their mistake the Caesarians dashed in and broke the line.'[3]

This is reasonable, for when two armies are locked in battle, nothing is more deadly than a rear attack on one of them. That Bogud, like Claudius Nero at the battle of the Metaurus, and Eumenes II at Magnesia, acted on his own initiative is improbable, because he was not well situated to see what was taking place on the right of Caesar's line. What is perplexing is: how was Bogud able to move at all? Gnaeus' camp 'was protected not only by the natural formation of the ground but also by the fortifications of the town itself,'[4] which presumably means that it was backed by it. How far from the camp Gnaeus deployed his original line of battle, and how far he advanced it down the slope to its second position – if he did so – are not stated. But wherever his final position was, it cannot have been at any great distance from the camp. How was it then possible, in face of Gnaeus' right wing cavalry, and in the restricted space between the rear of his line of battle and his camp, which space was occupied by some 5,000 to 6,000 auxiliary troops, for Bogud to advance with the facility he apparently did? It would appear that an entire phase of the battle – an extensive cavalry engagement between Caesar's left wing and Gnaeus' right wing cavalry – has been omitted by all authorities.

[1] Florus, II, xiii, 80–85. Livy (*Epitome*, CXV) says, 'Caesar at length gained a signal victory, after a most desperate engagement at Munda.'

[2] To the writer it would seem more probable that, when Caesar became aware of Labienus' movement, he sent a galloper to Bogud with an order to impede it; that Labienus' legion then fell back toward the Pompeian camp, and Bogud attacked the rear of Gnaeus' left flank.

[3] Vol. III, pp. 307–8, and 548–51.        [4] *Bell. Hisp.*, 28.

Pursued by the victorious Caesarians, the panic-stricken Pompeians fled to their camp and sought refuge in the fortress of Munda; in the one they fought fanatically until the last man was killed; in the other they were besieged. Among the slain were Labienus and Attius Varus. The casualties recorded were: 1,000 Caesarians killed and 500 wounded, and of the Pompeians some 30,000 are said to have perished.[1]

The battle would appear to have been the most stubbornly contested of any in the Civil War. According to Plutarch, Caesar, when he left the field, turned to those near him and said: 'That he had often striven for victory, but now first for his life;'[2] and Appian repeats that remark.[3] Finally, two things about the battle are worth noting: the one is that, although masses of cavalry were present, except for Bogud's Moorish horse, no mention is made of them; the other that, as at the battle of Zama, it was the horsemen of North Africa who decided the issue.

Although wounded, Gnaeus with some followers escaped from the battlefield to Carteia (El Rocadillo), a port on the Bay of Gibraltar; failed in his attempt to escape by sea, and soon after was captured by Didius' soldiers and beheaded. When other fugitives reached Corduba, Sextus learnt of the disaster, and on the plea that he would go to Caesar to discuss terms of peace, he abandoned its garrison and withdrew into hiding. Meanwhile Caesar left Fabius Maximus at Munda to invest it, and marched to Corduba, where he found Sextus' two legions at strife. One was for surrender, the other for continued resistance, and when the anti-Caesarians were about to set fire to the town, they were overpowered by Caesar's legionaries who, so we are told, massacred the incredible number of 22,000 people.[4]

From Corduba Caesar marched to Hispalis (Seville), thence to Asta (Mesa de Asta) and Gades (Cadiz). Wherever he went he found Pompeian factions still very active, which goes to show that, as both he and Pompey the Great had served in Spain before the outbreak of the war, Pompey's administration had appealed to the people more than his own. After he had left Spain, Sextus came out of hiding and gathered together large numbers of old Pompeians and vagabonds. According

---

[1] *Ibid.*, 31. On the face of them these figures are unreliable.

[2] Plutarch, *Caesar*, LVI, 3.

[3] Appian, *Civil Wars*, II, 104.

[4] *Bell. Hisp.*, 34. Dio (XLIII, 39, 2) says: 'He slew the slaves under arms and sold the rest', which seems more probable.

to Appian, 'he flew from place to place,' and spread terror through the whole of Spain.[1] He emulated Sertorius and relied on guerrilla warfare, and at the time of Caesar's assassination Asinius Pollio was still struggling with him.

From Gades Caesar returned to Hispalis, and accompanied by the youthful Octavius, the grandson of his sister Julia, together they travelled to New Carthage (Carthagena); thence to Tarraco, where they took ship, and by the middle of September, 45 B.C., Caesar was back in Rome.

## 5. CAESAR'S DEIFICATION

Sulla had been compelled to share his supremacy with the nobles who had assisted him in gaining it, and who ended by turning against him. After Munda Caesar shared his supremacy with no one; therefore it was unlimited. The devotion of his soldiers was his, and he had at his disposal incalculable wealth. With it he could have bought out all opposition of the knights and people, had it not been that they supported him; therefore there was no need to carry out a proscription in order to enrich himself. 'The plebeian electors and the citizens of the tribes,' writes Carcopino, 'were actually no more than the sheep of Panurge, and with closed eyes they followed Caesar wherever it pleased him to lead them. . . . It is,' he adds, 'a characteristic of "Caesarism" that, in the name of the people, the people surrendered to him the decision which politically annihilated them.'[2] This surrender is reflected in the honours he already had received, and in the additional ones conferred upon him when news of Munda reached Rome.

He was decreed a thanksgiving of fifty days; that in honour of the victory a temple of Liberty should be built at the public cost; and that the title of *Imperator* should be bestowed upon him for life and made hereditary. He was offered the magistracies, even those of the *plebs*, elected consul for ten years, and supreme financial control was surrendered to him. Also it was decreed that an ivory statue of him and his chariot should appear in the processions at the public games with the statues of the gods; that another statue should be set up in the temple of Quirinus,[3] with the inscription 'To the Invincible God'; and yet another on the Capitol beside the former kings of

[1] Appian, *Civil Wars*, IV, 83.
[2] *Histoire Générale* (edit. Glotz), 'Histoire Romaine', vol. II, 'César', Jérôme Carcopino, p. 927.
[3] The name of the deified Romulus.

Rome. Thus they deified him, and 'declared him a monarch out and out'.[1]

Immediately after his return to Rome Caesar made his will, and in it he adopted Octavius as his son and principal heir. Soon after, his arrogance was such that he committed the unprecedented blunder of celebrating another triumph, this time over his fellow citizens whom he had conquered in Spain. To gratify his two generals, Fabius Maximus and Quintus Pedius, he allowed them triumphs of their own, which, as Dio says, 'occasioned ridicule' – a dangerous weapon to place in the hands of his adversaries. He ignored the Senate and the people; set out to justify his title of *Imperator* in perpetuity, and acted as though he were an Oriental sultan.

His aim, so far as it can be judged from his actions, was to consolidate his own position and reduce the Senate to a nullity. With an energy and completeness, which in after centuries was only rivalled by Lenin in the October Revolution, he set to work.

He proclaimed a general amnesty, pardoned nearly all of his adversaries and promoted many. Like Sulla, he added to the praetors and quaestors, respectively increasing their numbers to 16 and 40, so as to meet the increased demands of the provinces, and handed the treasury over to two of his prefects. Like Sulla, he increased the membership of the Senate from 600 to 900, and swamped it with his partisans – centurions, private soldiers, scribes, sons of freedmen, and even Gauls – whom Syme calls 'a ghastly and disgusting rabble'.[2] Further, he reinstated those who had been degraded by the censors; admitted to office the sons of the proscribed; prohibited citizens between twenty and forty years of age to be absent from Italy for more than three successive years, and decreed that at least a third of the herdsmen of the great landowners should be men of free birth. Also he established a special body of police to enforce his sumptuary laws.[3]

He appointed commissioners to carry out the allotment of land for his discharged veterans, and in the footsteps of Gaius Gracchus he projected the establishment of colonies in which to settle 80,000 citizens, and ordered the rebuilding of Carthage and Corinth as two of them. Also he bestowed Latin rights upon Sicily, in Gaul and in Spain,

[1] Dio, XLIII, 45. In Classical times deification was equivalent to canonization in Christian.

[2] *The Roman Revolution*, p. 78. Also Cicero: 'Ye gods what a following! what *âmes damnées* in your phrase! . . . what desperate gangs' (*Ad. Att.*, IX, 18).

[3] For these and other acts see Suetonius, *Div. Iul.*, XLI–XLIII.

and to secure the eastern provinces against extortion, he abolished the existing tax system, and reverted to the earlier practice, which allowed their cities and districts to collect and pay tribute without the intervention of Roman middlemen.[1]

Like so many autocrats before and after him, his ambition was to leave to future generations visible monuments of his greatness. Suetonius and others relate that in Rome he intended to build a temple to Mars greater than any in existence; a theatre of vast size, and a great state library on the model of the one at Alexandria; to drain the Pontine marshes; transform Ostiain to a great commercial and naval harbour, and among other notable works, cut a canal through the isthmus of Corinth.

At the same time he was engaged on planning a war against the Dacians, who had poured into Pontus and Thrace, and on preparing his long contemplated campaign against Parthia: to expunge the shame of Carrhae; possibly also to crown his autocracy with glory, and in the eyes of the people become a second Alexander. For that campaign he ordered sixteen legions and 10,000 cavalry to be mustered.[2]

For the year 44 B.C., he selected Antony as his partner in the consulate; Hirtius and C. Vibius Pansa consuls for 43, and Decimus Brutus and Munatius Plancus for 42. Meanwhile he assigned Decimus Brutus to rule Cisalpine Gaul, appointed Gaius Trebonius and Tillius Cimber governors of Asia and Bithynia, and made Marcus Brutus *praetor urbanus*, and Gaius Cassius *praetor peregrinus*,[3] all of whom were to become leading tyrannicides.

Early in the new year (44 B.C.), in spite of Caesar's autocratic behaviour, the Senate resolved that further honours should be conferred on him, and the following were bestowed:

That he should be sole censor for life; that '*Pater Patriae*' ('Father of his Country') and his image be stamped on his coins – a symbol of monarchy; that his birthday be celebrated by public sacrifices; that the month of *Quintilis* (July), in which he was born, be renamed '*Julius*', and that when he appeared in the Senate he should sit on a gilded chair and in the garb the kings had formerly worn. Further, it was elected that his decrees, past and future, were binding, and that magistrates on assuming office should take an oath not to violate them; that his

---

[1] See Appian, *Civil Wars*, V, 4, and Dio, XLII, 6, 3.

[2] Appian, *Civil Wars*, II, 10.

[3] The former tried causes between Roman citizens, and the latter between strangers.

person was sacrosanct, and by oath the senators bound themselves to protect his life. 'And finally they addressed him outright as Jupiter Julius and ordered a temple to be consecrated to him and to his Clemency, electing Antony as their priest like some *flamen dialis*.'[1]

According to Dio, when at first the senators began to honour him, they hoped that he would be reasonable; 'but as they went on and saw that he was delighted with what they voted – indeed he accepted all but a very few of their decrees' – by way of ridicule the majority 'wished to make him envied and hated as quickly as possible, that he might the sooner perish.'[2] Nevertheless, 'Caesar was encouraged by these very measures to believe that he should never be plotted against ... and consequently he even dispensed henceforth with his bodyguard ... [and] accepted the privilege of being watched over by the senators and knights.'[3]

When the Senate had resolved to confer upon Caesar the above mentioned honours, with the exception of Cassius and a few others, the senators were received by him in the temple of Venus Genetrix, and instead of rising to greet them, he remained seated. This indignity deeply offended them. 'To an insult which so plainly showed his contempt for the Senate,' writes Suetonius, 'he added an act of even greater insolence.' At the Latin Festival someone placed a diadem – the emblem of royalty – on his statue, and when two of the tribunes had it removed, 'Caesar sharply rebuked and deposed them, either offended that the hint of regal power had been received with so little favour, or, as he asserted, that he had been robbed of the glory of refusing it.'[4] Since the days of Tiberius Gracchus no tribune had been subjected to such an indignity.[5]

On February 15, the *Lupercalia*, an ancient fertility festival in honour of Pan, was held in Rome, and immediately previous to it Caesar had accepted the dictatorship for life.[6] As such he took his seat in his gilded chair on the *Rostra*, and when the *Luperci*, came running into the Forum, Antony, who was one of them, as priest of the *Juliani* mounted the platform, attempted to bind the diadem upon Caesar's

[1] For above see Suetonius, *Div. Iul.*, LXXVI; Dio, XLIV, 4–7; Appian, *Civil Wars*, II, 106.

[2] '. . . Some actually ventured to suggest permitting him to have intercourse with as many women as he pleased'. (Dio, XLIV, 7, 3.)

[3] Dio, XLIV, 7, 2–4; see also Suetonius, *Div. Iul.*, LXXXVI, and Plutarch, *Caesar*, LVII, 4.

[4] Suetonius, *Div. Iul.*, LXXIX, 1–2.

[5] See *supra*, Chapter I, p. 22.          [6] Dio, XLIV, 8, 4.

head, and as he did so exclaimed: 'The people offer this to you through me.' At the sight, 'some few clapped their hands, but the greater number groaned.' Thereupon Caesar rejected it; replied: 'Jupiter alone is King of the Romans'; and 'sent the diadem to Jupiter on the Capitol.' Then the people shouted with joy.[1]

Did Caesar stage this demonstration because he desired to be acclaimed king; or did he seize upon the opportunity the *Lupercalia* offered publicly to refuse the diadem, and thereby silence rumours? Intrinsically these questions are superfluous, and the question which should be asked is: could he avoid becoming king *de jure*, since his dictatorship for life had made him king *de facto*? 'It is a sensible argument', writes R. A. G. Carson, 'that Caesar did not, as many still hold, continue to hanker after the diadem and the title *rex*; for when he held the substance of power, why should he seek the outward forms of it which might arouse political antagonisms?'[2] On the other hand, Carcopino holds that, in order to rule he must be a king so as to be the equal of kings, 'and we cannot doubt that his intention was to be called king by his Roman subjects.'[3]

Whether either of these conjectures be true, neither answers the crucial questions: How could Caesar render his absolute power, whether *de facto*, or *de jure*, or both, acceptable to the people? Actually, and seemingly unrecognized by him, his deification had already made him more than king; absolute kingly power is mortal, but absolute divine power is immortal; therefore the second is vastly the more vital. After his death it was his divinity Octavius inherited, and not his monarchy. Undoubtedly, the most realistic critic of the many who have tackled this subject is the emperor Napoleon. He said: 'If Caesar wanted to be king, he would have got his army to acclaim him as such.'[4] For this, no better opportunity could have been devised than the Parthian campaign.

## 6. CAESAR'S ASSASSINATION

At the next meeting of the Senate, the regal question again cropped up. Lucius Cotta, one of the priests in charge of the Sibylline Books, announced it was written in them that the Parthians could be conquered only by a king, and therefore that Caesar should be given that

[1] Dio, XLIV, 11, 2–3; and Appian, *Civil Wars*, II, 109.
[2] *Greece and Rome*, vol. IV, No. 1, March, 1957. 'Caesar and the Monarchy', p. 52.  [3] *Op. cit.*, p. 1003.
[4] *Correspondance*, vol. XXXII, p. 88.

title.[1] Dio says that those who at the time were conspiring against him, of whom Gaius Cassius and Marcus Brutus were the leaders, believed the prophecy to be true, and 'because a vote would be demanded of the magistrates, among whom were Cassius and Brutus, owing to the importance of the measure, and they neither dared to oppose it nor would submit to remain silent, they hastened forward their plot before any business connected with the measure could come up.'[2] Appian also mentions the Sibylline Books, but differs from Dio in that the conspirators believed that, should Caesar conquer the Parthians, 'he would be a king without a doubt.'[3]

When the conspiracy was first hatched is not known. Later, Cicero accused Cassius, Trebonius, and Antony of having on two occasions planned it;[4] but he is an unreliable authority. Such evidence as there is points to Cassius as the ringleader,[5] and it was he who prevailed on Marcus Brutus, Cato's nephew and son-in-law, to join the conspiracy. Both had fought under Pompey against Caesar, had been pardoned after Pharsalus, and, as already mentioned, had been made praetors by him. While Cassius hated Caesar, and Caesar suspected him,[6] Brutus was devoted to Caesar until his return from Spain, and Caesar's affection for him led some to suppose that he was his natural son.[7] In all there were more than sixty conspirators, and many had been Caesar's close and trusted friends.

The avowed object of the plot was tyrannicide, which in the eyes of both Greeks and Romans was righteous and just. A perpetual dictatorship conflicted with every concept of the Republic, and the plotters were well aware that under Caesar's autocracy their opportunities for financial gain and political power would vanish, and the prestige of the Senate would be obliterated by further dilutions. In short, the way of life the senators had been following since the Second Punic War would end. Their struggle against reforms had opened with the murder of the Gracchi, and they fondly imagined that it could be closed by the murder of Caesar. Blinded by their arrogance and corrupted by their avarice, they overlooked the causes of the struggle, and persuaded themselves that were Caesar removed the republican machinery would

---

[1] Suetonius, *Div. Iul.*, LXXIX, 3.
[2] Dio, XLIV, 15, 4.                    [3] Appian, *Civil Wars*, II, 111.
[4] Cicero, *Philippics*, II, 26 and 34.
[5] Suetonius, *Div. Iul.*, LXXX.
[6] Plutarch, *Caesar*, LXII, 4–5; and *Brutus*, VIII, 9.
[7] Appian, *Civil Wars*, II, 112.

at once begin to function. How Caesar's army was to be dealt with would seem altogether to have escaped them.

When it became known to them that Caesar was to leave Rome and set out on his Parthian campaign on March 18, after which date his person would be secured against attack, they decided to strike on March 15 (the Ides of March) when the Senate was to meet Caesar in a hall which adjoined the theatre of Pompey.

On the night of March 14, accompanied by Decimus Brutus, Caesar supped with Lepidus, and as they sat over their wine, one of them – probably Lepidus – put the question: 'What sort of death was the best?' To which Caesar replied: 'That which is unexpected.'[1] On the following morning Calpurnia implored her husband to cancel the meeting of the Senate, because in a dream she had seen him streaming with blood. As the sacrifices proved unfavourable, Caesar sent for Antony and instructed him to dismiss the Senate.

These prognostications, and a host of others recorded by the classical historians, are in fact unnecessary embellishments of the drama, because Caesar was under no illusions about his pretended friends. Plutarch mentions that he suspected Cassius,[2] and Suetonius states that 'if any dangerous plots were formed against him, or slanders uttered, he preferred to quash rather than punish them. Accordingly he took no further notice of the conspiracies which were detected.'[3] Already, some days previously, when Hirtius had urged him to recall his body-guard, he had set the suggestion aside, presumably because the members of the Senate had sworn to protect him, and his *dignitas* forbade that he should either doubt their loyalty, or quake before their treachery. It was an irrational decision, an act of pride and not of reason, and, like Nebuchadnezzar, 'in pride he was [to be] deposed from his kingly throne.'[4]

Early on the Ides of March the conspirators posted a party of gladiators, provided by Decimus Brutus, in Pompey's theatre, in case their services should be needed; then they assembled in the adjoining hall to await Caesar. When, at the appointed hour, he did not come, they grew anxious, and sent Decimus Brutus, 'who was so trusted by Caesar that he was entered in his will as his second heir,'[5] to fetch him. Brutus, 'his devoted friend',[6] urged him to come, and succeeded in persuading him to change his mind by saying: 'If he was fully resolved

---

[1] Plutarch, *Caesar*, XLIII, 4.
[2] *Ibid.*, LXII, 5.
[3] Suetonius, *Div. Iul.*, LXXV, 4.
[4] Daniel, V, 20.
[5] Plutarch, *Caesar*, LXIV, 1.
[6] Dio, XLIV, 18, 1.

to regard the day as inauspicious, it was better that he should go in person and address the Senate, and then postpone the business.'[1]

Caesar then stepped into his litter, and on the way to the Senate, a teacher of Greek philosophy, Artemidorus by name, thrust into his hand a roll of paper in which the conspiracy was divulged, and said: 'Read this, Caesar, by thyself, and speedily.'[2] Caesar took it, but was prevented by the crush of the people from doing so.

Because it was customary for the magistrates, when about to enter the Senate House, to take auspices, Caesar did so. They proved inauspicious. Nevertheless, in defiance of the portents, he laughed at Spurinna, the soothsayer, and called him a false prophet, 'because the Ides of March were come without bringing him harm.' Spurinna replied, 'that they had of a truth come, but they had not gone.'[3]

Caesar entered the hall, and because Antony was a powerful and courageous man who might give trouble, Trebonius engaged him in conversation at its entrance. When Caesar had seated himself on his gilded chair, Tillius Cimber came forward and petitioned him for the recall of his brother, who had been banished. When Caesar rejected his appeal, Cimber seized hold of his purple robe, and pulled it away to expose his neck. It was the signal for the attack. Casca, who was close to Caesar, aimed a blow with his dagger at his throat, but missed it. Cimber then seized Caesar's hand; nevertheless, Caesar sprang from his chair and threw Casca to the ground. The other assassins then closed on him. Cassius wounded him in the face, and when Brutus struck him in the thigh, Caesar cried out in Greek: 'You too, my child?'[4] He then fell dead at the foot of Pompey's statue. In all he received twenty-three wounds, but in the opinion of the physician Antistus, 'except the second in the breast,' none was mortal.[5]

The conspirators had intended, once Caesar was slain, to make a speech in the Senate; but in panic the senators had fled, and instead they ran out of the hall to exhort the people 'to restore the government of their fathers'.[6] As the people were too terror-stricken to respond, with their gladiators the assassins hastened to the Capitol, took counsel and decided to bribe the populace. 'They thought,' writes Appian, 'that

[1] Plutarch, Caesar, LXIV, 3.　　　　　[2] Ibid., LXV, 1.
[3] Suetonius, Div. Iul., LXXXI, 4.
[4] Ibid., LXXXII, 3. Dio (XLIV, 19, 5) says: 'Thou too, my son?'
[5] Suetonius, Div. Iul., LXXXII, 3.
[6] The following is based on Appian, Civil Wars, II, 118–48. His account of events immediately following the murder is the fullest of all classical historians.

the Roman people were still exactly the same as they had heard they were at the time when the elder Brutus[1] expelled the kings.'

Antony and Lepidus were for avenging Caesar, but they feared Decimus Brutus who, as governor of Cisalpine Gaul, had a large army at call. As consul, the former summoned the Senate, and acted with consummate skill. To those – the vast majority – who condemned Caesar, he pointed out that because he had been their chosen ruler, his acts remained valid. Therefore his first question was: Are you willing to resign the offices to which he appointed you? 'Having lighted this kind of firebrand among them,' they rose *en masse* and protested against new elections, or that their claims should be submitted to the people. Then, to those who called for peace, he replied: 'That is what we are striving for . . . but it is hard to get security for it where so many oaths . . . were of no avail in the case of Caesar.' Next, he turned to those who demanded vengeance and said: 'I myself would join you and would be the first to call for vengeance if I were not the consul.' He concluded his speech by saying: 'I move that all the acts and intentions of Caesar be ratified and that the authors of the crime be by no means applauded, for that would be neither pious, nor just, nor consistent with the ratification of Caesar's acts.' The following decree was then passed: 'There shall be no prosecutions for the murder of Caesar, but all his acts and decrees are confirmed, because his policy is deemed advantageous to the commonwealth.'

Caesar's will was then publicly read. In it Octavius was adopted by Caesar as his son; his gardens were given to the people as a place of recreation, and every Roman living in the city received 300 sesterces (£3). When it was learnt that Decimus Brutus had been adopted by Caesar as his second heir, there was a great disturbance among the people who considered it 'shocking and sacrilegious' that as his adopted son he should have conspired against him.

When Caesar's body was brought into the Forum, a countless multitude ran together to guard it, and Antony delivered the funeral oration – a masterpiece of incisive rabble-rousing.

He began by enumerating the decrees which in admiration of his merits had been voted to Caesar by the Senate and the people, and by which Caesar had been declared to be 'superhuman, sacred, and inviolable'. As he recorded each one he turned and pointed at Caesar's corpse. 'Nobody', he said, 'who found refuge with him was harmed, but he, whom you declared sacred and inviolable, was killed, although

1 First consul in 509 B.C.

he did not extort these honours from you as a tyrant, and did not even ask for them.' He next 'recited the oaths by which all were pledged to guard Caesar and Caesar's body with all their strength, and all were devoted to perdition who should not avenge him against any conspiracy'. Lastly, he uncovered Caesar's body, 'lifted his robe on the point of a spear and shook it aloft;' at which the people went mad with rage. They set fire to the senate-chamber; tore to pieces an unfortunate poet whom they mistook for Cinna the tribune, and burnt the houses of the murderers, who fled the city.

Finally, Caesar's corpse was brought into the Forum, and cremated 'where in olden time stood the palace of the Kings of Rome'. A fitting place for his funeral pyre, for as Fowler says: 'If ever there was a king, Caesar was one.'[1]

Thus it came about that Cicero, who had gloated over the assassination, wrote to Atticus:

'So now I see it was folly to be consoled by the Ides of March: for though our courage was that of men, believe me we had no more sense than children. We have only cut down the tree not rooted it up.'[2]

Indeed prophetic words, for Caesar's mighty ghost was to stalk the battlefields of yet another civil war; to end thirteen years later with the battle of Actium, when the century of revolution passed into history.

[1] *Julius Caesar*, W. Warde Fowler (edit. 1935), p. 365.
[2] *Ad Att.*, XV, iv (May 24, 44 B.C.). One of several letters with the same refrain.

# XIV

## As Statesman and General

### I. AS STATESMAN

IN Mommsen's opinion, 'Caesar was a statesman in the deepest sense of the term . . . a consummate statesman . . . the sole creative genius produced by Rome, and the last produced by the ancient world.' This is a monumental overstatement. Except for his settlement of Gaul, and his reform of the taxation of the eastern provinces, as a statesman he created nothing; neither a rejuvenated republic, nor an acceptable monarchy, let alone anything resembling the Principate, which his adopted son, Octavian – an incomparably greater statesman – did.

Further, the great German scholar compared him with Cromwell, who, he writes, 'also transformed himself from a leader of opposition into a military chief and democratic king, and who in general, little as the Puritan hero seems to resemble the dissolute Roman, is yet in his development as well as in the objects which he aimed at and the results which he achieved of all statesmen perhaps the most akin to Caesar.'[1]

This is a just estimate as the reader will discover if he turns to Clarendon's history of the Great Rebellion; for when the obvious differences between Caesar and Cromwell are set aside, Clarendon's judgement of the latter is startlingly true of the former.

'He was one of those men [he writes] . . . whom his very enemies could not condemn without commending him at the same time: for he could never have done half that mischief without great parts of courage, industry, and judgement. He must have had a wonderful understanding in the natures and humours of men, and as great a dexterity in applying them; who . . . without interest or estate, alliance or friendship, could raise himself to such a height, and compound and

[1] *Op. cit.*, vol. IV, pp. 424–8.

knead such opposite and contradictory tempers, humours, and interests into a consistence, that contributed to his designs, and to their destruction, whilst himself grew insensibly powerful enough to cut off those by whom he had climbed, in the instant that they projected to demolish their own building ... he attempted those things which no good man durst have ventured on; and achieved those in which none but a valiant and a great man could have succeeded ... yet wickedness as great as his could never have accomplished those designs without the assistance of a great spirit, an admirable circumspection and sagacity, and a most magnanimous resolution. . . .

'After he was confirmed and invested Protector by the humble Petition and Advice, he consulted with few upon any action of importance, nor communicated any enterprise he resolved upon, with more than those who were to have principal parts in the execution of it. . . . What he once resolved ... he would not be dissuaded from, nor endure any contradiction of his power and authority; but extorted obedience from them who were not willing to yield it.'[1]

Both Caesar and Cromwell were opportunists and autocrats, and as Cromwell once said of himself, that why he mounted so high was because he did not know the end ordained for him, may with equal truth be said of Caesar. Neither had a policy he could define, other than, on the one hand, the complete surrender to the will of the Lord, and on the other, to the will of Caesar. Therefore the one dealt with each situation as the Lord commanded, and the other as he himself determined. Both preached tolerance and were intolerant, and when both had attained to supreme power, both were at a loss what to do with it.

It may with justice be argued that Caesar did not live long enough to do so. Nevertheless, at the time of his assassination, rather than devote himself to the elimination of the causes which since the days of Marius had precipitated civil strife, he was about to wage yet another campaign which, if successful, was unlikely to do more than extend the area of trouble. The truth would appear to be that he was too much of a general to be a creative statesman.

[1] *The History of the Rebellion and Civil Wars in England*, Edward Earl of Clarendon (1807 edit.), vol. III, part II, book XV, pp. 983–4.

## 2. THE BASIC PROBLEM

In a remarkable letter addressed to Caesar, either in 50 or 49 B.C., Sallust wrote:

'By far the greatest blessing which you can confer upon your country . . . will be either to do away with the pursuit of wealth or to reduce it so far as circumstances permit . . . wherever riches are regarded as a distinction, there honour, uprightness, moderation, chastity and all the virtues are lightly rated. . . . First of all then, deprive money of its importance. Let no one be given greater or less opportunity according to his wealth. . . .'¹

This was to suggest a form of socialist state capitalism which, whether good or bad, could only be established by a revolution. But as Caesar was not a revolutionary, let alone one of the Lenin type, it was politically impracticable, and even had he been willing to consider it, he had first to win the Civil War.

In 46 B.C., when he had done so, Sallust again wrote to him to re-establish harmony by casting out the evils of discord.

'This can be done [he wrote] if you check the frenzied indulgence in extravagance and pillage, not by calling men back to the old standards, which from the corruption of our morals have long since become a farce, but by fixing the amount of each man's income as the limit of his expenditure. . . . We must therefore for the future rid ourselves of the money-lender, to the end that each one of us may take care of his own property. This is the only right way to administer a magistracy for the people and not for the creditor, and to show greatness of soul by enriching the state, not by pillaging it. . . .

'Finally, wise men wage war only for the sake of peace and endure the toil in the hope of quiet; unless you bring about a lasting peace, what mattered victory or defeat?'²

What Sallust failed to see was that, although the money-lender was

¹ 'Letter to Caesar on the State', vii. This is little more than a paraphrase of what Sallust wrote in his *War with Catiline* (X, 3-4), namely: 'Hence the lust for money first, then for power, grew upon them; these were, I may say, the root of all evils. For avarice destroyed honour, integrity, and all other noble qualities; taught in their place intolerance, cruelty, to neglect the gods, to set a price on everything.'

² 'Speech on the State, addressed to Caesar in his Later Years', V and VI. For the genuineness of this citation and the preceding one see the Loeb Classical Library edition of Sallust, pp. xviii and xix.

one of the main causes of the general corruption, he was not the cause of civil strife. How could a lasting peace be assured, unless the control of the army, upon which Caesar's authority was based, were surrendered to the Senate and the people; and should it be, how could they guarantee a lasting peace as long as the Marian military system continued to flourish?

In the circumstances in which Caesar was placed, it was impossible for him to contemplate such a surrender of power without becoming party to his own destruction, and without benefit to the Republic. What was his alternative? We are not told, and the high probability is, he did not know, other than to hold fast to his dictatorship, in which case the lasting peace would be measured by his life. That would appear to have been his outlook; because, according to Suetonius, 'he was wont to declare that it was not so much to his own interest as to that of his country that he remain alive; he had long since had his fill of power and glory; but if aught befell him, the commonwealth would have no peace, but would be plunged into civil strife under much worse conditions.'[1] Because he was not immortal, that was as much as to say: '*Après moi le déluge.*'

This hopeless outlook is referred to by Cicero in a letter to Atticus, dated April 7, 44 B.C., in which he mentions that Caesar's friend, Gaius Matius, had said to him: 'If Caesar with all his genius could not find a solution, who will find it now?'[2] How came it that Caesar was faced by this fateful dilemma, and unless it could be solved to the good of the State, 'what mattered victory or defeat?'

### 3. CAESAR'S STATECRAFT

In the normal meaning of the word, Caesar was not a statesman, that is, a man whose main tasks in peacetime are to establish justice, harmony and prosperity within his country, as well as to guarantee its security against aggression from without; and in wartime, as Sallust so wisely urged, to wage war for the sake of a lasting peace.[3] Instead

[1] *Div. Iul.*, LXXXVI.

[2] *Ad. Att.*, XIV, i.

[3] In his letter to Atticus of February 27, 49 B.C., Cicero quotes with approval Scipio's views on the ideal statesman. They are: 'As a safe voyage is the aim of the pilot, health of the physician, victory of the general, so the ideal statesman will aim at happiness for the citizens of the state to give them material security, copious wealth, wide-reaching distinction and untarnished honour'. Cicero's comment on this is: 'Absolute power is what [Pompey] and Caesar have sought . . . neither of them looks to our happiness. Both want to be kings'. (*Ad. Att.*, VIII, xi.)

he was a demagogue of genius and an astute politician, who strove to undermine the authority of the Senate and impose his will on the Republic. Not peace but power was his aim, and it is understandable that, until he had gained it, he was compelled to struggle for it within the vicious environment of his day.

Wherever power was to be found he wooed it: the *plebs*, who so largely controlled Rome; the rising intelligentsia, who could arouse the rabble; the financiers and property owners, who bought and sold the magistracies and bribed senators, tribunes and jurors; and above all the legions, who could place the Republic at his mercy.

Only after the battle of Thapsus, when he gained absolute power, was he in a position to change his aim, and by then he was so entangled in the means by which he had gained it, and so indebted to those who had helped him, that he found himself the slave and not the master of power. For instance, should Sallust's diagnosis of the main cause of corruption be accepted, how was it possible for him to revolutionize finance without antagonizing his most powerful supporters – the financiers and bankers? But it would appear unlikely that he ever contemplated such a revolution, because he was in no sense of the word a revolutionary statesman, and as a legislator he showed little originality.

'His measures [writes Professor Marsh] were all based on well-established precedents. . . . In the means he took to dispose of his veterans and to reduce the number of the Roman rabble he followed on the lines which C. Gracchus had pointed out; in his debt legislation he adopted the solution of Valerius Flaccus in a milder form; in his requirement that the great ranches of Southern Italy should be operated partly by free labour he re-enacted a provision of the Licinian laws on a more limited scale; when he compelled the Knights to invest half their capital in land, he tried to accomplish what Sulla actually did by the proscription and the advance of many of the equestrians to the senate. . . .'[1]

Sir Frank Adcock says much the same:
'The notable features of Caesarian legislation,' he writes, 'so far as time has spared it, are its direct and radical removal of acknowledged abuses, its insistence on order and good administration, its resource in dealing with present perplexities. At the same time, it is difficult to

[1] *A History of the Roman World from 146 to 30 B.C.*, Frank Burr Marsh (1957 edit.), p. 255.

discover anything which is a marked breach with the past or anything which looks far beyond the present.'[1]

His peace policy was a continuation of his war policy by identical means. On March 26, 46 B.C. – that is, at the opening of the Civil War – in a letter to Atticus, Cicero wrote that Caesar had replied to one of his as follows:

'You are right to infer of me . . . that there is nothing further from my nature than cruelty. . . . I am not moved because it is said that those, whom I let go, have departed to wage war on me again, for there is nothing I like better than that I should be true to myself and they to themselves.'[2]

As we have seen, his clemency was a profitable war policy; nevertheless, as a peace policy it was exceedingly dangerous to carry clemency to such an extreme as to reinstate his pardoned enemies who – it would seem he overlooked – would continue to be true to themselves.[3]

In September, 46 B.C., Cicero wrote to Aulus Caccina, one of the few Pompeians Caesar refused to reinstate:

'I often admire the sobriety and justice and wisdom of Caesar. . . . Why, how warmly he has welcomed us all! Cassius he has made his legate; Brutus he has made governor of Gaul; Sulpicius of Greece; Marcellus, with whom he was more indignant than any one, he has recalled with every consideration for his honour.'[4]

What is so perplexing is that, although he welcomed his former adversaries, he took no steps to conciliate them, and yet must have been aware that the extravagant honours and powers he had accepted would antagonize them. It would seem that in the last years of his life absolute power unhinged his mind.[5] What would one think today, if at the conclusion of the Second World War Sir Winston Churchill had accepted at the hands of his Cabinet the appointments of Prime Minister

---

[1] *C.A.H.*, vol. IX, p. 701.

[2] *Ad. Att.*, IX, 16.

[3] On May 14, 44 B.C., Hirtius told Cicero that many of Caesar's followers held that 'his clemency was his destruction, and that, if he had not practised clemency, such a thing [his assassination] could not have happened to him'. (*Add. Att.*, XIV, 22.)

[4] *Ad. Fam.*, VI, vi, 10.

[5] His erratic behaviour also points to this. When Quintus Fabius died on the last day of his consulship in 45 B.C., Caesar forthwith nominated Gaius Caninius Rebilius in his place for the few remaining hours. Also, when he was about to set out for Parthia, he designated Octavius, at the time a mere lad, Master of the Horse, and he appointed Dolabella – a notorious scoundrel who during his absence in 47–46 B.C. had fomented rebellion in Italy – consul in his own stead.

for life, Commander-in-Chief of the Armed Forces, Lord Chief Justice, Chancellor of the Exchequer, etc., etc., and on top of these extravagances had been addressed as 'Jehovah Churchill'?

In the circumstances his ambition had created, to pack the magistracies with his recent enemies was to transform his clemency into a high explosive. It may have exalted his *dignitas* by differentiating him from the common run of men, and have endowed him with an Olympian sense of superiority; but it in no way allayed the bitterness of his pardoned enemies, who continued to nurse their resentments and plot against him.

In these circumstances, to march against Parthia and leave the plotters behind him is incomprehensible bad statesmanship. It was to repeat Sulla's error of 87 B.C., when he left Cinna consul in Rome and marched against Mithridates.[1] Incidentally, it was also bad generalship, for, as Napoleon has pointed out, the Romans were nearly always defeated by the Parthians, because the legions were unsuited to their mode of fighting,[2] and Caesar's experiences against the Numidians, a somewhat similar foe, should have made this clear to him. As far as his reputation both as a statesman and a general is concerned, it may well have been that his assassination was the culmination of his good fortune. Either to have repeated the history of Sulla, or to have met the fate of Crassus, would have been a sorry ending of his amazing career.

It may have been statesmanlike not to be vindictive, and proscribe his enemies as Sulla had done. But was it good statesmanship to place them in positions of authority, any more than it was good generalship to warn Pompey through Vibullius of his arrival in Epirus? A year after his assassination Cicero did not think so. On April 17, 43 B.C., he wrote to Marcus Brutus:

'You say that we should display more zeal in banning civil wars than in wreaking vengeance on the vanquished. I heartily disagree with you, Brutus, and I cannot defer to your leniency. No, a wholesome sternness carries the day against the vain show of leniency! Why, if we choose to be lenient, there will never be a lack of civil wars.'[3]

So it came about: clemency, when carried to its extreme, unleashed vengeance, and vengeance put spurs to yet another fratricidal struggle.

Nevertheless, in contrast with his deficiencies in statecraft, his abilities as a demagogue enabled him to become the idol of the people, and his genius as a soldier to reach the dizzy height of absolute master

---

[1] See *supra*, Chapter I, p. 30.
[2] *Op. cit.*, vol. XXXII, p. 29.       [3] *Ad. Brut.*, VI, i, 5.

of the Roman world. Of this amazing feat a recent historian has written:

"To Caesar the art of government meant the promotion of any measure, however inconsistent with his previous or even present professions, that promised to advance the next step in his plans; his only long-range objective which can be definitely identified is the enhancement of his power. For this he indulged in a lifetime of double talk, professing slogans of democracy, while debasing and destroying the powers of the electorate, and insisting on constitutional technicalities, while persistently undermining the constitution. In the end, his prescription for government turned out to be a surprisingly simple one: to reduce its mechanism to the simplest and most primitive of all institutional forms, personal absolutism, and to employ it for one of the simplest and most primitive of all purposes, foreign conquest.'[1]

## 4. AS GENERAL

Like Cromwell, Caesar was an amateur soldier of genius, neither trained nor educated for war, and, so far as is known, not even interested in military affairs until he was approaching middle age. But unlike Cromwell, who won the English Civil War with his new Model Army, Caesar's army, it would seem, in no way differed from that of his uncle Marius, which in Numidia had failed to bring Jugurtha to book, and later, under Pompey, had failed to subdue Sertorius in Spain. As earlier discussed, its deficiencies were lack of trained cavalry and efficient light infantry to add elasticity to the rigid defensive and offensive tactics of the legions. Also, should Dr Holmes's surmise be correct,[2] that Caesar had no wagon train, and depended on his allies to provide the vehicles needed to supply it, or else to requisition them in the districts he operated in, then the most serious of its deficiencies was an organized commisariat.

These were innovations Caesar should have introduced; yet, in the twelve years of his campaigning, as we have seen, his sole one was,

---

[1] *Death of a Republic: Politics and Political Thought at Rome 59–44 B.C.*, Professor John Dickinson (1963), pp. 365–6. Compared with this, Tenny Frank's estimate of him is: that the earlier years of his career 'reveal him as a reckless and unscrupulous demagogue', and that 'His consulship in 59 reveals very little statesmanship'. But later, when in 'sole responsibility' (for reasons not stated) he revealed himself to be 'a statesman of unparalleled insight, sympathy, and effectiveness'. (*Op. cit.*, pp. 332–4.)

[2] See *supra*, Chapter IV, p. 82.

when in Africa, to order each of his legions to train 300 of its men as light infantry to co-operate with his cavalry against the Numidian horsemen.[1] The truth is, Caesar was not an organizer; careful preparations – adequate supplies, sufficient fighting forces, and many other requirements needed to assure the success of a campaign – were either distasteful to him, or lost to sight by reliance on his genius to solve all difficulties, as well as his eagerness to respond immediately to every challenge whatever at the moment his means might be.

As far as can be gathered from his *Commentaries*, and from those compiled by Hirtius or others, not one of his campaigns was adequately prepared, and some not prepared at all. In his campaign against the Helvetii, because Rome, like Great Britain in after centuries, was never ready for war, he may be excused. But his two invasions of Britain were amateurish in the extreme: no provisions were made to carry in the ships supplies of corn, or provide reserve vessels, or extra anchors, cordage, tackle, etc., in the event of loss or damage by storm. So we read, when disaster came there was 'great dismay throughout the army', because 'there were no other ships to carry [the troops] back.' We are told that 'everything needful for the repair of ships was lacking; and as it was generally understood that the army was to winter in Gaul, no corn had been provided in these parts against the winter.'[2] Caesar mentions these deficiencies as if they were acts of God, instead of due to his own negligence. Unfortunately for him, the British chieftains soon became aware of his lack of corn, and they decided to prevent him from foraging, which, as we have seen, led to the near destruction of his 7th Legion.[3]

Seldom was his army adequately fed. At Ilerda it was reduced to near starvation, and at times during the blockade of Dyrrachium it subsisted on roots. At Alexandria, no sooner had Caesar occupied the royal palace than he sent out urgent appeals to various states and people to supply him with corn, and his campaign in Africa was little more than a food hunt. Strangely enough, his constant references to his corn-supply have led some historians to assume the excellence of his commissariat, whereas his almost daily anxiety concerning it was due to its uncertainty. For instance, Holmes writes: 'He knew that a well-organized commissariat is the foundation of success in war; and the

[1] See *supra*, Chapter XII, p. 278. It would appear to have been no more than a temporary expedient.

[2] *B.G.*, IV, 29.

[3] See *supra*, Chapter V, p. 122.

truth of this is borne in at every turn upon the reader of his memoirs.'[1] Had it been well organized, why should it be necessary for Caesar to mention it to the reader at every turn? Like all smooth-working services, its efficiency would be taken for granted.

It is also inexplicable why he never attempted to raise, organize, and train efficient cavalry and light infantry, arms which since the days of Marius had ceased to be recruited from Roman citizens, and on the outbreak of war were provided by allies and the *auxilia*. Syme says that 'Gallia Comata ... provided ... the best cavalry in the world.'[2] If so, how came it that, under Caesar and Crassus, Gallic cavalry were next to useless against Numidian and Parthian horsemen?

At the opening of the Gallic War, Caesar's 4,000 cavalry were requisitioned from the Aedui and their allies, and, as we have seen, soon after he took the field the Aeduan contingent, under Dumnorix, betrayed him.[3] So unreliable were they that, when he agreed to parley with Ariovistus, in order to provide himself with a reliable escort, he mounted his 10th Legion on their horses.[4] At times the cavalry problem became farcical, and one out of several incidents referred to in preceding chapters is sufficient to illustrate it. In his campaign on the Rhine, in 55 B.C., when he found himself opposed by a coalition of doubtful loyalty, which demanded his immediate attention, as he had disbanded his Gallic cavalry for the winter, he could do nothing until he had replaced them, and actually was compelled to requisition 5,000 horsemen from the chieftains whose good faith he suspected.[5] His near defeat at the hands of the Nervii, in 57 B.C., was largely due to the failure of his cavalry to discover the whereabouts of the enemy, and in 52 B.C., immediately before Vercingetorix fell back on Alesia, their failure to reconnoitre ahead placed his column of march in a critical situation.[6]

The inefficiency of his light-armed auxiliary troops, of whom he must have had thousands with him in all his campaigns, was such that, although they were useful as hewers of wood and drawers of water, they were valueless as soldiers. In Publius Crassus' operations in Aquitania, in 56 B.C., it is mentioned that, although Crassus 'had no great confidence in his auxiliaries for actual fighting,' he found them useful 'in handing up stones and missiles and carrying sods to make a ramp,' and that they 'gave the appearance and impression of fighting

---

[1] *Op. cit.*, vol. II, pp. 232–3.  [2] *Op. cit.*, p. 75.
[3] See *supra*, Chapter V, pp. 103–4.
[4] See *supra*, *ibid.*, p. 108.  [5] See *supra*, *ibid.*, p. 119.
[6] See *supra*, Chapter VI, p. 148.

troops.'[1] On the rare occasions Caesar mentions them, it is more often than not to give an appearance of strength to his legionaries.

They were totally useless as or against guerrillas, as were also the legionaries; of that Caesar was fully aware. It will be remembered that during his second expedition to Britain he was opposed by Cassivellaunus' guerrilla tactics, and he declared that his legions were incapable of countering them, because 'the enemy never fought in close array, but in small parties with wide intervals; and had detachments posted at regular stations, so that one party covered another in turn, and fresh, unspent warriors took the place of the battle weary,' whereas his legions could only fight in regular formations.[2]

These defects in the organization of Caesar's army detrimentally influenced both his strategy and tactics. His defective system of supply frequently compelled him to change his area of operations to his disadvantage; his untrained, barbaric cavalry at times led him into critical situations; and when his enemy took to guerrilla warfare, because of his lack of trained light infantry he could do nothing to respond to him. It is astonishing that a soldier of his outstanding intelligence, who apparently was acquainted with the works of Xenophon[3] and the history of Alexander,[4] could have failed to realize how defective his army organization was.

## 5. AS STRATEGIST

These deficiencies were a serious handicap in both the Gallic and Civil Wars. Nevertheless, in the first, when compared with the unorganized tribal levies of the Gauls, Caesar's army was so superior in discipline, training, and tactics that, with the exception of guerrilla warfare, the fortunes of war were heavily loaded against them. And in the Civil War, although the organization of the Pompeian armies was identical with his own, when it broke out Caesar's legionaries were for the greater part veterans inured to war, whereas the bulk of Pompey's was either unsalted or composed of raw recruits.

A still greater advantage was that in Caesar's army unity of command prevailed, while in Pompey's it was lacking. Even more important,

---

[1] B.G., III, 25. In 51 B.C., when proconsul of Cilicia, Cicero issued a circular letter in which he stated that, because of the injustice of Roman rule, 'the auxiliaries . . . are either so feeble that they cannot give us much assistance, or else so estranged from us' that they cannot be trusted (Ad. Fam., XV, i, 5).

[2] See supra, Chapter V, p. 125; and B.G., V, 16.

[3] Suetonius, Div. Iul., LXXXVII.          [4] Plutarch, Caesar, XI, 3.

while Pompey was no more than an able soldier, Caesar was a political genius who could relate war with politics, and devise a grand strategy in which war was subordinated to a clearly defined policy that appealed to the masses of Romans. It has been discussed in Section (1) of Chapter VIII, and is reminiscent of Alexander the Great's policy of reconciliation, but on a more restricted scale and with a more practical aim. While Alexander's was to establish the brotherhood of mankind, Caesar limited his to the brotherhood of all good Romans. Or, as he put it: 'Let us see if by moderation we can win all hearts and secure a lasting victory,'[1] which also meant a lasting peace. But of what a lasting peace entailed he gives us no inkling.

Although in Gaul his conquests were based on a strategy of annihilation, at times – more particularly when in difficulties – he had resorted to leniency – that is, to a strategy of moderation – and had found that it paid. It will be recalled that, in his second expedition to Britain, after he had crossed the Thames and when Cassivellaunus was planning a surprise attack on the Roman naval base, by forbidding his legions to ravage the land of the Trinobantes Caesar won their submission and broke up Cassivellaunus' tribal coalition.[2] Again, when after the fall of Alesia he was eager to wind up the Gallic revolt, he treated the Bituriges with so unaccustomed a lenity that soon after they sought his aid against the Carnutes who were ravaging their lands, and immediately after he brought all opposition to an end by his clemency toward the Bellovaci.[3]

Whether it was these changes in policy which led him to appreciate the value of a strategy of moderation, or whether it was that in the Civil War he was loath, as he said, to kill his kith and kin, we do not know. Nevertheless, the fact remains that, as soon as civil war became a certainty, peace became the main plank in Caesar's war policy, and remained so until he won the battle of Pharsalus. Whether during that period he believed he could persuade Pompey to end the struggle by negotiations would seem doubtful. What would appear to be more probable is, that throughout his aim was to consolidate his moral base by justifying his cause, and win over the goodwill of both the masses and the propertied classes in Italy. With reference to this, it is of interest to recall that, as early as the first year of the war in Gaul, before he advanced against Ariovistus he sought peace with him, in order to put him in the wrong should he refuse his terms, and thereby

[1] See *supra*, Chapter VIII, p. 182.     [2] See *supra*, Chapter V, pp. 125–6.
[3] See *supra*, Chapter VI, p. 160.

justify his attack on him in the eyes of the Senate and the Roman People.

It was that policy and not his legions which had compelled Pompey to withdraw from Italy into Greece, and up to his victory at Pharsalus his audacity in crossing the Adriatic in face of Pompey's command of the sea was justified by the security that same policy had enabled him to establish in his rear in Italy and Spain. After Pharsalus the end was in sight, and, in order to extinguish the Civil War, all that remained to be done was to mop up the fragments of the Pompeian army and proclaim a general amnesty. To recapitulate:

Instead of following Cato and the bulk of the fugitives to the Province of Africa, he decided – probably rightly – to pursue Pompey. But when early in October, 48 B.C., he arrived at Alexandria and learnt of Pompey's assassination, it needs no hind-sight on the part of the reader to discern that his next strategic objective was the destruction of the fugitives before they could recruit another army. But instead of proceeding to Italy, he cast strategy to the winds, abandoned the Civil War for a campaign in Egypt, to be followed by another in Pontus, and thereby gave the fugitives a full year to recoup in.[1] That this extraordinary strategical lapse was not what might be called an accidental aberration is supported by the fact that, in 54 B.C., he had committed a similar blunder, but of lesser magnitude. Instead of consolidating his position in Gaul, he invaded Britain with a full scale expeditionary force, and the price he had to pay for that piece of strategic folly was the fostering of the Gallic Revolt.

What are we to make of these two Caesars? On the one hand, the man who won Italy with an olive branch; who corralled Pompey's legions in Spain as if they were cattle; and who won the battle of Pharsalus against overwhelming odds. On the other, the man who abandoned the Civil War for a love affair with Cleopatra; who launched a punitive war on an Oriental potentate of such little repute that Cicero had never heard of him; and who, when he had given his opponents a year and more to recruit in, set out against them so un-

---

[1] On this Napoleon is emphatic. In his 'Précis des Guerres de Jules César' he says: The Alexandrian War gave the Pompeians nine months' respite in which to make ready for the war in Africa and a new campaign in Spain. 'These two campaigns, which demanded all his genius and good fortune to achieve victory, need never have been fought had he after Pharsalus rapidly moved against Cato and Scipio in Africa, instead of proceeding to Alexandria'. (*Correspondance*, vol. XXXII, p. 63.)

prepared that, within a day or two of landing in Africa, he was urgently calling for reinforcements and supplies of corn.

It would appear that he was a strategical Jekyll and Hyde: at times a clear-sighted genius, and at others blind to strategical realities. Unless this were so, how are these erratic changes in outlook to be accounted for?

## 6. AS TACTICIAN

As a leader of men Caesar stood head and shoulders above the generals of his day, and it is more as a fighting than as a thinking soldier that his generalship has been judged. It is not, as Professor Last affirms, that 'he bequeathed to the generals who followed him no receipt for victory except one beyond their reach – to be Caesar.'[1] Rather is it, that the generals, and apparently also the historians, have failed to analyse his tactics.

First, it must be borne in mind that normally the battles of his day were parallel engagements in which the aim was to exhaust and then penetrate the enemy's front. They were methodical operations in which, when both sides were similarly trained and organized, success depended largely on superiority of numbers. Caesar modified these tactics by basing his campaigns, not on superiority of numbers and meticulous preparations but on celerity and audacity. By surprising his opponent he caught him off-guard, and got him so thoroughly rattled that either he refused his challenge to fight and in consequence lost prestige, or, should he respond, was morally half-beaten before the engagement took place.[2]

When the Civil War was about to open, his adversaries expected that he would await the arrival of his legions at Ravenna. Instead, although he had no more than a single legion at hand, he raced into Italy and threw Rome into convulsions. Similarly, after the conquest of Spain, he sped to Brundisium, and in spite of the wintry weather, insufficiency of transports, and the fact that several of his legions were still on the line of march, he said to his men: 'I consider rapidity of movement the best substitute for all these things,' and 'that the most potent thing in war is the unexpected'.[3] Under cover of it he crossed the Adriatic.

[1] See Preface, p. 13.

[2] Suetonius (Div. Iul., LX) says: 'He joined battle, not only after planning his movements in advance but on a sudden opportunity, often immediately at the end of a march, and sometimes in the foulest weather, when one would least expect him to make a move.'     [3] See supra, Chapter X, p. 210.

In his operations against Ambiorix the speed of his advance prevented Acco, chief of the Senones, withdrawing to his strongholds, and compelled his submission. At the opening of the Gallic Revolt, when he crossed the snow-bound Cevennes, his speed dumbfounded the Arverni; and soon after, it was the speed of his march on Orléans which threw its inhabitants into panic. When, at a critical moment during the siege of Gergovia, he learnt of the revolt of the Aedui, without a moment's hesitation he set out to suppress it, did so, and returned to Gergovia, having marched 50 Roman miles in a little over 24 hours.

The tactical innovation of speed proved so profitable that, coupled with Caesar's apparent dislike for preparations, due to his eagerness to clinch with his enemy as rapidly as possible, at times his forces were insufficient to take advantage of the enemy's surprise. 'In the art of war, as in mechanics,' wrote Napoleon, 'time is the grand element between weight and force.'[1] In other words: celerity multiplies weight – numbers – which implies that force depends on weight as well as on celerity. Therefore weight, when multiplied by celerity, must be sufficient to make good a surprisal. It would seem that Caesar never grasped this, with the result that at times his over-eagerness to surprise his enemy with insufficient forces landed him in a critical position. Even though he escaped annihilation, as he always succeeded in doing, he lost the initiative until he was reinforced: his Alexandrian and African campaigns are outstanding examples of this.

Bound by no rule, on occasion he acted with caution. As we have seen, in his campaign against the Helvetii, he knew that they could not escape him because they were impeded by an immense supply train, and when their two assaults failed, instead of attempting to annihilate them, as he might have done, he deprived them of the greater part of their wagon-train and forced their surrender. Again in the Ebro campaign, when on several occasions he could have destroyed the Pompeians in battle, and when his officers urged him to do so and his men threatened to mutiny if he did not, he stuck to his plan: to avoid battle by manœuvring his enemy away from water and compel him to capitulate; which he did without the loss of a man, and was thanked by the enemy for having spared them.

Well aware that a soldier, when engaged in front, dreads nothing more than an attack in rear, and that, therefore, the rear of a line of battle is psychologically its weakest point, whenever opportunity offered Caesar combined a rear attack, or threat of one, with his frontal

[1] *Correspondance*, vol. XII, No. 9997.

attack. At the most critical moment of the last day's fighting at Alesia, when he came to Labienus' relief with four cohorts and a body of cavalry, it will be remembered that, while on his way, he ordered part of the cavalry to ride round 'the outer entrenchments [unseen] and attack that enemy in rear.' It was the suddenness of this unexpected attack that detonated the panic which compelled the Gauls to abandon the relief of Alesia, and led to its capitulation.[1] Again at the battle of the Nile, when his initial attack was making no headway, he sent a few cohorts unobserved to assault the Egyptians in rear, an operation which led to a panic and won him the battle.[2] Also it would appear almost certain that it was Bogud's attack on the rear of Gnaeus Pompey's left wing at Munda which led to the destruction of his army at the very moment when Caesar's was in dire peril.

In this context it is interesting to recall that, in Caesar's first attack on the Heptastadium, to distract the Egyptians on Pharos, he sent several galleys round the northern side of the island to threaten their rear;[3] and that, prior to the battle of Thapsus, he instructed part of his fleet to be prepared at a given signal to sail close inshore to a point in rear of Scipio's camp and cause confusion in his army.[4]

During his many campaigns he suffered only two serious defeats, at Gergovia and at Dyrrachium; also two comparatively minor setbacks; the one at Ilerda and the other at the assault of the Heptastadium: in each his troops panicked. At Gergovia because the signal of retreat was unheard, and because the attacking Romans mistook the Aeduan contingent for the enemy, and at Dyrrachium because the Caesarians were surprised. In both his defeats Caesar's responsibility lay, not so much in the immediate causes of these mishaps, but in the fact that, prior to both, he had failed to concentrate all the troops he might have. Before he advanced on Gergovia, he detached four legions, under Labienus, to operate against the revolted Senones and Parisii; and prior to his blockade of Pompey, instead of retaining with him the whole of Antony's reinforcements, he detached two of his legions and 500 cavalry, under Domitius Calvinus, to operate against Scipio. In the circumstances which faced him, it is impossible to justify these detachments, unless the reason was that he could not feed more troops than he actually had with him at Gergovia and Dyrrachium. But whatever it was, there can be little doubt that with four additional legions at the one, and two at the other, both defeats might have been avoided.

[1] See *supra*, Chapter VI, pp. 156–7.  [2] *Ibid.*, Chapter XI, p. 255.
[3] *Ibid.*, Chapter XI, p. 250.  [4] *Ibid.*, Chapter XII, p. 279.

Although the one coincided with the defection of the Aedui, and the other restored Pompey's prestige, these defeats did not place Caesar in his most critical situations. Those were: at the battle of the Sambre, at the ambush near Dijon, and at the battles of Ruspina and Munda. In each he revealed his astonishing ability to seize hold of a most desperate situation, and, through sheer force of will and faith in his own genius, transmute what to a normally able general would have been certain defeat into victory. This complete confidence in himself, whatever the circumstances might be, made him one of the greatest of fighting generals of the Classical age.

# Postscript

'May it be my privilege to establish the State in a firm and secure position, and reap from that act the fruit that I desire; but only if I may be called the author of the best possible government, and bear with me the hope when I die that the foundations which I have laid for the State will remain unshaken.'

AUGUSTUS[1]

I N this postscript on the solution of Caesar's problem, it is not our intention to trace Octavian's rise to power from the time he arrived in Rome to claim his inheritance until, in 31 B.C., with the aid of Vipsanius Agrippa, he defeated Antony and Cleopatra at Actium and became master of the Roman world. Instead, it is to describe in brief how as such he solved Caesar's problem and established a peace which was to last for over 200 years.

When he contemplated the empire he had won and its heterogeneous local governments and peoples, he realized that it was far too large and complex to be ruled by the council of a city state; that instead it demanded some form of one-man rule, and that his problem was how to disguise it. From the outset he decided not to tamper with the constitution of the Republic, or contemplate monarchy; but instead establish what Mommsen has called a diarchy, in which Caesar's ghost would be wrapped in Cato's shroud.

Firstly, in 28 B.C., he declined all honours calculated to remind the Romans of the kingly power;[2] adopted the title of *princeps* ('first citizen'),[3] and called his system the Principate. Secondly, he accepted all the old conventions – consuls, tribunes, magistrates, elections, etc. Thirdly, instead of ignoring the Senate and insulting its members as Caesar had done, he went out of his way to consult it and placate them. Lastly, on January 13, 27 B.C., at a session of the Senate, he renounced all his extraordinary powers and placed them at the disposal of the Senate and the people.[4] And when the senators begged him to resume

[1] Suetonius, *Div. Aug.*, XXVIII, 2.
[2] *Res Gestae Divi Augusti*, 6.
[3] Dio, LIII, 3.
[4] *Res Gestae*, 34.

325

them and not abandon the Commonwealth he had saved, he yielded to their request and consented to assume proconsular authority over an enlarged province, which included Spain, Gaul, Syria, Cilicia, and Cyprus, while the Senate was left with the remaining provinces. Thus in semblance the sovereignty of the Senate and the people was restored; but in fact, because his enlarged province comprised the majority of the legions, and Egypt, over which he ruled as king, was apart from the reckoning, the basis of political power passed into his hands. Three days later the Senate decreed that the title 'Augustus' (the Revered) should be conferred upon him.

Because his first task was to safeguard the empire and assure internal tranquillity, it was imperative that his army should be one he could implicitly trust, and the merits of the policy he adopted are recognized by Dio, when in his review of the empire he makes Maecenas proffer him the following advice:

'You will be wise to maintain a permanent force raised from the citizens, the subjects and the allies distributed throughout the provinces as necessity requires. . . . We cannot rely on forces called out for the occasion owing to the distance which separates us from the borders of the Empire. If we allow all our subjects of military age to have arms and to undergo military training, there will be civil wars; but if we check all military activities, we shall run the risk of having nothing but raw and untrained troops when we need an army to help us.'[1]

Therefore Augustus decided to form a standing army of professional soldiers, sworn to serve him loyally for a term of sixteen years – later extended to twenty. And when after Actium he found himself left with some sixty legions,[2] a number far in excess of defensive requirements, he disbanded over half of them, and stationed the remainder in the provinces to defend the frontiers.

Standing armies were by no means a novel innovation, but in the past they had consisted of forces on a peace-footing, which, when a crisis arose, were brought on to a war-footing by raising emergency legions. Because it was these *ad hoc* legions which in the past had enabled generals to defy the State and foment civil wars, Augustus did away with their need by maintaining his standing army on a permanent war-footing.[3]

[1] Dio, LII, 27 (abbreviated).
[2] Parker, *op. cit.*, p. 75. Syme, *op. cit.*, p. 304, mentions about seventy legions.
[3] Dio, LII, 27. Its weakness, which later became apparent, was the lack of a central reserve.

Down to 13 B.C., the discharged legionaries were provided with grants of land and were settled in colonies. After that date a pension was substituted for land,[1] and to raise the funds needed, Augustus created a military treasury fed by new taxes.[2] Further, he opened the path of promotion to the common soldier, and on occasion appointed centurions in command of legions; disbanded his German body-guard, and replaced it by nine Roman cohorts – the famous Praetorian Guard – three of which were permanently quartered in Rome. Also he created a police force of four cohorts to keep order within the city.

To prevent the growth of a purely professional officer-class, Augustus combined the officer's military and civil career. Should an officer shape well after he had served for several years as military tribune, he 'would be pushed forward,' writes Professor Smith, 'by Augustus in his civilian administrative career to the praetorship, after which as an ex-praetor he would acquire further military and administrative experience, until he finally attained the consulship, which led to the government of an Imperial province. In this way Augustus was able to prevent the growth of a professional officer-class in his completely professional army;'[3] a danger hardly less dangerous than the creation of emergency forces. In addition to these reforms, by paying the provincial governors adequate salaries, he rendered illegal their freedom to enrich themselves by requisition.[4]

Thus Augustus solved the problem to which Caesar could find no answer.

The hidden forces which had impelled them along such different historic paths are revealed by Sir Frank Adcock in his chapter on 'The Achievement of Augustus' in *The Cambridge Ancient History*. With profound discernment he writes:

'Caesar had embodied faith in his own star and his own genius; Octavian stood for faith in Rome. At Ilerda, Pharsalus, Thapsus, Munda, it was Caesar who had conquered; at Actium it was Rome and Italy. . . . Caesar's dictatorship had been the crowning *reductio ad absurdum* of Roman constitutional forms: Augustus meant the old Republic to be a reality so far as it could.'[5]

[1] Dio LIV, 25, 5; and *Res Gestae*, 17.
[2] Suetonius, *Div. Aug.*, XLIX.
[3] *Service in the Post-Marian Army*, R. E. Smith (1958), p. 73 (see Dio, LII, 20).
[4] Dio, LII, 23, 1; and LXIII, 15, 5.
[5] Vol. X (1934), Chapter XVIII, pp. 585 and 587.

# Index